Handbook to Practical Disaster Preparedness for the Family

Handbook to Practical Disaster Preparedness for the Family

Arthur T. Bradley, Ph.D.

Foreword by
Curtis A. Bradley

Handbook to Practical Disaster Preparedness for the Family

Author: Arthur T. Bradley, Ph.D.

Email orders: orders@disasterpreparer.com

Website: http://www.disasterpreparer.com

Special thanks are extended to Siobhan Gallagher and Bridget Flanagan for editing the book's content, Marites Bautista for designing the layout, and Bryan Macabanti for illustrations.

ISBN 10:   145367887-5
ISBN 13:   978-145367887-9

Printed in the United States of America

This book is dedicated to family,
both yours and mine.
May they all be kept safe no matter how
dark the skies.

CONTENTS

FOREWORD

The world of late has been in upheaval: earthquakes, tsunamis, hurricanes, terrorist strikes, pandemics . . . the deadly list grows with each passing day. It is as if we are being given a warning to ready ourselves for things to come. Whether that warning is from God or simply a result of our own empirical observations is up to every individual to decide. What is undeniable is that the world is openly demonstrating its ferocity.

Every generation faces its own unique challenges. Our grandparents and great grandparents weathered world wars, food shortages, deadly pandemics, and nearly total financial ruin. They did so with grit and determination and by coming together as communities—sharing in their collective need to survive. This connectedness has all but disappeared, save for the most rural areas of our country. The sad truth is that, today, many people don't even know their neighbors' names.

Recently, however, there has been an awakening in our country. People are realizing that there truly is strength in numbers. Churches, fraternal organizations, veterans groups, friends and neighbors are discussing more and more how best to prepare for uncertain challenges. Food storage, water purification, backup electrical power, and community protection are all being considered.

Having learned much from my many roles in life, including marine, police officer, father, and priest, I can attest to the three things necessary for survival: knowledge, preparation, and determination. This book you hold in your hands represents the first of those three steps. The author has done his part to lay out commonsense approaches to meet your family's needs during nearly any crisis. The rest is up to you.

Now let's get to Chapter One. Time may be short!

Curtis A. Bradley
Shichidan, 7th Degree Black Belt
Tracy's Kenpo Karate

CHAPTER 1

INTRODUCTION

Chapter 1 Notes

CHAPTER 1

INTRODUCTION

R ight out of the gate let me tell you what this book is NOT. It is not a book about fighting off hordes of flesh-eating zombies, should they ever rise from the grave. Nor will it describe how to survive a shipwreck by feasting on coconuts and roasted iguana. Finally, it is not intended to help you survive our planet being sucked into the cosmic fireball affectionately known as our Sun. If you wish to prepare for those types of events, I respectfully suggest that you continue your search for a more suitable text.

This book is designed to help your family prepare for more common-place, yet still potentially deadly disasters. The list is long and varied, and includes hurricanes, tornados, terrorist attacks, earthquakes, pandemics, financial collapse, widespread blackouts, and much more. My hope is that this handbook will accomplish three things: (1) motivate you to become better prepared, (2) illustrate how to prepare effectively, and (3) help you to realize your place in a larger movement.

If you are going to become a true "prepper," you should start by learning the disaster preparer's mantra. Let's all say it together—ready, here goes . . .

"The sky is falling! The sky is falling!"

It helps if you wave your hands wildly above your head for effect. Seriously, give it a try. It is best to get this silliness out of your system now; that way you won't succumb to it later. Besides, you might as well say it a few times because you are almost certainly going to be accused of thinking it—even if only by way of stage whispers and snooty grins.

Why bother?
You better know
the answer in your
"heart of hearts."

At the root of this incredulity, lies a very basic question: *"Why?"* Why bother to prepare at all? Behind this question is the unspoken assertion that preparing for a disaster is unnecessary. It can be argued that most of us live in a fairly safe and stable world. What are the chances that you will ever need large stores of food or water? When will you actually use the carefully stocked first-aid kit that you keep in the car's trunk? Wouldn't your time, money, and energy be better served by focusing on life's "knowns" rather than its "unknowns?"

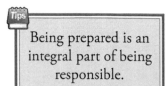

Being prepared is an
integral part of being
responsible.

The answer to that question is a resounding YES! Disaster preparedness (sometimes abbreviated as DP) should never distract you from meeting life's other needs and responsibilities. Your kids will still need to go to college; your family will continue to benefit from the yearly get-away vacation; and you will undoubtedly have a better chance of advancing in your job if you remain vigilant at keeping your boss happy. People who neglect important areas of their life in order to focus on uncertain doom are losing sight of what's important—not to mention failing to see life's daily joys. With that said, it is still quite possible to live a full, rewarding life while preparing for hard times. Not only is it possible, but as the head of a household, I would argue that achieving this kind of balance is your responsibility.

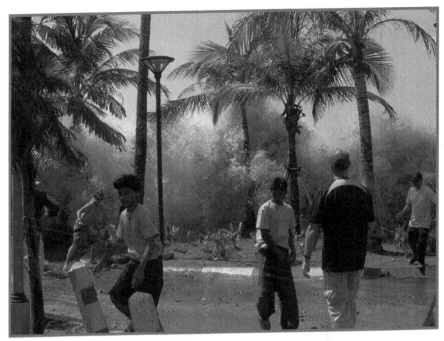

Indian Ocean tsunami, 2004

Events have made me who I am, neither a hardcore survivalist nor an all-trusting soul. I am a Boy Scout in the truest sense of the word—dedicated to family, country, and good citizenship. As you may already know, an enabling element of those ideals is being prepared. I will never forget the helplessness that I felt in witnessing the horrific terrorist attacks of September 11, 2001. That event forced me to accept that our world is not as safe as we like to believe.

Before I could even catch my breath, the world shook again with the tragic Indian Ocean tsunami of 2004. I remember sitting with my family that fateful Christmas, the holiday cheer forever interrupted by the suffering that hundreds of thousands of our brothers and sisters felt across the world.

These events drove me to take actions that one day might save lives. And what better contribution can anyone give this world than to save another life? When things go terribly wrong, the few reach deep for courage to make it better for the many. It has always been that way.

Tips

Effective preparation requires prioritizing your needs based on the likelihood and impact of events.

What makes this book different from others is that it presents a practical approach to becoming prepared. As many books have demonstrated, it is easy to simply recommend that you keep everything you could ever need on hand. It doesn't seem to matter that it costs five times your salary, weighs a couple tons, and compromises many important aspects of your life. In my view, preparedness is best served by keeping all things in perspective. This premise will become clearer as you make your way through this book.

There are plenty of hardcore *preppers* who believe that everyone should be ready for Armageddon. These survivalist types will almost certainly criticize some of my recommendations as not going far enough. Who knows for sure—they may be right! But I tend to take a more pragmatic approach. My motto is *"prepare for what makes sense."* It is highly unlikely the world will end tomorrow. Even if it does, it is equally unlikely that anything you do today will ensure your survival through the cataclysm. Better to be prepare for the challenges you might actually face—harsh weather, power outages, loss of income, being stranded on the road, and so on.

But we still haven't answered the underlying question: "Why?" That single question is arguably the most important one in this entire book. If you don't know the answer, then you will likely lose your dedication to preparedness somewhere along the way. Also, without a clear rational answer that you truly believe in your heart, you will never win over family or friends—and establishing a network of fellow *preppers* is an important part of the readiness process.

Don't lose your way. Anything can happen!

The short answer is that the world is not as safe as we would like to believe. It is a chaotic system with limitless inputs and outcomes. ***Anything can happen.*** If you can keep these three simple words in mind, they will help you along your way. When people ask why you are going to such trouble to prepare for darker days, smile and say, "Anything can happen." Who can possibly contest that simple statement?

Life is wholly unpredictable. Ninety-nine percent of the time everything works great. The world spins like a top, the skies are clear, and your refrigerator is full of milk and cheese. But know with certainty that the world is a dangerous place. Storms rage, fires burn, and enemies attack. No one is ever completely safe. Not you. Not your children. Not the richest man alive. We all live as part of a very complex ecosystem that, at its core, is unpredictable and willing to kill us without remorse or pause.

Don't believe me? Read on.

A SHOPPING LIST OF DISASTERS

There are countless ways in which the world can kill you. Many are simple accidents of nature, while others are the result of more malicious intent. Regardless of the cause, dead is still dead, and that eventuality is something we are all trying to avoid (or at least postpone). Remember the simple truism that nearly everyone who died as the result of a disaster fully believed they would live to see another day.

To help get everyone on the same page, as well as illustrate the point of how merciless our world can be, let's start by defining the word "disaster." One succinct yet informative definition is given below.[1]

> **disaster** - *a calamitous event, especially one occurring suddenly and causing great loss of life, damage, or hardship, such as a flood, airplane crash, or business failure.*

The key words here are *calamitous event, suddenly, great loss of life, damage,* and *hardship*. None of which sound appealing, but particularly distressing when put together in a single sentence! When described in this way, it becomes clear why we are interested in mitigating the hardship caused by such a crisis.

Disasters can generally be divided into five broad categories: natural, pandemic, man-made, war/terrorism/crime, and personal. The cause of each type of disaster may differ, but the impacts are often the same (e.g., loss of electricity, water contamination, food shortages, evacuations, mass casualties). The goal

Types of Disasters
- Natural
- Pandemic
- Man-made
- War/Terrorism/Crime
- Personal

therefore is to come up with a comprehensive preparedness plan that addresses these impacts regardless of the specific cause.

> **Natural Disasters**
> - Flood
> - Earthquake
> - Snow storm
> - Tornado
> - Hurricane
> - Winter freeze
> - Ice storm
> - Thunderstorm
> - Heat wave
> - Wildfire
> - Famine
> - Drought
> - Volcanic eruption
> - Landslide
> - Sinkhole
> - Tsunami
> - Hail
> - Avalanche
> - Asteroid strike

NATURAL

Natural disasters are events stemming from the dynamic nature of our universe. The world is constantly changing, and that grand-scale motion wreaks havoc. This category of disaster includes the four horsemen of death and destruction: earthquakes, tsunamis, hurricanes, and floods. Natural disasters cause extensive property damage and unbelievable loss of life. Even a quick listing of some of the worst natural disasters in the last 50 years is sobering. [2,3,4,5]

EARTHQUAKES AND TSUNAMIS

Location	Date	Impact
Haiti	January 2010	est. 230,000 dead
Sichuan, China	May 2008	est. 70,000 dead, 18,000 missing
Kashmir, Pakistan	October 2005	est. 80,000 dead, 3 million homeless
Sumatran Coast	December 2004	est. 225,000 dead
Bam, Iran	December 2003	est. 31,000 dead
Manjil-Rudbar, Iran	June 1990	est. 40,000 dead, 60,000 injured, 500,000 homeless
Tangshan, China	July 1976	est. 242,000 dead
Peru	May 1970	est. 66,000 dead

Eruption of Mount Saint Helens, 1980 *(photo by department of Natural Resources, State of Washington)*

VOLCANIC ERUPTIONS

Location	Date	Impact
Mount Pinatubo, Philippines	July 1991	Blanketed 290 square miles with ash; more than 800 dead
Nevado del Ruiz, Columbia	November 1985	est. 25,000 dead
El Chichon, Mexico	April 1982	est. 2,000 dead
Mount Saint Helens, Washington	May 1980	Largest historic volcanic eruption in the 48 contiguous states; deposited ash across 11 states; 57 dead

DROUGHT AND FLOODS

Location	Date	Impact
North Korea	mid-1990's	est. 600,000 dead
Ethiopia	1984-85	1 million people+ dead
Uganda	1980	21% of the population (est. 50,000) dead
India	1965-67	est. 1.5 million dead from starvation and disease

HURRICANES, CYCLONES, AND FLOODS

Event, Location	Date	Impact
Cyclone Nargis Burmese Peninsula	May 2008	est. 100,000 dead
Hurricane Katrina United States Gulf Coast	August 2005	Massive coastal destruction; 80% of New Orleans flooded; est. 1,800 dead
Hurricane Mitch Honduras and Nicaragua	October-November 1998	Unknown dead; 2.4 million homeless
Floods Yangtze River, China	August 1975	Widespread famine; est. 85,000 dead
Floods Hanoi, Vietnam	August 1971	est. 100,000 dead
Bhola Cyclone Bangladesh	November 1970	est. 500,000 to 1 million dead

Cyclone Nargis, 2008

Even this cursory survey of recent natural disasters makes it clear that large scale catastrophes causing terrible loss of life are not uncommon events. Again, these are only the *major* natural disasters in the last half century. There are countless others of a lesser scale not listed.

Weather events are often the first type of natural disaster that comes to mind. If you live in Colorado, you have experienced the isolation of heavy winter snowfalls. If you are on the Florida coast, you know well the destructive forces of hurricanes. And if you have ever had to pack your family into a coat closet in rural Alabama, you can appreciate the very real threat tornados pose. Regardless of where you are in the world, dangerous weather events can and do affect you.

There are, however, many other types of natural disasters that cause worry, death, and grief all over the planet. How has your family been affected by natural disasters?

Spanish influenza, 1918

PANDEMIC

A pandemic is loosely defined as a very widespread disease or illness—perhaps across a nation, perhaps around the world. For as long as I've been alive, and probably much longer, people have been predicting that a "superbug" will eventually destroy our world (or at least set it back a few centuries). Given the list of potential candidates that make the daily news, including H1N1 Swine Flu, SARS, AIDS, Marbug virus, Ebola, H5N1 Avian Flu, and many others, it is certainly easy to understand their pessimistic predictions.

MAN-MADE

Man-made disasters are usually the result of things going wrong in our complex technological society. They include: blackouts, hazardous material spills, air pollution, house fires, radiation leaks, food or water contamination, and industrial chemical releases. In the best case, they simply rob us of our modern luxuries for a brief time. In the worst case, they impact the entire ecosystem in which we live.

Man-Made Disasters	
➢ Electrical blackout	➢ Radiation leak
➢ Hazardous material spill	➢ Food/water contamination
➢ Air pollution	➢ Industrial chemical release
➢ House fire	➢ Oil spill

A profound example of a man-made calamity is the 1986 Chernobyl nuclear power plant accident that, according to the World Health Organization, exposed six million people to dangerous levels of radiation and left a portion of our planet nearly uninhabitable.[6]

WAR/TERRORISM/CRIME

Disasters caused by malicious intent are perhaps the most terrifying because their impact is limited only by the perpetrator's knowledge and available resources. Consider that humans are the only species to have ever existed who possess the ability to destroy the planet (in so far as to make it uninhabitable for mankind). Recently, there has been significant emphasis around the globe on combating the threat of terrorism. Some argue that such attention has improved our level of safety, while others quickly dismiss that view as naïve.

Chernobyl nuclear accident, 1986

Terrorist attacks of 9/11 *(photo by FEMA News/Bri Rodriguez)*

PERSONAL

Sometimes a disaster is nothing more than an unfortunate turn of events in your personal life—perhaps an illness, loss of job, or unexpected financial burden. Typically, it causes hardship through financial pressures or physical disability. Serious personal misfortunes like these must also be included in your emergency plans since they disrupt your life in much the same way as other disasters.

DEFINING "BAD" AND "REALLY BAD"

All things are relative. What is considered to be a disaster by one person, might be thought of as little more than an inconvenience by another. To sort this out, it is helpful to have a general method of ranking disaster events. There are no recognized rating systems, so one will be arbitrarily created for the sake of discussion. This admittedly unscientific system is designed solely to illustrate the point that the term "disaster" may be used to describe a wide range of events.

Let's rate disasters by three important metrics: *area affected, duration,* and *severity.* Let's further rank each metric from 1 to 4, where 1 represents the

Table 1-1 Arbitrary Disaster Ranking

Category	Area Affected	Duration	Severity
1	Local	<5 days	- Limited disruption to services/utilities - Food/water/fuel available - Government/financial institutions intact
2	Regional	5-14 days	- Limited disruption to services/utilities - Limited food/water/fuel - Government/financial institutions intact
3	National	15-60 days	- No services/utilities available - No food/water/fuel available - Limited disruption to government/financial institutions
4	Global	>60 days	- No services/utilities available - No food/water/fuel available - Collapse of government/financial institutions

best case, and 4 represents the worst case. Table 1-1 puts values to the categories. Again, keep in mind this is just an arbitrary rating system. But it gets your head in the right place—thinking about how broad disasters can be, how long they can last, and what impacts they might have on you and those you love.

To make sense of this, consider two examples—one at each end of the disaster spectrum.

Example 1:

Your community is hit by a winter ice storm. Power goes out, and the roads are treacherous to drive on. A few grocery stores have managed to stay open, and water and propane fuel are still available and unaffected. Within a few days, the ice melts and things return to normal. Using our rating system, we would define this disaster as 1-1-1 (Area Affected: Cat 1), (Duration: Cat 1), and (Severity: Cat 1). All in all, this is a mild disaster with limited impact.

Example 2:

Now, let's consider something more devastating. A large volcano erupts without warning in the center of the United States. It spews ash up to six feet thick across the entire country. The weather becomes unpredictable, daylight is limited, and there are no services (medical, fire, police) or utilities (phone, power, water, gas) available. Roads are completely impassable, so escaping the worst hit regions is not an option. The government is overwhelmed and quickly unable to function. Financial institutions worldwide are crippled. Worst of all, the effects of the disaster could be felt for a decade or more. This disaster would rank as 4-4-4 (Area Affected: Cat 4), (Duration: Cat 4), (Severity: Cat 4).

> **Tips**
> Think this sounds impossible? Do a little research on the super volcano lying under Yellowstone National Park, affectionately named "The Beast" by geologists.[7]

Again, the key point of this rating exercise is to recognize that disasters come in many shapes and sizes, not all of which require the same preparation.

PREPARING VERSUS *PREPARING!*

Just as there are various degrees of disasters, there are also many different levels of preparedness. This brings us to one of the most important points in this book: ***Know what you are preparing for.***

> **Tips**
> Realize from the beginning that you can't prepare for everything.

You can't prepare for everything. Instead, try to draw a line in the sand based on what you see to be the greatest threats to your family. Then target your efforts to mitigate the impact of those threats. Do you want your family to be capable of riding out a particularly bad winter storm? Or are you preparing for something much worse? Only you can answer these questions. And your priorities may change over time. Perhaps you will begin by simply reviewing and updating your homeowner's insurance, and filling the pantry with extra canned goods. Later, you might feel compelled to take a more exhaustive look at things. Taking that next step might lead you to develop emergency preparedness skills (e.g., first aid, home maintenance, gardening, canning), establish a network of fellow *preppers,* and more closely monitor world events that might portend of an impending disaster.

The point here is that you need to maintain a realistic understanding of how well your preparations will carry you through different situations. As a Green Beret soldier once advised me, "know your capabilities, but more importantly, know your limitations." Accept that being prepared does not necessarily require planning for the end of the world. A better starting place is to focus on meeting your family's needs during the most likely disaster events.

WILDERNESS SURVIVAL

People often confuse disaster preparedness with wilderness survival. Many books treat them as one and the same, and that is a critical shortcoming. Let's distinguish between the two. Disaster preparedness is having a wood-burning stove for keeping your family warm on cold winter nights when the power fails. Wilderness survival is building a lean-to using branches and shoestrings. Both are important and can save your life. Even though there will be times when the line gets blurred, there should be no illusion about it. This book is focused on disaster preparedness, *not* wilderness survival. There are two reasons for this.

First and foremost, preparing for likely disasters will serve the vast majority of people much better than honing their "live off the land" skills. Perhaps some, such as avid hikers or pilots, might fall outside this rule, but for most of us it is far more likely that we will be facing a power outage than a charging moose.

 The second reason is that disaster preparedness is something that can be taught using a book. Regardless of the number of ways someone describes how you clean a squirrel with a pocketknife, it requires hands-on instruction and a heck of a lot of practice in order to become proficient. Much of what is contained in this book, on the other hand, is simply designed to help you identify the needs you may experience during hard times.

This is not to suggest that wilderness survival is unimportant. On the contrary, it just might save your life one day. Those blessed few who truly possess the skill to survive in extreme wilderness conditions are to be saluted.

AVOIDING PITFALLS

There are dozens of disaster preparedness (DP) books available. Some titles are unique and informative, while others do little more than rehash the Air Force Survival Guide. Even with the breadth of choices, there remain many unanswered questions and a great deal of misinformation. An overriding objective in writing this handbook was to pull together a collection of useful information that avoided the shortcomings common to other DP books.

Some of the biggest shortfalls are discussed below. They are listed here only to illustrate what you should watch out for when conducting your own research.

Back to Basics - Much is written on the need to become self-sufficient by generating your own power (a.k.a., "getting off the grid"), growing your own food, retrieving your own water, and essentially checking out of modern society. This approach is not particularly practical or even desirable for most people.

List Driven - Preparing is often conveyed by exhaustive lists of tools, clothing, food supplies, and other gear. Unfortunately, this hoarding can cost tens of thousands of dollars with a questionable return on the investment. The approach tends to be popular because, let's face it, we all love lists!

> **Tips**
> Unless all civilization breaks down, you don't have to be self-sufficient to be prepared.

They itemize what you need in a format that allows checking a box—thereby getting one step closer to readiness. The assumption with exhaustive stockpiling is that the world's supply chain will collapse, forcing your family to live for a year or more on only what you have stockpiled.

Try not to get overly
excited by lists.
Preparing is not just
about collecting "stuff."

If history is to be our guide, then this doomsday assumption is very unrealistic. Most of the recommended supplies would prove costly and unnecessary. You would likely end up with a jumble of stuff collecting dust in a "junk" closet until a spring cleaning forced them to be sold at a garage sale.

Food Focus - Countless pages in dozens of DP books have already been dedicated to food topics, from bulk storage to basic recipes, canning techniques, sprouting, and even grinding your own wheat. All of this I personally find very interesting, and if you share that interest, I encourage you to investigate. However, as you will discover, the food plan presented in this book is built around very different goals.

If ever there was a
time to be a skeptic,
it is when your life is
on the line.

Hearsay - Unfortunately, much of the information circulated in the DP community is unsubstantiated—based as much on folklore as fact. I am, and advise that you be, very skeptical of unreferenced information. People *think* they know lots of

A worst case scenario

things, but more often than not, the knowledge is unproven and untested. Always ask yourself, "How do I know this is true?" The best answer is to put it to the test yourself. Second to that, is to locate a well-documented report of someone else testing the idea.

Scare and Prepare - Scare tactics are often employed as motivators for disaster preparedness. Worst-case "what if" scenarios are employed— another nation threatening a preemptive nuclear strike, an Earth-destroying asteroid heading our way, the latest plague mutating and become airborne—you get the idea. Once an author has scared the pants off you, he may spend another 50 pages emphasizing that you can survive anything if you are adequately prepared.

I do not engage in the *scare and prepare* method. The fact that you are reading this book tells me that you already know the world is a dangerous place and want to prepare. Preparation motivated by fear is ill-advised.

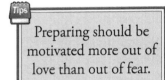

Preparing should be motivated more out of love than out of fear.

Remember, you already dealt with this when you ran around waving your hands wildly, shouting, "The sky is falling, the sky is falling." Besides, I believe that preparing should be motivated more out of love than out of fear.

TOME OF ALL KNOWLEDGE

It would be easy to write an 800-page book on disaster preparedness. There are scores of topics that could be studied, many of which would be of secondary value at best. This book aims toward a basic nuts and bolts approach rather than being the "tome of all knowledge."

My objective was to write a book that you can share with your family and friends. In fact, my intent was to create a book to give to *my* children and friends, and all those whom I care enough about to help them make it through tough times. In the end, it is not quite Strunk and White's *The Elements of Style,* but at least it doesn't rival the girth of Margaret Mitchell's *Gone with the Wind.*

This book is intended to be a study guide—something that can be read as a whole or quickly referenced by individual sections. While the organization is similar to many other DP books, the content is a compilation of personal recommendations based upon my own research. The ultimate goal is simple: to ensure that you and your family are more confident, prepared, and secure in this very unpredictable world.

YOU are responsible for your family's safety. Don't wait to take action. Start today.

Let's be clear about one thing. Disaster preparedness is all about you. If you choose to read this book and take no action, then fine, you are a little smarter than you were at the onset—although arguably no better prepared. On the other hand, if you find yourself loading up the supermarket cart with some extra cans of tuna, or tossing a gas can and blanket into your trunk "just in case," then it was all worth it.

CANDOR

Years ago I worked as a college professor, and one thing I came away with is that teaching is most effective when done with empathy and candor. For that reason, I am writing this book with the same tone and honesty that I would want to see if I were reading it. Try to think of us as two friends out in the shop changing the spark plugs while drinking cold ones (Coke or Coors, your choice). We will work through the discovery process together. I will read through the Chilton's guide, and you turn the wrench. One thing that may not be obvious yet is that a significant part of surviving a disaster is leaning on your fellow citizens, sharing resources, and finding strength in numbers. We might as well start out that way.

ORGANIZATION OF BOOK

The bulk of this handbook is organized around the basic needs that must be met in order to survive. At the beginning of each chapter, is an example scenario designed to help you consider your current level of readiness. At the end of the chapters, are quick summaries of the important points for easy future reference.

Also at the end of each chapter, is a brief list of recommended supplies. The lists are intentionally kept short, limited to actual needs, not "nice to haves," and are crafted with generality in mind—focusing more on the general need than the specific items. You should tailor the lists such that your supplies are practical and effective in meeting *your* specific needs. Taking an individual approach to preparation will help you pull together a DP plan that works for you and your family.

Also, you will likely be better served if you start thinking like MacGyver—learning to make the most of what you have on hand. Even with a house full of supplies, there will undoubtedly be challenges that require you to adapt and use what you have in ways you never before considered. Recognizing how to use things for other than their intended purpose may in fact be the most valuable DP skill you can develop.

> **Tips**
> Learning to use things for other than their intended purpose is an important DP skill.

In addition to the chapters that discuss basics needs, are three that focus on other topics. The first addresses special needs, specifically those of children, pregnant women, the elderly, people with disabilities, and pets. This section is a must read for most families. Second is a chapter on the importance of establishing a support network. You will be stronger and more capable in a group of like-minded families. Finally, the last chapter of the book encourages you to test your level of preparedness by rehearsing several scenarios in order to test your plan *before* an actual disaster occurs. In my experience, this is the best way to reveal any preparations you may have overlooked.

At the end of this handbook are a number of worksheets, designed to help you organize your family's information. Feel free to photocopy them for easier use.

Worksheets

- ➢ Food storage list
- ➢ Telephone numbers
- ➢ Important papers
- ➢ Home assessment
- ➢ Home hazards checklist
- ➢ List of medications/allergies
- ➢ Leave behind note
- ➢ Personalized DP plan

WEB REFERENCES

I have endeavored to research the covered topics extensively, and limit recommendations to only those areas where sound conclusions could be drawn—eliminating any guesswork that might get you killed.

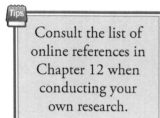

Consult the list of online references in Chapter 12 when conducting your own research.

One advantage of living in the 21st century is that nearly any kind of information can be found from one's own living room via the Internet. This convenience speeds up research to be sure, but unfortunately it also leaves a fleeting trail for others to follow. The question then becomes how does a writer reference his work to sources that might change on any given day?

My answer to this challenge is to do three things:

1. All the web links may be found in the bibliography at the end of the book for easy reference. They include websites from private organizations (e.g., American Red Cross, WebMD) and government services [e.g., Centers for Disease Control and Prevention (CDC), Federal Emergency Management Agency (FEMA)]. Websites for large institutions such as these are typically better managed than those of smaller organizations, and change less frequently. When changes do occur, there is often a link to redirect you.

2. A complete listing of the referenced websites may also be found at *www.disasterpreparer.com*. The webpage will be periodically updated to reflect any known changes in the reference web links. If you identify a dead link or changed content, please email me via this website.

3. More than one reference is cited whenever possible. Duplicate sources should enable you to locate supporting information in the event of a dead link.

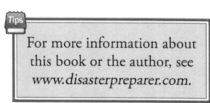

For more information about this book or the author, see *www.disasterpreparer.com*.

CHAPTER 2
STAYING ALIVE

CHAPTER 2

STAYING ALIVE

E ffective preparation of any kind requires a clear understanding of the goals you are trying to achieve. In the case of disaster preparedness, the primary goal is to minimize the impact of a crisis—whether it's a house fire, earthquake, or flood. At an absolute minimum, this means you want to survive, but in most cases you also expect to maintain a reasonable quality of life. A comprehensive DP plan should help you and your family to accomplish both.

CORNERSTONES TO PREPARING

Disaster preparedness requires much more than just stocking up on food and water. A thorough approach is developed around five cornerstones (see tip box). As you work through the discussion of the 14 basic human needs, consider each of these cornerstones to establish the most effective preparedness plan.

> **Cornerstones**
> 1. Leverage existing safety nets.
> 2. Stock extra consumables.
> 3. Collect tools and supplies.
> 4. Develop useful knowledge and skills.
> 5. Establish a support group.

Of the five, developing useful knowledge and skills is arguably the most important. As you will see throughout the book, many of the recommendations emphasize what you need to *learn,* rather than what you need to *buy.* The truth is most of us already have plenty of stuff. Rather, it's our know-how that is seriously lacking. That is where this book comes in—to teach you critical skills, such as how to store food, purify water, make your house safer, generate electricity, find disaster information on the Internet, protect your family, and much more.

WHERE TO BEGIN

If the thought of pulling together a personalized DP plan feels a bit overwhelming, don't be discouraged. It's hard enough to prepare for a single catastrophe let alone ready your family for dozens of possible scenarios. You already know that your family will need food and water, but how do you pull together something more comprehensive?

Preparing for many different disaster scenarios requires careful planning.

There are two possible methods. The first is to list as many disaster situations as you can think of, and then identify what your family would need in order to survive them. The problem with this approach is that there is significant overlap of needs from one disaster to another. There is also the risk that you might overlook a specific scenario, leaving your family vulnerable.

The second approach is to identify your family's fundamental needs that must be met in order to survive nearly any situation. You then tailor the specifics of that list to the type and severity of the disaster. This is the preferred approach because it results in a more general solution, one without the tedious repetition.

HUMAN NEEDS

An excellent discussion of human needs was presented by the humanistic psychologist Abraham Maslow. As a humanist, he proposed that people not only try to survive, but also prosper and live meaningful lives. In our current society, this trait often manifests in professional achievement or the pursuit of advanced consciousness and wisdom. The assertion is that people wish to be "fully functioning." Under most conditions, humans are not only interested in meeting their most basic physical needs, but also in living full and consequential lives. As conditions deteriorate,

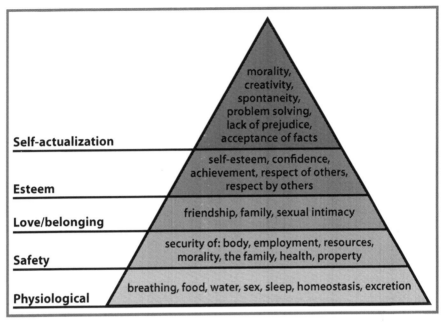

Maslow's hierarchy of needs

however, people are forced to focus on meeting only their most fundamental needs, the ones that help keep them alive. This necessary retrogression is frequently seen when a major disaster strikes.

Maslow established a hierarchy of needs, often illustrated using a pyramid.[7] In his hierarchy, he identified the most basic survival needs as physiological. Included in these are food, water, air, and sleep. Above those, are needs associated with safety and prosperity. Even farther up the hierarchy, are more personal needs, such as friendship, self-esteem, and morality.

As far as disaster preparedness, you need to concern yourself primarily with *physiological, safety,* and to a lesser extent the *love/belonging* needs. The abstract needs above those are better suited to self-improvement studies. If you consider Maslow's hierarchy and apply a little common sense, you can quickly identify eight basic needs that must to be met in a disaster situation: food, water, shelter, light, heating/cooling, air, sleep, and hygiene/sanitation.

This is a short list compared with all the perceived necessities you might require in the course of your normal daily life (e.g., fashionable clothes, premium coffee, a comfortable bed). But unlike those desires, the

Basic Needs
- Food
- Water
- Shelter
- Light
- Heating/cooling
- Air
- Sleep
- Hygiene/sanitation

Supporting Needs
- Medicine/first aid
- Communication
- Electrical power
- Financial security
- Transportation
- Protection

sustained loss of any one of these eight primary necessities will almost certainly lead to your demise. The goal of preparation, therefore, is to meet these needs regardless of the crisis. There are also six secondary needs that directly or indirectly support your survival and help to maintain a reasonable quality of life. They include: medicine/first aid, communication, electrical power, financial security, transportation, and protection.

Together these two lists comprise fourteen areas that should be addressed by a comprehensive preparedness plan. It seems logical therefore to organize this handbook around these needs. By the end of the book, you should have a good understanding of these subjects. And with that knowledge, you will be ready to tailor your own personalized DP plan.

YOUR PERSONALIZED DP PLAN

What exactly is a disaster preparedness plan, and how do you go about making one? Despite the wealth of information published on the subject of emergency preparedness, you will find it difficult to find a direct answer to this question. It's also equally unlikely that you will find an actual example of what a comprehensive DP plan might look like. Rest assured that this question will be tackled head on. Not only will you understand what a DP plan should include, but you will also have examples to guide you in creating a customized plan for your family.

A disaster preparedness plan is a personalized summary of how you will meet your family's needs—those listed above, or others that you identify. There are many ways to organize the details, but the simplest is to create a table that pairs the dangers your family may face to the steps you will take to mitigate their impact. Keep in mind that your family's DP plan will be unique because it is built around their specific needs as well as the methods you choose to meet those needs.

A blank DP Plan worksheet is included in the *Appendix* to help you better organize your approach. Feel free to make as many copies as necessary to detail your preparations—perhaps using one page for your water plan, another page for your food plan, etc.

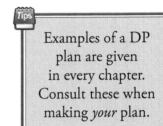

Examples of a DP plan are given in every chapter. Consult these when making *your* plan.

Each chapter also includes an example of what a corresponding DP plan might look like. Feel free to create your own format if you don't like the one provided. It's also not a bad idea to document your plan on the computer since doing so allows you to make changes quickly and easily. Remember, a DP plan is nothing more than a manner in which to get your preparations down on paper. There is no one right way.

SURVIVAL IN A BUCKET?

We all love one-stop shopping. It's easy, and there's little thought required. Capitalizing on that line of convenience thinking, several Internet-based companies now offer prepackaged disaster preparedness kits. Most are stored in airtight buckets or easy to carry backpacks. If you read the retailer websites, you might be convinced that preparing involves nothing more than forking over $99 and finding a shelf on which to store the bucket of goodies.

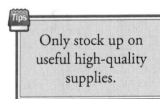

Only stock up on useful high-quality supplies.

Let's take a look at one such disaster preparedness kit meant for a family of four, all conveniently stored in a five-gallon waterproof bucket:

- 12 energy bars
- 12 8-oz. water boxes
- 4 space blankets
- 1 pair disposable medical gloves
- 5 five-hour emergency candles
- 1 whistle

- 4 light sticks
- 4 thin plastic ponchos
- 4 small packs of tissues
- 1 tube tent
- 4 lightweight dust masks
- 1 pair work gloves
- 12 plastic bags
- 1 small first-aid kit
  (adhesive bandages, gauze,
  tweezers, antibiotic cream)

- 50 water purification tablets
- 1 GI-style can opener
- 50 feet of nylon cord
- 1 small Swiss Army knife
- 50 waterproof matches
- 1 solar radio with flashlight
- 1 package of toilet chemicals
- 1 roll of duct tape

Wow, that seems like quite a list! Now, let's imagine being in a real life situation and see how well the supplies hold up.

One of many DP kits available from MayDay Industries

Example scenario:

Assume that your family of four lives on the East Coast, and a hurricane blows through. Thousands of power poles are downed, leaving you without electricity for two weeks. Gasoline is in very short supply, supermarkets are unable to restock, and local water reserves are contaminated due to flooding. The temperature is about 85 degrees during the day and 50 degrees at night. There are subsequent bouts of heavy rain. Worst of all, a large tree has fallen through the roof of your house. And, though not prevalent, there are scattered incidents of looting.

Let's test this kit against your family's fourteen fundamental needs:

- **Food**—The energy bars will keep your family alive for an additional day or two over having nothing at all. But the less than appetizing meals certainly won't help the morale of your hungry family. The GI-style can opener will open any canned food, but it's slow, difficult to use, easy to lose, and won't hold up for long.
- **Water**—The purified water will last your family of four about six hours (assuming a minimum of one gallon per person/day). After that, you will have to either boil or treat the city water in an effort to nullify whatever contaminants have entered the water supply.
- **Shelter**—There are no tarps or tools in this kit to patch the hole in your roof, so your shelter is slowly being destroyed by the deluge of rain.
- **Light**—The kit's single solar radio with flashlight will be inadequate for your family to function at night. The five emergency candles will likely only last a single evening. After that, your family will be forced to hunker down as soon darkness arrives.
- **Heating/Cooling**—The temperatures are mild enough that you can survive without heating or cooling. Daytime temperatures will make it uncomfortably warm, as well as increase the need for drinking water. Evening temperatures will be chilly, forcing you to depend on the blankets you already have to keep everyone warm. Space blankets are unsuitable for anything except short-term wilderness survival. They are typically small, easily torn, hard to wrap yourself in, and of questionable benefit over a simple tarp.

- **Air**—In this scenario, there are no dangers to your air supply. However, if there were, the kit offers only lightweight dust masks that would be ineffective against most airborne threats.
- **Sleep**—Sleeping in your home is still possible for a while, but conditions will quickly become unhealthy because of sanitation issues.
- **Hygiene/Sanitation**—The few packages of tissues and the potty bucket are inadequate for your family's personal hygiene. Without an ample supply of water, your family faces risk of disease from poor sanitation. Also, the inability to maintain an accepted level of cleanliness will drastically drive morale down.
- **Medicine/First Aid**—The first aid supplies provided are completely insufficient for anything beyond a scraped knee. If anyone in your family becomes injured or ill (both very possible), you will be faced with a very serious situation.
- **Communication**—There is nothing in the kit to help contact family or friends, no evacuation plan, no games or activities to keep children entertained, and no information about emergency services.
- **Financial Security**—The kit does nothing to help your financial security. In particular, there are no home inventory sheets included to help itemize property damage.
- **Transportation/Navigation**—The small radio might offer information to help decide if evacuation is necessary. However, with this kit alone, you will have no spare gasoline, no alternate means of transportation, and no maps of the surrounding area.
- **Protection**—The kit offers no personal protection beyond a small pocketknife. Should looters invade your home thinking it empty, your family will be helpless to defend themselves.

The bottom line is that, upon further analysis, the bucket DP kit falls far short of meeting your family's post-hurricane needs. Test this kit against other scenarios, such as a winter storm, terrorist strike, or widespread blackout. No doubt you will agree that it does little to improve your chances of survival, let alone make the situations more tolerable.

This criticism, however, isn't directed toward any company offering such kits. Having a bucket of supplies is better than having nothing at all. So in one sense, they are to be applauded for identifying a very real need.

It is, however, strongly recommended that you take a more practical approach to disaster preparedness.

Preparing will require you to do significantly more than just order a bucket of supplies. It will require you to take numerous actions, including assessing your family's needs, stocking supplies, shoring up your shelter, mitigating potential hazards, and preparing for likely threats. At the end of your efforts, you will be rewarded with knowing that your family is far better prepared to handle real world challenges.

> The best DP kit is not the one with the most supplies, but the one with the right supplies.

Now let's get on with it.

CHAPTER 3

FOOD

CHAPTER 3

FOOD

Challenge

A series of coordinated terrorist attacks on the country's food transportation system have left grocery stores unable to restock their supplies. Shelves are quickly emptied, and it may take up to three weeks for shipments to be resumed. How will you feed your family?

When preparing for a disaster, food is often the first need that comes to mind. A good illustration of this is when people rush to purchase milk and bread at the first warning of a bad storm. Admittedly, some people also turn their attention to batteries, generators, and bottled water, but those needs are usually considered after their stop at the grocery store.

Your access to food can be cut off in two different ways. The first is local in nature when stores are forced to close due to an immediate crisis—most often inclement weather. The second situation is one in which the food supply itself is disrupted. What is the likelihood of that? Not as remote as you might think. Minor disruptions occur all the time, often caused by weather events or contamination. For example, recently there was a winter freeze that ruined much of California's citrus crop, and an outbreak of *E. coli* poisoning that forced the recall of the nation's spinach. More significant disruptions can be caused by many incidents, including a prolonged power outage, transportation problems, major weather events, or an attack on the food supply system.

Did you know that most supermarkets only stock about a week's supply of food? This "just in time" supply system serves everyone well under normal circumstances. The supermarket owner doesn't suffer the overhead of having to hold large stockpiles of goods. And the consumer is guaranteed fresh goods that haven't sat on a shelf for extended times.

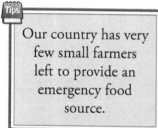

Our country has very few small farmers left to provide an emergency food source.

Ask yourself what would happen if the grocery stores were forced to shut down, or if the food supply was disrupted and stores could no longer be resupplied in a timely manner. Where would your family get food? There are very few small farmers left in the country, so local farmers' markets wouldn't be much help. Likely it would fall to the government to provide emergency rations, and let's face it; our government hasn't always shown itself to be efficient or timely when it comes to disaster relief.

A self-replenishing food source is the only way to truly be prepared for a long-term disruption.

The only way to be truly prepared for a long-term disruption of the food supply system is to have a self-replenishing food source, such as a farm or livestock. Unfortunately, this is not a practical option for most people. Landlords just wouldn't understand cows in the apartment! Many experts suggest doing the next best thing—stockpiling large quantities of non-perishable food. This book challenges that premise. Instead, the recommendation here is for a modest food storage plan that will meet your family's needs in all but the very worst disaster scenarios.

There are four fundamental questions to consider when preparing a well thought out food storage plan. As it turns out, the answer to the first question determines the answers to the other three.

> **Fundamental Food Questions**
> 1. How much food should you store?
> 2. What types of food?
> 3. How should you store it?
> 4. How long will the stored food last?

HOW MUCH FOOD SHOULD YOU STORE?

The question of how much food to store ties directly back to the more fundamental question posed in Chapter 1. What you are preparing for? The answer ultimately determines the quantity of supplies of every type that you will need. Short-term food interruptions, such as a snowstorm that prevent you from getting to the store, are unlikely to require more than a week's supply. Whereas a terrorist attack on the food supply system might cause shortages lasting weeks or even months—albeit likely limited only to certain food types.

Making preparations requires you to draw the line somewhere. Some *preppers* gravitate towards extreme, "end of the world" food storage plans but fail to consider the likelihood of such events or the costs associated with that kind of preparation. The recommendations in this book strive to be more practical and pocketbook friendly.

When it comes to food storage, a reasonable approach is to keep a 30-day supply. Perhaps you are shaking your head in disbelief. You're recalling the advice of numerous experts who suggest having an entire year's supply of food stockpiled.

> **Tips**
> A 30-day food supply is adequate for all but the most catastrophic of events.

That level of food storage is impractical, wasteful, and almost always unnecessary.

Let's start with *impractical*. Consider that the average American consumes about 2,000 pounds of food per year. Now imagine a family of four storing *four tons* of food in a location that is both temperature and humidity controlled. Not only storing it, but rotating it, and keeping it from spoiling or being ruined by pests. A challenge indeed!

Storing such a large quantity of food would likely be very *wasteful* as well. You would need to master techniques to keep food from becoming contaminated—most likely using nitrogen-purged air-tight containers. Even when you did become skilled at food storage, you would still experience loss due to spoilage, rodents, and insects. This means that you would be required to regularly inspect a huge stockpile of food, discarding and replacing things that were no longer consumable. This would be a costly and time consuming process.

Finally, ask yourself which disasters would require you to have such a large food cache. Go back and examine the *Shopping List of Disasters* in Chapter 1. Of all the disasters listed there, only a few truly catastrophic scenarios would require you to have more than a month's food supply (e.g., asteroid strike, world-wide drought, global war—a truly world changing event). The bottom line is that the sacrifices incurred from storing large quantities of food would very likely be *unnecessary*.

Consider the impact of every family in America following this recommendation to keep a full month's supply of food. No one would ever have to race to the store when weather threatens. Catastrophic disasters would still cause worry, but the 30-day supply would give families time: time for the nation's emergency management services to provide relief, time for people to rally with friends and family to pool resources, and time to evacuate to areas where shortages were not as severe.

As with every aspect of preparedness, however, your food storage plan is just that—yours! If you decide that a month's supply isn't enough to protect your family, then by all means store more. But be forewarned, having a large food cache can be expensive and wasteful.

WHAT TYPES OF FOOD?

The next step in creating a food plan is deciding what to store. Table 3-1 is an example of what a few entries in a food storage list might look like. A blank food storage worksheet is given in the *Appendix*. Make a copy of the worksheet, and then fill it in with the food items your family enjoys eating. You may find it helpful to use different color highlighters to color code the foods, indicating if the item is stored in the pantry, refrigerator, or freezer.

Table 3-1 Sample Food Storage List

Food Category	Type	Full Stock Qty	Full Stock Size	Current Stock	Qty Needed
Vegetables	Green Beans	4	12 oz. can	1	3
	Frozen Corn	2	12 oz. bag	2	-
Rice and Beans	Brown rice	2	16 oz. bag	1	1
	Pinto beans	3	12 oz. bag	1	2
Dairy	Milk	2	Gallon	1	1
	Milk, dry	1	16 oz box	1	-

Keep the food storage list and a pencil near your pantry, perhaps taped to the door. As you consume items, change the "Qty Needed" to reflect what needs to be restocked. When you take your next trip to the supermarket, bring the worksheet with you as a shopping list. Don't forget to replace the old list with a new blank one.

Feel free to vary it up each week by making food substitutions, such as replacing canned peaches with raisins, but try to stay true to your general dietary goals—discussed in detail later in this chapter.

Far too often, food storage plans consist mostly of bland, easy-to-store food. This is usually a result of trying to store massive quantities of food where shelf life and getting enough calories in the diet are the driving requirements. Unfortunately, little thought is put into how unhappy the menu will make the person having to eat it.

Shying away from very large food plans frees you up to store a wide variety of commercially available food. This type of food plan can revolve around three requirements: (1) nutrition, (2) taste, and (3) shelf life. Your family will thank you for adopting a consumer view in your preparations. No more dehydrated banana chips or molasses-flavored cookies.

To stock up, go no further than your local grocery store or discount warehouse. Storing foods with a very long shelf life, such as military Meals Ready-to-Eat

> **Tips**
> Stock up on food that your family enjoys and is accustomed to eating.

(MREs) are thankfully no longer necessary. If you have ever eaten MREs (or their predecessor, C-Rations), you likely understand. A meal or two can be fun, but eating them as your three squares a day gets old very quickly. *I say this as an ex-Army grunt who has eaten his fair share of both.*

> **Tips**
> Gardening, sprouting, canning, and dehydrating are all very interesting, but not necessary for establishing a modest food cache.

There is a line of thinking in the DP community that preparing is synonymous with getting "back to basics." Many books have lengthy discussions on gardening, sprouting, canning, and dehydrating. Any activity that has you eating healthier is certainly to be encouraged, but understand that these activities aren't necessary to pull together a reasonable food storage plan. Therefore, they are not discussed at length here. If you are interested in learning about these food topics, you should have no trouble finding numerous books specializing in them.

When deciding what types of food to store, sound advice can be found by consulting the New USDA food pyramid.[8] The food pyramid was recently updated, and though you may still find it flawed, it provides well-researched guidance to proper nutrition. Contrary to popular belief, creating a stockpile does not mean that you have to store food oddities—don't go out and buy a huge tub of beef jerky thinking that it would make great "survival food." Stick to what your family eats and enjoys *now*.

> **Tips**
> When selecting canned goods, opt for those with pull tops. This eliminates the need for can openers, and does not affect the shelf life.

Said another way . . . ***store what you eat, and eat what you store.*** This makes rotation a snap; you put the newest food to the rear, and eat that which is oldest.

Canned and boxed foods will be perfectly fresh 30 days after purchase. Breads and raw meats must be frozen to maintain a 30-day supply. Canned meats are also readily available (e.g., Spam, tuna, chicken). As far as dairy, many items have adequate refrigerator life, such as cheese, yogurt, and butter. Shelf stable milk and hard cheeses are options that don't require refrigeration. Shelf stable milk is created using ultra high tempera-

Borden's shelf stable milk

ture pasteurization, and has a shelf life of several months. It is offered through several manufacturers, including Borden, Nestle, and Parmalat, and is readily available at grocery and warehouse stores. For even longer storage, you can keep powdered products, even if just as a backup.

Be careful not to stock up too heavily on frozen or refrigerated foods because this leaves your food supply susceptible to the loss of electricity. There are, however, a few tricks to keeping food cool during a power outage (i.e., up to a few days).

- Put blocks of dry ice in the refrigerator and freezer.
- Keep the refrigerator and freezer stocked full with little empty space, even if it is just filled with containers of frozen water.
- Minimize the times you open the refrigerator or freezer.

If you do find yourself with extra food that will go to waste due to thawing, invite the neighbors over for a big cookout. Goodwill toward others, especially in times of crisis, can go a long way toward making lifelong friendships. Even if you don't like your neighbors and are not driven by "the common good," your generosity may well lead to a prudent exchange of resources.

THE NEW FOOD PYRAMID

You already know what your family likes to eat, but it wouldn't hurt to review the food pyramid to ensure that you pull together a balanced, nutritious food

Use food storage as a chance to improve your family's eating habits.

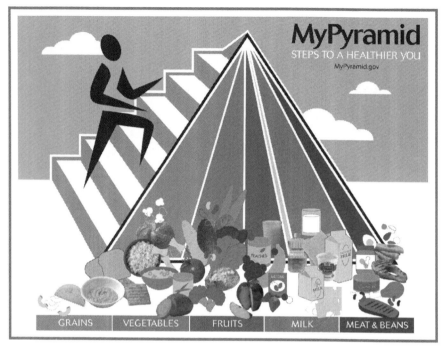

New food pyramid *(illustration by MyPyramid.gov)*

storage plan. Much of what follows might seem better suited to a guide on nutrition, but an important part of being prepared is stocking your cupboards, refrigerator, and freezer with the right kinds of food.

In 2005, the United States Department of Agriculture (USDA) released a significant update to the food pyramid. It is divided into five basic food groups as well as oils/fats. There are also two other categories not explicitly shown by pyramid slices:[8]

- Physical Activity—illustrated by the person climbing the stairs
- Discretionary Calories—represented by the uncolored tip at the top of the pyramid

Recognizing that everyone is different, the USDA has created an online tool that allows you to create your own personalized food plan. Recommendations are based upon age, sex, size, and activity level. There are also many other useful features, including menu planners, meal tracking worksheets, nutrition tips, food ratings, and more. Go to *www.mypyramid.gov* to try the interactive tool.

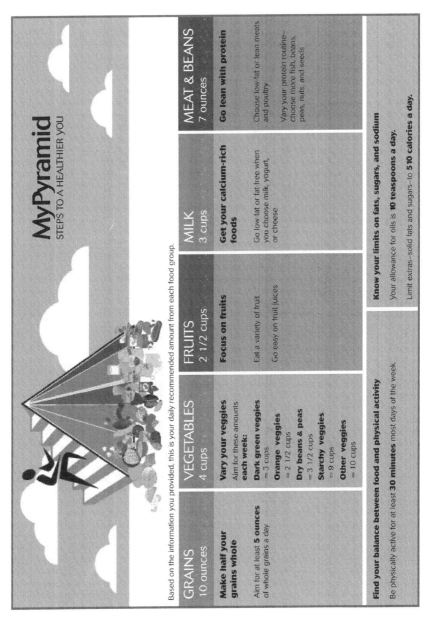

MyPyramid
STEPS TO A HEALTHIER YOU

Based on the information you provided, this is your daily recommended amount from each food group.

GRAINS 10 ounces	VEGETABLES 4 cups	FRUITS 2 1/2 cups	MILK 3 cups	MEAT & BEANS 7 ounces
Make half your grains whole	**Vary your veggies**	**Focus on fruits**	**Get your calcium-rich foods**	**Go lean with protein**
Aim for at least **5 ounces** of whole grains a day	Aim for these amounts each week:	Eat a variety of fruit	Go low-fat or fat-free when you choose milk, yogurt, or cheese	Choose low-fat or lean meats and poultry
	Dark green veggies = 3 cups	Go easy on fruit juices		Vary your protein routine—choose more fish, beans, peas, nuts, and seeds
	Orange veggies = 2 1/2 cups			
	Dry beans & peas = 3 1/2 cups			
	Starchy veggies = 9 cups			
	Other veggies = 10 cups			

Find your balance between food and physical activity
Be physically active for at least **30 minutes** most days of the week.

Know your limits on fats, sugars, and sodium
Your allowance for oils is **10 teaspoons** a day.
Limit extras—solid fats and sugars—to **510 calories a day.**

Sample dietary plan *(illustration by MyPyramid.gov)*

This sample plan recommends consuming 10 ounces of grains, 4 cups of vegetables, 2½ cups of fruits, 3 cups of milk/dairy, and 7 ounces of low-fat meat each day. The specific quantities will vary based on weight, age, and activity level, but the general profile will remain very much the same. Use the new food pyramid's dietary plan to help establish a nutrituous food inventory.

GRAINS

The foundation of the food pyramid is built on grain products, such as breads, cereal, pasta, tortillas, popcorn, oatmeal, and rice. When possible, choose foods made with whole grains over those with refined or enriched grains. The food pyramid recommends that at least half of your grains be whole grains.

Whole-grain foods are made with the entire grain kernel (i.e., bran, germ, and endosperm) and as a result offer more fiber and vitamins, and have been shown to reduce the occurrence of several diseases.[9,10,11] Refined grains are processed such that the bran and germ are removed. This is done to give the grain a finer texture and extend the shelf life. The drawback is that removing them also removes much of the fiber and B vitamins. Whole-grain foods are thus healthier, and since they are higher in fiber, they also keep your digestion on track while helping you to feel full longer.

Courtesy of Country Living Productions

It is also possible to store raw wheat for grinding, but this requires a grain mill (either electric or manual). For very large food stockpiles, a grain mill becomes necessary because raw wheat lasts longer than ground wheat. For the 30-day plan however, it is not required.

Don't forget to store baking items (e.g., baking powder, baking soda, salt, yeast, sugar, corn starch) if planning to bake your own foods. Home-baked goods are considered healthier because they contain less preservatives. Also include spices and flavorings, such as vanilla, cinnamon, cocoa, and chili powder. As always, the bottom line is to store what you know how to use.

FRUITS AND VEGETABLES

You have heard it a thousand times: Americans don't eat enough fruits and vegetables. People use a host of excuses ranging from not liking the taste, to restaurants not offering enough choices. Excuses aside, everyone knows that fresh produce contributes to better health, and is thus deserving of a more concerted effort. Americans in general would be better served by moving away from meats and sweets and toward fruits and vegetables.

You can get your recommended servings of fruits and vegetables many different ways—fresh, cooked, frozen, canned, dried, or even as juice (not the sugar-loaded stuff). Nutritionists recommend eating a variety of fruits and vegetables with different colors and textures. The reason for this is that each food has unique properties that contribute to good health. Try using this excursion into disaster preparedness to take two actions:

1) **Try new foods**—Try those fruits and vegetables that you have passed by so many times in the grocery store fearing that you wouldn't like the taste. You may stumble upon a gem while contributing to your own good health. Besides, having a broad appreciation of a variety of foods is a valuable DP skill since it will help you adapt to dietary changes introduced by food shortages.

2) **Eat a more balanced diet**—Consume more fruits and vegetables, and try some of the whole-grain products available today. Eating more fruits and vegetables will likely help you lose any unwanted pounds, thereby improving your health and helping you to be more physically active. Physical ability is often important when facing the challenges associated with a disaster, such as repairing your roof, hiking down to the river for water, or clearing the roadway of fallen trees.

DAIRY

It is no surprise that the food pyramid recommends consuming primarily low-fat dairy products. They are significantly lower in calories and saturated fat than the full-up versions. A diet low in saturated fat is believed to help maintain low cholesterol, which is an important part of heart health.[12]

Dairy products can include such things as milk, cheese, yogurt, pudding, and ice cream. For those who are lactose-intolerant, there are many lactose-free dairy products now available.

PROTEINS

Protein sources include a wide variety of meat, poultry, fish, beans, eggs, nuts, and seeds. The food pyramid recommends that you opt for lean meats, fish, and poultry with the skin removed. Try to avoid processed meats since they often contain added sodium and other ingredients that can best be described as "miscellaneous animal parts."

Protein can also be found in a wide variety of beans and peas. Eggs are another good source of protein, but be aware that the yolks are high in cholesterol (containing about 70% of your recommended daily allowance). A healthier choice is to eat only the whites if you are going to eat eggs often.[13]

As far as nuts and seeds, the medical community has recently recognized that eating 1½ ounces of nuts per day may reduce the risk of coronary heart disease.[14] Keep in mind that nuts are high in calories, and an ounce is only a small handful (about ¼ cup).

FATS, OILS, SWEETS

Most people have no trouble getting enough fat in their diet. From butter, to mayonnaise, to cooking oil, to animal fat, to candy bars, fat is everywhere! You can't escape it.

Oils are simply fats that are liquid at room temperature. Most are high in monounsaturated or polyun-
saturated fats, low in saturated fats, and have no cholesterol. Notable exceptions are coconut and palm
kernel oil, which are high in saturated fats—very undesirable. Cooking oils include canola oil, corn oil,
cottonseed oil, olive oil, safflower oil, soybean oil,
and sunflower oil.

Solid fats are just that—fats that are solid at room temperature. This includes food items such as butter, margarine, vegetable shortening, beef
fat (tallow, suet), and pork fat (lard). Solid fats come from many animal
products and can also be made from vegetable oils through a process
called hydrogenation. The American Heart Association (AHA) recommends that you consume fats and oils with less than 2 grams of saturated fat per tablespoon, such as canola, olive, and soybean oils.[15]

The AHA also recommends limiting
dietary fat to 30% of total calories. How
easy is this to do? Consider that whole
milk gets about 48% of its calories from
fat, peanut butter—75%, and steak—
52%.[16] It's quite easy to see why people

Tips

Even under the worst
of times, it is hard to
imagine not getting
enough fat in our diets.

routinely exceed the 30% calories-from-fat recommendation. Short of
having to live on lean, wild rabbits, it is difficult to imagine a case where
inadequate fat intake would become a health concern.

Sweets and sweeteners fit best into this category too. Sweeteners include
such things as sugar, brown sugar, honey, maple syrup, corn syrup, and
artificial sweeteners. Consider stocking a collection of sweeteners for
fresh-baked goods, as well as a small supply of your family's favorite
sweets (e.g., candy bars, brownie mix). They can help make life a bit more
pleasurable, which can offset some of the hardship.

FOOD SUMMARY

The message here is that *now* is a good time to introduce your family to
a balanced, nutritious diet. The new food pyramid can help you craft a
healthy eating plan. As far as food storage, increase your stockpile of

foods to a minimum of 30-days supply, being careful not to rely too heavily on frozen or refrigerated foods. Also, remember to store what you eat and eat what you store—no need for "survival food." This strategy keeps waste to a minimum. Perhaps this food storage plan lacks the adventuresome feel of storing a bunker full of military rations. It is, however, practical and would serve your family well in hard times.

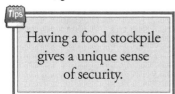

Having a food stockpile gives a unique sense of security.

One final thought on food storage—of all the steps in the DP process, stockpiling food will provide you with the most unique sense of security. Every time your family asks, "What's for dinner?", and you have dozens of choices at your fingertips, you can't help but feel better prepared. Try it, and you will quickly discover the comfort in having well-stocked cupboards.

HOW DO YOU STORE IT?

The difficulty of storing food is directly proportional to how much you decide to store. Larger storage plans present significant challenges, including storage space, rotation, infestation, and spoilage. If you are on board with the 30-day food plan, then the biggest challenge is simply finding enough space.

Large food pantry

To help you better appreciate just how much food is required for 30 days, go to your cupboards and count up how many full meals you have (breakfast, lunch, and dinner). If you are like most families, your current stockpile is somewhere around five to seven days, with lots of little extras that don't necessarily fit into a specific meal. Take a moment to imagine what 30 days of food might look like. Would it even fit in your cupboards? Probably not. More than likely you will have to be a bit creative and free up some closet space or perhaps keep extra food in out of the way places. Many people find that the wasted space under a stairway can be easily converted to a convenient food pantry.

Canned and boxed foods are best stored in dry conditions where temperatures are kept fairly constant, ideally between 40°-60°F.[17] Keep food away from appliances or heating vents where undue heat could cause spoilage. Storage places could include a basement, under your stairs, closets, a utility room, kitchen cupboards, or even under your bed. Due to wide temperature swings, storing extra food in the garage or attic is probably a bad idea. Try to keep all but canned foods off the ground to minimize potential problems with bugs, rodents, or moisture. If you are tight on space, check out *www.shelfreliance.com*, a provider of slanted shelves that allow efficient storage of canned foods, and make rotation a snap.

If you have opted for a larger food storage plan, then you will need to do your homework and learn important storage methods; most of which depend on storing bulk food in airtight containers. Plastic buckets and mylar-foil bags are effective at keeping out air, bugs, and light—all of which can compromise your food cache. Don't store food in garbage bags because the bags may contain pesticides and are made of plastic resins that are not recommended for contact with food.[18] A good deal of advice regarding large food plans can be found in Spigarelli's *Crisis Preparedness Handbook*.[19]

When storing refrigerated foods, the temperature should be kept between 34°-40°F.[20] Cool temperatures help slow the growth of bacteria, extending the shelf life of foods.

Courtesy of Taylor

To ensure that you have the proper refrigerator temperature, check it in several places using a small refrigerator thermometer. Make sure that the highest reading is no more than 40°F. Here's your first big investment—a $10 thermometer!

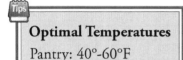

Optimal Temperatures

Pantry: 40°-60°F

Refrigerator: 34°-40°F

Freezer: 0°-5°F

Frozen foods should ideally be kept at 0°F but never above 5°F.[20] Once again, you can use the refrigerator thermometer to ensure you have the proper setting. As a rule of thumb, if your freezer can't keep a block of ice cream brick solid, then it is set too high. It is a good idea to put a freeze date on your freezer foods if they aren't already dated by the store. Also, freeze foods in moisture-vapor-proof packages, such as zippered freezer bags, or airtight freezer containers. Poorly sealed freezer packaging can lead to freezer burn.

HOW LONG WILL STORED FOOD LAST?

You might think that if you limit your food supply to 30 days, then spoilage won't be of much concern. While it is true that a smaller storage plan does remove much of this worry, there are still several reasons why every *prepper* should be aware of the shelf life of different foods.

1. During a crisis, food poisoning can be potentially life threatening. Knowledge of food safety is therefore critical.
2. Even with a modest 30-day food plan, spoilage can still affect some of your supplies (e.g., thawed meats, fresh produce, dairy).
3. In situations where you are forced to scavenge for food, you will need to assess whether that food is safe to eat.
4. If you ever decide to adopt a larger food storage plan, shelf life is critical to planning your stockpile and establishing a rotation schedule.

The first thing to know about shelf life is that it is affected by many factors and is therefore impossible to precisely predict. Food can degrade and become dangerous to consume due to either microbial or non-microbial causes. Some forms of microbial growth are easily seen, such as the fuzzy mold that grows on food that sits in your refrigerator for too long.

Other types of bacteria are more difficult to detect. Eating contaminated food is dangerous because it can cause a variety of different foodborne illnesses, a discussion of which is given in the next section. The time it takes for microorganisms to affect foods depends on the particular methods used in production as well as storage conditions.

Non-microbial spoilage includes moisture gain or loss, chemical effects leading to changes in color or flavor, light-induced rancidity or vitamin loss, and physical damage (e.g., bruising of fruits/vegetables, denting of cans).[21] Beyond spoilage, food can also be ruined by rodents or insects.

Foods can develop an unpleasant odor, flavor, texture, or appearance due to bacterial spoilage. Don't initially taste test food to see if it's spoiled. Rather, begin by checking it for

When in doubt, throw it out!

bulging, bubbles or foam, mold, or cloudiness. If it looks okay, check to see if it smells sour, cheesy, fermented, or putrid. Next, touch the food to see if it has become slimy. Finally, if it passes the visual, smell, and touch tests, taste a small quantity to see if it tastes okay. If the food has become sour, bitter, chalky, or mushy, spit it out immediately.[19]

If any of the above characteristics are noted, the food should be immediately discarded. Your senses are trying to warn you! Food can also be mishandled, causing bacteria to grow rapidly. A well known example is that leaving hot dogs sitting in the sun for several hours at a picnic will cause them to spoil prematurely.

Food that is properly handled and stored at 0°F will remain safe almost indefinitely. Only the quality of food (e.g., tenderness, flavor, aroma, juiciness, and color) suffers from lengthy freezer storage.[23] This rule applies to freezer burn as well. Freezer

Food kept frozen at 0°F can remain safe almost indefinitely.

burn occurs when air reaches the food's surface and dries the product, usually due to the food not being wrapped in air-tight packaging. Freezer-burned food *is* safe to eat. Simply cut away the affected areas before or after cooking.

For additional information on food safety, check out the Department of Health and Human Services website, *www.foodsafety.gov*. It contains useful

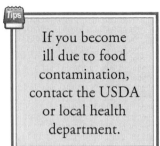

If you become ill due to food contamination, contact the USDA or local health department.

information regarding food safety, food poisoning, and current recalls.

If you should ever become ill, and suspect it is due to food contamination, save the packaging materials. Label any remaining food as "Dangerous," and freeze it for future examination by health officials. If the food is a meat or poultry product, call the USDA Meat and Poultry Hotline at 1-888-674-6854. If it is something other than meat or poultry, or is from a restaurant, contact your local health department. To locate the phone number for your local health department, consult the Health Guide USA website.[24]

FOODBORNE ILLNESSES

In times of crisis, you definitely don't want illness added to your list of troubles. Traveling to a doctor may prove difficult or even impossible, and medical facilities are likely to be overwhelmed. Having to rough it out during a disaster can be bad enough, but doing so while hovering over the toilet can make it nearly intolerable. The following sections provide brief descriptions of seven important foodborne illnesses found in the United States (and throughout the world). The purpose of reviewing them is to become familiar with their symptoms and likely causes. This information is drawn from several references.[25,26,27,28,29,30] Later, some simple but effective ways to prevent food poisoning are discussed.

SALMONELLA

How you get it: *Salmonella* is a rod-shaped motile bacterium that occurs widely in animals, especially poultry and swine. *Salmonella* is frequently contracted by eating food contaminated with

animal or human feces (a.k.a., fecal-oral contamination). Contamination often occurs when the food preparer doesn't wash his hands after using the toilet. Other possible sources include undercooked eggs, poultry, or meat; and unpasteurized milk or juice.

What it causes: Onset of salmonellosis typically occurs within 1 to 3 days. Acute symptoms can last a few days to a week and may include nausea, vomiting, abdominal cramps, diarrhea, fever, and headache. Additionally, arthritic symptoms may follow 3 to 4 weeks after the onset of acute symptoms. The Food and Drug Administration (FDA) estimates that 2-4 million cases of salmonellosis occur annually in the United States.

CAMPYLOBACTER JEJUNI

How you get it: *Campylobacter jejuni* is a slender, rod-shaped bacterium that causes campylobacteriosis. Most cases result from eating raw or undercooked poultry, or from cross-contamination. The bacteria are often found in healthy cattle and birds. Surveys show that 20-100% of retail chickens are contaminated. However, properly cooking chicken *will* kill the bacteria. *C. jejuni* is also contracted from contaminated water and unpasteurized milk.

What it causes: Onset of symptoms usually occurs 2 to 5 days after ingestion of the contaminated food or water. Symptoms can include diarrhea, fever, abdominal pain, nausea, headache, and muscle pain. The illness generally lasts 7 to 10 days, but relapses are also common. *C. jejuni* may also spread to the bloodstream and cause a life-threatening infection. Surveys have shown that *C. jejuni* is the leading cause of bacterial diarrheal illness in the United States. The FDA estimates that there are at least 2-4 million cases annually.

CLOSTRIDIUM PERFRINGENS

How you get it: *Clostridium perfringens* is a sporeforming, rod-shaped bacterium that is widely distributed in the environment, and can be found in decaying vegetation, marine sediment, and the intestines of humans and domestic animals. Consumption can cause *C. perfringens* food poisoning. Eating of improperly prepared meat or meat dishes (e.g., gravy, stew) is the main source of infection. Food may be either undercooked or prepared too far in advance of consumption. This bacterium is often referred to as the "cafeteria germ" because most outbreaks occur at institutional kitchens in hospitals, school cafeterias, prisons, and nursing homes.

What it causes: Symptoms usually start 8 to 22 hours after consumption and include abdominal cramps and diarrhea. The illness is usually over within 24 hours, but less severe symptoms may persist for 1 to 2 weeks. Symptoms may last longer in the elderly. *C. perfringens* is the third most common foodborne illness in the United States with an estimated 250,000 people affected annually.

E. COLI

How you get it: *Escherichia coli* are a large and diverse group of bacteria. Some strains are harmless, while others can cause diarrhea, urinary tract infection, or respiratory illness. The most commonly identified Shiga toxin-producing *E. coli* (STEC) is *E. coli O157*. When you hear reports about outbreaks of *E. coli,* they are usually referring to this particular strain. Infections are caused by fecal-oral contamination (i.e., ingesting small quantities of human or animal feces). This can be caused by

consuming contaminated food or water, drinking unpasteurized milk, or coming into direct contact with human or animal feces. Other possible sources include undercooked hamburger, and unpasteurized milk or juice.

What it causes: Symptoms of STEC infections include severe stomach cramps, diarrhea (sometimes bloody), vomiting, and a mild fever. Most people recover within a week. Onset of symptoms may begin anywhere from 1 to 10 days after infection. Very young victims may develop hemolytic-uremic syndrome (HUS), which may cause acute kidney failure. The FDA estimates that 70,000 cases of *E. coli O157* occur each year in the United States.

SHIGELLA

How you get it: *Shigella* are non-sporeforming, rod-shaped bacteria that cause shigellosis. Shigellosis is primarily a human disease, not found in animals except monkeys and chimpanzees. There are several different types of *Shigella* bacteria, but Groups B and D account for almost all the cases in the United States. The organism is frequently found in water polluted by human feces. The disease is most often spread through fecal-oral contamination. It is particularly common with toddlers who are not fully toilet-trained. Shigellosis can also be contracted by eat-

ing contaminated food. Uncooked salads (e.g., potato, tuna, shrimp, macaroni, and chicken), raw vegetables, milk and dairy products are all foods that may be contaminated. Water can also become contaminated if sewage runs into it, or if someone infected with shigellosis swims in it.

What it causes: Symptoms usually occur 12 to 50 hours after ingestion and may include abdominal pain, cramps, diarrhea, fever, vomiting, blood/pus/mucus in the stool, and difficulty defecating. Shigellosis typically resolves in 5 to 7 days. A severe infection can occur in children under age 2 resulting in high fever and seizures. An estimated 300,000 cases of shigellosis occur annually in the United States.

CLOSTRIDIUM BOTULINUM

How you get it: *Clostridium botulinum* is a spore-forming, rod-shaped bacteria that produces a potent neurotoxin. Seven types of botulism are recognized (A-G), of which types A, B, E, and F cause human botulism. Food botulism is a rare but severe type of food poisoning caused by the ingestion of foods containing the potent neurotoxin formed during growth of the organism. The toxin is heat-sensitive and can be effectively destroyed if heated to 176°F for a minimum of 10 minutes. Sausages, meat products, canned vegetables, and seafood products are the most frequent vehicles for human botulism. Most of the outbreaks in the United States are associated with inadequately processed home-canned foods, but commercially produced foods have also been involved (e.g., Castleberry's hot dog chili in 2007).

What it causes: The botulism toxin causes paralysis by blocking motor nerve terminals. The flaccid paralysis progresses downward, usually starting with the eyes and face, moving to the throat, chest, and extremities. When the diaphragm and chest muscles become paralyzed, respiration is impaired and death from asphyxia can result. The incidence of this type of poisoning is very low, but the mortality rate is high. Annually, there are on average 10 to 30 outbreaks of food botulism in the United States.

STAPHYLOCOCCUS AUREUS

How you get it: *Staphylococcus aureus* is a spherical bacterium capable of producing a highly heat-stable enterotoxin that causes illness in humans. The most common way of contracting Staphylococcal food poisoning is through contact with food workers who carry the bacteria, or by eating contaminated foods. It is usually associated with meat products, poultry and egg products, homemade salads (e.g., egg, tuna, chicken, potato, macaroni), cream pastries and pies, and dairy products.

What it causes: Onset of symptoms is usually rapid and may include nausea, vomiting, retching, abdominal cramping, and exhaustion. In severe cases, headache, muscle cramping, and changes in blood pressure and pulse rate may occur. Recovery may require a few days. The incidence rate of staphylococcal food poisoning is unknown due to poor reporting of the illness and frequent misdiagnosis.

AVOIDING FOOD POISONING

The CDC estimates that 325,000 hospitalizations and 5,000 deaths occur every year in the United States due to foodborne illnesses.[27] To help combat food poisoning, a partnership between the USDA Food Safety and Inspection Service and the FDA Center for Food Safety and Applied Nutrition established the *Fight BAC!* campaign.[31] Their recommendations are obvious, yet important. Millions of people get food poisoning each year from not following these simple steps.

Avoiding Food Poisoning

➢ Clean
➢ Separate
➢ Cook
➢ Chill

1. **Clean** - Wash hands, kitchen utensils, and surfaces with hot, soapy water. Many foodborne illnesses occur due to fecal-oral contamination. This is often caused by someone with "dirty" hands touching the food, a utensil, or a kitchen surface. After washing, a weak bleach solution (1 tbsp bleach to 1 gallon water) can also be used to sanitize cutting boards or utensils. Always rinse fresh fruits and vegetables with tap water, scrubbing lightly.
2. **Separate** - To prevent cross-contamination, separate raw meat, poultry, and seafood from ready-to-eat foods. Use separate cutting boards and knives. Never place cooked or ready-to-eat foods on a plate or surface that had raw meat on it previously.
3. **Cook** - Cook foods to safe internal temperatures. Table 3-2 gives minimum safe internal temperatures for various food types. Use a

Table 3-2 Minimum Internal Temperatures[30,32]

Category	Food	Temp. (°F)
Ground Meat & Meat Mixtures	Beef, Pork, Veal, Lamb	160
	Turkey, Chicken	165
Fresh Beef, Veal, Lamb	Steaks, Roasts, Chops	145
Poultry	Chicken, Turkey, Duck, Goose	165
Pork, Ham	Fresh Pork	160
	Fresh Ham	160
	Precooked Ham	140
Eggs & Egg Dishes	Eggs	Firm
	Egg dishes	160
Leftovers & Casseroles	Leftovers	165
	Casseroles	165
Seafood	Fish	145
	Shrimp, Lobster, Crab	Flesh opaque

    clean thermometer to test temperatures. Color is not a reliable indicator of doneness. Also, keep cooked foods hot until they are eaten. Bring sauces, soups, and gravies to a boil when reheating.

4. **Chill** - Refrigerate leftovers and takeout foods within 2 hours. Refrigerate perishables as quickly as possible after purchase. Keep cold foods cold (34°-40°F for refrigerated, 0°F for frozen). Never defrost food at room temperature. Most food can be thawed in one of three ways: in cold water, in the microwave, or in the refrigerator. Food thawed in the microwave or in cold water should be cooked immediately.

Having your family follow these four simple steps will significantly reduce their chances of contracting food poisoning. A few additional suggestions that will further reduce the likelihood of contamination are listed below.

• Make sure that poultry is adequately cooked. The meat juice should run clear, not pink.

- Don't eat raw or undercooked eggs, or homemade products with raw eggs, such as salad dressings, mayonnaise, ice cream, cookie dough, and frostings.
- Don't consume unpasteurized milk or juices.
- Avoid swallowing water from swimming pools, lakes, ponds, or streams.
- If your tap water has been declared unsafe, cook or peel all fresh produce.
- Follow strict hygienic practices when home canning, especially with low-acid foods, such as green beans and corn. Boil all home-canned foods for 10 minutes before eating.

PRODUCT DATING

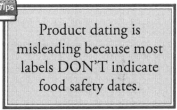

Tips

Product dating is misleading because most labels DON'T indicate food safety dates.

Except for infant formula and some baby food, product dating is generally not required by federal regulations. State food dating requirements vary. If calendar dating is used (a.k.a., "open dating"), it will include both month and day. Also, a phrase must be included to indicate the meaning of the date, such as "use by" or "best before."

Fortunately, manufacturers have voluntarily labeled the vast majority of foods with freshness dates. However, there are several different types of phrases associated with these dates, and this can cause confusion about what is safe to eat. Take a moment to go through your cupboard and locate the dates on various types of food products. They are not always easy to find—sometimes hidden under flaps or stamped into the paper. An understanding of the following food dating terms will help you put meaning to the dates.[23,33,34]

"USE BY" OR "BEST IF USED BY" OR "BEST BEFORE" OR "BEST" OR "USE" DATE

This is the last date a product is deemed to be at its best. This date recommendation is based solely on flavor or quality. It *is not* a food safety date, however, highly perishable foods may present a safety risk if consumed after this date.

"SELL BY" DATE

This date indicates the last day the product can be sold. The "sell by" date tells the retailer how long to display a product. The date is quality driven, and *is not* a food safety date.

"EXPIRATION" DATE

The expiration date indicates the last date a food should be eaten or used. This *is* a food safety date.

Foods that are not already labeled by the manufacturer should be manually labeled following the guidelines given in shelf life tables (see next section).

SHELF LIFE TABLES

Many published tables detail the expected shelf life of pantry foods. The tables presented here are based on input from several sources.[20,25,30,35,36,37] Keep in mind that shelf life tables generally represent conservative estimates, and in many cas-

When storing pantry food, remember three words: *cool, dry,* and *sealed.*

es, food will last longer. For example, there are tales of people eating canned food after 20 or more years of storage. That's not something to be recommended, but you get the point.

The most important recommendation regarding pantry food is to keep it cool, dry, and tightly sealed. Heat and moisture are bacteria's best friends and will speed up the spoilage process. Air, on the other hand, will dry out exposed food and cause flavor and color changes due to oxidation.[38]

Another way to extend the shelf life of food from the grocery store is to buy the freshest products available. Check the dates on packages whenever in doubt. Dusty cans or icy deposits may indicate old stock. Don't purchase dented or bulging cans as this may indicate spoilage. Also, don't purchase frozen goods whose boxes are discolored due to having been wet as this might indicate that they were inadvertently thawed during transport or during stocking. Feel free to cherry-pick the foods from the back of the shelf to find those that are freshest.

Table 3-3 Cupboard Storage Chart

Food	Recommended Storage Time
Baking powder	18 months
Baking soda	2 years
Beans/peas, dried	1 year (airtight container)
Biscuit, brownie, muffin mixes	9 months (airtight container)
Bouillon cubes, granules	1-2 years
Bread crumbs (dry)	6 months
Bread	3-5 days
Cakes - purchased or prepared - mixes	 1-2 days 1 year
Canned foods, unopened	2+ years
Catsup, chili sauce - unopened - opened, sealed well	 1 year 1 month (refrigerate)
Cereal, ready to eat - unopened - opened, sealed well	 6-12 months 2-3 months
Cheese, grated Parmesan - unopened - opened, sealed well	 10 months 2 months (refrigerate)

Food	Recommended Storage Time
Chocolate	
- unsweetened	18 months
- semi-sweet	18 months
- syrup, unopened	2 years
- syrup, opened, sealed well	6 months (refrigerate)
Cocoa	Indefinitely
Cocoa mixes	8 months
Coconut, shredded or canned	
- unopened	1 year
- opened, sealed well	6 months (refrigerate)
Coffee	
- cans or bags, unopened	2 years
- cans or bags, opened	2 weeks (airtight container)
- instant, unopened	1-2 years
- instant, opened	1-2 months (airtight container)
Coffee creamers, dry	
- unopened	9 months
- opened, sealed well	6 months
Cookies	
- homemade	2-3 weeks (airtight container)
- packaged	2 months
Corn syrup	up to 3 years (refrigerate to extend life)
Cornmeal	1 year (airtight container)
Cornstarch	18 months (airtight container)
Crackers	3 months
Fish, canned	3-5 years
Flour	
- white	6-8 months (airtight container)
- whole wheat	6-8 months (airtight container)

Food	Recommended Storage Time
Frosting	
- canned, unopened	3 months
- mix, unopened	8 months
Fruit	
- dried	6 months (airtight container)
- fresh	3-5 days (longer in refrigerator)
Fruit juice	
- canned	9 months
- juice/drink boxes	9 months
Gelatin	18 months
Grits	1 year (airtight container)
Honey	1 year - if crystallized, warm opened jar in hot water.
Hot roll mix	18 months
Hot sauce	2 years
Jellies/jams	1 year (refrigerate after opening)
Marshmallows	2-3 months (airtight container)
Mayonnaise	
- unopened	4-6 months
- opened	2 months (refrigerate)
Milk	
- condensed, unopened	1 year
- evaporated, unopened	1 year
- nonfat dry	6 months (airtight container)
- shelf-stable, unopened	2-3 months
Molasses	
- unopened	2 years
- opened	6 months (refrigerate)
Mustard, prepared yellow	
- unopened	2 years
- opened	6-8 months (refrigerate)

Food	Recommended Storage Time
Nuts	
- in shell, unopened	4-6 months
- vacuum can, unopened	1-3 years
- vacuum can, opened	3 months
Pancake syrup	
- unopened	18 months
- opened	3-4 months (refrigerate)
Pasta	
- spaghetti, macaroni, etc.	2 years (airtight container)
- egg noodles	6 months (airtight container)
Peanut Butter	
- unopened	6-9 months
- opened	2-3 months
	Natural peanut butter must be refrigerated after opening.
Pie crust mix	8 months
Pies and pastries	2-3 days
	Refrigerate whipped cream, custard fillings.
Popcorn, unpopped	2 years (airtight container)
Potatoes	
- instant mix	6-12 months (airtight container)
- fresh	2-4 weeks (keep in dark place)
Powdered drink mix	18-24 months
Pudding mix	1 year
Rice	
- white	2 years
- brown, wild	6-12 months
- flavored or herb	6 months

Food	Recommended Storage Time
Salad Dressing - bottled, unopened - bottled, opened - made from mix	 10-12 months 3 months (refrigerate) 2 weeks (refrigerate)
Shortenings (solid)	8 months
Sauces and gravy mixes	6-12 months
Soft drinks	6 months
Soup mixes, dry	1 year
Soy sauce - unopened - opened, sealed well	 3 years 9 months
Spices and herbs	6 months-2 years depending on type (airtight container)
Sugar - brown - confectioners - granulated - artificial sweeteners	 4 months (airtight container) 18 months (airtight container) 2 years 2 years
Syrup - unopened - opened	 18 months 1 year (refrigerate)
Tea - bags - instant - loose	 18 months (airtight container) 3 years 2 years (airtight container)
Toaster Pastries	2-3 months (airtight container)
Vanilla (and other extracts) - unopened - opened, sealed well	 2 years 1 year

Food	Recommended Storage Time
Vegetables, fresh	
- onions	2 weeks
- potatoes	2-4 weeks
- sweet potatoes	1-2 weeks
Vegetable Oils	
- unopened	6 months
- opened	1-3 months
Vinegar	
- unopened	2 years
- opened	1 year

REFRIGERATOR / FREEZER STORAGE

Just as there are storage guidelines for shelved foods, there are also recommendations regarding the usable lifetime of refrigerated and frozen foods. The storage times listed here assume that food has been stored in appropriate airtight containers, and that temperatures are maintained properly (i.e., 34°-40°F for refrigerated and 0°F for frozen). Note that the freezer storage times are provided for optimum quality only, since food can be stored almost indefinitely in a properly cooled freezer.

Table 3-4 Refrigerator and Freezer Storage Chart

Product	Refrigerator	Freezer
Eggs		
- Fresh, in shell	4-5 weeks	Don't freeze
- Raw yolks or whites	2-4 days	1 year
- Hard-boiled	1 week	Don't freeze
- Egg substitutes, unopened	10 days	1 year
- Egg substitutes, opened	3 days	Don't freeze
- Mayonnaise	2 months	Don't freeze
TV Dinners, frozen casseroles	Keep frozen until ready to eat	3-4 months

Product	Refrigerator	Freezer
Deli & vacuum-packed products		
- Egg, chicken, macaroni salads	3-5 days	Don't freeze
- Stuffed pork, lamb, or chicken	1 day	Don't freeze
- Store cooked convenience meals	3-4 days	Don't freeze
- Vacuum-packed dinners	2 weeks	Don't freeze
Raw Meats and Poultry		
- Ground beef, turkey, pork, veal	1-2 days	3-4 months
- Steaks	3-5 days	6-12 months
- Pork chops	3-5 days	4-6 months
- Roasts	3-5 days	4-12 months
- Tongue, kidneys, liver, heart	1-2 days	3-4 months
- Chicken, turkey—whole	1-2 days	6-12 months
- Chicken, turkey—parts	1-2 days	6-9 months
- Giblets	1-2 days	3-4 months
- Bacon, store-packed	7 days	1 month
- Bacon, vacuum-packed	1-2 months	6-12 months
- Sausage, raw, store-packed	1-2 days	3 months
- Sausage, factory-packed		
unopened	1-3 months	6-12 months
opened	1-2 days	3 months
Cooked Meats and Poultry		
- Poultry		
Fried chicken	3-4 days	4 months
Chicken nuggets	1-2 days	1-3 months
Cooked poultry dishes	3-4 days	4-6 months
- Beef, pork, veal		
Cooked meat	3-4 days	2-3 months
Cooked meat dishes	3-4 days	2-3 months
- Gravy and meat broth	1-2 days	2-3 months
- Soups and stews	3-4 days	2-3 months
- Ham, fully cooked		
whole	7 days	1-2 months
half	3-5 days	1-2 months
sliced	3-4 days	1-2 months
canned	6-9 months	Don't freeze

Product	Refrigerator	Freezer
Fish & Shellfish		
- Lean fish	1-2 days	6 months
- Fatty fish	1-2 days	2-3 months
- Canned fish, opened	3-4 days	2 months
- Shellfish	1-2 days	3-6 months
- Cooked fish	3-4 days	4-6 months
- Smoked fish	14 days	2 months
Hot Dogs, Lunch Meat		
- Hot dogs		
opened	1 week	1-2 months
unopened	2 weeks	1-2 months
- Lunch meats		
opened	3-5 days	1-2 months
unopened	2 weeks	1-2 months
Breads, Pastries, Cakes		
- Bread/rolls		
unbaked	2-3 weeks	1 month
baked	Don't refrigerate	2-3 months
- Cookies		
dough	3 months	3 months
baked	Don't refrigerate	6-12 months
- Cakes		
batter	Don't refrigerate	1 month
baked, unfrosted	3 days	2-4 months
baked, frosted	3 days	1 month
- Fruit pies		
unbaked	1-2 days	2-4 months
baked	2-3 days	6-8 months

Product	Refrigerator	Freezer
Cheese		
- Cottage, ricotta	1-2 weeks	4 weeks
- Soft cream, opened	5 days	Don't freeze
- Hard and wax-coated	1-2 months	6-8 months
- Sliced	2 weeks	Don't freeze
- Parmesan, Romano—grated	2 months	Don't freeze
- Processed	3-4 weeks	6-8 months
Fruits/Vegetables	Varies, based on type and freshness	6 months (blanching may be required)

FOOD SAFETY AND TERRORISM

The terrorist attacks of September 11, 2001, brought renewed focus on shoring up the country's defenses. In 2002, Congress and the president together enacted the Public Health Security and Bioterrorism Preparedness and Response Act.[39] The law is worth reading and can be found at the FDA website on Food Defense and Terrorism.[40]

The Bioterrorism Act is divided into five sections:

- National Preparedness for Bioterrorism and Other Public Health Emergencies
- Enhancing Controls on Dangerous Biological Agents and Toxins
- Protecting Safety and Security of Food and Drug Supply
- Drinking Water Security and Safety
- Additional Provisions

There are numerous goals and provisions outlined in the document. How well they will actually protect the population against a terrorist attack on the food, water, or drug supply is anyone's guess.

Radioactive Effects on Food

Food exposed to radioactive fallout requires cleaning prior to eating. Radioactive particulates should be rinsed off canned foods before

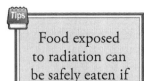

Food exposed to radiation can be safely eaten if handled properly.

opening. Boxed foods can also be cleaned off and consumed if the food is sealed inside an airtight bag. Produce should be washed and peeled to remove any radioactive fallout. Foods that can't be thoroughly cleaned, such as opened cans or breads, should be discarded.[41]

MISCELLANEOUS

SPECIAL NEEDS

When stockpiling food, it is important to consider any special needs that your family may have. This includes baby food, pet food, and food for those with dietary restrictions. See *Chapter 16: Special Needs* for more information.

MULTIVITAMINS

There tends to be two camps of people: those who swear by multivitamin supplements, and those who believe they are a waste of money. The people in favor of daily multivitamins will argue that the diet of the average American is sorely lacking in important nutrients. Those opposing the use of vitamins will cite studies that show that high levels of some vitamins and minerals have been shown to cause health problems as well as interfere with medications.[42,43,44,45]

Fortunately, almost everyone seems to agree that daily multivitamins should be taken during times of bodily stress, such as when pregnant, confined indoors for an extended period, or eating a restricted diet. Therefore, in situations where food quantity and selection might be limited—such as during a disaster—taking a multi-vitamin supplement seems both reasonable and prudent.

PETS

For most people, pets are members of the family. Don't forget to keep the same 30-day supply of food for your pets. For dogs and cats, this isn't usually difficult—stocking a spare bag of dry food in the cupboard, or rotating canned food. Of course, if you run out of pet food, it may be possible (depending on the type of animal) to improvise by feeding your pets

Don't forget the needs of your four-legged friends.

"scraps" from your meals. It might not be the healthiest diet, but it beats starving. Fortunately, most animals quickly adapt to scavenger mode when the need arises.

A much more complete set of recommendations regarding pets is given in *Chapter 16: Special Needs.*

NON-FOOD ITEMS

Take a good inventory of the consumable non-food items in your kitchen, making sure that you have an adequate supply. This list would include such items as aluminum foil, plastic wrap, paper products, plastic utensils, plastic storage bags and containers, and napkins.

There is certainly no need to go out and purchase a new set of kitchen supplies, but you should do a quick inspection of your utensils and pots and pans. During a disaster would be a poor time to realize that your only manual can opener is being held together by zip ties.

Using disposable paper products can help reduce water consumption.

Most families have a shelf lined with cookbooks. It would be wise to select one of your favorites (perhaps an all-purpose cookbook from Betty Crocker, Better Homes, or Mark Bittman) and familiarize yourself with different recipes. If you are stranded at home for an extended period, you may need to improvise by pulling together dishes using only the particular ingredients you have on hand. Learning a few shortcuts and substitutions *now* means you won't find yourself staring at a cupboard full of supplies during a crisis wondering how best to use them. Also, knowing how to cook using your microwave or barbeque grill can be especially handy for situations with limited electrical power (see *Cooking* in *Chapter 8: Heating/Cooling*).

DP PLAN EXAMPLE

Table 3-5 Sample DP Plan Entry - Food

Need: Food			
Danger	**Goals**	**Needs**	**Implementation**
Shortage	Feed family for 30 days without resupplying	Sufficient food for three meals a day for a family of five Additional food to supplement a needy elderly neighbor Pet food for household pets	Create pantry by installing shelving in closet under stairs. Keep a few days of food in the kitchen cabinets, and the bulk of pre-packaged and canned foods in the pantry. Keep a food storage list inside pantry door. Rotate food with each weekly purchase.
Loss of refrigeration	Don't compromise food supply with power outage	Bulk of food stockpile that doesn't require refrigeration	Limit refrigerated or frozen food to no more than 7 of the 30-day supply. Keep additional frozen foods in the garage freezer. Use water bottles as necessary to keep refrigerator and freezers full.

Quick Summary - Food

➢ Store a minimum of 30 days of non-perishable food.

➢ Consult the USDA food pyramid when deciding what to store. See *www.mypyramid.gov.*

➢ Store what you eat, and eat what you store.

➢ Rotate your food. Newest to the back; oldest to the front.

➢ Always keep pantry food cool, dry, and tightly sealed.

➢ Sweeteners, oils, and seasonings are not critical to survival but can ease the hardship by making food more enjoyable.

➢ Consult product labels and shelf-life tables to determine how long foods will store safely.

➢ Don't forget to stock up on non-food and special need items.

➢ Food poisoning can turn a bad situation into a deadly one. Practice the four steps (clean, separate, cook, and chill) to avoid food poisoning.

Recommended Items - Food

❑ A stockpile of food
   a. Minimum of 30 days of food that generally satisfies the guidelines of the USDA New food pyramid and does not rely heavily on refrigeration
   b. Any special needs foods, including baby food, pet food, and dietary restricted foods

❑ Refrigerator/freezer thermometer to properly set the temperatures

❑ Non-food items (e.g., aluminum foil, paper products, plastic utensils, plastic storage bags, napkins, cooking utensils)

❑ General all-purpose cookbook

CHAPTER 4

WATER

Chapter 4 Notes

CHAPTER 4

WATER

Challenge

Heavy rains have flooded the nearby water treatment facility, introducing two dangerous pathogens (Giardia and Shigella) into the water supply. Local authorities have issued an order to use bottled water or boil all tap water. The rains are expected to continue for the next five days. How will you provide clean drinking water for your family? Do you understand the risks that these pathogens pose?

Never underestimate the importance of having clean, drinkable water. A useful saying is that humans can live three minutes without air, three days without water, and three weeks without food. Given that air quality is often not a problem in many disasters, it leaves water as the primary need—certainly much more important than food for short-term survival. Also, take a moment to consider that even in the best of times, over a billion people on this planet don't have access to clean drinking water.[46]

There are two approaches to making sure that you have water in a crisis. You can either maintain a permanent stockpile of water, or you can have empty containers ready to fill when a disaster is approaching. The obvious advantage of the permanent stockpile is that you are always ready. The disadvantage is that water is heavy, bulky, and can be a mess if not handled correctly. Also, unless treated with a water preserver, it must be poured out and refilled about every six months—see *Storing Water* further in this chapter.

Regardless of your approach, one thing holds true. If a disaster is imminent, store as much water as possible. If you don't have enough water containers, then fill bathtubs, buckets, pots, barrels, and anything else you have available. Remember that water is not only used for drinking, but also hygiene and sanitation. Don't neglect to account for those needs. As discussed in *Chapter 3: Food,* many of the worst bacteria-related illnesses are a result of fecal-oral contamination. Keeping yourself and your environment clean is extremely important in times of crisis.

Finally, don't forget to account for your pets. If you have a couple of cats, they probably won't have much impact on your water consumption. However, if you have two German Shepherds, three cats, and a donkey, you should definitely determine their water usage and budget accordingly!

SANITATION

When water is in short supply, the toilet is going to be your biggest enemy. The amount of non-potable water (i.e., water not fit for drinking) needed depends on how old your toilet is, and how frugal you are with your flushes. If your toilet was made prior to 1982, it probably takes 5 to 7 gallons per flush. That is a lot of water. Newer toilets require only about 2 to 3 gallons per flush. This conservation is an excellent reason to upgrade at least

Sun-Mar composting toilet

one toilet if you happen to live in an older home. If your budget doesn't allow the upgrade, consider putting a few heavy glass jars or bottles in the tank to displace some of the water—thereby reducing the amount used with each flush.

When city water is no longer available, there are four obvious choices for sanitation:

1. Dig a hole or trench outdoors—this can get old in a hurry, as well as be a source of disease.
2. Use a potty bucket with disposable liners—smelly but manageable with the correct supplies.
3. Use a self-contained composting toilet—an excellent, but expensive alternative (see *www.lehmans.com*).
4. Ration your water, and continue to use your conventional toilet—the least impact to your family, but one that requires access to a significant amount of water.

If you opt to use your toilet, you will need to store, or have access to, enough non-potable water for at least one flush per person per day. The idea is to flush the toilet only after bowel movements. A great way to remember this is to keep in mind the saying, "If it's yellow, let it mellow. If it's brown, flush it down." A tad vulgar perhaps, but you won't forget it.

There are two ways to flush a toilet when water has been disconnected. The first is to cut off the incoming water valve (usually just behind the toilet), pour water into the back of the tank, and flush as usual. This works fine, but can be a little messy. The second method is to pour the water directly into the bowl. If unfamiliar with plumbing, you might think that the toilet would overflow. However, as the water level rises, a partial vacuum is created as water spills over the dam in the back of the toilet boil. This vacuum pulls the water out of the bowl and down into the sewage pipe.

One final note about operating toilets with external water sources: once you are finished flushing, add a little water to the toilet bowl. If the water level is too low, it will allow sewer gas to enter the home.

SEWER BACKFLOW

One other topic that fits in the category of sanitation is sewage backflow. Your sewer or septic system is designed to remove sewage from your home, but that same piping can inadvertently bring sewage back up into your home. This most frequently occurs when flood water flows into the sewer system and floats raw sewage up through a home's toilets, tubs, and sinks—disgusting to be sure!

Install a backflow valve to prevent sewage from backing up into your home from flooded sewage systems.

The surest way to prevent sewage backflow is to install a backflow valve on your sewage line. The backflow valve allows sewage to flow in only one direction—that is, *out* of your home and not back into it. If you are a handyman with a bit of plumbing experience, you can probably do this job yourself. Otherwise, contact your local plumber. If possible, have the backflow valve installed somewhere convenient to access. This way, if you ever have a clog associated with the backflow valve, you can easily clear it.

HYGIENE

This might be a good place to emphasize the importance of maintaining good personal hygiene during times of crisis. Simply put, you must keep your hands clean of fecal matter and other contaminants. Many serious infections, including salmonellosis and *E. coli*, can be the result of contamination from tiny amounts of fecal matter entering your body through the mouth, nose, or eyes. These bacterial infections can be especially deadly when access to medical care is limited.

When you use the toilet, or touch anything else that might be contaminated (e.g., a sick person, garbage can, raw meat), you must wash your hands thoroughly. Likewise, before handling food, you should always assume your hands are dirty and wash them. For these reasons, budget a gallon of water for hygiene per person per day. This recommendation exceeds those of many other DP books, but hygiene is critical to preventing illness and should not be shortchanged.

Washing has one primary goal; to remove the contaminants from your skin. The soap foam bonds to the contaminants, and water rinses them away. Teach your children the proper way to wash their hands (see tip box).[47]

Washing Hands

1. Use warm water if possible.
2. Lather soap into a thick foam.
3. Scrub hands thoroughly for at least 20 seconds.
4. Rinse thoroughly.
5. Air dry, or use a disposable towel.
6. Use towel to turn off faucet.

Hand sanitizers with 60% or more alcohol are an excellent alternative to hand washing when water is not available. They do a great job of killing pathogens but don't remove waste, blood, or dirt from your skin. As with soap and water, most sanitizers *don't* provide extended protection. They only kill what is currently on your hands. There are a few lotion-based sanitizers that claim to provide several hours of protection, but it is not clear that they are an adequate substitute for periodic hand washing.

Disposable baby wipes can also be used to clean your hands and body, but most wipes are not alcohol-based and don't clean as well as soap and water. Using larger, disposable bathing wipes can be an excellent temporary replacement for taking showers or baths. Campers have used bathing wipes for years, and they can really help you to feel refreshed.

It is also a good idea to have plenty of heavy-duty garbage bags and twist ties on hand. Plastic bags are handy for getting rid of food remnants, medical waste, and contaminated clothing. They can also be used to seal leaks, gather water, serve as a rain poncho, act as a toilet, and much more.

Finally, if you need to clean a hard surface, such as a countertop, door knob, or toilet, and are out of Lysol or other germ-killing cleansers, you can call upon bleach to serve as a powerful disinfectant. Simply mix 1 part bleach to 9 parts water.[48] Just be careful not to spill the mixture

Homemade Disinfectants
1 part bleach to 9 parts water
or
hydrogen peroxide + vinegar
applied separately

on carpet or clothing since it will cause whitening. If the surface will later be used for preparing foods, it should be rinsed first with clean water.

An alternative to using bleach is to spray the infected surface with 3% hydrogen peroxide (i.e., the standard drug store concentration), and then again with white vinegar. This combination has been shown effective at killing *E. coli, Salmonella,* and *Shigella,* and is safe to use without additional rinsing.[49] Don't combine the vinegar and hydrogen peroxide in the same bottle. Also, keep the hydrogen peroxide in an opaque bottle since light will degrade the solution.

ADDING IT ALL UP

To determine your family's daily water needs, simply add up the water required for drinking (1 gallon per person), hygiene (1 gallon per person), and sanitation (2 to 7 gallons per person depending on your toilet type). Drinking and hygiene needs must be met with potable water, but sanitation can be handled with non-potable water. It is recommended that you store (or have access to) enough water to support your family for a minimum of 14 days.

For a family of five, this corresponds to: 5 people $\times$ 2 gallons per day $\times$ 14 days = 140 gallons of potable water. And if toilets are to be used (assuming 3 gallons per flush): 5 people $\times$ 3 gallons per day $\times$ 14 days = 210 gallons of non-potable water.

It should go without saying that storing 350 gallons of water is something that requires prior planning. If you are fortunate enough to have access to a large body of water, such as a swimming pool, stream, or lake, you can draw upon it for your non-potable needs. Using outside sources like these significantly reduces your storage requirements.

> **Tips**
> The average American uses about 100 gallons of water per day.

The average American household uses about 94,000 gallons of water each year.[50] Using the 2000 Census estimate of 2.59 people per household, this consumption figure converts to about 100 gallons per person per day! Compare this to the 5 gallons of water recommended per person (2 gallons of potable, 3 gallons of non-potable). Suffice it to say, your family should be prepared to live on much less water than they are accustomed to. The days of lounging in the hot shower will be a thing of the past.

STORING WATER

The shelf life of water is difficult to predict because it is based on many factors, including the purity of the source, storage temperature, lighting, and type of storage container. In some conditions, water can be stored safely for several years, while in others, it can become contaminated in a matter of months. Follow the water storage guidelines (in tip box) for achieving the best shelf life.

Water Storage Guidelines
- ➢ Use FDA-approved DOT #34 opaque containers
- ➢ Store out of light
- ➢ Keep away from pesticides, gasoline, paint, or chemicals
- ➢ Store where it won't freeze
- ➢ Cycle every 6 months unless treated with a water preserver
- ➢ Pre-treat if it comes from untreated sources (e.g., well)

It is a good idea to have both large and small containers for your water storage. The large containers are efficient at storing sizable quantities of water in a small space. But if you are forced to relocate, or simply have to go out in search of additional water, you will need containers light enough to transport. A gallon of water weighs approximately eight pounds, so portable containers shouldn't be over about six gallons in size (less if you are unable to handle 50 pounds). Keep two sets of portable containers.

Water storage containers

Use one set for retrieving potable water and the second set for retrieving non-potable water. By keeping them separate, you eliminate the risk of cross-contaminating your containers.

Prepare your potable water containers in advance of any disaster. Containers should be cleaned following these simple steps:

1. Mix 1 tablespoon of unscented liquid household bleach (i.e., 5-6% sodium hypochlorite) into one gallon of water.
2. Pour the solution into the container, rubbing or brushing it on the threads and mouth.
3. Shake it around in the container, and then let it sit for 10 minutes.
4. Rinse the container thoroughly with clean water.

TREATING WATER

> **Tips**
> Water can be pre-treated with 4 drops of bleach per gallon of water.

Unscented household bleach can also be used to pre-treat water prior to storage by adding 4 drops per gallon and mixing well. However, pre-treating water with bleach is only recommended if the water comes from an untreated source, such as a well or rural township water. Most cities pre-treat their water before it is piped to customers, so further pre-treating is unnecessary and won't increase the shelf life of the water. Additional pre-treating won't cause any harm, but it may leave an unpleasant odor and taste.

Commercial concentrated water preservers, such as 7C's Safety & Environmental's Water Preserver, can be added to water to significantly increase the shelf life. These products are made of stabilized sodium hypochlorite, which is designed to prevent microorganisms for a minimum of five years. If you have large water storage containers (e.g., 55-gallon drums, 250-gallon Super Tankers), then using a water preserver makes sense. However, if you are just using jerry cans or smaller containers, it isn't difficult to simply cycle your water every six months.

Courtesy of 7C's Safety & Environmental, Inc.

CONTAMINATION

The Environmental Protection Agency (EPA) has estimated that 90% of the world's fresh water is contaminated and unsuitable for drinking without some form of purification.[50] The days of kneeling down on a hike and sipping from the stream are long gone. Don't make the mistake of thinking that just because water looks clear or tastes good that it is free of contaminants. That includes frozen water, which can house hepatitis A, *Salmonella,* and *Cryptosporidium* for months.[51] The CDC estimates that 88% of the world's cases of diarrhea are the result of unsafe water, inadequate sanitation, and poor hygiene. Water-related illnesses rank as one of our planet's deadliest killers, resulting in the death of 1.5 million people annually, most of them children.[52]

The EPA classifies water contaminants into six categories (see tip box). Based on these categories, the agency publishes a long list of contaminants and sets their maximum allowed levels in drinking water.[53] Likewise, the National Sanitation Foundation International (NSF) certifies that water filters remove those contaminants to a specified

> **Water Contaminants**
> ➢ Pathogens
> ➢ Organic chemicals
> ➢ Inorganic chemicals
> ➢ Disinfectants
> ➢ Disinfection by-products
> ➢ Radionuclides

level of effectiveness. Contaminant removal is tested by adding an influent and then measuring the effluent. In other words, they start with clean water, add a contaminant, pass the water through a filter and see how much of the contaminant has been removed. For a filter to be certified as effective against a contaminant, it must meet or exceed the NSF requirements.[54]

It is instructive to compare the EPA safe-water requirements to the list of contaminants removed by NSF-certified water filters. For example, the EPA requirements dictate that drinking water contain less than 0.015 mg/L of lead, and the NSF certification process requires that water contaminated with 0.15 mg/L of lead be reduced down to a maximum of 0.01 mg/L (about 93% removal)—just within the EPA limit. It becomes clear that EPA requirements and NSF certification align closely to first dictate, and then test, water quality.

PATHOGENS

Pathogens are microscopic organisms that include protozoa, bacteria, parasitic worms, fungi, and viruses.[55] They can generally be classified into one of three broad categories: parasites, bacteria, and viruses. For detailed information about many different water contaminants, see the Center for Disease Control and Prevention's online listing.[56]

> **Tips**
>
> Pathogens are classified as parasites, bacteria, and viruses.

PARASITES

Parasites include worms, lice, and protozoa. All can be transmitted through water, but for modern societies, protozoa represent the greatest waterborne parasitic threat. Protozoa are single-celled organisms that may have more than one nucleus. They are generally found in water as microbial cysts and cause serious gastrointestinal illness when ingested. Their source is human or animal fecal waste, and they typically range from 2 to 30 microns in size. A micron (a.k.a., micrometer) is 1/1,000,000 of a meter. Fortunately, parasites of this size are large enough to be easily removed by quality water filters (i.e., those with an absolute pore size of less than 1 micron).

Giardia

BACTERIA

Bacteria are single-celled microorganisms without a nucleus, generally measuring from 0.2 to 4 microns in size. They are found in every habitat; growing in soil, seawater and fresh water, and even deep in the Earth's crust. Many bacteria are not harmful, and some are even beneficial to your health. There are approximately 40 million bacterial cells in a gram of soil and 5 million in a single teaspoon of fresh water.[57] Some of the bacteria found in water are the result of transfer from fecal waste. As with parasites, ingestion usually results in severe gastrointestinal illness, along with other associated infections. Larger bacteria are effectively removed by conventional water filters, while other smaller bacteria are more difficult to remove.

Salmonella

VIRUSES

Viruses are essentially raw genetic material with a protective coating called a capsid. They infect healthy cells and inject their genetic characteristics into them. In turn, those contaminated cells quickly replicate.

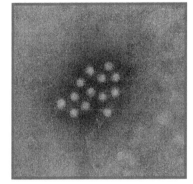

Consuming virus-contaminated water can cause gastrointestinal illness, weakness, fever, liver disease, and paralysis. Viruses are very small in size, measuring from 0.004 to 0.3 microns in size. Because of their tiny size, most water filters will *not* effectively remove viruses. However, there are a few filters that do remove them by taking advantage of the fact that viruses will attach to larger particles under certain conditions.

Hepatitis A

For a conventional filter to effectively remove a contaminant of any type, the absolute (not average) pore size of the filter membrane must be smaller than the contaminant. Table 4-1 provides a quick comparison of general filter requirements to remove several common pathogens.

Depending on where you look, you will find conflicting data regarding the size of different microorganisms. That's because the microorganisms can be many different sizes depending on the conditions in which they grow. How then do you decide if a filter will remove a particular pathogen? The best way is to review the test data for the specific filter in question. Certified filters will provide performance information such as "removes 99.99% of *Cryptosporidium*." Much more information about selecting a water filter is given later in this chapter.

Table 4-1 Filter Absolute Pore Size Recommendations

Microorganism Type	Microorganism	Recommended Absolute Filter Pore Size (microns)
Protozoa	Giardia lamblia	
	Cryptosporidium	1
	Entamoeba histolytica	
Bacteria	Escherichia coli	
	Vibrio cholera	
	Shigella	0.2-0.4
	Campylobacter	
	Salmonella	
Virus	Hepatitis A	
	Norovirus	N/A—see note
	Poliovirus	
	Rhinovirus	

Note: Due to the very small size of viruses, most filters don't adequately remove them. However, there are a few exceptions, as noted later in the chapter.

ORGANIC AND INORGANIC CHEMICALS

The EPA tests drinking water for a long list of organic and inorganic chemicals.[53] These include chemicals discharged from various types of factories (e.g., petroleum, plastic, metal, coal-burning, pulp), runoff from herbicide treatments, corrosion from plumbing, and erosion of natural deposits. Consumption of chemical contaminants can cause cancer as well as damage to the body's basic systems and organs.

Most conventional membrane filters do a poor job of removing chemicals. However, distillation and reverse osmosis systems have been shown to be effective treatment methods.

DISINFECTANTS AND BY-PRODUCTS

Disinfectants are chemicals added to water during the purification process to kill microbes. These additives include chloramines, chlorine, and chlorine dioxide. By-products created by the water treatment process include bromate, chlorite, haloacetic acids, and total trihalomethanes. Consuming high levels of these increases the risk of cancer as well as liver, kidney, and neurological disorders.

Tips

Distillation and reverse osmosis are the best ways of removing chemical contaminants.

Fortunately, these additives and by-products are often able to be removed with a quality, carbon-based water filter.

RADIONUCLIDES

Drinking water in the United States has very low levels of radioactive contamination (a.k.a., radionuclides). Most of what is present in water occurs naturally as result of erosion of natural deposits of certain minerals. Radioactive contamination can also be the result of the introduction of human-made nuclear materials, such as from an accidental spill or improper disposal practices. Examples of radioactive contamination include alpha/beta particles, uranium, and radium 226/228. Long-term exposure to high levels of radionuclides in drinking water causes an increased risk of cancer. Exposure to uranium in drinking water also causes kidney damage.[58]

Conventional membrane filters will not remove radionuclides. Three methods that have been shown to reduce radionuclides are: ion exchange devices used to remove water hardness, reverse osmosis systems, and lime softening.[59]

LOCAL LEVELS

If you are interested in learning about the levels of contaminants in your local water supply, go to the EPA's website, *www.epa.gov/safewater,* and find the link for your area. If your water provider doesn't post its findings on the EPA website, you may have to contact your provider directly. It is both informative and well advised to understand the water quality issues facing your community.[60]

Investigate your water quality at *www.epa.gov/safewater.*

Even in the best of times, maintaining the purity of your drinking water requires careful attention. You may find that your local drinking water falls short of EPA guidelines. During disasters, water quality can quickly degrade, or worse, can be completely shut off. To adequately prepare for contamination or shortage, you will need a well thought-out water management plan.

PURIFICATION

Unless you have a large storage tank of clean drinking water, or can draw water from an uncontaminated source, such as an underground well, you will likely need some method of purifying water from non-potable sources. Let's start by quickly examining the water purification process that large treatment facilities use.

The purification process consists of six fundamental steps:[61]

- **pre-treatment**—screen to remove large debris, and perform limited softening and chlorination
- **pH adjustment**—adjust alkaline/acidic level
- **coagulation/flocculation/sedimentation**—clarify to remove particles

- **filtration**—remove smaller particles
- **disinfection**—kill pathogens using chemicals and UV light
- **additional treatments**—fluoridate, hard/soft condition, and remove radium

Strict replication of these steps on a small scale is not practical. However, the basic goals of purification still apply—remove the debris and kill or remove the impurities. Unfortunately, there is a great deal of misinformation about how to make non-potable water safe. Even within the DP community, confusion abounds. The information presented here will make clear the efficacy of different methods.

There are six primary techniques that can be used independently or in conjunction to purify water (see tip box). Each method has its respective advantages and disadvantages. Let's begin with a discussion of each the various techniques, followed by several recommended approaches to purifying water.

> **Purifying Water**
> ➤ Boiling
> ➤ Filtering/purifying
> ➤ Chemical disinfection
> ➤ Distillation
> ➤ Reverse osmosis
> ➤ Ultraviolet light

BOILING

Boiling is *the* optimal way of killing microorganisms. It is simple and effective at neutralizing all types of pathogens, but it will not improve the taste of water. Nor will it remove particulates or chemical impurities. Tests have shown that microorganisms are destroyed by the time water reaches the boiling point (212°F). Boiling the water for extended durations (e.g., 10 to 30 minutes) as suggested in some texts is unnecessary.[50] The generally accepted guidance is to bring the water to a rolling boil for one minute. After that, let the water cool naturally, providing a final measure of safety by ensuring that the water remains at high temperatures for an extended time.

Boiling is an excellent method of purifying already clear water, such as tap water, that has become infected with a pathogen. The main drawback is that it is slow and requires a heat source. Boiling is also not optimal for purifying water from natural sources, such as a lake, since it doesn't remove any particulates or debris and won't improve the taste.

FILTERING/PURIFYING

Filtering can be as simple as passing water through a handkerchief, or as sophisticated as forcing it through a nearly solid substance that allows little else but water molecules to pass through. Water coming from natural sources, such as a lake or river, is often filtered in stages—a coarse filter first to remove the dirt and debris, followed by a much finer filter to remove pathogens. The idea is to get as much crud out of the water as possible before trying to purify it. This approach greatly helps to prevent clogging of the filter.

The terms *filter* and *purifier* are often used interchangeably by retailers, even though they refer to very different things. *Filter* is a general term describing any device that can be used to remove contaminants from water. This could be as crude as a simple coffee filter, although typically it refers to a device that contains some sort of fine membrane. Most general purpose water filters remove protozoa and select bacteria. Contrary to popular belief, they *do not* remove minerals, heavy metals, or salt.

> **Tips**
> Purifiers are the cream of the water filter crop—able to reduce all types of pathogens to safe levels.

A water *purifier* is a special type of filter, one with a very specific definition. The EPA defines a purifier as something that reduces *all* pathogens to safe levels—exceeding log-6 protection for bacteria (99.9999% removed), log-3 for *Cryptosporidium* (99.9% removed), and log-4 for viruses (99.99% removed).[62] When you see something described as a "certified purifier," you should recognize that the device offers broad protection from waterborne contaminants.

Water filters can be grouped into one of three categories: point-of-entry (POE), point-of-use (POU), and portable. A POE filter attaches to the main water line, filtering water throughout the entire house. A POU filter sits on the countertop or under the sink and filters only a single tap. Finally, portable units are lightweight pump-driven or gravity-fed devices often used when camping or traveling. Pitchers and other filtered dispensers can also be categorized as portable units.

Having a quality POU or POE filtering system will ensure that you can very likely continue to use your city's water even if it becomes contaminated. This provision relieves the burden of trying to find clean or treated water. Having a POU or POE filter obviously does not help in the event that water service is completely shut off. For those situations, you will need to locate an alternate water source, and use a pump-driven or gravity-fed water filter as necessary.

Whether choosing a POU or POE system, select one with an absolute pore size of 1 micron or smaller. This rating indicates that the filter will not pass anything larger than 1 micron in size. A filter with 1 micron absolute pore size will safely remove all protozoa (e.g., *Cryptosporidium, Giardia*) and provide some protection from bacteria (e.g., *E. coli*

Katadyn's Pocket filter

and *Salmonella*). However, it is unlikely that the filter will protect you from viruses since they are significantly smaller than 1 micron.

Fortunately, there are a few select water filters that have been independently verified to eliminate all forms of pathogens (i.e., bacteria, protozoa, and viruses) without the use of chemical disinfectants. These filters are classified as true water purifiers, and offer a simple one step process to removing pathogens (discussed in *Selecting a Water Filter*).

CHEMICAL DISINFECTION

Two widely used halogen chemicals for killing waterborne pathogens are iodine and chlorine (along with their respective derivatives). Popular products include Micropur MP1 chlorine dioxide tablets and Potable Aqua's titratable iodine tablets. These tablets are easy to use and have shelf lives of at least four years if unopened—one year if opened.[63,64] Another product, Polar Pure iodine crystals, is a little more difficult to precisely administer but is much less expensive and offers the advantage of having a nearly indefinite shelf life.[65]

Polar Pure

MSR's MIOX

If you have no other means, you can use household bleach or 2% tincture of iodine to disinfect water. These products are as effective as the commercial chemical water disinfectant products (e.g., MP1), but not as convenient to use. Also, bleach has a much shorter shelf life—requiring replacement every six months to maintain potency.[66]

Halogen disinfectants (a.k.a., electronegative chemicals) of this type are considered effective against bacteria, somewhat effective against viruses, and of limited value against protozoa. The reason for this limitation is that protozoa cysts have protective coatings around them. *Cryptosporidium* in particular is resistant to halogen treatment.[67]

Finally, there is one device (Mountain Safety Research's MIOX) that uses salt, water, and electricity to create a foamy brine of oxidizing agents. When added to water, the brine will neutralize protozoa, bacteria, and viruses. Disposable test strips are used to verify that the water has been adequately treated. Independent tests have shown MIOX meets the EPA Guide Standard and Protocol for Testing Microbiological Water Purifiers (a.k.a., EPA Guide Standard).[68] Suffice it to say that this level of purification is exceptional—far better than iodine or chlorine. One noticeable disadvantage of the mixed oxidant method is that it requires a four-hour treatment time for *Cryptosporidium.*

DOSING

If using commercial chemical disinfectants, such as Polar Pure or Micropur MP1, the dosages are clearly marked on the package. However, if you are using bleach or iodine to disinfect water, you will need to measure your own dose.

Chemical Disinfection

1. Add halogen per Table 4-2.
2. Mix the water thoroughly.
3. Splash the disinfected water onto the container's threads.
4. Wait 30 minutes. Increase the wait time to 2 hours for very cold water.

Table 4-2 gives the recommended dosages for disinfecting clear and cloudy water using bleach or iodine. The recommended dose for bleach is 2 drops per quart of water, which translates to approximately 5-6 parts per million (assuming a bleach solution with 5-6% sodium hypochlorite). Similarly, the recommended dose for iodine is 5 drops per quart of water, corresponding to approximately 5 parts per million (assuming a 2% tincture of iodine solution). After treating with either chemical, let the water sit covered for 30 minutes, giving time for the halogen to work. Treated water should have a detectable chlorine or iodine odor.

In general, the more turbid the water, the more disinfectant you need to add.[72] Consequently, most references suggest doubling the concentration for cloudy water—as indicated in Table 4-2. Although effective, the increased dose introduces a strong chemical taste. An alternative approach is to filter the water first to clear it up, and then use the standard dose of halogen. A second alternative is to double the dose of disinfectant and then filter using a small-pore filter to remove some, although not all, of the unpleasant chemical taste.

Table 4-2 Ratios for Purifying Water with Bleach or Iodine.[69,70]

Water Quantity	Clear Water	Cloudy Water
1 Quart/Liter	Bleach - 2 drops Iodine - 5 drops	Bleach - 4 drops Iodine - 10 drops
1 Gallon	Bleach - 8 drops (1/8 tsp) Iodine - 20 drops	Bleach - 16 drops (1/4 tsp) Iodine - 1/2 tsp
5 Gallons	Bleach - 1/2 tsp Iodine - 1 tsp	Bleach - 1 tsp Iodine - 2 tsp
10 Gallons	Bleach - 1 tsp Iodine - 2 tsp	Bleach - 2 tsp Iodine - 4 tsp
55 Gallons	Bleach - 5½ tsp Iodine - 11 tsp	Bleach - 11 tsp Iodine - 22 tsp

Notes:
1. 1 drop = 0.05 mL
2. Water that has been disinfected with iodine is not recommended for pregnant women, people with thyroid problems, those with known hypersensitivity to iodine, or continuous use for more than a few weeks at a time.[71]

> **Tips**
>
> The taste of chemically-treated water can be especially objectionable to children.

Very cold water (i.e., water below 40°F) slows the reaction time of the halogen, leading to the suggestion once again to double the normal dose of disinfectant. An alternative to this is to allow the water to warm before treating it. A second alternative is to permit the halogen to work for two hours instead of 30 minutes when disinfecting very cold water.[73]

One drawback of using chemical disinfectants is the objectionable smell and taste of the treated water. There are several things that can help with this:

- Avoid using higher doses by first clarifying the water or allowing the disinfectant to work longer.
- Use a filter subsequent to the chemical disinfection process.
- Mix in a powdered fruit drink mix, such as lemonade or Kool-aid, that contains ascorbic acid (vitamin C). The ascorbic acid helps convert the chlorine and iodine to tasteless chloride and iodide.
- Allow the treated water to air out for a couple hours before drinking.

If you plan to use a chemical disinfectant, it is advisable to try out several methods to determine which yields the best-tasting solution for your family.

Personal aside: In a very unscientific taste test of chemical treatment methods, my own family concluded that iodine-treated water was by far the worst smelling and tasting, bleach-treated was second, MIOX-treated water third, and water treated with Micropur MP1 ready-to-use tablets was the least objectionable.

DISTILLATION

Distillation is a process of boiling water and then collecting the water vapor as it condenses. This method of purifying water is extremely effective at removing all types of pathogens (i.e., bacteria, protozoa, and viruses). Distillation and reverse osmosis are also the only methods discussed that do an excellent job of removing chemical contaminants.[74]

A disadvantage of using distillers is that they are slow, typically taking about six hours to yield one gallon of water. They also require electricity

Courtesy of Nutriteam

to operate, which given the amount of time they have to run, might be a significant problem during many disasters.

REVERSE OSMOSIS

Osmosis is the process of flowing from low concentrate level to high. It is the reason drinking seawater can kill you. The seawater in your stomach draws water out of your body trying to dilute the high concentrate of salt, eventually leading to dehydration and death.

Reverse osmosis (RO) is the process of flowing from high concentrate to low. Pressurized water is forced through a very fine membrane while discharging excess water and concentrate (pollutants in this case). Reverse osmosis systems are usually constructed of several stages, including a pre-filter, semi-permeable membrane, pressurized storage tank to hold the treated water, and carbon adsorption post-filter.

Reverse osmosis systems do an excellent job of removing all forms of pathogens as well as chemical impurities. However, they require high water pressure (typically > 40 psi), and therefore may necessitate the use

Courtesy of Watts

of an electric pressure-boost pump in some homes. They also waste a great deal of water, turning out only 5-10% of the incoming water. The remaining water is flushed away with the pollutant. To create 1 gallon of purified water might take 8 to 18 gallons of incoming water.[75] Finally, reverse osmosis systems require periodic maintenance, including replacing the pre- and post-filters annually and the membrane every few years.

REVERSE OSMOSIS VERSUS DISTILLATION

Be forewarned that there are two very vocal groups of water filter marketeers—those who sell distillation devices, and those who sell reverse osmosis systems. Salesmen for distillation devices will claim that reverse osmosis removes important minerals. Likewise, those selling reverse osmosis systems will claim that distillation causes the water to taste flat. Both salesmen will claim that the competing technique doesn't remove contaminants as well as the one they are selling.

There is a little bit of truth in both arguments. Yes, distilled water can taste flat. And yes, reverse osmosis does remove minerals. But both issues are not really problematic. The flat taste can be eliminated by aerating the water—simply pour the water back and forth between containers and allow it to sit for a few hours. Also, the loss of minerals from reverse osmosis is not usually considered a health concern since Americans get most of their minerals from the foods they eat. The good news is that both types of systems filter water exceptionally well, removing all forms of pathogens and many chemical contaminants.

ULTRAVIOLET LIGHT

It is also possible to disinfect water using ultraviolet (UV) light. This treatment method has been used for years by large water treatment facilities, but it has only recently been available for the home user, traveler, or hiker. Two units are widely available: Meridian Design's Aqua-Star and Hydro-photon's SteriPEN. The AquaStar includes a heavy plastic bottle with an enclosed UV light source. The SteriPEN is a small, portable UV light pen used to stir water in a glass or bottle. Both claim to have been independently certified to meet the EPA Guide Standard.[76]

Courtesy of Hydro-Photon

Using either of the portable UV devices is quick and easy (taking only 30-80 seconds) and has been shown to be very effective against all types of pathogens. The UV light effectively disrupts the microbes' DNA, preventing them from multiplying. Unlike chemical disinfectants, ultraviolet light is also effective at neutralizing protozoa such as *Giardia* and *Cryptosporidium*.[77]

However, neither device will remove impurities (e.g., dirt, particulates, chemicals) or help improve the taste of the water. There are also some concerns over the effectiveness of the devices in turbid water. For example, independent testing showed that the SteriPen did a poor job of purifying muddy water.[78] For this reason, it is recommended that water be clarified prior to using a UV light purification device.

Those limitations aside, portable UV purifiers do offer a convenient method of purifying small quantities of water.

SUNLIGHT

When no other methods are available, sunlight can be used to decontaminate water. This method of solar water disinfection (a.k.a., SODIS) takes advantage of the ultraviolet emission of the sun to kill waterborne microorganisms and is used in developing countries around the world.[79]

The SODIS method is easy to follow:

1. Wash the bottles thoroughly with soap and water.
2. If necessary, perform basic filtering to clarify the water.
3. Fill the bottles with water, and close the lids.
4. Expose the filled bottles to direct sunlight for a minimum period of time.
5. Drink directly from the bottles, or pour the water into a clean cup.

SODIS

The method is simple, however, you must use colorless, transparent, polyethylene terephthalate (PET) bottles no larger than 2 liters in size. Glass and other plastic materials can block the ultraviolet light needed to purify the water. Fortunately, most convenience-sized beverage bottles sold in the United States are made of PET materials.[80]

At a water temperature of 86°F, a minimum of six hours of direct, summer sunlight is needed for mid-latitude regions. Colder water requires longer, as do cloudy conditions. For example, on days that are 50-100% overcast, water decontamination requires a full two days of exposure.[79]

The SODIS method has been proven to reduce cases of diarrhea caused from *some* waterborne pathogens. However, it has not been shown to kill *all* waterborne pathogens. Also, it is not clear that SODIS will kill trace contamination on the threads of the bottle. For these reasons, it should be considered a last resort for water decontamination.

RECOMMENDED METHODS

With all the advantages and disadvantages in hand, it becomes easier to select the optimal purification methods. Remember the two goals of purification: remove debris/particulates, and neutralize the pathogens. Given the methods discussed, to remove anything requires either filtration, distillation, or reverse osmosis. Fortunately these methods also improve the taste of water—something that can be important to many finicky drinkers. Refer to Table 4-3 for a comparison of water purification methods.

For general in-home use, an EPA-certified purifier, water distiller, or reverse osmosis system are all perfectly adequate. However, for disaster preparedness, a certified purifier is preferred over a distiller or a reverse osmosis system. This preference is because the purifier doesn't require electricity like distillation, and doesn't waste water like reverse osmosis. Table 4-4 summarizes the benefits and drawbacks of the three preferred POU and POE methods.

When it comes to portable systems, the only single-step solution that removes particles and neutralizes pathogens is a certified purifier. If

Table 4-3 Comparison of Purification Methods[74]

Method/ Device	Neutralizes Pathogens	Removes Particulates	Removes Chemicals	Affects Taste	Portable	Notes
Boiling	All	No	No	Leaves water tasting flat	Yes	The best method of killing pathogens.
Filter (1 micron pore size)	Protozoa – All Bacteria – Limited Viruses – Limited	Yes	Some	Improves	Yes	Filter effectiveness varies greatly based on pore size and membrane technology.
Certified Purifier	All	Yes	Some	Improves	Yes	Purifiers are proven to remove all forms of pathogens.
Chemical Disinfectant	Protozoa – Limited Bacteria – All Viruses – Limited	No	No	Introduces chemical taste	Yes	Slow to neutralize protozoa.
MIOX	All	No	No	Introduces salty taste	Yes	Slow to neutralize protozoa.
Distillation	All	Yes	Yes	Improves, but may leave water tasting flat	No	Requires electricity. Very slow.
Reverse Osmosis	All	Yes	Yes	Improves	No	Wasteful. Requires high water pressure. May require electricity for booster pump. Removes minerals.
Ultraviolet Light	All	No	No	No	Yes	Does not work as well in cloudy water.

Table 4-4 Comparing Preferred POU and POE Methods

Method	Neutralizes all Pathogens	Improves Taste	Needs Electricity	Wastes Water
Purifier	Yes	Yes	No	No
Distiller	Yes	Yes	Yes	No
Reverse Osmosis	Yes	Yes	Maybe	Yes

you are willing to combine two methods, then several other options exist. For example, combining boiling, UV light, or the MIOX with a standard filter can neutralize pathogens, clarify the water, and make it more palatable.

SELECTING A WATER FILTER

When selecting a water filter, you should know that all water filters are not created equal. Many manufacturers promise "clean water" using vague claims about their products that are impossible to fully understand. When it comes to filters, it is definitely *let the buyer beware*. Don't assume anything. When buying a used car, you want to see the Carfax report to verify that things are as the seller claims. In the case of water filters, you need to see the impurity removal test data.

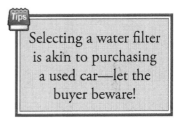

Selecting a water filter is akin to purchasing a used car—let the buyer beware!

If you can't find independent technical data showing how well the filter removes a certain type of contaminant, then you should assume that the filter falls short in that area. Remember, manufacturers want to convince you that their product is the best, so if they are not showing you the data then they likely have something to hide. Table 4-5 lists several misleading terms that you may see in water filter advertisements. In general, these claims indicate nothing about the capabilities of the filter.

Table 4-5 Making Sense of Filter Claims

Claim	Meaning
Registered with the EPA	All filters that use a chemical disinfectant must be registered. It is not an indication of their effectiveness.
Tested/Approved by the EPA	The EPA does not test or approve filters.
Nominal pore size of *x* microns	"Nominal size" indicates the average pore size, not absolute. The filter could have pores significantly larger than the average size—making it ineffective at filtering smaller pathogens.
Effective against *Giardia*, etc.	Claiming to be effective without providing specific data is meaningless.

There is also a great deal of confusion over the difference between filters and purifiers. As discussed previously, for a product to be described as a water purifier, it must be highly effective at removing, killing, or inactivating *all* forms of pathogens.[81] The word "filter" is a broader term describing any device used to remove contaminants, regardless of its effectiveness.

In reality, there are very few filters that can be classified as true water purifiers. This is largely due to the difficulty in filtering out viruses. Two exceptions worth noting are the General Ecology Seagull IV series (sink mount), the General Ecology First Need (portable). These purifying systems have been independently certified to meet the EPA Guide Standard without the use of chemical purification. Other filters may outperform these purifiers for specific contaminants, in particular *Cryptosporidium,* but the noted models offer a unique one-step solution to purifying water without the use of chemicals, UV light, or boiling. General Ecology also offers an emergency preparedness conversion kit (EPK) that converts their Seagull IV POU purifier to a portable pump-driven system.

Courtesy of General Ecology

CERTIFICATION

Filter certification can also be confusing because there are three sources of official water filter certification, all of which are accredited by the American National Standards Institute (ANSI):

- National Sanitation Foundation International (NSF)[82]
- Underwriters Laboratories (UL)[83]
- Water Quality Association (WQA)[84]

Each of the organizations has its own certification program (e.g., WQA Gold Seal, UL Water Quality Mark), but all require testing to the same ANSI/NSF standards.

Standards set the requirements for each the four different purification methods: filtering, UV light, reverse osmosis, and distillation. These standards require that careful testing verifies that the filter reduces specific contaminants by a certain amount (e.g., 99.9% removed). Construction, product labels, and sales literature are also inspected. Periodic re-certification and inspection are required. The key ANSI/NSF standards relating to point-of-use (POU) water filters are listed below.[85]

- Standard 42: *Drinking Water Treatment Units - Aesthetic Effects*
- Standard 53: *Drinking Water Treatment Units - Health Effects*
- Standard 55: *Ultraviolet Microbiological Water Treatment Systems*
- Standard 58: *Reverse Osmosis Drinking Water Treatment Systems*
- Standard 62: *Drinking Water Distillation Systems*

To verify that a product was tested by an official lab, go to the NSF, WQA, or UL website and search their database of certified products. Testing by any of these three accredited organizations is expensive. As a result, many companies elect to have independent testing done by universities or other outside labs. Accordingly, they may state that their product is "tested to the NSF/ANSI standards by an independent lab." Most independent test labs are reputable, and the results are considered accurate. Regardless of who does the testing, the results should be published and available for the customer's review.

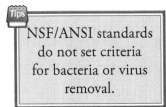

NSF/ANSI standards do not set criteria for bacteria or virus removal.

Given the list of ANSI/NSF standards, it would seem that selecting a POU water filter would be as easy as finding one that is certified to Standards 42 and 53. Or, if using alternative technologies (e.g., ultraviolet light, reverse osmosis, distillation), you would ensure that the product meets the associated standard (i.e., Standards 55, 58, or 62 respectively). In general, this selection criteria is sound. However, there is one important point to note: a significant shortcoming of Standard 53 is that it has no criteria to check effectiveness against bacteria or viruses. Broadening of the standard to include bacteria and viruses has been discussed for many years. Until that effort is complete, Standard 53 is of limited value in selecting a filter system.

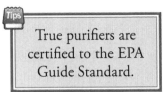

True purifiers are certified to the EPA Guide Standard.

The NSF has recognized this shortcoming and has been working on standards that address all pathogens.[86] As a stop gap, NSF currently tests to Protocol P231, which aligns with the EPA Guide Standard.

If you decide to purchase a water purifier, find one that is certified to the EPA Guide Standard. If the retailer does not clearly advertise this qualification, rest assured the product is not certified. Certification is like winning an Olympic gold medal; you are going to display it for everyone to see.

CHANGING FILTERS

Filter elements must be changed periodically, or the filter will lose its effectiveness. The element can become clogged with debris (usually indicated by reduced water flow), or the surface of the filter can become saturated, leading to reduced performance.[87] The time between filter changes is dependent on the condition of the water being filtered. If you are pumping water directly from streams or lakes, you will need more frequent filter changes than if you are filtering tap water.

Follow the manufacturer's recommendations whenever possible. Beyond that, change the filter anytime you notice the flow rate has decreased or the water begins to have an unpleasant taste or odor. Regardless of performance, change the water filter element at least annually.

Portable filters that are used infrequently should be cleaned after each use. This will prevent bacterial growth. A simple way to do this is cycle a weak bleach solution (i.e., 1 tbsp bleach into 1 gallon of water) through the unit. Then allow the filter to air dry.

> Tips
>
> Portable filters should be cleaned after each use.

WATER SOURCES

The fundamental goal of your water plan should be to have access to enough potable and non-potable water to see your family through a two-week disaster. Given the resources necessary to store hundreds of gallons of water, it is likely that in some situations you may find yourself in need of more water than you have stored.

Alternative Water Sources

- ➤ Hot water heater
- ➤ Water pipes
- ➤ Toilet
- ➤ Waterbed
- ➤ Swimming pool
- ➤ River, lake, or spring

In the best case, you can simply turn on the tap. The water may require purification before drinking, but at least you won't have to forage for water. In the worst case, however, your local water service may have been cut off due to excessive contamination, shortages, or sabotage.

When tap water is no longer available, you will need to locate alternate water sources. There are likely many such sources around you.

HOT WATER HEATER

Your hot water heater is an excellent source of potable water. Many units are 75 gallons or larger in size, giving you a sizable emergency stockpile. Water can be drained out the bottom of the tank through the built-in spigot. The five-step process to drain the tank is straightforward. Like all preparation steps, however, you need to practice on your particular water heater before a crisis hits. Don't assume that you can do it and then find yourself in an "oh, crap" moment later.

Draining Hot Water Heater

1. Turn off power or gas to the water heater.
2. Turn off the incoming water supply.
3. Attach one end of a hose to the spigot, and put the other end into a bucket below the level of the spigot.
4. Open the pressure relief valve near the top of the tank, or turn on a hot water faucet in the home.
5. Open the spigot and collect the water in the bucket. Careful, it is hot!

WATER PIPES

When water is shut off by your local water authority, it may still be possible to drain the water in your home's pipes for potable water needs. However, to have access to the water in your pipes, you must first prevent it from draining back out of your home. This is done by installing an anti-siphon water valve on your incoming main water line. The anti-siphon valve automatically closes when the water pressure gets too low, thereby keeping the water safely stored in your home's pipes.

> ### Draining Water Pipes
> 1. Turn off the incoming water main.
> 2. One by one, turn on all of the taps at the highest elevation, collecting the small amount of water that comes out of each. Leave the taps open.
> 3. Turn on the taps at the lowest elevation, collecting the water that comes out—this might take several minutes.
> 4. Once all of the taps stop outputting water, close them.

Personal aside: I was able to recover just over two gallons of water from the pipes in my two-story home. Cut off the water main, and try this water recovery process in your own house to have a better idea of the expected yield.

TOILET

The water from the toilet tanks (not bowls) can be used for drinking, but you should purify it first. Purification is needed because bacteria and rust can collect in the tank. Use a portable filter to retrieve the water, or simply scoop the water out with a cup and soak up any remaining water at the bottom with a rag or sponge.

Depending on your particular model of toilet, this could yield anywhere from 2 to 7 gallons of water per toilet.

WATERBED, SWIMMING POOL

If you have a waterbed or swimming pool, it can act as an excellent secondary source of water. However, according to the NSF, the water from a waterbed or swimming pool should only be used for non-potable needs.[88] High levels of chemicals and/or organic contaminants may be present, and no method has been proven effective at making this water completely safe.

RIVER, LAKE, OR SPRING

The water from rivers, lakes, or other fresh water sources can be used directly for non-potable needs, or for potable needs (e.g., drinking, bathing) if purified first. If the water contains visible particulates, such as dirt or twigs, use a coffee filter or clean bandana to do a cursory filter before purification. Regardless of how clear the water may appear to be, assume all natural water sources are contaminated. If the water is very shallow, use a rag or sponge to soak it up.

Sea water should not be used for potable needs unless purified with a desalination device. Never drink brackish water since it will dehydrate you, and can lead to death.

NATURAL COLLECTION

When you have exhausted all known water sources, it may be necessary to extract water from the environment around you. Extraction techniques are referred to as *natural collection*. Collection of this sort should be considered a last resort. Despite what you may have read in various survival manuals, natural collection is very difficult and requires skill, materials, and patience.

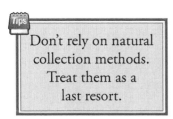

Natural Collection Methods

➤ Rain collection
➤ Dew collection
➤ Transpiration
➤ Solar still

Don't make the mistake of relying on natural collection without having spent the necessary time and energy learning how to do the extraction effectively. There are very few people, for example, who can build a solar still and get more water from it than they put out in sweat building it. Before relying on any natural water collection method, practice it ahead of time! Don't wait until you are dying of dehydration to figure out that you don't know what you are doing.

Tips

Don't rely on natural collection methods. Treat them as a last resort.

RAIN COLLECTION

Rain water can be an excellent source of natural water. The obvious (and significant) disadvantage of collecting rain water is that rainfall is unpredictable. Also, given that in most places it usually rains one inch or less with each rainfall, you will need a large surface area to collect enough water. A child's inflatable swimming pool works well. A six-foot diameter pool collects about 18 gallons of water if it rains one inch.[89]

Tips

A kid's inflatable swimming pool makes a great rain collector.

An alternative is to use a clean, waterproof tarp tied up into a mild "V" shape, sloping downward into a large container. With a 10 ft. × 12 ft. tarp, you can collect up to about 70 gallons of water from a one-inch rainfall.[89] Be sure to secure your tarp so that it won't be blown down by heavy winds. The idea is to face the tarp into the wind, allowing rain to blow onto the surface, down the channel, and into your water storage container.

Another good method of collecting rainwater is to place buckets (or rain barrels) under your home's gutter down-spouts. The large surface area of your roof will yield significant water. People have been doing this for years to collect water for use in their gardens, as well as prevent flooding of their yards.

A final, albeit less effective, option for collecting rain water is to hang bed sheets outside your windows. Let them get drenched in the rain, and then bring the sheets inside and ring the water out into a container. Repeat for as long as the rain continues.

All rain water should be purified by one of the recommended methods before drinking.

DEW COLLECTION

In heavily vegetated areas, dew can be collected off plants early in the morning or immediately after a rainfall. This can be done by dragging absorbent rags across the surface of plants. Once the rags become

> **Tips**
> Dew collection can yield significant water with nothing more than a rag and a bucket.

saturated, wring them out into buckets. Continue the process until the yield starts to decrease as temperatures rise.

The advantages of dew collection are that it requires only minimal supplies and can yield fairly good results even in the wilderness. The two drawbacks are that the collection process can be mildly arduous, and once again water must be purified before drinking. The method is also not effective in areas with limited vegetation.

Personal aside: Following a rainfall, I was able to collect 12 cups of water in one hour using only a sturdy paper towel and a small bucket—a significant yield.

TRANSPIRATION

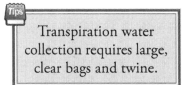

> **Tips**
> Transpiration water collection requires large, clear bags and twine.

Transpiration bags use evaporation and condensation to collect water. Large clear plastic bags are secured over the green foliage of non-poisonous plants. Plants with large root systems work best. The opening of the bag is tied off to make it as airtight as possible. Using a cloth or paper as a gasket in the mouth of the bag will also help. The bag creates a greenhouse effect causing the plant to release water vapor. The vapor then condenses on the inner surface and pools in the bottom corner of the bag (see illustration).

The amount of water released through transpiration varies by temperature (as temperature rises, yields increase), relative humidity (as humidity rises, yields drop), plant type, and soil moisture. The biggest advantage of using transpiration bags is that they can be placed with very little energy, allowing for many bags to be used in parallel. However, practical yields are often minimal (perhaps only a cup per bag per day, depending on conditions). Also, be aware that transpiration bags can kill the plants.

A modest secondary benefit can be had by wiping dew from the outside of transpiration bags during the early morning hours.

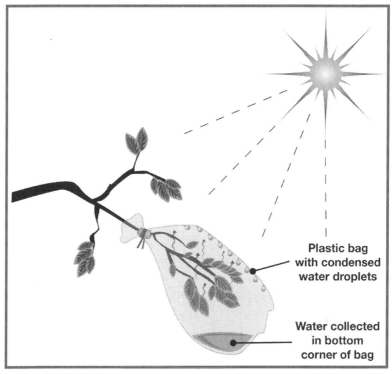

Plastic bag
with condensed
water droplets

Water collected
in bottom
corner of bag

Transpiration

SOLAR STILL

The solar still is a well known natural water collection method also based on the greenhouse effect. Two simple models are the single-sloped box still and the pit still (see illustration on next page). With the single-sloped still, a sealed box is constructed with a dark insulator material lining the bottom, a sloped clear glass or plastic barrier on top, and a way of introducing and removing the contaminated and distilled water.

The pit solar still is the type you will find in most survival manuals. It consists of a large hole in the ground, perhaps 3 feet across, covered with a clear plastic barrier. A collection cup is placed in the center of the pit, and a water source (e.g., shredded vegetation, urine, brackish water) around the cup. A rock is put on top of the plastic to form an inverse apex centered over the cup. Rubber tubing can be used to drink water from the cup so as not to disturb the still.

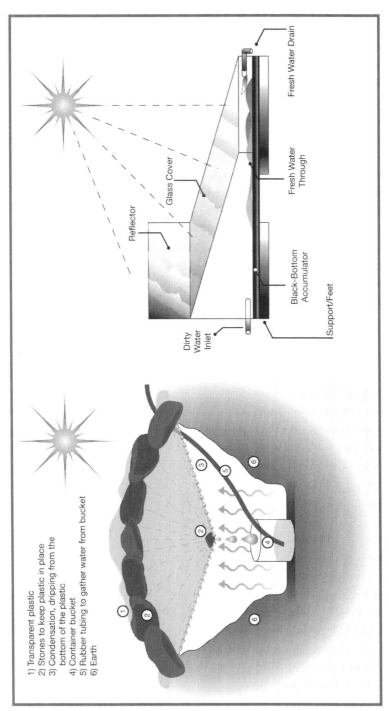

1) Transparent plastic
2) Stones to keep plastic in place
3) Condensation, dripping from the bottom of the plastic
4) Container bucket
5) Rubber tubing to gather water from bucket
6) Earth

Reflector

Glass Cover

Fresh Water Drain

Fresh Water Through

Black-Bottom Accumulator

Support/Feet

Dirty Water Inlet

Solar stills – pit style and single-sloped box

Both types of stills operate in a very similar manner. Solar energy heats the ground or black background. Moisture inside the greenhouse evaporates, rises, and condenses on the underside of the clear barrier. The solar-distilled water then runs down the slope and drips into a collection channel or cup.

One significant advantage of the solar distillation process over other natural collection methods is that the water recovered *does not* require purification. Plants, sea water, and even urine can be used as the originating source of water. All will ultimately produce clean, drinkable water.

However, there are three notable problems with the solar still. First, it requires materials (plastic, collection cup, and tubing) and a shovel for digging the hole. The still also takes significant energy to set up. Finally, it is very difficult to make work effectively.

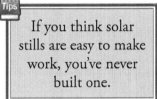

If you think solar stills are easy to make work, you've never built one.

Experts who have evaluated the effectiveness of the solar still suggest that many things can go wrong—causing it to provide very little if any water. Problems can include failing to get the plastic sufficiently tight, wind disturbance, insufficient transparency of plastic, improper angle to the sun, and a host of other things.[90] Some experts swear by solar stills. Others will warn you away.

DP PLAN EXAMPLE

Table 4-6 Sample DP Plan Entry

Need: Water			
Danger	**Goals**	**Needs**	**Implementation**
Shortage	Access to enough water for family of 5 to survive for 14 days	Potable: Minimum of 28 gallons per person = 140 gallons Non-potable: Enough water to flush the commode 5 times per day @ 3 gallons per flush = 210 gallons	Store 250 gallons of treated potable water in a Super Tanker container. Access neighbor's swimming pool for non-potable use. Use 5 gallon buckets for water retrieval. Use two rain barrels on main house gutters.
	A 2-day supply transportable by car	Transportable: Minimum of 4 gallons per person = 20 gallons	Transport water using four 6-gallon blue water jerry cans
Contamination	Neutralize or remove all pathogens in water coming from at least one tap in the house	POU water filter purifies tap water A backup plan in case filter becomes inoperable	Install a Seagull IV water purifier on the kitchen tap. Boil water as the backup plan.

Quick Summary - Water

➢ Store, or have access to, enough potable water to maintain your family for 14 days, assuming 2 gallons per day per person.

➢ Have access to enough non-potable water for at least one toilet flush per person per day for 14 days. Water quantity varies based on toilet model.

➢ Hygiene is critically important during a disaster because falling ill can leave you weak and unable to handle the situation's hardships.

➢ Store potable water in FDA-approved containers out of light and away from chemicals or gasoline.

➢ If keeping a permanent stockpile, rotate the water every six months or treat with a water preserver.

➢ Water pre-treatment is usually unnecessary for tap water.

➢ Pathogens found in water include protozoa, bacteria, and viruses. To purify the water, you must remove, kill, or neutralize the pathogens.

➢ Recommended home POU or POE purifying methods include: certified purifiers, distillers, and reverse osmosis systems.

➢ Recommended portable purifying methods include: certified purifiers, or combining filtering with boiling, UV light, or chemical treatment.

➢ Use secondary sources as necessary, including your home's hot water heater, water in house pipes or commode tanks, swimming pool, waterbed, and rivers or lakes.

➢ Do not try to purify seawater without a desalination device.

➢ Depend on natural collection methods only as a last resort. Natural methods include rain collection, dew collection, transpiration, and solar stills.

➢ Test your water collection methods before an emergency.

Recommended Items - Water

❑ Water Storage
   a. Large water containers to allow for 28 gallons of potable water per person stored in FDA approved containers—e.g., 55-gallon water storage barrels with pump, Super Tankers, Aquatank water bags
   b. Two sets of smaller water containers for retrieving and transporting water (one set for potable water, one set for non-potable water)—e.g., plastic jerry cans, 2-liter bottles, five-gallon buckets, WaterCubes, dromedary bags

❑ Water retrieval
   a. Garden hose and bucket for draining the hot water heater

❑ Chemical disinfectant for preparing containers, treating water, and cleaning surfaces.
   a. Jug of household bleach, dropper

❑ A home POU or POE water purification system
   a. A purifier that meets the EPA Guide Standard, *or*
   b. Water distiller, *or*
   c. Reverse osmosis system

❑ A portable water purifier
   a. A purifier that meets the EPA Guide Standard, *or*
   b. UV light, *or*
   c. MIOX device

❑ Supplies to stay clean
   a. Adequate supply of hand soap, alcohol-based hand sanitizer, and hand/body wipes
   b. Supply of large plastic bags and twist ties

❑ Sanitation needs
   a. Access to enough non-potable water for at least one toilet flush per person per day, *or*
   b. A potty bucket, plastic bags, and treatment chemicals, *or*
   c. A self-contained composting toilet

CHAPTER 5
SHELTER

CHAPTER 5

SHELTER

Challenge

Your microwave oven short-circuits in the middle of the night, igniting a house fire. The fire smolders for several hours before spreading, filling the house with smoke. Do you have the correct smoke alarms to detect the slow-burning fire? How will your family evacuate the house if the primary exit is impassible? Can your children escape without your help? Does everyone know what to do once they get out of the house?

There is a well understood order to wilderness survival: shelter, water, and then food. The idea is simple enough. You must first protect yourself from the environment, whether it is the heat of summer, the frost of winter, or the drenching rains of spring, before worrying about what you are going to eat or drink. This generally holds true for disaster preparedness as well. The only difference is that you are not typically required to build a shelter. Rather, you will need to effectively use and protect the shelters you already have.

> In order of importance: shelter, water, and then food.

Your home—a generic expression for a house, apartment, townhouse, mobile home, etc., is the shelter that your family will most likely depend

Your home as a shelter *(photo by FEMA/Dave Gatley)*

on when confronting a disaster. Certainly there may be times when you are forced to evacuate, in which case you will have to secure a new shelter. However, for most situations, your family will be much better served by staying put. As shelters go, your home is far superior to anything you can construct ad hoc. If you don't believe this, try spending a cold, rainy night in your yard under the best shelter you can build in half a day. You will quickly come to enjoy the comforts provided by your home, even with the power, water, and gas all turned off.

There are certain threats that require specialized shelters. For example, buried or hardened shelters offer the best protection from radioactive fallout.[91] They can be built from conventional materials (stone block, concrete, etc.), or they can be made from such things as fuel tanks, shipping containers, steel culverts, Quonsets, or pre-made fiberglass inserts. However, they are not generally the best solution to more common disasters.

Take a look at the list of disasters in *Chapter 1: Introduction,* and you will see that, for most situations, a buried bunker doesn't really offer any advantage over a conventional house. Specialized shelters of this sort are also very expensive for a private individual, not to mention nearly impossible for people living in metropolitan areas. For these reasons, this chapter focuses on issues related to using a conventional residence as an effective shelter. A section in *Chapter 14: Transportation* discusses the special case where you find yourself on the road depending on your automobile to serve as an emergency shelter.

In general, there are three important steps in preparing your home to be an effective shelter.

1. Assess what protection your home provides.
2. Make improvements to increase that level of protection.
3. Safeguard your home to prevent loss, damage, or deterioration.

ASSESSING AND MAKING IMPROVEMENTS

Begin by evaluating the safety that your home provides. Factors that weigh into this evaluation are construction, geography, and distance from likely threats.

- **Construction**—What is your house made from? Brick, wood, vinyl, sheet metal? Are there any specific threats to which your house's construction will be particularly vulnerable? Are there large exposed windows, and if so, can they be shuttered? Do you have a basement that might flood? Is the construction solid? Can you identify any obvious weaknesses, such as an exposed carport with insufficient supports or a roof with loose shingles?
- **Geography**—In which part of the country do you live? What weather events are most likely to affect you? Are there any specific geological threats such as mudslides, avalanches, earthquakes, rockslides, or sinkholes? Does the landscape offer any natural protections? Are you on the coast where ocean-related weather events, such as hurricanes or nor'easters, pose very real concerns? Is your home situated in a valley that might flood from heavy rains? Are you close to a river or lake that could overflow its banks? Are you off the beaten path, making it difficult for repair crews to get to you?
- **Distance from likely threats**—Do you live near a nuclear or industrial plant that might release an airbrone contaminant? Are you in a metropolitan area (e.g., New York, Los Angeles) that might experience a terrorist attack? Do you live near a railway or airport at which a major crash might occur?

List of Threats

- Flood
- Earthquake
- Snow storm
- Tornado
- Hurricane/typhoon
- Winter freeze
- Ice storm
- Thunderstorm
- Lightning
- Heat wave
- Wildfire
- Drought
- Volcanic eruption
- Landslide
- Tsunami/tidal wave
- Avalanche
- Home invasion
- Pandemic
- Blackout
- Hazardous material spill
- Air pollution
- Water pollution
- Radioactive material release
- Chemical release
- Food contamination
- Fire
- Military attack
- Biochemical attack
- Riot
- Hail
- Sinkhole
- Airplane/train crash

Consider the list of threats in the tip box. How likely is each to affect you? How much protection would your home offer? What steps can you take to improve that level of protection?

To make your home threat assessment a little easier, a blank worksheet is included in the *Appendix*. Table 5-1 serves as an example of what a threat assessment entry might look like. This particular example is assessing a home against floods.[92,93,94]

Assessments are completely subjective—you can rate your home at whatever level you think appropriate. The point of the exercise is to have you think about your home's vulnerabilities, and then take steps to reduce them. Realize that many of the threats listed are unlikely, requiring little or no preventive action. Again, the key to practical preparation is to identify the likeliest (or most worrisome) threats first and make improvements to reduce their impact.

Personal aside: Many years ago, I lived in a mobile home in rural Alabama. I scrutinized the weather regularly, fearing the announcer would utter the single word we all

---

Table 5-1 Example of Shelter Assessment (Flood)

Threat	Likelihood (1-10)	Protection (1-10)	Steps to Improve
Flood	8	5	1. Determine the base flood elevation (BFE) for the area.*
	I live on the east coast where flooding is common, usually due to nor'easters and hurricanes.	My home is situated atop a small hill, 42 feet above sea level. It has gutters to route water effectively off the roof. Unfortunately curbside water drains are directly in front of the house and thus prone to backup and flooding.	2. Ensure that water-resistant materials have been used in places below BFE. If not, replace them as appropriate.
			3. Raise the water heater and other appliances above BFE level.
			4. Install backflow valves in sewer pipes to prevent backups.
			5. Install flood shields or natural built-up barriers near basement windows and doors.
			6. Install sump pump system for basement.
			7. Check yard grading to ensure adequate water drainage.
			8. Use rain barrels on the two main gutters.
			9. Landscape using vegetation that resists soil erosion.
			10. Seal walls in basement with waterproofing compounds.
			11. Add flood insurance coverage.

*BFE is the height that a flood has a 1% chance of reaching or exceeding for a given year—a.k.a., the 100-year flood level. Maps showing your BFE and flood zone designation are available online at FEMA's Map Service Center.[95]

dreaded—tornado. When twisters were spotted anywhere in the vicinity, alarms would sound for miles, and my family would race to a small brick building that the landlord provided for just such occasions. The lesson that I took away from the experience was that it is very important to understand what protections each type of shelter offers. In my case, the small reinforced brick building was much more likely to survive the winds of a tornado than a mobile home constructed of sheet metal and particle board. With that said, I never felt the need to evacuate when thunderstorms, ice storms, blackouts, or winter snow threatened. And in general, I think I got it right. My rather fragile house was perfectly capable of handling certain dangers, but ill-equipped for others.

MAINTENANCE

A home is only as good as the elbow grease put into it. It needs to be maintained with diligence. Major systems include roofing, heating and cooling, appliances, plumbing, electrical, and structural. Each system should be regularly inspected, and any problems discovered should be repaired without unnecessary delay—an empty pocketbook being the most likely cause of a "necessary delay." Think of your house as your personal fortress against the dangers of the world. In doing so, give it the attention that it deserves.

One of the first things you should do is learn how to shut off your utilities (e.g., electricity, water, and gas). Don't just *think* you know how to shut them off. Go through the motions a couple times. Keep the necessary shutoff tools near the cutoff points. This way you won't have to hunt for them when trouble is knocking on your door. One word of caution: don't actually shut off your gas. It may require a professional to come out to turn it back on. That can be a hassle, not to mention expensive.

Even if you do maintain your home properly, damage will undoubtedly occur. Perhaps high winds or a fallen tree are to blame. In the case of a quickly passing disaster, you can simply head to your local home improvement store, or call your insurance company to hire appropriate contractors to make repairs.

Home Repair Supplies

➤ A good set of hand tools
➤ Basic home repair materials
➤ Home fix-it books
➤ Cleanup equipment

If the danger is more prolonged, you may need to make impromptu emergency repairs to patch a leaky roof, cover a broken window, or replace a cracked pipe. For these home repairs, you will need a few tools and supplies. However, it is not necessary to have a toolkit that would make Bob Vila proud. Your money is better spent elsewhere. For now, a basic set of tools that you know how to use (e.g., hammer, screw drivers, wrenches, hand saw, pliers, pry bar) will suffice.

Likewise, limit your construction materials to only those needed to perform emergency repairs on your home (e.g., fasteners, plastic sheeting, PVC fittings, duct tape). You don't need pallets of sheetrock or bags of concrete. Just keep it simple. Pick up a few home fix-it manuals to help you understand the basics of home repair.

It's a good idea to have some cleanup equipment on hand too, such as shovels, an axe, wheelbarrow, heavy broom, and a chain saw if you can afford one. All of these items can be very useful for cleaning up after a major storm blows through.

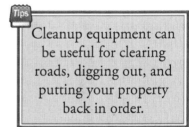

Tips

Cleanup equipment can be useful for clearing roads, digging out, and putting your property back in order.

As for proficiency, that comes with practice and perhaps a bit of one-on-one instruction from a local handyman. Developing some basic know-how will not only help you to make emergency repairs, but also to appreciate the details of your home's construction.

Personal aside: When a particularly nasty nor'easter blew through town a few years ago, I had to carefully hang outside my second story window to secure a large tarp over a leaky window. It was an unpleasant (and very wet) job, but I did feel fortunate to have had the right materials available to keep my house from becoming a swimming pool.

HARDENING YOUR HOME

There is one particular area that often doesn't get the attention it deserves, and that is hardening your home from intruders. It is not necessary or even wise to be paranoid, but it is important to be honest enough to accept that bad things can happen to good people. Home invasions and burglaries occur in nearly every community, and during times of crisis, even otherwise law-abiding people may feel compelled to take desperate actions.

Try this simple 30-day challenge. Imagine for a moment that a nasty-looking thug comes up to you and says, "In 30 days, I am going to break into your home and scare the hell out of you and your family."

What would you do? Call the police—for sure. Get a gun—probably. One thing for certain is that you would turn your attention to hardening your home and preparing your family. The point in posing this ridiculous scenario is to motivate you to take some precautionary steps that might one day prevent you from becoming a victim of theft, burglary, or home invasion.

It is possible to transform your house into a "hard target" without turning it into a maximum-security prison. Consider some of the many proven methods used to improve your home security and deter criminals.[96,97,98,99,100]

BE MORE CAUTIOUS

> **Tips**
> The first step in being safer at home is becoming more cautious.

Before you even think about hardening your home, teach everyone in your family to be more cautious. Even simple actions like keeping all your doors and windows locked, whether you are at home or away, will go a long way toward keeping your family safe. It is estimated that 90% of all illegal entries occur through doors.[100]

Be careful about how you open your door, and who you open it to. Never blindly open the door—always look first. Ideally have a peep-hole, chain lock, or floor-mounted retractable door stop to help you better assess the situation. If you see an unexpected repairman, or a suspected evangelist or solicitor, simply don't open the door to them. They will get the message and move on to the next house. If an unknown person persistently knocks on your door, call a neighbor to come over to back you up. Finally, never allow your children to open the door unattended.

Personal aside: When I was in college, one night at around 1:00 AM someone began banging on my apartment door. Purely by coincidence, I was up that night cleaning my handgun from a day at the range. I foolishly answered the door without checking the peephole, thinking that someone was in trouble—perhaps needing medical attention. What I found was a scruffy-looking man who smelled of booze and whose intention never became fully known. When he saw the pistol hanging loosely at my side, he apologized and hastily stumbled away. I was fortunate that my mistake didn't cost me my life.

MAKE IT HARDER FOR A PERSON TO SURPRISE YOU

Take steps to make it harder for someone to surprise you. Consider installing an electronic home security system. Even if the system just serves as a noise-maker, it will alert your family when someone tries to enter your home while you are asleep. The noise may also be sufficient to scare away an intruder.

Tips

A guard dog can be a wonderful companion and an almost unbeatable security system.

An alternative is to have a guard dog act as your early warning system. But don't rely wholly on your pet's natural instincts. Take time to teach your dog that security is an important part of his/her role in the family. A point of distinction is in order. A *guard dog* is a dog that will make noise when someone tries to enter your home. It could be as tiny as a Chihuahua. An *attack dog* is a dog that will viciously attack an intruder. Unless you live alone and know how to handle a trained attack dog, you should definitely limit yourself to a guard dog. They are much easier to train, and can serve as a loving companion.

Courtesy of Heath Zenith

Keep the exterior of your home well lit using flood-lights and motion-detector lighting under the eaves or in the yard. Keep bushes and tree limbs cut back to prevent anyone from hiding outside your home, or using trees to access your upper floors. Put gravel or pebbles under the windows as a noise deterrent. Also, consider planting thorny bushes, such as Barberry or Hawthorne, in front of the windows.

DON'T BROADCAST YOUR WEAKNESS

Never let anyone other than family or friends know when you or your spouse will be out of town. If the house is empty, use light timers to make it seem like someone is at home. It is also useful to create the illusion of additional security by keeping a large set of boots or a dog bowl with the word "Killer" on the front porch. A home security sign in the yard can act as a similar deterrent.

HARDEN YOUR DOORS AND WINDOWS

A simple step to improving a door's security is to install longer screws in the hinges and strike plate.

Shore up your doors and windows. Install heavy-duty, solid-core external doors and deadbolt locks with 1 inch or longer bolt throw. Replace hinge screws with longer wood screws (2 inches for doors, 3 inches for frames). Replace strike plates with high-security models. At a minimum, replace your existing strike plate screws with 3-inch wood screws. If it isn't possible to install adequate locks, consider using inexpensive security bars that wedge between the doorknob and floor (e.g., Master Lock 265), or keyless security latches that are many times stronger than deadbolts (e.g., Meranto DG01-B).

If you have a glass window in your door, it may be possible to install shatterproof plastic or security glass—assuming it doesn't already have it. If that's not possible, you can line the glass with security film, such as 3M's Prestige.

Don't use double-cylinder locks in your home because they introduce a fire safety hazard.

For French or double doors, use inset-keyed slide bolts at the top and bottom to lock in place the lesser-used door. For sliding glass doors, you can drill a hole in the door and frame and insert a locking steel pin, use a window bar, or insert a rod (wood or metal) in the bottom track to prevent it from being forced open.

A lock is only secure if the intruder doesn't already have the key. Don't hide a key outside—especially not under the mat, above the door frame, or in nearby flower pot. It is much better to give a spare key to a neighbor or relative. If you move into a new home, immediately rekey the locks. You might also consider using battery-operated electronic locks that can be easily reconfigured with new codes,

Courtesy of Schlage

should they ever be compromised. Don't use a deadbolt requiring a key on both sides (a.k.a., a double cylinder lock), since it might slow your family's escape in the event of a fire.

If windows are *not* going to be used as fire exits, you can nail or screw them closed, install keyed latches, or cover them with metal grillwork. If the window may act as a potential fire escape, consider using a removable window bar (e.g., Master Lock 266), or quick release, hinged interior bars. An alternative for high-risk windows, sliding glass doors, and storm doors is to cover them with protective security film (e.g., 3M's Prestige).

HARDEN YOUR BASEMENT AND GARAGE DOORS

Due to their privacy and weak construction, basements and garages are often easier points of entry for intruders. To help mitigate these

> **Tips**
> Garage and basement doors are easy targets for someone wishing to break into your home.

vulnerabilities, install solid-core exterior doors to your basement and garage, and consider using motion-sensor lighting outside. Be sure to include your garage and basement in your home security-system.

If you have automatic garage door openers, reprogram them to be different from the factory setting (usually done by changing a couple of internal switches). The same goes for changing the code to the external keypad. Treat your garage remote with the same level of care as you would a house key. Also, if you are guilty of accidentally leaving your garage open at times, consider getting an electronic garage door monitor.

Most garages have manual slide bar latches on each side that can lock the door in place from the inside, making forcing the garage difficult. An alternative to a slide bar is to drill a hole in the track and use a bolt or padlock to keep the door's rollers from moving. Both of these security measures are handiest for use at night or when away on vacation.

SECURE THE COMMUNITY

> **Tips**
> A neighborhood watch program is a great way to find neighbors interested in being part of a DP network.

An important part of home security is being part of a community that looks out for one another. In many neighborhoods this manifests as a formal watch program. If your community doesn't have a neighborhood watch program, then at least work to establish an "I'll watch your back if you'll watch mine" mentality with your neighbors.

SAFE ROOM

During certain events (e.g., terrorist threats, contaminant leaks, tornados), your family may be safer confined to a small fortified place within your home.[101] Unless you already live in a small home or apartment, it probably makes sense to create a "safe room." This is a secure area that you and your family can retreat to when a serious disaster threatens.

Select a structurally sound room in your home, perhaps a basement or large closet. Ideally, pick an interior room with access to a toilet, running water, and a telephone. Stock the room with a complete set of emergency supplies, including blankets, food, water, medicine, a first-aid kit, flashlights, AM and weather radios, batteries, a cell phone, children's toys, a space heater, and weapons.

BIOCHEMICAL CONSIDERATION

If, because of your location, you feel that you are at risk of a chemical or biological threat, you may wish to locate the safe room on the upper floor of your home. Gases tend to settle, so the upper rooms are likely to have less airborne contamination. Also, you will want to consider storing some additional items for protection from biochemical hazards.

- Duct tape and plastic sheeting for sealing around doors, windows, and heating/cooling vents.
- A HEPA air filter. When properly sized to the room, HEPA filters have been shown to be effective in removing vapor contaminants and some poison gases.[102]
- Gas masks or protective hoods, carefully adjusted to fit each family member. Inexpensive disposable respirators, such as N95 masks, can also be used.
- Disposable biochemical protection suits, such as Tyvek F.

For additional details and recommendations regarding sheltering in place and safeguarding against airborne hazards, see *Chapter 9: Air*.

As with every other preparation, creating a safe room is about weighing risks versus costs. If you live close to an industrial plant, then a room designed to protect your family from chemical leaks probably ranks high on your action list. If you don't live close to a potential biochemical

Tyvek F biochemical suit

threat, then you may want to tailor the room to better handle other threats—putting your money and efforts toward the most likely dangers first.

You may wonder if it is possible to seal the room so well that suffocation becomes a risk. The only documented case found was in 2003 when three Israeli citizens suffocated in a sealed safe room.[103] Their mistake, however, was not in over sealing the room, but in burning a coal-fueled heater in the safe room. The heater consumed oxygen as it burned, eventually creating a deadly deficit. Fuel-burning appliances should *never* be used indoors without proper ventilation. See *Chapter 8: Heating/Cooling* for more heating safety recommendations.

From the evidence available, it appears to be very difficult to seal a room in your home well enough to endanger your family from suffocation. With that said, it would still be prudent to keep an eye out for signs of oxygen shortage and CO_2 buildup. Symptoms include headache, fatigue, shortness of breath, euphoria, and nausea.[104,105] If anyone confined to the safe room experiences these symptoms, everyone should immediately seek fresh air.

Tips

There is no evidence to support the myth that a sealed room poses a suffocation hazard.

SAFEGUARDING YOUR SHELTER

Given that your home is likely one of your most important financial investments, as well as your family's primary shelter during most disasters, every effort should be made to ensure that it is protected from damage.

Safeguarding your Shelter

1. Minimize hazards in and around your home.
2. Equip your home with safety devices.
3. Adequately insure your home.

MINIMIZING HOME HAZARDS

Set aside an hour every couple of months to inspect your home for hazards (i.e., things that could endanger your family or your home). Make a checklist, and then work your way through the needed improvements over time—starting with the most important first.

Below are sample outdoor and indoor home hazard checklists. A blank home hazards checklist is included in the *Appendix*.

OUTDOOR

	Clear heavy vegetation away from the home.
	Remove any dead trees that pose a threat from falling or catching fire. Ideally, even live trees should be far enough away to prevent them from hitting your home, should they fall.
	Secure items that might act as flying debris, such as a swing set, barbeque grill, bicycles, deck furniture, or trash cans.
	Keep gutters clear to facilitate proper water drainage from roof.
	Inspect and clean chimneys or wood-burning stove vents.
	Inspect roofing for loose or worn shingles and degraded seals.
	Check gas lines for signs of corrosion or leaks.
	Make sure land is properly graded for water runoff.
	Store flammables (e.g., gas, paint thinner, cleaners, oily rags) in approved containers, away from heat, and in areas with adequate ventilation.
	Check under home for leaks, water-damage, termites, or mold.
	Insulate or drain any external pipes (e.g., sprinklers) that might freeze.
	If flood prone, raise heating/cooling units above the Base Flood Elevation (BFE) level.
	Make sure your house number is visible from the street so emergency vehicles can easily locate the home.

INDOOR

Check that electrical outlets and extension cords aren't overloaded.
Check for frayed electrical cords.
Check that all electrical outlets near sinks are equipped with properly wired ground fault protection.
Connect all sensitive electronics to surge protectors (certified to UL1449 330V).
Use correct wattage light bulbs in lamps and lighting fixtures.
Check all safety devices at least twice a year (smoke alarms, fire extinguishers, CO alarms).
Inspect underneath sinks and around toilets for leaks.
Ensure that poisonous substances, such as cleaners, pesticides, medicines, and alcohol are locked up or high enough that young children can't reach them.
Eliminate clutter in your home, clearing emergency escape routes.

In earthquake-prone areas:
   - Place large, heavy items on lower shelves.
   - Hang pictures and mirrors away from beds.
   - Secure water heater by strapping it to wall studs.

SAFETY DEVICES

Home safety is about being responsible and protective of what is most precious to you—your life and those of your family. This is one of those rare times when there is a clear right thing to do; and that is to take every reasonable precaution when it comes to keeping your family safe.

> **Tips**
> Equipping your home with the proper safety devices is *the* single biggest action you can take to increase your family's chance of disaster survival.

Fortunately, there are a small set of safety devices that can *significantly* reduce your chances of dying from an accident in your home. Safety devices are like insurance; most of the time they cost you money and give nothing more than peace of mind in return. But if tragedy strikes, nothing could be more valuable. Don't skimp on properly equipping your home.

SMOKE, HEAT ALARMS

According to the U.S. Fire Administration, fires kill more Americans than all other natural disasters combined.[106] Did you miss that? **Fires kill more Americans than all natural disasters combined!** Forget hurricanes, storms, Earth-destroying asteroids, or volcanic eruptions. If you want to make a big impact in reducing your chances of dying from a disaster, take steps to reduce your risk of dying in a fire.

The National Fire Protection Association (NFPA) reports that an average household will have *five* fires through the course of a person's lifetime; roughly one every 15 years.[107] Most will be small fires, perhaps

Fire—a very real threat!

a greasy pan in the kitchen, or a candle igniting a tablecloth—easily managed by the homeowner. The odds of having a fire large enough to be reported to the fire department are 1 in 4, and the chances of someone in your household being injured in a fire are 1 in 10.

According to the NFPA, residential fires kill an average of 3,000 Americans each year, and injure another 13,000.[108] Perhaps the most tragic part is that 63% of residential fire deaths occurred in homes with no working smoke alarms. For your family's sake, take a stand against fire by being thoroughly prepared.

Tips
House fires give an average of only three minutes warning!

Early detection is the key to surviving a house fire. Install smoke detectors in the hallways outside sleeping areas as well as in the bedrooms. Keep a minimum of one on every level of your home, even if there are no bedrooms. Put one in the kitchen, as well as the attic, and at the top of the basement stairs. The idea is to put smoke detectors between hazard areas and people areas—providing you with the earliest possible warning. Think about where a fire could start, and where you might be sitting, sleeping, or working; then put a detector between the two locations.

There are three types of smoke alarms available today.

- Ionization alarms—detect flaming, fast-moving fires quickly
- Photoelectric alarms—detect smoldering, smoky fires quickly
- Dual sensor alarms—combined ionization and photoelectric sensors in one unit

Since both types of fires (i.e., fast-moving and smoldering) are possible, you should equip your home with both ionization and photoelectric alarms, or better yet, use dual sensor alarms. Note that alarms using strobe lights rather than sound are also available for people with hearing disabilities.

Smoke detectors can be powered from batteries or from your home's electrical system. House-powered units with battery backup are preferred. If your house was built after 1993, the alarms installed during construction are *interconnected* alarms—meaning that when one sounds off, it should trigger the others to sound also. This is a great advantage

Kidde strobe fire alarm

over individual alarms because it ensures that you will receive the greatest warning possible. Did you know that house fires give an average of only three minutes warning for occupants to escape?[109]

If you are installing additional smoke alarms after construction, you will likely have to settle for battery-only models since they are much easier to install. Once again, it is best to select units that are interconnectable—now readily available from First Alert, Kidde, and other manufacturers.

The U.S. Consumer Product Safety Commission recommends replacing your smoke alarm batteries at least once a year.[110] A simple way to remember this is to change the batteries when the time changes in the spring or fall. Always test a smoke alarm after you change the batteries. This is done by pressing the test button on the unit. When you purchase a new smoke detector, you may wish to test the sensitivity of the unit. This can easily be done by lighting a few matches together, blowing them out, and holding them up to the smoke detector. Once the alarm sounds, quickly blow the smoke away, or spray a fine mist of water to clear the air.

You might be surprised to learn that children often don't wake up when a smoke alarm sounds. Studies have shown that even at ear-piercing levels,

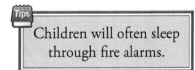

Tips

Children will often sleep through fire alarms.

children often remain asleep.[110] To overcome this, there are special "voice" smoke alarms available, some even allowing you to pre-record your own voice as the alarm. Voice alarms of this type have been shown to be more effective at waking sleeping children.

Hint: If you accidentally set off the smoke alarm in the kitchen, spray a fine mist of water underneath it, rather than turning off the alarm. Alternatively, kitchen smoke detectors can be replaced with heat detectors to make them less susceptible to triggering from burning food.

FIRE EXTINGUISHERS

It is important to equip your home with fire extinguishers. The NFPA recommends that you keep at least one primary extinguisher (size 2-A:10-BC or larger) on every level of your home. Supplement these with smaller extinguishers in the kitchen, garage, and car to further reduce your family's changes of being injured or killed in a fire.

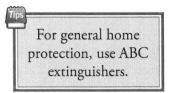

Tips

For general home protection, use ABC extinguishers.

Fire extinguishers spray water or chemicals that either cool burning fuel, displace or remove oxygen, or stop chemical reactions. They must be approved by nationally recognized testing labs, such as Underwriters Laboratory (UL). Fire extinguishers are labeled with an alpha-numeric classification, based on the type and size of fire they can effectively extinguish. It is important to understand the labeling conventions used on fire extinguishers.

Fire extinguisher labeling

The letters A, B, and C, represent the type of fire for which the extinguisher is approved: type A is used for standard wood, paper, and combustible material fires, type B is for grease, gasoline, and oil fires, and type C is for electrical fires. A multiclass extinguisher (e.g., BC, ABC) is effective on more than one fire type. For general home protection, use ABC multiclass fire extinguishers. This type of extinguisher is good for nearly any kind of fire except very hot grease fires, chemical fires, and those that burn metals.[111]

The numbers convey information about the size of fire that the extinguisher can put out. The number in front of the A indicates the number of 1.25 gallon units of water that the extinguisher is equivalent to when fighting standard combustible fires. The number in front of the B rating indicates the square footage of a grease, fuel, or oil fire that the extinguisher can put out. There is no number associated with the C rating.

> **Tips**
>
> Caution: Class A air-pressurized water extinguishers (APW) should never be used on grease, electrical, or chemical fires!

For example, an extinguisher labeled 1-A:10-BC is rated to be equivalent to $1 \times 1.25 = 1.25$ gallons of water for standard combustible fires, and is capable of putting out a grease fire measuring 10 square feet in size.

It is tempting to equip your home with the largest fire extinguishers on the market, but realize that family members must also be able to handle them effectively. A good compromise might be to keep a combination of smaller and larger units distributed throughout the house.

For recommendations regarding the latest fire extinguisher models, consult online reviews, such as the GALT website.[112] If the recommended models are not available in your area, simply find a suitable replacement.

Using an Extinguisher

A fire extinguisher is only as good as its user. Unfortunately, most people don't know how to properly operate a fire extinguisher—understandable since the average person doesn't have an opportunity to practice. To gain this much-needed and valuable experience, set up a well-controlled practice session. It is worth the cost of an extinguisher or two for you and your family to learn how to put out a fire.

Practicing *PASS*

Start by picking a suitable location—ideally, a sandbox in the back yard away from everything else. Be absolutely certain that the location is safe. Please don't burn down your house trying to learn how to use a fire extinguisher! Keep a garden hose ready in case you need to put the fire out quickly. Once you have the site ready, build a small controlled fire that is within the capability of your extinguisher. Give each family member a chance to practice putting the fire out.

Have them follow OSHA's *PASS* method (in tip box).[113]

PASS Method

➤ *PULL* - Pull the pin. This will also break the tamper seal.
➤ *AIM* - Aim low, pointing the extinguisher nozzle or horn at the base of the fire. Don't point at the flames, but rather at the material that is actually burning.
➤ *SQUEEZE* - Squeeze the handle to release the extinguishing agent.
➤ *SWEEP* – Sweep from side to side, aiming at the base of the fire until extinguished.

When fighting a house fire, try to keep your back facing a clear escape path. If the room becomes filled with smoke, leave immediately. Realize that many fires can't be put out with a single fire extinguisher. If you don't get to the fire early, it is better to evacuate your family and let things burn. The primary purpose of having fire extinguishers is to save lives. Property comes second.

ESCAPE LADDERS

If you have upstairs bedrooms, you need a way to escape from them without relying on the main corridors of your home. Some rooms may have direct access to the roof, which can serve as a fire escape by allowing you to go out onto the roof, and hang and drop down to the ground. If a bedroom doesn't have roof access, or if the roof is too high to hang and drop from, you will need to equip the room with an escape

ladder. These ladders must be easily accessible. Keeping them buried under fifty pounds of clutter in the bottom of a closet isn't going to help anyone. Escape ladders must be long enough to reach the ground, able to simultaneously support multiple people, and easy to use by those sleeping in the bedrooms.

Courtesy of Bold Industries

Check your windows periodically to make sure they can be easily opened. Windows can become stuck or "painted shut" when not frequently used. Escape ladders (or roof access) are of little value if the windows can't be opened. Breaking out the window glass and trying to climb through it is both difficult and incredibly dangerous.

Ideally, the windows should be able to be opened by the people who sleep in the bedrooms. If it is a child's room, then he or she should be able to open the window and deploy the escape ladder. This obviously introduces the risk of a child opening the window and falling out. You as a parent have to weigh that risk against the risk of your child perishing in a fire. Many families conclude that emphasis

Tips

Each family member must be able to escape without assistance.

should be placed on falling safety when the child is very young, and then on independent evacuation when the child gets a little older. Whatever methods you choose for escape, practice them so that everyone is clear and confident about their respective actions.

CARBON MONOXIDE ALARMS

Carbon monoxide (CO) is a deadly, colorless, odorless gas produced by the incomplete burning of fuels such as liquid petroleum, oil, kerosene, coal, and wood.[114] Grills, fireplaces, furnaces, hot water heaters, fuel-burning engines, and automobiles all produce CO. If equipment is used correctly (e.g., grill used outdoors), and working properly (e.g., fireplace properly vented), then CO won't build up in the home. However, leaks can occur and judgment can lapse, especially during times of crisis. Having one or more CO detectors in your home is a wise precaution.

Carbon monoxide poisoning is deadly, killing about 200 people in the United States each year.[114] Symptoms of CO poisoning include headache, fatigue, lightheadedness, shortness of breath, nausea, and dizziness. If you experience any of these symptoms when operating fuel-burning appliances, such as a range, fireplace, or gas dryer, get fresh air immediately! Then call your fire department and report the situation.

Below are a few rules to follow to minimize your chances of CO poisoning.

Never . . .

- Leave your car running in the garage.
- Burn charcoal inside your home, garage, vehicle, or tent.
- Use gas appliances such as a range, oven, or clothes dryer to heat your home.
- Use portable, fuel-burning camping equipment inside your home, tent, or vehicle.

CO detectors are cheap, small, and very low maintenance—only requiring the occasional battery change. It is especially important to have a unit with battery backup because people tend to use equipment that generates carbon monoxide (e.g., space heaters, generators, cooking grills) when power is interrupted. The best places to put CO detectors are in the locations where the risks reside, such as the garage, near the furnace, and in your safe room.

Most units have a small display that indicates the current CO level, as well as the highest level recorded since the last reset. When a threshold level is exceeded, an alarm will sound. Independent reviews of several units can be found online through Consumer Search.[115] Don't worry if you can't find the particular models recommended. Buying name brand units with the features you want will usually serve you well.

RADON TESTING

Radon is a colorless, odorless, radioactive gas released by the natural decay of uranium in rock, soil, and water. Once produced, radon rises from the ground and into the air that your family breathes. The gas decays into radioactive particles that

> Radon is a poisonous radioactive gas that kills 20,000 Americans each year.

become trapped in your lungs. These particles eventually release small bursts of energy that cause lung tissue damage.[116]

Radon is the leading cause of lung cancer among non-smokers. The gas is attributed with causing about 20,000 deaths annually in the United States. That is more deaths than can be attributed to drunk driving, falls in the home, or drowning.[117] It affects about the same number of people as house fires, but with a much higher fatality rate. There are no symptoms from overexposure, and there are no treatments either. Once the damage is done, it's done.

Fortunately, detecting radon is easy and inexpensive. Based on recent testing by Consumer Reports, it is recommended that you use the Accustar Alpha Track Test Kit AT 100.[118] This is also the model currently sold through the National Safety Council (NSC). These units are cheap and simple to use— just a small plastic sensor that you place on a shelf in the lowest level of your home. Leave the device out for at least 90 days, and then return it to the laboratory for analysis.

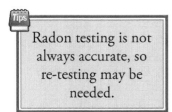

Tips

Radon testing is not always accurate, so re-testing may be needed.

In the event that the home test results indicate levels higher than 2 pCi/L, you should repeat the test. Home tests are not always accurate. If the second test disagrees with the first (i.e., first indicated high, second indicated low), then perform a third test before making a conclusion. If two of the three tests indicate elevated levels (i.e., greater than 2 pCi/L), you should to hire a professional radon test company to confirm the findings and take appropriate action.

Remedying high levels of radon requires installing a radon-removal system consisting of a fan-driven, vented system to suck radon away from your home. Correcting the problem can be rather expensive, but given the potential consequences to everyone in the house, there is no question about the necessity of the repair. More information on radon testing and correction is found on the NSC's website.[119]

Personal aside: My own experience is a good example of the confusion that can come with radon testing. My first radon test result indicated that my home had levels of 5.6 pCi/L, well above the 2 pCi/L maximum. Of course, I became concerned. I placed the second unit at a different point in the same room, and those levels were less than 1 pCi/L. Finally, I repeated the test a third time in yet another location in the room, and it also came back as less than 1 pCi/L—no action required. The question burning in my mind was why did the first unit show such a high level? I ultimately concluded that since I had placed the first unit adjacent to several granite book ends, they must have outgassed some radon into the sensor.

MISCELLANEOUS ITEMS

The most important safety items were discussed first: smoke alarms, fire extinguishers, CO detectors, radon detectors, and escape ladders. Consider these safety devices to be on your must-have list. Depending on your particular situation, there are a few additional safety items that you may want to consider.

Radiation Threat

Radioactive materials can be released into the environment either unintentionally (e.g., nuclear power plant accident), or intentionally (e.g., atomic bomb explosion, act of terrorism). If you feel that your family is in danger of a radioactive threat, then you may wish to equip your home with a radiation detector.

There are two types of radiation poisoning: radioactive contamination and radiation exposure. Radioactive contamination occurs when you come into contact with radioactive materials. Contamination is usually the result of radioactive particulates being inhaled, consumed, or coming into direct contact with your body. Contact with radioactive materials causes tissue and organ damage, and can ultimately lead to death. This is distinctly different from radiation exposure, which is being exposed to the energy that radioactive materials emit—high-frequency rays penetrating the body, such as when you receive an x-ray. Excessive radiation exposure can cause sickness, burns, cancer, and death.

Radioactive contamination is not the same as radiation exposure.

There are pills, such as potassium iodide, that can be taken to help reduce the amount of radioactive contaminant that your body will absorb. However, they will not protect you from radiation exposure. These preventive measures are discussed in greater detail in *Chapter 9: Air*.

Nuclear danger

On average, Americans are exposed to about 300 to 400 milliRems of radiation per year (where a milliRem is 1/1000 of a Rem), most of which is a result of radon, background radiation, and medical imaging.[120] The recommended maximum dose is 5,000 milliRems per year, with a total dose of not more than 1,000 milliRems multiplied by a person's age.[121]

A relatively inexpensive radiation detector that fits on your keychain is offered from NukAlert. It claims to reliably detect radiation levels from 100 milliRems per hour to more than 50 Rems per hour, and can operate for 10 full years without a battery replacement. The detector remains active 24 hours a day, and sounds different alarms depending on the exposure level.[122]

Courtesy of NukAlert

If you detect increased levels of radiation, you should immediately contact your local emergency management services. The best way to protect yourself from radiation exposure is to put distance between you and the source. If evacuation is not possible, then put as much solid material (e.g., dirt, concrete, water) as possible between you and the outside world. In the event of radioactive contamination, you should remove your clothing (putting it into a plastic bag away from other people), wash yourself thoroughly, and contact local authorities.[123]

Additional Fire Safety

For additional fire safety, you may want to consider stocking emergency escape hoods and gel-soaked blankets. Escape hoods can help you get through a smoky building without being overcome by toxic fumes. Gel-soaked blankets are designed to help protect from heat and flame as well as treat burns.

In general, both hoods and gel blankets are good products. Their only drawback is that they both require time to equip. And when it comes to a fire, time is ev-

> **Tips**
> When it comes to escaping a fire, time is everything.

Courtesy of Water-Jel

erything. Do you really want to take the time to locate and put on your escape hood or blanket? Escape hoods in particular are not easy to put on properly. More often than not, you will be better served by getting out of the house as quickly as possible.

With that said, if you do find yourself in a room with the only exit clouded with smoke or blocked by heat, the use of an escape hood and/or gel-soaked blanket could very well save your life. You need to assess the likelihood of this situation and prepare accordingly. If you know that evacuating would be

> **Tips**
> If you are trapped in a room with the exit blocked, consider knocking or kicking out the wallboard to get to an adjacent room.

time-consuming or require you to pass close to where a fire might originate, then one or both of these products might be prudent investments. Escape hoods, for example, are popular choices for people who work in high-rise buildings. More information about respirators and escape hoods is given in *Chapter 9: Air*.

Pet Fire Safety

If you have pets in your home, consider getting pet alert stickers. These decals are placed in conspicuous places on your home, usually near the

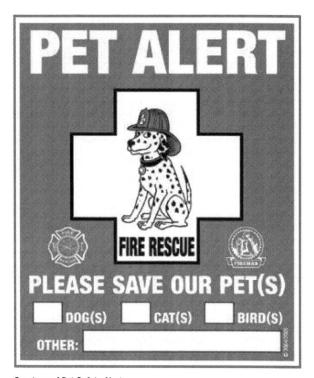

Courtesy of Pet Safety Alert

front door, to inform firefighters of how many, and what type, pets you have in the home. If a fire breaks out while you are away, the stickers will let firefighters know that your home is not empty, and that you wish for them to make every effort to rescue your pets.

ADEQUATELY INSURE YOUR HOME

Many people mistakenly assume that the government will step in and help out those who lose property in a disaster. While it is true that mitigating actions are sometimes taken, such as the offering of low-interest building loans, it is generally up to the individual to rebuild and replace what is lost. This is where insurance comes in.

Property insurance is like every other aspect of disaster preparedness. Start by assessing the most likely risks to your home, and then target your insurance to protect from those risks.

Test your knowledge of homeowner's insurance by considering two scenarios involving the same thunderstorm:

Case 1: High winds tear your roof off. Rains pour through the exposed roof and flood your home.

Case 2: Heavy rains flood your yard. The water rises to the point that it floods the ground floor of your home.

Did you recognize that these are considered two very different events by an insurance company? Unless you have specific flood insurance, you are likely not covered against Case 2.

Review your current homeowner's (or renter's) insurance policy to answer a few basic questions.

Basic Home Insurance Questions

1. Are you adequately insured? Are any supplemental structures (e.g., carport, fence, swimming pool) covered?
2. Do you have replacement cost or actual cash value (ACV) insurance?
3. What are your deductibles? Are they reasonable?
4. Are you protected against earthquake or flood? Should you be?
5. Does your insurance provide for temporary housing? What about debris removal?
6. Do you have (or should you have) any special riders covering jewelry, guns, or collectibles?

Based on your answers to these questions, contact your insurance agent to make adjustments. Be sure to ask appropriate questions of your agent, and select the coverage that adequately protects your investment. Remember, as a general rule, it is wiser to have a higher deductible and better coverage than a lower deductible and limited coverage.

Insist on replacement cost insurance on both your home and contents. If you don't, you could be out many thousands of dollars in the event of a disaster. With actual

> **Tips**
> Replacement cost insurance will fully replace your belongings. Actual cash value (ACV) insurance will pay you only a prorated amount.

cash value (ACV) insurance, the insurer could give you only a fraction of the replacement cost due to their assessment of depreciation. Also, remember to adjust your insurance when property values increase or improvements are made.

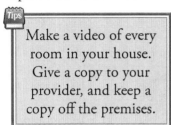

Make a video of every room in your house. Give a copy to your provider, and keep a copy off the premises.

If you do suffer a loss, your insurance company will require you to provide a detailed description of those items damaged. There are many horror stories of insurance companies failing to pay for items by claiming that the owner never had them and is therefore committing fraud. For your protection, take a video recording of your home and its contents. Walk through every room slowly, verbally discussing all of its contents—noting specific brands, where it was purchased, how long you've had it, etc. Don't forget to include the garage, yard, basement, and attic.

Make at least two copies of the recording. Leave one with your insurance agent, and another one with a friend, family member, or somewhere else outside of the home. Each year when you renew your policy, distribute an updated video. Keeping a video record or your belongings not only protects you, but also makes it much easier for a claim to be processed.

DOCUMENT AND RECORD

Should your property ever become damaged due to an event covered by insurance, you should immediately document the damage. Once again, the best way to do this is with a video camera. Don't discard anything that was damaged, no matter how unusable, since the remnants could serve to better substantiate your claim.

Keep a record of all conversations that you have with your insurance company, appraisers, contractors, and relief organizations. Request that all agreements, repair estimates, and property appraisals be provided in writing. If you purchase emergency relief supplies, such as clothing or food, or if you have to pay for temporary lodging, be certain to keep all receipts. Provide copies of these receipts to your insurance agent as quickly as possible.

EVACUATION

There are two types of evacuations. The first is forced by an immediate threat, such as a house fire, and the second by an imminent, but not yet present threat, such as an approaching hurricane.

In the case of an immediate threat, the rules are simple. Get your family away from the threat as quickly as possible. Don't stop to grab anything that is not absolutely necessary. It is a good idea to identify exits from each room in your home—the primary escape route likely being the main door, and the secondary route through a window. You should practice evacuation with your family, with everyone managing to get out the house without assistance (very young children excluded). Also, agree on a family gathering point outside the home.

You might think that preparation like this will frighten your children. On the contrary, children like to have a clear understanding of the world around them. Many times our sheltering of children to protect them can in fact cause confusion and lead to dangerous misunderstandings. Rather than shoulder all the responsibilities yourself, explain the dangers to everyone, as well as what actions each person is expected to take. Not

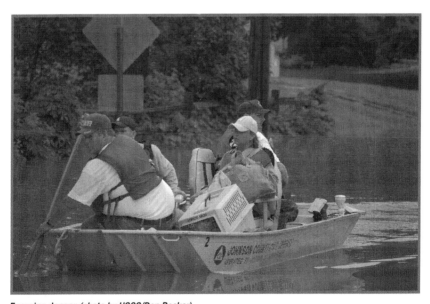

Escaping danger *(photo by USGS/Don Becker)*

only does this empower each individual, but it also makes it more likely that your family will successfully escape, even when you are unable to lead them.

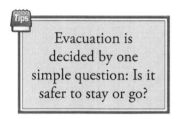

When a threat is approaching, but hasn't yet arrived, perhaps giving you hours or even days notice, you will need to make a calculated decision regarding evacuation. The decision hinges on whether you weigh the danger of staying to be greater than that of leaving. The window of time allowing safe evacuation may be short, so understand that you may be stuck with the consequences of your decision.

> Evacuation is decided by one simple question: Is it safer to stay or go?

As you consider evacuation, take some basic steps to prepare for your possible departure.

- Fully fuel your vehicle and any spare gas cans. Have enough fuel to travel at least 500 miles.
- Identify multiple escape routes from the area being affected. Also, pick at least one alternate retreat location in case traffic flow prevents you from traveling to your preferred one.
- Listen to TV or radio broadcasts to determine when is the best time to evacuate and what the recommended escape routes are.
- Pack your vehicle with supplies, including those you might need for roadside emergencies (see the auto disaster kits in *Chapter 14: Transportation.*)

If you decide to evacuate, take additional steps to prepare your home.

- Unplug all electronics except for refrigerators and freezers.
- Turn off unused utilities.
- Lock all doors and windows.
- Brace windows, doors, and garage doors as best you can (if appropriate to the threat).
- Write down the GPS coordinates of your home's location. Some disasters are so destructive that even locating your home can be nearly impossible without a set of absolute coordinates.
- Pack your most valuable items in the car. These could be gold coins or old photo albums—you be the judge.

- Let family and friends know when you are leaving and where you will be heading. If you can't convey this information, then consider leaving a note attached to the front door that indicates who you are, where you have gone, as well as contact information of those who might know your whereabouts. A blank "leave behind note" is given in the *Appendix* for this purpose. Realize that leaving a note like this may make your home susceptible to looting, but that is a price worth paying to give rescuers vital information should you go missing.
- Put on shoes and clothes that will suit you well should your car break down. Be prepared to spend the night in your car.
- Be watchful for washed-out roads, downed power lines, or other roadside hazards. Don't drive into flooded areas! It is very easy to underestimate the depth of water on roadways. If you absolutely must cross a flooded area of still water (not flowing), one person can carefully walk ahead of the vehicle to check for water depth. But this should be done only as a last resort.

There are times when you may be forced to evacuate but feel uncomfortable taking valuable items with you (e.g., jewelry, coins, guns). Leaving them behind in an empty house is also undesirable. One option is to bury them in the yard or under the house in small sections of PVC pipe with threaded or pressure-fitted plastic end caps. They don't have to be buried particularly deep, just far enough beneath the soil that they aren't noticeable. This is a reasonable option for locations that might experience looting. Be sure to check the tubes for water tightness before burying them.

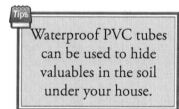

Tips

Waterproof PVC tubes can be used to hide valuables in the soil under your house.

WHEN YOU HAVE NO PLACE TO GO

Some disasters will leave you without a shelter. Hurricane Katrina, for example, displaced tens of thousands of people from New Orleans. Many of those sought temporary shelter in the Superdome. There were countless subsequent stories telling of crimes of opportunity including robbery, rape, battery, and murder. If even a small portion of them are

Hurricane Katrina, 2005 *(photo by FEMA/Andrea Booher)*

true, the anarchy described is certainly not something you would wish upon your family.

There are many lessons to be learned from Katrina, both by individuals and by our government. Certainly one lesson is that government-provided emergency shelters are less than ideal. They are not the comforting environments that you want to put your family in during times of great stress.

It is almost always better to seek out family and friends first. If you are already part of a preparedness network, someone will likely have the means (and inclination) to put you and your family up for a short time. If you have nowhere else to go, look for a private shelter—perhaps a neighborhood church or civic organization (e.g., Masons, Elks). Your chances of being treated humanely and meeting likeminded individuals are arguably better than they would be at a government-run shelter.

If you are displaced, consider taking some of the following actions.

- Set up a post office box for mail delivery.
- Write to request duplicates of important documents and identification cards that may have been lost, such as birth certificates, social security cards, and driver's licenses.

- Use the public library or other free services to access email and the Internet. This can be a good way to keep family and friends informed of your situation.

Longer term housing needs can be addressed by checking with local homeless assistance programs. The Department of Housing and Urban Development maintains a website with information on homeless programs for various communities across the United States. The website also contains information about receiving counseling and applying for transitional or Section 8 housing assistance.

Homeless Assistance Programs
www.hud.gov/homeless/index.cfm

TENTS, TARPS, AND TEEPEES

Some of you may wonder why this book doesn't contain details on constructing ad-hoc shelters, such as lean-to's, teepees, and dome shelters. Remember, this guide is targeted toward disaster preparedness, not toward wilderness survival. As such, the decision was made not to fill the pages with detailed plans for building shelters from tarps and twine.

The truth is that, without a great deal of practice, you probably wouldn't be able to build a very good shelter anyway. Also, consider what the chances are of being stranded outdoors without any form of shelter. Keep in mind that your car is a great shelter, much better than anything you can build with makeshift supplies. In the event that you are stranded outdoors without a shelter or a vehicle, it seems inconceivable that you will have the necessary supplies, tools, and blueprints with you to build a protective shelter. From a preparedness standpoint, the best thing you can do is to not put yourself in that very precarious situation.

DP PLAN EXAMPLE

Table 5-2 Sample DP Plan Entry

Need: Shelter			
Danger	**Goals**	**Needs**	**Implementation**
Damage to structure or contents	Mitigate extent of damage to house	Threat assessment	Complete threat assessments and make improvements for likeliest threats.
		Hazards checklist	Complete home hazards checklists.
		Ability to turn off utilities	Practice turning off utilities; keep cutoff tools nearby.
	Safeguard against losses to structure or contents	A safety net to recover losses	Insure home with replacement cost insurance and extra riders for firearms, etc.
Fire	Detect fires	Smoke alarms	Install dual sensor smoke alarms in garage and attic. Check all smoke detectors in March and November.
	Extinguish a fire	Fire extinguishers	Put a 2-A:10-BC extinguisher in upstairs bedroom, and another in downstairs hallway.
	Escape from a fire	Way to escape from every room	Identify escape routes from every room. Equip upstairs rooms with escape ladders.
Carbon monoxide	Detect high levels of CO	CO detectors	Install CO detectors in living room and garage.
Radon	Detect high levels of radon	Radon test kit	Test lowest level of house for radon using long-term test kit.

Quick Summary - Shelter

> Make seeking adequate shelter your family's first priority.

> Your home is likely to be the most effective shelter during a crisis.

> Assess the level of protection that your shelter offers to specific threats, and then make improvements to increase that protection.

> Complete a hazards checklist, removing potential threats to your home.

> Fires kills more Americans than all natural disasters combined.

> House fires give an average of only three minutes warning.

> Equip your home with as many safeguards as possible, including smoke detectors, carbon monoxide sensors, and fire extinguishers.

> Know how to cut off your utilities, and keep the necessary tools close by.

> Set up a safe room in your house that is easy to heat, protect, and seal from chemical and biological threats.

> Adequately insure your home and car. Elect to have replacement value insurance for your home and contents.

> Follow OSHA's *PASS* method to extinguish a fire.

> When evacuating, seek family and friends first, but also consider church, civic, and government services.

> If evacuating, stock your vehicle with emergency supplies (see *Chapter 14: Transportation*), and be prepared to spend the night in your car.

Recommended Items - Shelter

❑ Basic repair and cleanup supplies
  a. A good set of hand tools
  b. Basic home repair materials (e.g., nails, plastic sheeting, duct tape, tarps, PVC fittings, glue, wire, twine)
  c. A few home fix-it books
  d. Shovel, axe, a wheelbarrow, a heavy broom, and a chain saw—if you can afford one

❑ Home safety equipment
  a. Smoke alarms
  b. Carbon monoxide alarms
  c. Radon test kit
  d. ABC fire extinguishers
  e. Pet fire safety decals
  f. (Optional) Smoke hoods, Water-Jel blankets

CHAPTER 6
LIGHT

Chapter 6 Notes

CHAPTER 6

LIGHT

Challenge

Electrical power has been lost due to an ice storm, and it is expected to remain off for the next few days. How will your family function at night?

Although not the first thing to come to mind when considering disaster preparedness, light can play a critical role in not only surviving, but also thriving in dangerous situations.

Light serves four basic DP functions:

1. Allows operation in darkness
2. Deters animals and intruders
3. Provides a sense of comfort
4. Interacts with our bodies to maintain good health; helping to create vitamin D, preventing infection, and combating depression

Without light, you are limited to operating only during daylight hours as it is simply too dangerous to work in the dark. How many times have you tried to get up in the night to perform a simple task, only to jam your toe against an unexpected chair or walk nose-first into a door jamb? Imagine

> **Tips**
>
> For countless years, light has helped people cope with their fears of the dark.

how dangerous it would be if you were forced to hike outside into the dead of night to relieve yourself.

Light has another very real benefit. Having a steady reliable light source allows people to better use their senses, and that helps alleviate the fear that darkness brings. With light, comes a feeling of being in control. Much of survival is keeping the right frame of mind— not melting down. Having a sense of control can help prevent you from making irrational, and perhaps life-threatening, mistakes.

Consider for a moment that about one quarter of the world's population (over 1.6 billion people) lives without electricity and is limited to performing most activities during daylight hours.[124] These people know the challenges of trying to function in darkness, and if put in our shoes, could compensate well during this type of crisis. However, the same cannot necessarily be said for the rest of us.

COMPARING LIGHT SOURCES

> **Light Source Metrics**
>
> ➤ Intensity
> ➤ Duration
> ➤ Safety
> ➤ Portability
> ➤ Heat output
> ➤ Energy cost

Light comes from a variety of sources, including natural, electrical, fuel-burning, and chemical. Each source has inherent advantages and disadvantages when comparing them by six metrics: intensity, duration, safety, portability, heat output, and energy cost.

The six metrics give you a way to qualitatively compare the suitability of different light sources. There is no one best light source. Rather, you must select a source that best meets the needs specific to your situation. For example, a very bright flashlight that only burns for an hour without a change of batteries would be a logical choice for hiking to safety from a stranded car. Likewise, a fragile gas lantern that emits both heat and light for an entire night would be a better choice for extended home use.

NATURAL LIGHT

Natural light is light generated by the world around us. This includes sunlight, starlight, and moonlight (i.e., sunlight reflecting off the moon).

Make the most of natural light since it is free in terms of energy cost. Do most of your work during the daylight hours. If you are experiencing a prolonged disaster, use the daytime to prepare for the arrival of nightfall—shoring up shelters, gathering supplies, and seeking out any needed assistance. Whenever possible, evacuation should also be done during the day.

Accomplish as much as possible during daylight hours.

ELECTRICAL LIGHT

Electrical light is light created by electrical current passing through filaments or solid-state devices. For increased brightness, efficiency, and life, the filaments are sometimes surrounded by special gases (e.g., krypton).

If you have electrical power available, then light is probably not much of a concern. Modern incandescent light bulbs burn for a couple thousand hours each, so even without a single spare bulb in the house it is unlikely that you will be faced with a situation where you are without enough light to function.

Unfortunately, electrical power is often the first utility to fail when a disaster strikes. Without an electrical power source, you are left to use portable light sources that run off of batteries (e.g., lanterns, flashlights) or consume fuel (e.g., candles, lamps, lanterns).

FLASHLIGHTS

Over the past several years, flashlight technology has advanced significantly with the arrival of high-efficiency white light-emitting diode (LED) bulbs. LED flashlights operate for much longer on a set of batteries than conventional incandescent units, and the LED bulbs never need replacing. The downside is that quality high-output LED flashlights are rather expensive.

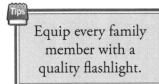

Equip every family member with a quality flashlight.

There are many good flashlight manufacturers, including Surefire, Pelican, Streamlight, and Maglite. Flashlight intensity can vary anywhere from 5 to over 500 lumens, with most products outputting between 50-115 lumens.[125] You should consider a quality flashlight as one of the fundamental pieces of your preparedness gear. Everyone in your family should have his or her own dedicated flashlight. This not only increases their utility, but it also helps alleviate fear.

Courtesy of Surefire

Select flashlights that are highly visible, such as those decorated with reflective tape and bright colors. This makes them much easier to find when you accidentally misplace them.

You will need an adequate supply of batteries for flashlights and electric lanterns. Before stocking up, however, see *Chapter 7: Electrical Power* for a discussion of battery types.

SHAKE LIGHTS

Recently, so-called "shake lights" were introduced to the flashlight-loving public. These flashlights work on the Faraday principal of generating electrical energy by moving a magnet through an inductive coil. In theory, having a battery-less flashlight sounds fantastic. Simply give the unit a shake, and bright light pours out the end.

Unfortunately, there are several problems with shake lights. First and foremost, many of the flashlights are not very durable—being closer to

Courtesy of Applied Innovative Technologies

toys than tools. The second drawback is that the light they generate is neither bright nor long-lasting. The output from shake lights range from 7 to 13 lumens. Compare this to the 140 lumens that a more compact Surefire 9AN rechargeable LED flashlight emits.

Shake lights require that you physically shake them to store up electrical energy. For example, you might have to shake the flashlight for a minute to get 5 to 10 minutes of light. Also, since they contain a fairly powerful magnet, you must keep them away from sensitive electronics (e.g., laptop computer, cell phone, iPod). They are not good choices for children or the elderly because of the effort required to recharge them. If you plan to purchase a shake light, read reviews to find the better quality choices.[126] Applied Innovative Technologies' Nightstar products are recognized as some of the highest-quality shake lights on the market.

ELECTRIC LANTERNS

Electric lanterns are used to illuminate wider areas. Nearly all electric lanterns use krypton, fluorescent, or LED bulbs. Each bulb type presents a tradeoff between light output, energy use, and bulb life (see Table 6-1).[127]

Electric lanterns are powered from batteries (typically D-cells), and some are also equipped with hand cranks—you turn the handle every few minutes to keep it going.

Lanterns are particularly useful in lighting your shelter because they use reflectors to spread the light out rather than focus it as a beam. Electric lanterns don't put out much heat, so they are not good choices to warm up an area. They are however safe (i.e., not a fire hazard), and most models are fairly durable.

Courtesy of Coleman

Table 6-1 Lantern Bulb Comparison

Bulb Type	Light Output	Energy Use	Bulb Life (hours)
Krypton	Brightest	Highest	1000's
Fluorescent	Bright	Lower	10,000's
LED	Dimmest	Lowest	100,000's

FUEL-BURNING LIGHT

Since the discovery of fire, people have been burning fuel of one kind or another to produce light and heat. Fuel-based lighting includes bonfires, torches, candles, and oil lamps/lanterns. The big advantage of fuel-burning light is that heat is also produced, thus serving two important needs. Of course, heat may not always be desirable, such as when you are confined to a small shelter in the middle of summer.

Consider carefully the risk of fire when making your light source selection.

There are also several disadvantages to using fuel-burning light sources. They require you to stockpile and handle combustible fuel. This can be dangerous, messy, and smelly. Also, when fuel is burned, fumes and/or smoke may be emitted. However, the most significant drawback to any fuel-burning source is the very real risk of fire that it introduces. Consider this risk carefully when making your light source selection. Introducing additional danger into what is already a hazardous situation means extra care must be taken.

FIRE

If you have the supplies, a fire can be a great way to generate both light and heat. To safely burn a fire indoors, you must use a fireplace or wood-burning stove with an adequate ventilation system. The burning of wood or any other combustible material releases carbon monoxide, which is deadly if allowed to build up in a room. See *Chapter 8: Heating/Cooling* for additional details on indoor heating.

Fires are particularly useful when stuck outdoors and trying to stay warm or cook food. Knowing how to start a fire is one of life's necessities, like learning to swim. For that reason, you should do a bit of research on fire starting. There are countless books, articles, and websites that offer techniques for starting fires. But be warned, actually starting a fire is not the same as reading about how to start a fire! You need to learn about such things as selecting dry tinder, ensuring air flow, and taking advantage of the chimney effect. Someone telling you how to do it won't be enough (which is why I haven't done so here). This is a skill that can only be learned by doing. Once you are ready to test your fire-building skills, hold a class for your family, teaching everyone the basics. It is convenient to combine this class with the "how to use a fire extinguisher" class recommended in *Chapter 5: Shelter.*

CANDLES

Candles are the staple of many emergency supply kits. They are inexpensive and burn for many hours. They don't put out much light, but the placement of a few candles in a small room will allow you to function. Some candles even put out enough heat to do very minor cooking (e.g., Nuwick).

There are also lanterns that use candles as their light source, such as Uco's Candlelier and Eastern Mountain Sports' candle lantern. Candles are simple to use, reliable, and easily stored. However, they introduce a fire hazard, so once again caution is needed.

UCO's Candlelier

FUEL-BURNING LAMPS / LANTERNS

Fuel-burning lamps and lanterns are good alternatives to electric lanterns. Their merits are compared in Table 6-2. The distinction between *lamps* and *lanterns* is subtle but important.

Lamps are kerosene-filled vials topped with a cotton or felt wick inside a glass globe. To adjust the lamp's brightness, you adjust the wick up or down, leaving more or less exposed. Once lit, lamps must remain stationary because the oil can spill, and the wick is very fragile while burning.

Lanterns are designed to be portable hand-held lights, and are usually equipped with a handle. Fuel-burning lanterns emit both light and heat by expressing flaming

Courtesy of BriteLyt

Table 6-2 Comparing Electric to Fuel-burning Lanterns

	Electric	Fuel-burning
Brightness	Poor-Fair	Good-Excellent
Fire hazard	No	Yes
Emit odors	No	Yes
Durable	Good	Poor-Fair

gas onto a cloth mantle saturated with a rare earth oxide. As the oxide heats, it emits visible light. Lighting a lantern requires manual pumping to build up the gas pressure, and takes practice to get right. Lanterns that use pressurized propane tanks eliminate the need for pumping.

Nearly all lamps burn kerosene, but lanterns may burn different fuels, including lamp oil, white gas, or propane. Only kerosene or lamp oil should be burned indoors in a lantern. Other fuels emit dangerous levels of carbon monoxide.

Only burn kerosene or lamp oil indoors.

Fuel-burning lamps and lanterns are very good sources of light and modest secondary sources of heat. For convenience, it is a good idea to use a lamp or lantern that burns the same type of fuel as your heating and cooking equipment. Both lamps and lanterns require frequent maintenance, so be sure to keep an ample supply of mantles, chimneys, and wicks.

There are many good choices for lamps and lanterns, including Aladdin, BriteLyt, Coleman, and others. Each has its particular strengths and weaknesses. For example, Aladdin lamps emit a good deal of light, but are expensive and very easy to break. BriteLyt lanterns run on multiple types of fuel and are more durable, but are expensive and can be tricky to operate.

Lamps and lanterns share the same disadvantages as other fuel-burning methods. They introduce a risk of fire, require you to store and handle dangerous fuel, and emit an odor when burning that can be offensive to some people. Because of the fire hazard, you may prefer to use electric versus fuel-burning lanterns when children are present.

CHEMICAL LIGHT

Light sticks are a relatively new invention, and are useful for a variety of military as well as commercial purposes. They operate by a chemical process that causes chemiluminescence. The sticks generally contain hydrogen peroxide and color dye inside a plastic sleeve, as well as a glass vial filled with phenyl oxalate ester. When you break the glass vial, a chemical reaction occurs, causing light to be emitted.[128]

This chemiluminescent process can be accelerated by heating up the light stick. For example, if you put the light stick in boiling water, it will glow very bright. Likewise it can be slowed down by cooling the stick. If you want a light stick to last until the next day, store it in the freezer.

Plastic sleeve

Glass vial with
phenyl oxalate ester

Hydrogen peroxide
and dye

Mixing occurs

Chemiluminescence

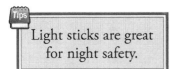

Light sticks are great for night safety.

Since light sticks are waterproof and don't require electricity, you can use them under water as well as in environments where explosives are present. For general DP purposes, light sticks are primarily used for night safety. Each person can wear a light stick, making it easier to keep track of everyone's location without consuming flashlight batteries. Light sticks are not a replacement for flashlights or lanterns. They output only a few lumens and provide merely a soft glow. However, if no other means exists, they can be used as a low-intensity flashlight by cutting open one end of the foil package and allowing light to shine out through the open end.

LIGHT INTENSITY

Light intensity is an important metric when comparing light sources. Obviously, you want as bright a light as possible; unfortunately there is no single measurement unit to indicate this brightness. Rather, light intensity is reported using several different units, making pre-purchase comparisons difficult. However, with a bit of patience and a dose of math, different light sources can be fairly compared.

Consider this section to be a mathematic aside that is not essential for you to understand when selecting the most appropriate light source. If you feel your eyes glazing over at the sight of equations, simply skip over them and find yourself the brightest flashlight or lantern you can. For those curious about the details of light intensity, read on.

Light is measured in two different ways. One method describes the amount of light actually emitted at the source—defined as *radiance*. The other method defines the amount of light that illuminates an area some distance away—defined as *illuminance*.

Radiance is the amount of light emitted from a source and is usually measured in candelas (English units) or lumens (metric units). One candela is roughly the amount of light emitted by a single birthday candle. If the light source emits light in every direction, then you simply multiply the number of candelas by 12.6 to get the number of lumens. More generally, you must know the radiation angle (i.e., the vertex angle of the cone of the flashlight) to convert between candelas and lumens. Below

Table 6-3 Converting Watts to Lumens

Bulb type	Approx. Conversion (Watts to Lumens)
Tungsten incandescent	17
Halogen/krypton	20
Compact fluorescent	70

is the equation to convert between lumens and candelas. If you are not a mathematician or engineer, you may need to break out your scientific calculator to apply it.

$$\# \; lumens = \# \; candelas \cdot \left[2\pi \cdot \left(1 - \cos\left(\frac{angle}{2} \right) \right) \right]$$

For example, assume you have a flashlight specified as emitting 100 candelas and having a 10° angle of radiance. Converting from candelas to lumens would be done as shown.

$$\# \; lumens = 100 \cdot \left[2\pi \cdot \left[1 - \cos\left(\left(\frac{10°}{2} \right) \right) \right] \right] = 2.39$$

Fortunately, lumens have become the norm by retailers of flashlights and lanterns, so it is rare that you will need to convert from candelas.

Electric lanterns that use krypton or fluorescent bulbs are usually specified in watts rather than lumens. There is no direct conversion between watts and lumens because they measure different quantities. Some approximate conversions are given in Table 6-3, and can be used to provide an estimate of equivalent light intensities.[129,130,131]

For example, a 100-watt incandescent light bulb is roughly equivalent to 1,700 lumens. Likewise, a 13-watt compact fluorescent bulb is equivalent to about 900 lumens.

Illuminance is a measure of how much light falls on a given surface some distance away. It is usually measured in foot-candles (English units) or lux (metric units). The foot-candle is the amount of light a birthday candle shines on a surrounding sphere of one-foot radius. To convert between the two, multiply the number of foot-candles by 10.8 to get the number of lux. No special equations are needed for this one. Thank goodness.

Think of illuminance as how bright an area is. For example, a bright office is lit to about 400 lux, moonlight represents about 1 lux, and midday sunlight might reach as high as 100,000 lux.[132]

Most of you will probably never need to be numerically rigorous in comparing light sources. The proof is in the pudding—turn the flashlight on in a dark room and see how well it works. For the few who are curious about this sort of thing, you can draw upon these simple terms and conversions.

DP PLAN EXAMPLE

Table 6-4 Sample DP Plan Entry

Need: Light			
Danger	Goals	Needs	Implementation
Blackout	Function safely at night for a minimum of two weeks	Portable lighting	Equip each family member with a Surefire G2L flashlight. Stock three changes of spare batteries.
			Keep supply of light sticks on hand for outdoor night safety.
		Area lighting	Light main living area and bedrooms with six Garrity hand-crank rechargeable LED lanterns.

Quick Summary - Light

➤ Light provides both comfort and a measure of safety to your family. It also allows you to function safely and effectively in the dark.

➤ Lighting sources include natural, electrical, fuel-burning, and chemical.

➤ Take advantage of sunlight by accomplishing as much as possible during the day.

➤ When comparing different light sources, consider six metrics: intensity, duration, safety, portability, heat output, and energy cost.

➤ Recent advances in LED technology enable electrical light sources to be very energy efficient.

➤ Fuel-burning light sources are very bright and radiate heat. However, they also introduce a fire hazard.

➤ Fires should never be built indoors without proper ventilation due to the risk of CO poisoning.

➤ Assign a flashlight to every person in your family. Use lanterns (electric or fuel-burning) for wider-area illumination.

➤ Most shake flashlights have questionable durability, limited light output, and short storage duration.

➤ Light sticks can increase night safety, but are not a replacement for flashlights or lanterns.

Recommended Items - Light

❑ Portable illumination
    a. A quality flashlight for each family member
    b. Spare batteries

❑ Area illumination
    a. Electric lanterns and spare batteries, *or*
    b. Fuel-burning lanterns and fuel in approved containers

❑ Night safety
    a. Light sticks

CHAPTER 7
ELECTRICAL POWER

ELECTRICAL POWER

Challenge

Your city has suffered a direct hit from a powerful hurricane. Thousands of power poles are taken down by high winds, leaving your community without electricity. Authorities indicate that it will be anywhere from two to four weeks before power is fully restored. How will you perform basic functions like keeping warm at night, washing clothes, cooking food, and lighting your home?

O ur modern society depends on electrical power for its needs and conveniences; from providing heat, to cooking, to powering our televisions and telephones, we need electricity. Unfortunately, electrical power is often the first service to fail in a crisis. Loss of power can be the result of many different events, including downed trees, power grid failures, vehicle collisions, ice storms, and high winds to name just a few.

Being without electricity for a few hours is usually little more than annoying, perhaps missing your favorite football game, or having to eat dinner by candlelight. However, as those who have experienced extended blackouts can testify, being without electrical power for more than a few days can introduce real hardships.

TERMINOLOGY

The flow of electricity is analogous to the flow of water.

Let's begin with an explanation of a few electrical terms. A useful analogy compares electricity to water. Just as water flows through pipes, electricity flows through wires. Water pressure forces water to move, and electrical pressure, known as *voltage,* forces electrons to move. The higher the pressure, the more water (or electrons) flow in a given amount of time. This flow of electricity—quantified by counting the number of electrons that pass in a given amount of time—is called *current,* and is measured in amps. If you multiply the voltage and current together, the result is *power,* which is measured in watts. More generally, the resultant is in volt-amps, but for our purposes, we can neglect this detail. Power can be thought of as the amount of usable energy at any given time that is being delivered to a device.

There are two types of current: *direct current* (DC), and *alternating current* (AC). With DC, current flows in one direction—from point A to B, perhaps from the battery to your cell phone. Alternating current is a bit more complicated. With AC, current flows from point A to B, and then reverses direction, flowing from B back to A. For your house power, this reversing action occurs 60 times in a single second, with the number of cycles being measured in the unit of hertz (Hz). If you live outside the United States, the AC frequency may be different (perhaps operating at 50 Hz), but the principles of alternating current flow remain the same.

HOUSE POWER

Your electric power company generates AC electricity and distributes it to your home using overhead or buried wires. For efficiency reasons, this electricity is transmitted at very high voltages (perhaps hundreds of thousands of volts). When the electricity gets close to your neighborhood, it is stepped down to a more usable voltage using transformers. The electricity is then routed into your home over three wires: two 120-volt "hot" lines, and one "neutral" line. The three wires can be configured as 120 volts and 240 volts (see figure on next page).

House wiring

Most of the electronic items in your home are powered by 120 volts AC. Your dishwasher, house lights, televisions, and stereos all require standard 120-volt AC power. A few high-power appliances, such as clothes dryers, air conditioners, and stoves, may require 240 volts. Portable devices that plug into an electrical socket for recharging (e.g., laptop, handheld gaming device, cell phone) convert the 120-volt AC voltage into a DC voltage either internally or through a small converter module in the cable or plug.

To develop a DP plan for electricity, start by determining your electrical needs—both AC and DC, and then select and size a method to provide this level of electricity.

AC POWER SOURCES

Providing your own AC power is generally done in one of two ways: using fuel-burning generators or battery-powered inverters. Other more

Generating AC power is done using generators or inverters.

exotic options, such as steam, hydroelectric, and wind-powered generators, are generally not practical for individuals due to high costs and low-power output.

GENERATORS

Generators are fuel-burning engines that generate AC electricity. Most run on standard gasoline, diesel, propane, or natural gas. They are rated according to the maximum power they can produce—typically measured in 1000's of watts (a.k.a., kilowatts). Generators must be placed outdoors because, like all gas-powered engines, they vent poisonous exhausts. They also require regular maintenance, including changing the oil, replacing spark plugs, and cleaning filters.

Generators are classified as either *standby* or *portable*. Standby generators are permanent units mounted outside your home or office to provide backup power. They are usually configured to automatically turn on when power drops out. Most standby generators are fueled by propane or natural gas. They are very expensive, but offer an excellent solution to power outages. If money is no obstacle, then having your home configured with a large standby generator is the optimal solution to meeting your electrical needs.

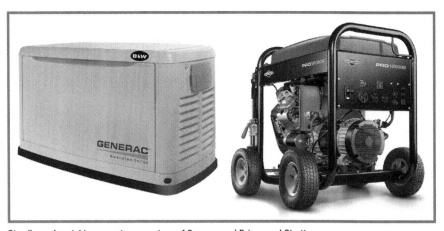

Standby and portable generators, courtesy of Generac and Briggs and Stratton

Portable generators are the type seen frequently at home repair stores. As their name implies, these units are wheeled outdoors and put into service only when the need arises. Portable generators typically run on either gasoline or diesel fuel.

The biggest shortcoming of portable generators is that they burn a lot of fuel. Using them as a direct replacement for your utility power is not practical. The best way to illustrate this is through an example.

Example: A 10-kilowatt gas-powered generator burns roughly 2 gallons of gas per hour. To run it for a full 24-hour day would require 48 gallons of gas. To run it constantly for a week would require over 300 gallons of fuel!

It is not practical to store this amount of fuel since it would present a tremendous fire hazard, and almost certainly void your homeowner's insurance policy. For this reason, portable generators are best used to provide short-term electrical power needs, sometimes spread across a long period of time. (See *Draw up a Schedule* for more details on effectively using a generator.)

A generator burns a lot of fuel. Limit your use to only a few hours each day.

If you are planning to use a generator for emergency power needs, you will need to make five important preparations (see tip box).

Preparing for Generator Use

1. Select the right size and type of generator.
2. Have the necessary hardware installed in your home.
3. Draft a schedule of how you will use it in an emergency.
4. Stockpile the necessary fuel.
5. Learn how to use the generator safely.

SELECT A GENERATOR

Begin by selecting the right type and size of generator. First, decide whether you need a standby or portable generator. Standby units are permanent systems professionally set up outside the home or business. Portable generators are the type you roll out of the garage when needed.

Next, select the type of fuel you wish to use. Most portable generators burn either gas or diesel. Generators that you find at your local hardware store will usually be gas-powered, portable units. Diesel generators are more expensive (perhaps double in price) but also more durable and require less fuel. Diesel fuel is also less combustible than gasoline.

Whatever type of generator you select, it should be large enough to meet your electrical needs. Resist the temptation to drastically oversize the unit. Generators are typically most efficient when the load is about 70% of the rated generator capacity.[133] To properly size a generator, make a list of those items that will require electrical power. Pay special attention to the voltage that your heating/air unit requires. If it runs on 240 volts, and you plan to power it during an emergency, you will need to select a generator that outputs both 120 and 240 volts.

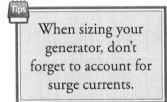

When sizing your generator, don't forget to account for surge currents.

Generators are sized with both "constant power" and "surge power" ratings. Make certain that the generator you select provides enough constant *and* surge power for your particular loads. Anything with a motor requires additional surge power during startup. Total constant power is determined by adding up all the constant power loads that will be running concurrently. To calculate total surge power, determine the extra surge power needed for your single largest appliance, and then add that difference to your total constant power value. You don't need to add up all the surge values because operationally you will ensure that you only start up one appliance at a time.

To make an accurate list of power usage, check appliance labels and product paperwork for power requirements. The amount of electricity listed on an appliance is the maximum it uses, such as when a refrigerator's compressor is running. The normal standby level may be much less. Some devices also consume a small amount of power even when turned off. To get the most out of your power source, it is best to unplug anything that isn't being used.

Table 7-1 lists example power requirements for common electrical appliances. Your loads may be different, but this table gives you a point of reference. You can also directly measure an appliance's power consumption using inexpensive electricity usage meters, such as the *Kill A Watt*.

Table 7-1 Wattage Reference Chart[133,134]

Tool or Appliance	Rated Watts (Running)	Surge Watts (Starting)	Required Voltage
Essentials			
Light bulbs	40-100	-	120
Deep freezer	500-600	1,200	120
Sump pump	800	2,000	120 or 240
Refrigerator	500-800	2,000	120
Water well pump	1,000-2,500	5,600-7,500	120 or 240
Electric water heater	4,000	-	120 or 240
Heating			
Heat pump	4,000-15,000	2 × Rated	120 or 240
Electric furnace	8,000-26,000	2 × Rated	120 or 240
Furnace fan (gas heater)	875	2,300	120 or 240
Space heater	600-1,800	-	120
Electric blanket	200-400	-	120
Cooling			
Central A/C (2.5 ton)	1,500-6,000	4 × Rated	120 or 240
Window A/C	1,200	3,000-4,800	120
Window fan	300-800	600-1200	120
Kitchen			
Microwave oven	800-1,000	-	120
Coffee maker	1,500	-	120
Electric range (one element on)	1,500	-	120 or 240
Toaster	800-1,000	-	120
Dishwasher	1,500	3,000	120
Oven	3,400	-	120 or 240

Tool or Appliance	Rated Watts (Running)	Surge Watts (Starting)	Required Voltage
Family Room			
Color TV	300	-	120
DVD/CD player	100	-	120
Stereo receiver	450	-	120
Computer system	300-800	-	120
Laptop	100	-	120
Other			
Security system	180-500	-	120
AM/FM clock radio	300	-	120
Garage door opener	480-750	-	120
Washing machine	1,150	3,400	120 or 240
Clothes dryer, electric	4,000-5,400	6,750	120 or 240
Clothes dryer, gas	700	2,500	120 or 240

INSTALL THE NECESSARY HARDWARE

Once you have selected your generator, decide how it is to be used. There are two different methods of using a generator: direct and whole house.

Direct Method

With the direct method, you plug lamps and appliances directly into the generator sockets. Every generator is equipped with a different set of sockets, so before purchasing, check that the generator has the right plugs for your appliances. All generators offer numerous standard 120-volt AC sockets, but some also provide 240-volt AC, or even 12-volt DC sockets—useful for recharging lead-acid batteries.

Since generators can only be used outdoors, heavy-duty extension cords are needed to connect your appliances to the generator. The direct method is inherently safe to your home's electrical system. It also

INSIDE HOME

MAIN
ELECTRICAL
PANEL

REFRIGERATOR

HEAVY DUTY
EXTENSION
CORD

OUTSIDE HOME

GENERATOR

Direct generator connection

requires very minimal setup since there is no hardware to install. A serious drawback of direct generator use, however, is that you can only power equipment that has a standard AC plug. This means that you can't easily power your water heater, house lights, or heat pump—all of which can be very important. Direct generator use is also inconvenient for powering several appliances located in different rooms of your house, since each one requires its own extension cord.

Whole House Method

With the whole house method, the generator is connected to your home's electrical system. This allows you to use your wall sockets and lights as

To power your home using a generator, you must use an interlock or transfer switch.

you normally do today. Using a generator to power your whole house requires that you install a mechanical interlock or transfer switch. This work should only be done by a licensed electrician. Mechanical interlocks and transfer switches are hardware devices that transfer the source from which your home draws electricity, choosing between the power company's lines or your generator. Interlocks and transfer switches both perform the same general function but in very different ways.

Whole house generator connection

The simpler of the two mechanisms is the mechanical interlock. An interlock manually switches your home's main breaker off anytime you switch your generator's breaker on. The interlock is a custom-fitted piece of metal that mounts inside your existing breaker box. This is the cheapest method to connect your generator to your home's electrical system, requiring only the mechanical linkage (installed inside your panel), a generator breaker (also installed inside your panel), and a power inlet box (installed outside where you wish to plug in the generator). Mechanical interlocks have the advantage of allowing you to power up any of

Courtesy of Interlockkit.com

your home's appliances using the existing secondary breakers.

Expect to pay a few hundred dollars to have a licensed electrician perform the installations. This is not a do it yourself job since wiring your home without a license can void your homeowner's insurance, not to mention kill you.

Mechanical Interlock Use

1. Turn off the main breaker.
2. Shut off all the home's circuit breakers.
3. Make sure the interlock is in the *home* position.
4. Connect and start the generator.
5. Slide the interlock into the *generator* position.
6. Turn on desired breakers one at a time, giving each load a moment to stabilize before throwing the next breaker.

If wired correctly, power will flow from the generator, through your existing breaker box, out to your selected lights and appliances. This flexibility to power anything in your home is a major advantage. No additional secondary breakers are required. The only disadvantage is that mechanical linkages don't allow you to see how much power is being drawn from your generator. However, given its cost and convenience, the mechanical interlock is the preferred method of connecting a generator to your home's electrical system.

A second method of using a generator is to connect it through a transfer switch that contains its own set of breakers. For this type of installation, the electrician moves wires from your main breaker panel and connects them to the transfer switch breakers—usually mounted next to your existing panel. The transfer switch has only a limited number of breakers, so you will likely have to make some sacrifices as to what systems you power from the generator.

This limitation forces you to allocate transfer switch breakers, starting with the most important loads first (e.g., water heater, cooking range, lights). If you use this method, select a transfer switch that has at least 12 breakers. Some transfer switches have large sockets that allow you to plug the generator directly into them using a heavy-duty cord. If the transfer switch doesn't have a socket, you must install a power inlet box

Reliance transfer switch

outside the house near the generator. One advantage of transfer switches is that they often have power meters to show the level of power going out to the house loads. This feature helps to prevent overloading of the generator.

Having an interlock or transfer switch is absolutely necessary to power your home's wall sockets and overhead lights. If you wire a generator directly into your home's electrical system without one of these isolation devices, you risk backfeeding the power lines, which can electrocute linemen working to restore electricity. There are stories of people turning off their main breaker and wiring a generator to their dryer socket in an emergency, but it is simply not worth the risk to your home, your family, and the hard-working linemen. Do it right or don't do it at all.

In theory, wiring a generator to your existing breaker panel using an interlock or transfer switch should enable you to use your home appliances just as you do today. In reality however, you will have to take into account the capabilities of the generator. It is very likely that the generator will be unable to power all your appliances simultaneously. For that reason, you will need to limit the electrical load to only what is absolutely needed at the time. This prioritizing is accomplished by keeping off some of the breakers in your main power or transfer switch panel. You may have to cycle some appliances in and out, perhaps waiting for the washing machine to finish before turning on your space heater. If you overload your generator, it will choke out the engine and may even damage the unit over time.

DRAW UP A SCHEDULE

Once you have compiled the list of equipment you want to power, and have all the hardware installed, draw up a schedule detailing how you will operate the generator. For most situations, it is best to run the generator for a couple of hours in the morning and a couple more at night. The goal is to take care of all your day's electrical needs during these few hours. Activities could include:

- Recharging your batteries and handheld devices (cell phones, laptops, radios)
- Heating or cooling the house
- Cooking the day's meals

- Cooling the refrigerator and freezer
- Heating the water in the hot water heater
- Tuning in to TV, radio stations, or shortwave broadcasts
- Washing and drying clothes
- Operating your water pump (if using an underground well) to flush commodes and replenish your water supply

Adopting a usage plan like this will still leave you without AC power for most of the day, so life is certainly not going to be normal. However, with brief periods of electrical power, your family will be able to better prepare for the coming day or night.

STORE FUEL

> **Tips**
> Consult your insurance provider regarding fuel storage to prevent voiding your policy.

Another important preparation is to stockpile sufficient fuel to handle your generator needs. Consult your homeowner's insurance provider and local fire department to determine how much fuel may be stored without voiding your policy or violating local law. The nation's Uniform Fire Code limits storage to 25 gallons, but local regulations may supersede this rule. If you want to prepare for a weeklong power outage and are operating on a four-hour daily schedule, you will likely need between 30 and 60 gallons of gas—some of which you may wish to pick up just before the emergency. The exact level depends on the size of your generator and how heavily you load it. If you have a diesel generator, you may only need about 20 to 40 gallons since they typically burn less fuel per kilowatt-hour.

Moeller gas caddy

Store fuel in UL-approved containers in a well-ventilated area (most likely your garage or a nearby shed). Never store fuel inside your home. Gas and diesel are both environmental hazards, and storing them underground is strictly regulated, making it very expensive for an individual to do so legally. Given these restrictions, you will probably end up using jerry cans, or slightly higher-capacity fuel caddies. Note that 60-gallon metal drums are the only large fuel containers approved by the Uniform Fire Code. However you decide to store it, fuel must either be in a container light enough to lift, or one that is able to be pumped or siphoned. Remember that siphoning only works when transferring to a level below the fuel level. If the fuel level in your gas container is at two feet off the ground, and your generator fuel tank is at three feet, you will not be able to siphon fuel into the generator.

Over time, gasoline deteriorates, losing octane and turning to a gummy lacquer-like substance. Under optimal conditions, gasoline can be stored up to one year.[135] Optimal conditions are defined as out of

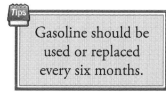
Gasoline should be used or replaced every six months.

sunlight, at a constant, moderate temperature (<80°F), and in a tightly closed container. A more conservative recommendation is to consume or replace your fuel within six months. This requirement presents a dilemma. Fuel has a relatively modest shelf life, and yet you only need it when power fails—something you certainly can't schedule.

Fortunately, fuel can be treated with special additives that help extend its shelf life. Two very popular products for this are PRI-D/G and STA-BIL. By adding a stabilizer, fuel may last for several years. These products mix at small ratios, so very little is needed. If you are going to store fuel, preservatives are a necessity.

Fuel stabilizers

OPERATE THE GENERATOR

To learn how to use a generator correctly, begin by consulting the operator's manual that comes with your specific unit. A few things are common regardless of the particular model. You will need to add oil and fuel, as well as install one or more filters. To start the generator, either use the pull string or electronic ignition button. Below are some additional operating tips.[136]

- Always operate the generator outdoors. Never use it in a garage, crawlspace, or shed. Generators exhaust a great deal of pollution that must be safely vented outdoors.
- Maintain a safety zone of at least four feet around the generator. Generators situated too close to a home can melt siding or cause a fire.
- Identify the exhaust port and ensure that it faces away from your home. Close all nearby windows or doors to prevent the exhaust from entering your house.
- Before refueling, shut down the generator and allow it to cool for a few minutes. Fuel spilled on a hot generator can ignite.
- Don't overfill the gas tank. Leave a couple of inches of space at the top to allow for the fuel to expand as it heats up.
- Wipe up any fuel spills before starting the generator.
- Keep the generator dry. Don't operate it in the rain unless it is covered with a overhead canopy.
- Be mindful of the generator's power rating, and try not to exceed it. A generator will choke out if overloaded.

INVERTERS

Inverters are a less expensive option for generating AC power. They convert DC battery voltage into AC voltage. Similar to generators, they are rated by the maximum power they output. Small inverters provide up to a few hundred watts, while larger ones can output several thousand watts. There is little need for inverters larger than this because they would quickly drain any reasonable-sized battery source.

Most inverters accept 12 or 24 volts DC as input, and output 120 or 240 volts AC through standard three-prong outlets. The 12-volt input makes

Northern Tool 800-watt inverter

them convenient to use since they can be connected directly to automotive or marine batteries.

Inverters are designed for direct plug applications only, routing power to your devices through extension cords. Don't connect an inverter to your home wiring. There is a danger of making the battery terminals live with the full 120-volt AC level.[137]

Most inverters are classified as *modified sine wave* devices. This means their output is not a true sine wave but a distorted representation. Normally this imperfection is not a problem since most electronic equipment will run fine without perfect sine wave power. However, some sensitive electronics, such as computers and televisions, may not operate properly with modified sine wave inverters. For those devices, you may need a more expensive, *true sine wave* inverter.

Inverters are not designed to power devices with high startup currents, such as washers, refrigerators, or heat pumps (see Table 7-1). Many inverters offer "soft start" circuitry to slowly bring up the current level. This

> **Tips**
>
> Caution: Many inverters don't have reverse polarity protection. To avoid damage, pay attention when connecting the battery input terminals.

may help power up some equipment with higher surge requirements.

Features you may wish to consider when selecting an inverter include:

- Overload and high temperature shutdown
- Low-voltage alarm and shutdown
- Soft starting to better handle surge currents
- Low idle current
- Overload protection
- Battery monitor

Inverters are not a direct replacement for generators for three reasons: they don't output as much power; they are not able to start up equipment with high surge currents; and they require large battery banks to output significant amounts of sustained power. An example will make this last point clear.

Large Load Example:

Assume you wish to use an inverter rated at 2,000 watts to power a space heater and a computer that require a total of 1,900 watts. You connect the inverter to a 12-volt, 100 amp-hour car battery (pulled out and sitting on the floor in this case). Although not precisely accurate, the 100 amp-hour rating will be taken to mean that the battery can output 100 amps for 1 hour, or 1 amp for 100 hours. The total available power is calculated as 12 volts × 100 amp-hours = 1,200 watt-hours.

The inverter is rated as 90% efficient, meaning that 90% of the power that goes into it is usable, and the remaining 10% is lost in heat. To output the 1,900 watts of AC power from the inverter requires 2,111 watts of DC power from the battery. This converts to only about half an hour of run time before the battery is completely drained (1,200 watt-hours capability ÷ 2,111 watts needed = 34 minutes).

This example illustrates that running a modest load of 1,900 watts for any reasonable length of time will require a significant bank of batteries. You might think that this limitation can be circumvented by keeping the battery in your vehicle and using it while the engine is running. The problem is that an alternator typically only outputs 600 to 800 watts, so it can't keep up with your load. The battery will still deplete rapidly. You may also experience car problems, such as overheating the alternator.

A particularly effective backup electrical system consists of a generator, battery bank, and an inverter. Teamed together, the three allow you to function with limited capacity throughout the entire day. The generator is used to provide high-current needs, such as cooking and clothes washing for a few hours each day. It is also used to recharge the battery bank. The batteries and inverter are used to provide for the day's lower power needs, such as radios, lamps, computers, and small appliances.

> When combined, a generator, inverter, and bank of batteries form an effective backup electrical system.

DC POWER SOURCES

Batteries provide DC power to portable devices, such as flashlights, cameras, cell phones, weather or pocket radios, and remote controls. There are many different types of batteries available, each with its respective advantages and shortcomings.

Batteries should be stored in a cool, dry location. Some people store batteries in the refrigerator thinking that the cool temperatures will help the shelf life. Studies have shown that the cool temperatures *do* help to slow the chemical reaction and increase battery shelf life, but only by a few percent—hardly worth the effort. Refrigerated batteries should always be warmed up prior to use. Not only do batteries have higher output levels when warmer, but if they are not allowed to warm, condensation can form inside the electronic device being powered.[138,139]

You will need to decide between single-use or rechargeable batteries. The advantages of single-use batteries are their low cost and good shelf life. Rechargeable batteries offer many more hours of use (assuming you can recharge them repeatedly), but generally suffer from poor shelf life and self-discharge. Most rechargeable batteries also require charging before using them the first time.

Below are tables comparing the most common types of single-use and rechargeable batteries.[140,141,142,143,144,145]

SINGLE-USE BATTERIES

There are four common types of single-use batteries: heavy duty, alkaline, nickel oxyhydroxide, and lithium. They can be compared using

Table 7-2 Single-Use Battery Comparison

Type	Energy Density	Shelf Life	Cost	Risk of Leaking	Comments
Heavy duty	Poor	2+ years	Low	Higher	Not recommended
Alkaline	Good	5+ years	Low	Higher	Acceptable for most uses.
Nickel Oxyhydroxide (NiOOH)	Very Good	6+ years	Moderate	Lower	Better than alkaline for high drain devices
Lithium (Li)	Excellent	10+ years	High	Lower	Best performing single-use battery

four metrics: cost, likelihood of leaking, energy density, and shelf life (how long they can sit on a shelf and still be usable, holding at least 70% of charge). See Table 7-2 for a comparison across these metrics.

Given their low cost and reasonable performance, alkaline batteries are the preferred choice for general purpose uses. For improved performance, such as in cameras, consider using nickel oxyhydroxide

Energizer Li batteries

batteries. Finally, if cost is not an issue and you want the very best, select lithium batteries for their outstanding performance and shelf life.

> To reduce the chances of batteries leaking, only pair up batteries that come from the same package at the same time.

RECHARGEABLE BATTERIES

Rechargeable batteries are compared using slightly different metrics, as shown in Table 7-3. The good news is that they aren't prone to leaking, and their energy densities are comparable to single-use batteries. Unfortunately, rechargeable batteries suffer from *self-discharge*. This means that even when just sitting on the shelf, they will discharge—some very rapidly. Their initial costs are also higher than single-use batteries, but they offer the advantage of numerous recharges, making them much cheaper to use over the long run.

Table 7-3 Rechargeable Battery Comparison

Type	Energy Density	Self-Discharge	Shelf Life	Cost	Comments
Nickel Metal Hydride (NiMH)	Good	30% per month	1-2 months	High	Acceptable for daily use
Low self-discharge NiMH	Good	1.5-3% per month	1-2 years	High	Best re-chargeable
Nickel Cadmium (NiCd)	Low	10-15% per month	3 months	Moderate	May have limited life due to memory effect
Lithium Ion (Li Ion)	Very good	5-10% per month	6 months	High	Suffers from declining capacity

Rechargeable batteries are great for daily-use devices because they can be recharged hundreds of times. However, because of their self-discharge and shorter shelf life, most are not ideal for disaster preparedness. To keep several sets of rechargeable batteries ready for use would require cycling them in and out of the charger every month—both inconvenient and easy to neglect. Most rechargeable batteries are also not suited for devices that are expected to last for many months, such as clocks or remote controls because once again, the self-discharge makes it necessary to do frequent battery cycling.

> **Tips**
> Low self-discharge NiMH batteries allow hundreds of recharges and have reasonable shelf life.

Low self-discharge NiMH batteries are a new addition to the battery world. They still allow hundreds of recharge cycles but have a much lower self-discharge rate, meaning that once charged, they will remain ready to use for a year or more. Low self-discharge NiMH batteries are also marketed as "ready to use," "pre-charged," or "hybrid" batteries, and generally come charged right out of the package. Although more expensive initially, pre-charged NiMH batteries are an excellent choice for nearly any need—including disaster preparedness.

Duracell pre-charged NiMH batteries

Lithium-ion batteries offer excellent initial energy capacity but suffer from a unique problem. They degrade in capacity about 20% per year due to rising internal resistance. After a couple of years, they are no longer usable for most applications. For this reason, lithium-ion batteries are not recommended. Additionally, they are typically only available in sizes suitable for camera use.

LEAD-ACID BATTERIES

Lead-acid batteries are large rechargeable batteries typically used in your automobile or boat. They have low energy-to-volume ratios, meaning they are large in size for the power they output. However, lead-acid batteries can supply the high surge currents needed to start motors. Most batteries have an output of a little over 12 volts when fully charged.

Lead-acid batteries are rated by several metrics, the most important of which is their sustained output capability (measured in amp-hours). The amp-hour rating indicates how much current over time the battery can deliver. A battery rated at 100 amp-hours would ideally be able to provide

When lead-acid batteries are heavily loaded, they won't live up to their amp-hour ratings.

1 amp for 100 hours, or 100 amps for 1 hour. In reality, batteries perform better with lighter loads, so a 100 amp-hour battery might actually be able to provide 1 amp for 120 hours, but only 80 amps for 1 hour.[146]

Excessive charging of lead-acid batteries can emit hydrogen and oxygen, which if not released, can explode. Fortunately most modern batteries are equipped with vents to release these gases. These self-venting batteries are known as valve-regulated lead-acid (VRLA) batteries. The two major types of VRLA batteries are gel cell (widely used) and absorbent glass mat (used primarily with high performance electric vehicles and motorcycles). Unlike previous-generation lead-acid batteries that required periodic inspection and adding water to account for electrolysis, modern sealed lead-acid batteries are relatively maintenance-free.

There are a several types of lead-acid batteries, but two are particularly important: starting batteries and deep cycle batteries.

Starting Batteries

Some lead-acid batteries are designed with numerous thin plates for maximum surge current, making them ideal for starting internal combustible engines. They are, however, not suited to deep discharge (i.e., draining them), which can cause permanent damage and lead to their premature failure. These types of batteries are often referred to as starting, lighting, ignition (SLI) batteries.

Deep Cycle Batteries

Deep cycle batteries are designed to be fully discharged without damage. They are useful for such things as electric vehicles, uninterruptable power supplies, boats, and photovoltaic systems. Their design also makes deep cycle batteries ideal for emergency power needs since you will want batteries that can be fully discharged and recharged repeatedly—perhaps recharging them each morning with a generator.

Deep cycle batteries are the battery of choice for disaster preparedness.

There are two ways to use lead-acid batteries when power fails. The first is to use them directly as DC power sources, providing power to your portable electronics or hand tools. The easiest way to do this is to use a power socket with battery clips. One end clips onto the battery; the other end is a conventional car cigarette lighter socket. This configuration enables you to plug your device into the socket using a standard car adapter.

The second method is to connect the lead-acid battery to an inverter, which then provides AC power. As illustrated in the *Large Load Example,* even a hefty car battery won't last very long (perhaps only minutes) when used to power home appliances. However, it can last for many hours if used for powering small loads. Again, an example will make this clear.

Small Load Example:

Assume you connect a 12-volt, 100 amp-hour, deep cycle, lead-acid battery to a modest 500-watt inverter with 90% efficiency. You use it to power a 10-watt emergency radio, and recharge both a cell phone (2.5 watts/hour) and three NiMH flashlight batteries (5 watts/hour). Assume it takes four hours to recharge your batteries and that you wish to listen to the radio during this time. The power needs are calculated as shown:

Emergency Radio: 10 watts per hour × 4 hours = 40 watt-hours

Cell phone (recharge): 2.5 watts per hour × 4 hours = 10 watt-hours

Flashlight batteries (recharge): 5 watts per hour × 4 hours × 3 batteries = 60 watt-hours

Total power needs = 110 watt-hours

With the inverter's 90% efficiency, the battery must provide 110 ÷ 0.9 = 121 watt-hours. This is only about 10% of the battery's 1,200 watt-hour capacity.

Recharging portable devices

For additional capacity, lead-acid batteries can be wired in parallel: positive terminals tied together; negative terminals tied together. Banks of batteries can power heavier loads such as lights, heaters, or a microwave oven. You should only connect batteries together like this if they are of the same charge level (i.e., fully discharged or fully charged).

RECHARGING LEAD-ACID BATTERIES

Given that lead-acid batteries will likely be your primary source of DC power, you will need an effective method to recharge them. If electrical power is available, such as a generator, then using a conventional battery charger is the quickest method. Note that some battery chargers can charge up parallel batteries concurrently. If your charger won't, then disconnect and charge each battery separately.

If electrical power is not available, you will need an alternative method to recharge your lead-acid batteries. From a practical standpoint, there are three ways to do this: solar arrays, wind turbines, and human-powered machines.

SOLAR POWER

Solar chargers exist for both NiMH and lead-acid batteries. Some chargers fit in the palm of your hand, while others may cover the roof of your home. At first glance, solar power would seem to be the perfect solution to your long-term energy needs. Simply hook your batteries up to the solar charger, and a short time later, your batteries are as good as new, right? Unfortunately, it is not quite that simple.

The problem with solar chargers is the very small amount of power they provide. Consider that small commercial solar chargers, designed to recharge AA and AAA batteries, output about 90 mA of current under full-sun conditions. Assuming six hours of bright sunlight each day, batteries would charge about 540 mA-hours per day. Typical high-capacity AAA and AA batteries are about 900 and 2500 mA-hours respectively. To fully recharge a set of four AAA batteries would require 3,600 mA-hours, taking about 7 days. Likewise, recharging four AA batteries would require 10,000 mA-hours and take about 18 days!

> **Tips**
> Solar chargers are very inefficient, taking days or even weeks to recharge batteries.

The solution to this slow recharge rate is to use larger solar panels. However, most large solar panels are only designed to recharge 12-volt or larger batteries. To charge small NiMH batteries requires you to convert the 12 volts coming off the solar panel to the 1.5-volt level needed for AA or AAA batteries. One method of doing this is to use a recharger, such as the Duracell Mobile Charger, that runs directly off 12 volts. A more general solution is to use an inverter, which allows you to use any recharger with an AC plug.

The problem of minimal solar-panel-energy-yield applies to larger lead-acid batteries as well. A modest solar panel charger measuring 17 in. × 13 in. might provide 400 mA of current in full sunlight. Considering that a heavy duty, lead-acid battery requires about 100 amp-hours, recharging will take 250 hours of full sunlight. If the sun shines with full intensity on the panel for 6 hours a day, it will take about 42 days to recharge the battery. If you increase the size of the solar panel to about 50 in. × 40 in., you might get 5 amps of charging current, reducing the recharge time down to a more manageable 20 hours (or three days of bright sunlight).

Backup electrical system

The point of the examples is to illustrate that using solar chargers to recharge batteries can be a slow process. The only way around this is to use very large solar panels. Despite this limitation, solar energy can be an excellent source of backup power. Just be realistic in your expectations.

WIND POWER

Wind is used to produce about 1.5% of the world's energy. In 2009, over 52 terawatt-hours of wind power were produced in the United States.[147] Large turbines can now be seen dotting the landscapes of Texas, Colorado, and Oregon. Wind power has become a practical supplement to coal and nuclear energy.

How viable a personal energy source it is depends largely on where you live. If steady, strong winds are prevalent in your area and you have unobstructed access to the wind, then it might yield tangible power. Wind turbines must be

> **Tips**
> The viability of wind power depends greatly on where you live, and the size and height of the turbine you erect.

Sunforce wind turbine

mounted high above the ground, such as atop a roof or tall pole, to gain unfettered access to the wind stream. Also, getting any significant power output requires a large turbine.

It is important to realize that a turbine's specified power output assumes ideal conditions (perhaps 35-mph winds). Practical yields can easily be a mere 10% of the values specified by the manufacturer. A turbine rated with a 400-watt output might only produce an average of 40 watts per hour.

The notable drawbacks to using wind turbines for personal use are cost, availability, and the unpredictable nature of wind. The hardware and installation costs of a small turbine with 26-inch blades and a mounting tower might cost you several thousand dollars. Larger wind generators are significantly more expensive. If a small turbine averages 3 amps of current 24 hours a day, it will yield a respectable 72 amp-hours per day—almost enough to recharge a deep cycle, lead-acid battery.

MECHANICAL MOTION

It is possible to convert mechanical energy to electrical energy by moving a permanent magnet through a coil of wire. When doing this, you are mimicking a generator. Three common methods to create this movement are to pedal a specially-equipped bicycle, use a hand pedal, or climb a stair-step machine.

Tips

Human-powered machines can create electricity, but the process is slow and arduous.

Bicycles give the greatest energy yield, with units from Windstream Power claiming to produce 10 to 16 amps. Recharging a 100-amp-hour lead-acid battery would take about 6 to 10 hours of steady pedaling—a *very* hard day's workout. Hand-pedaled units and stair steppers provide 3 to 4 amps of output power, driving the recharge time up to a whopping 25 to 33 hours.[148]

There are some advantages to human-powered recharge systems. They are available day and night, and are independent of sun and wind. Also, family members can take turns sharing the work load. The two significant disadvantages are the heavy exertion required and the limited power output.

Human-powered generator

DP PLAN EXAMPLE

Table 7-4 Sample DP Plan Entry

Need: Electricity			
Danger	**Goals**	**Needs**	**Implementation**
Power outage	Operate lights and appliances for a few hours each day for up to 10 days	AC power for house lights, primary heating unit, and appliances	Use a 10-kilowatt gas generator to power the whole house with select loads switched in and out.
			Have electrician install a mechanical interlock.
			Draw up a schedule that uses the generator 2 hours in the morning and 2 hours at night.
			Stock 25 gallons of stabilized fuel in 5-gallon jerry cans.
		DC power for recharging batteries, operating small loads (radios, cell phones, electric lanterns)	Use a 200 amp-hour deep discharge battery and 2,000-watt inverter.
			Sock low self-discharge NiMH batteries and chargers.

Quick Summary - Electrical Power

➤ Having a backup power source can make handling a disaster much easier.

➤ Power can be either direct current (DC) or alternating current (AC). Household appliances and lights run on AC, while most small portable devices use DC power.

➤ Generators and inverters are used to provide AC power.

➤ Determine your electrical needs in order to select the right-sized generator.

➤ Either plug directly into your generator using extension cords, or wire the generator to your house through a mechanical interlock or transfer switch.

➤ Limit fuel use by running your generator only a few hours each day. Develop a schedule of tasks to carry out during each power cycle.

➤ Check with your insurance company and fire department to determine how much fuel you are allowed to store.

➤ Add stabilizers to freshly-stored fuel to extend its shelf life.

➤ Inverters convert battery power into AC power, but are not suited to powering equipment with high startup currents.

➤ Lithium batteries have the highest capacity and longest shelf life of all single-use or rechargeable batteries. Alkaline are much less expensive, and are good general purpose batteries.

➤ Low self-discharge NiMH batteries are the only small, rechargeable batteries recommended for disaster preparedness. They are especially useful for powering radios and flashlights.

➤ When teamed with an inverter and recharger, lead-acid batteries are an excellent emergency power source.

➤ Rechargers that use natural energy include solar panels, wind turbines, and human-powered machines. All are viable methods of recharging batteries, but they suffer from limited output.

Recommended Items - Electrical Power

❑ Backup power source
  a. Electric generator system including: a gas or diesel generator, interlock or transfer switch, power inlet box, heavy-duty power cord, and maintenance items (e.g., filters, spark plugs), *and/or*
  b. Bank of deep cycle batteries, conventional charger, high-wattage inverter, and extension cords

❑ Backup fuel source
  a. Gas or diesel fuel in approved storage containers, treated with a stabilizer, *and/or*
  b. Solar, wind, or mechanical battery recharger

❑ Spare batteries
  a. Alkaline, *or*
  b. Low self-discharge rechargeable NiMH batteries with recharger

CHAPTER 8
HEATING / COOLING

Chapter 8 Notes

CHAPTER 8

HEATING / COOLING

Challenge

An arctic freeze has enveloped your community. Snow and ice have made roads impassable. Your heating unit unexpectedly shuts down, and it will be days before repairmen can service your home. Temperatures fall to dangerous levels each night. How will you keep your family warm?

There are numerous situations that can leave you without heating or cooling. In moderate climates, this may not be a serious concern, but most people are reminded annually of the bitter sting that winter brings. Staying warm becomes not merely a matter of comfort but one of survival. Conversely, there are places in the country where summer heat waves can bring suffering and even death if your home's temperature is not adequately controlled.

BODY TEMPERATURE

Simply put, getting too cold or too hot can kill you. At one end of the spectrum is hypothermia—literally freezing to death. At the other end is hyperthermia—overheating to the point of heatstroke. Both conditions are equally deadly and must be prevented.

HYPOTHERMIA

If more heat escapes your body than it can produce, you will cool and eventually develop hypothermia. Normal body temperature is 98.6°F. If your internal core temperature drops below 95°F, it signals hypothermia. Symptoms may include gradual loss of motor skills and mental acuity, fatigue, mumbling, slowed breathing, slurred speech, and cold, pale skin. Since symptoms usually develop gradually, victims are often unaware that they are succumbing to the cold. If the condition is allowed to progress, it can lead to death. In the United States alone, nearly 700 people die from hypothermia each year.[150]

Being in extreme cold without adequate clothing, wearing wet clothes (especially in windy conditions), or being exposed to very cold water, can all cause hypothermia. Treatment for hypothermia includes moving to a warmer environment, removing wet clothing, insulating from any cold surface, sharing body heat, and drinking warm beverages. Never massage the skin, apply direct heat using a heating pad or heat lamp, or drink alcoholic beverages.[150]

Prevention is best done by wearing clothing appropriate to the environment, including gloves, hat, and footwear. Avoid overexertion that can cause you to sweat. If you do become wet for any reason, change out of the wet clothes as soon as possible.

> **Tips**
>
> *Paradoxical undressing* is a hypothermic condition in which a person feels so hot that they undress.

Twenty to fifty percent of all deaths relating to hypothermia are associated with what is known as *paradoxical undressing*.[151] Though the causes are not entirely understood, it is a condition in which a person feels extremely hot even though his core temperature is falling to deadly levels. The victim begins to shed clothing in an effort to cool off, which only further speeds his demise. Unfortunately, the confusion and impaired judgment caused by hypothermia keep the person from recognizing the cause of their self-destructive actions.

HYPERTHERMIA

Hyperthermia is the condition in which your body absorbs or produces more heat than it can dissipate. The term is often used to describe several heat-related illnesses, including heat cramps, heat exhaustion, and heatstroke.

Heat cramps are the first stage of hyperthermia. Symptoms include profuse sweating, fatigue, thirst, and muscle cramps. Strenuous physical activity in hot weather is usually the cause, although exertion is not necessary if the environment is hot enough. Heat cramps can be treated by drinking fluids, especially those containing electrolytes, and resting in a cool location.

If you do not take the steps necessary to cool down when experiencing heat cramps, they will develop into heat exhaustion. You will become thirsty, giddy, weak, uncoordinated, nauseated, and continue to sweat profusely. Your body temperature will likely remain normal, but your pulse may become elevated, and your skin can feel cold and clammy. Heat exhaustion is a serious warning that you are getting too hot and need to immediately rest in a cool location and drink cold liquids.[152]

Continued exposure to heat or exertion could lead to heatstroke—a life-threatening condition. This occurs when your body temperature rises to 104°F or higher. Other symptoms may include cessation of sweating, hyperventilation (rapid, shallow breathing), muscle cramps, weakness, confusion, combativeness, irrational behavior, strong rapid pulse, and delirium. The high body temperature can cause irreversible brain damage, organ failure, and death.[153]

If you suspect you are suffering from heatstroke, get to a cool location and rest. Drink cold liquids, especially water and fruit juice, but avoid caffeinated or alcoholic drinks. If possible, shower, bathe, or sponge off with cool water. Additional medical attention may be necessary—see *Chapter 11: Medical/First Aid* for more treatment information.

COOLING

It may be hard to believe, but humankind survived for a very long time without air conditioning (A/C). You can too by applying a little common sense. If you find yourself without A/C, you can prevent heat-related illnesses by limiting your activities, drinking cold beverages, and establishing some basic air circulation in your home.

KEEPING YOURSELF COOL

Consider the following suggestions to keep *yourself* cool.

- Take it easy. Give yourself permission to be lazy.
- Drink plenty of cold, non-alcoholic liquids.
- Wear loose-fitting, warm-weather clothing, such as shorts and a t-shirt.
- Enjoy a Popsicle, frozen fruit, or other icy treat.
- Soak your t-shirt in water and sit in front of a fan or breeze.
- Take a cold bath or shower.
- Stay in the lowest level of your home. Heat tends to rise to the upper levels. Better yet, sit under a large shade tree outside.
- Fan yourself—improvise as necessary with a magazine, piece of cardboard, or other lightweight flat object.
- Soak your feet in a bucket of cool water.

KEEPING YOUR HOME COOL

Consider the following suggestions to keep *your home* cool.

- Close your blinds on windows facing the sun.
- Open windows on opposite sides of your house to create air circulation. If possible, use fans to draw off heat from the hottest parts of your house, and pull in cooler air from outside.
- Turn off anything creating unnecessary heat (e.g., lights, computer, dishwasher, television).
- Run appliances in the evening when it is cooler.
- Blow air across a bowl full of ice cubes or water frozen in 2-liter bottles to create a mini air conditioner.
- As a longer-term solution, plant shade trees around your home.

Beyond these basic preventive measures, no other special preparations are usually necessary to stave off heat-related illnesses. For most families, there isn't a pressing need to maintain a secondary cooling system for the home. With that said, if someone in your family is particularly susceptible to heat (perhaps an elderly parent, a young child, or even a pet), then you should plan accordingly. This usually means having backup electrical power to run fans or a small A/C system—see *Chapter 7: Electrical Power* for details on electrical preparations.

> The elderly and children are particularly susceptible to overheating, so monitor them closely.

HEATING

Keeping warm starts with having the right kinds of clothing and bedding. Your family should already have clothing appropriate to the climate in which you live, so additional garments aren't likely necessary. Bedding may be another matter. You are accustomed to maintaining a comfortable living environment by simply adjusting the thermostat. But what if that heat fails, and your home is left no warmer than the frosty outdoors? Your family's usual bedding probably won't be enough to stay warm at night.

The easiest way to prepare is to consider what your family would need to spend the night outdoors. Winter sleeping bags, down comforters, and heavy wool blankets should all come to mind. How much and what kind depends on where you

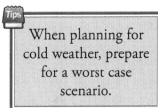

> When planning for cold weather, prepare for a worst case scenario.

live. Whatever blankets you select, plan as if Jack Frost is maliciously working against you—worst winter on record, heating system failure, a couple of windows broken out. Unrealistic yes, but keeping warm is critically important and not overly difficult to do with a few basic preparations. You can't go wrong by having extra blankets. If you end up not needing them, loan them to neighbors or friends who might be less prepared. Also, remember to stash blankets in the car for roadside emergencies—see the auto kits described in *Chapter 14: Transportation* for more information.

If you want to do much more than huddle under blankets, you will need some kind of area heating. Not only will heating help your family to function, but it will also help them to feel more comfortable—and that leads to a happier family.

LOSS OF HEAT

Heat can be lost in two very different ways, and each requires different preparations. The first is a disruption in your fuel source. For most people, this is manifested through a loss of electrical power or the shutting off of the gas supply. The second is when your heating unit fails, perhaps due to cold weather or just a case of bad luck. Regardless of the cause, a reasonable goal is to have sufficient heating supplies to support your family for a minimum of two weeks.

LOSS OF FUEL

Many situations can result in your heating system's fuel source being unavailable, whether that fuel is electricity, propane, or natural gas. For these occasions, you need a supplementary source of fuel and a method to use it in your heater. Depending on the type of heater, this provision is handled in different ways.

If you have an electric heating system, you can probably power it using a large generator. Take care to size the generator to handle both constant and surge current requirements—see *Chapter 7: Electrical Power*. If your heater burns propane or natural gas, you will need a backup fuel tank and a valve that allows you to switch over to that secondary source. You will also likely need a small backup electrical source to power the blower motor, thermostat, ignition system, and backup strip heating. This necessity can usually be met with a small generator or a battery and inverter.

If you have a wood-burning stove, kerosene heater, or other local heat source, you will probably not be directly affected by the centralized disruption of fuel. But once again, you may still require modest levels of electrical power for the blower or pellet auger. Investigate your particular system to fully understand its operational needs.

LOSS OF HEATING UNIT

If you have ever witnessed the numerous repair trucks servicing neighborhoods during a cold spell, you realize how frequently heating systems fail. This is especially true when the weather is unusually frigid, and the heater is worked harder than usual.

To be prepared for a heating system failure, you will need a backup heat source. Due to costs, having a fully redundant secondary heating system is probably not feasible. Instead, you may opt to have a smaller backup heater that is capable of heating only a portion of your home—enough to help you get by until your system can be serviced. There are many options for backup heating, including kerosene heaters, electric space heaters, and wood-burning stoves, all of which are discussed later in this chapter.

> Due to cost constraints, you may opt for a backup heating system that heats only an isolated area of your home.

Personal aside: On three separate occasions, and at three different residences, my family's heating system failed during harsh winter storms. In all three cases, I was unable to get a service person out to my house in less than 48 hours—leaving us to fend for ourselves. The first time, my family and I were ill prepared and had little choice but to abandon our house and seek a warm hotel. When the second incident occurred, we had enough blankets and knowhow to weather the event, albeit with a few shivers. By the third time, my family was equipped with a kerosene heater, a wood-burning fireplace, and stacks of blankets—making our home a welcome neighborhood refuge.

SAFETY FIRST

Before considering backup heat sources, realize that the dangers of improper use far outweigh the dangers of freezing to death. Two significant risks are worth noting: carbon monoxide (CO) poisoning and fire.

> When it comes to heaters, the dangers of fire and carbon monoxide poisoning far outweigh the dangers of freezing.

Any type of heater that burns fuel, such as wood, coal, propane, and kerosene, also produces CO. Carbon monoxide is a colorless, odorless gas, so you won't see or smell it. Symptoms of CO poisoning include headache, fatigue, lightheadedness, shortness of breath, nausea, and dizziness. If you experience any of these symptoms while operating fuel-burning heaters, get fresh air immediately! Carbon monoxide poisoning is deadly, killing about 200 people in the United States each year.[114] The surest way to prevent CO poisoning is never to use fuel-burning appliances indoors without proper ventilation. It is also a good idea to put a CO detector in any room where a fuel-burning appliance is used (see *Chapter 5: Shelter* for a discussion of safety devices).

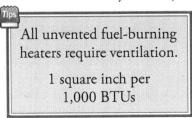

All unvented fuel-burning heaters require ventilation.

1 square inch per
1,000 BTUs

Using a fuel-burning heater requires either direct venting to the outdoors using a pipe that routes through the wall or ceiling or keeping the area well ventilated with open windows or doors. Most heaters come with manufacturer's recommendations regarding ventilation. Read and follow them. If recommendations are not furnished, a useful rule of thumb is to provide one square inch of window opening for each 1,000 BTUs of heater rating.[154] For example, a heater with a 20,000 BTUs/hour rating would require that a 10-inch wide window be open 2 inches (i.e., 20 square inches of opening). This recommendation should be treated as the minimum ventilation for *all* fuel-burning heaters that are not directly vented outdoors.

The second risk of using a fuel-burning heater is that you might catch your house or shelter on fire. Heaters must be kept away from flammable materials, and that means basically everything in your home except

Preventing Heater Fires

1. Keep the heater away from anything flammable.
2. Never leave the heater unattended.
3. Explain the dangers to everyone involved, and ask them to help keep a watchful eye. Be especially mindful of very young children who might tip the heater or burn themselves.
4. If the heater plugs into the wall, avoid using extension cords. If you must use one, select a heavy duty cord with at least 14 AWG wire.

stone, metal, or brick. Normal construction materials, such as sheetrock, wood flooring, and carpet, as well as furniture, clothing, and bedding can all catch fire from backup heaters. The hotter the heater, the more likely it is to cause a fire. For this reason, never leave heaters unattended, and solicit help from everyone involved to keep a watchful eye.

AMOUNT OF HEAT NEEDED

The amount of backup heat you need is largely determined by the climate in which you live. It is safe to say that if you live in Florida, you will need less backup heating than someone who lives in North Dakota. However, in all but the most temperate climates, some form of backup heat is advisable.

Start by assessing your current heat source. Does your house or apartment use a heat pump, gas furnace, or electric heater? If your heater burns fuel, such as natural gas or propane, does it also require electricity to power a blower? Perhaps you are out in the country and use a wood-burning stove or kerosene heater. If your primary fuel source was interrupted in the dead of the winter and remained out for two weeks, how would your family stay warm? The time to address this question is now while comfortably sipping iced tea, not when you can see your breath in the air.

Weatherproofing your home

> **Tips**
>
> Conserve heat by weatherproofing your home: seal gaps, insulate windows, and weatherstrip around doors.

Regardless of what type of secondary heating system you select, the first step is to conserve heat. Keep your house well sealed unless you are specifically using an unvented, fuel-burning heater. If you add up the gaps in an average home, they total about 14 square inches, and those gaps result in significant energy loss.[155] Obvious corrective actions include applying weatherstripping around leaky doors and window sashes, caulking gaps and joints, and using double-paned windows.

SELECTING A HEATER

When considering the type of backup heater to use, many factors will come into play, including cost, safety, heating area, and the climate in which you live.

Seven steps for selecting and readying a backup heating system are given below.

1. If your backup heater cannot heat your entire home, identify a well-insulated space in your house to where your family will retreat. It should have limited windows or doors to the outside, but easy access to a bathroom. If you decide to consolidate in the main living area of your home, seal off adjoining rooms.
2. Determine how much heat you will need (see *Sizing Your Heater*).
3. Select the most appropriate type of heater for your situation (see *Types of Heaters*).
4. Learn how to safely use your heater.
5. Install any necessary venting or duct work.
6. Stockpile the necessary fuel.
7. Test your heater on a very cold winter day to ensure it will meet your family's needs. Supplement or resize the heater as necessary.

SIZING YOUR HEATER

There are heaters available in nearly every size; some are big enough to heat a barn, while others are barely able to warm your feet. Properly sizing your backup heater can mean the difference between being cozy and being miserable.

Sizing a heater requires you to consider three things:

- The volume of air to be heated
- The heat that escapes through the walls, floor, and ceiling
- The minimum allowable temperature difference between indoors and outdoors on the worst possible winter day

If you're installing a large, fully-redundant heating system, such as a heat pump or furnace, have the retailer inspect your home to determine the correct heater size.

If you opt for a smaller, localized heat source, perhaps a wood-burning stove, kerosene heater, or electric space heater, you will need to determine the necessary heater size by making a few measurements and performing some simple calculations.

There are many online tools and resources to help you perform heater sizing.[156,157,158,159] Unfortunately, their methods and results frequently disagree. That is because precise heater sizing requires detailed knowledge of your home's exposure, orientation, insulation, sealing, and air flow. Each tool makes different assumptions, some more conservative than others.

The following guidelines are considered to be reasonable methods of estimating the required size of a heater. The three methods discussed are in order of increasing accuracy.

METHOD 1:

The simplest method to size a heater is to multiply the square footage to be heated by 25. The result is the number of BTUs/hour needed to stay warm.

For example, if you wish to heat 200 square feet, you would need a heater capable of outputting a minimum of:

$$200 \times 25 = 5,000 \text{ BTUs/hour}$$

METHOD 2:

A second slightly more accurate method requires measuring the volume of air to be heated and specifying the minimum temperature difference desired between your home and the outdoors. Once again, a straightforward equation can be used to estimate the heater size.

$$Volume \times \Delta T \times 0.133$$

For example, to heat a room measuring 200 square feet and having 8-foot ceilings, would require heating 1,600 cubic feet of air. If the outside temperature can fall as low as 10°F, and you wish to maintain the inside temperature at 60°F, the temperature difference is 50°F. The minimum heater size then would be determined to be:

$$1,600 \times 50 \times 0.133 = 10,640 \text{ BTUs/hour.}$$

METHOD 3:

An even more accurate method takes into account your home's level of insulation, but no longer considers the specific temperature difference you are trying to achieve. This method has you multiply the size of the area to be heated by an insulation factor (given in Table 8-1).

$$Area \times Insulation\ Factor$$

Table 8-1 Insulation Factors.[160]

Category	Insulation	Factor
Poor Insulation	No insulation in walls, ceilings, or floors; no storm windows; windows and doors not well sealed	90-110
Average Insulation	R-11 insulation in walls and ceilings; no insulation in floors; no storm windows; doors and windows fairly tight	50-70
Good Insulation	R-19 insulation in walls, R-30 in ceilings, R-11 in floors; tight-fitting storm windows or double-pane windows	29-35
Super Insulation	R-24 wall insulation, R-40 in ceilings, R-19 in floor; tight-fitting storm windows or double-pane windows; vapor barrier sealed carefully during construction	21-25
Earth-sheltered	Earth-sheltered house with little exposure; well insulated	10-13

For a house with average insulation, heating a 200-square-foot area would require between:

Best case: $200 \times 50 = 10,000$ BTUs/hour

Worst case: $200 \times 70 = 14,000$ BTUs/hour

SUMMARY

As you can see, the three estimates range anywhere from 5,000 to 14,000 BTUs/hour. With these methods you can get a first-order estimate of your heating needs (perhaps by taking the

Sizing a secondary heater can often be a process of trial and error.

average of the three). Once you have that estimate, you will need to select a heater that functions well in your house for the temperature extremes you are likely to experience. This can often be a process of trial and error—buying a heater that you think will work, and then supplementing or replacing it as needed.

Most heaters are specified by British Thermal Units per hour (BTUs/ hour). Sometimes retailers will get sloppy and simply state the value as BTUs, but they are always referring to BTUs/hour. A BTU is defined as the amount of heat required to raise one pound of water one degree Fahrenheit. It makes sense that a heater should be rated by how much heat per hour that it outputs.

Electric heaters are an exception to this method of specification. They are sized in watts rather than BTUs/hour. For comparison purposes, you can convert from watts to BTUs/hour by multiplying the number of watts by 3.4. For example, a standard 1,500-watt electric space heater will output heat comparable to a 5,100-BTUs/hour propane heater. There are other considerations to make this conversion more accurate, such as energy efficiency, but the factor of 3.4 is a reasonable estimate.

Another method to size an electric heater is to assume that every square foot requires about 10 watts of power.[161] This is not precise and does not consider cubic feet or temperature drop, but it gives a preliminary estimate. Using this method, a 200-square-foot room would require 2,000 watts of electric heating (or roughly 6,800 BTUs/hour).

TYPES OF HEATERS

There are many possible sources of backup heat, each with its respective advantages and disadvantages. A list of likely candidates is given in the tip box.

Backup Heaters
➤ Fireplaces
➤ Masonry heaters
➤ Wood/Coal/Pellet stoves
➤ Electric space heaters
➤ Kerosene space heaters
➤ Oil-filled radiators
➤ Propane or natural gas heaters

Regardless of the type of heater you select, you should fully understand the dangers associated with it. If you select an electric, propane, or kerosene space heater, pick a unit that has an automatic shutoff feature in case it is accidentally tipped over. It is worth repeating that any heater that burns fuel, whether it is wood, propane, kerosene, or gas, must either be vented to the outdoors or reside in a well-ventilated room to prevent carbon monoxide buildup.

FIREPLACES

Modern fireplaces typically come with artificial logs and glass covers and are designed more for style than heat. They offer a wonderful instant fire ambiance, but unfortunately, they don't output much heat to the room. To improve their utility, many instant-on fireplaces can be equipped with internal blowers that help to circulate the heat. If using blowers, don't forget to address this requirement in your electrical power preparations.

Fireplaces are terribly inefficient, but using a Texas Fire Frame can help.

If you have a traditional stone or brick wood-burning fireplace, then you can get a little more heat from it—but not much. Wood-burning fireplaces are very inefficient, losing about 90% of their heat up the chimney.[162] This can be improved through the use of a "Texas Fire Frame" or other fireplace radiant grate that focuses heat back into the room, perhaps raising the efficiency up to 30%.

More heat directed into room

Texas Fire Frame

Another option is to install a wood- or pellet-burning stove insert into the fireplace. Stoves inserts significantly improve the efficiency as well as reduce smoke emissions.

MASONRY HEATERS

Modern masonry heaters are based on traditional designs dating back to the 14th century. They are known by many names, including Russian stoves, Kachelofen, Tulikivi, Grudofen, and Contraflow heaters. Each heater consists of a large stone or brick burn box, a chimney, and a labyrinth of channels to trap the heat and smoke. This trapped heat is transferred to the masonry hearth and surrounding walls. The fire itself only burns for a brief period of time, but the heat is radiated out from the masonry for 12 to 24 hours, meaning that only a single fire may be needed for an entire day's heat. This slow, steady release of heat is the primary advantage of masonry heaters over other heating methods.

> Even with a small morning fire, masonry heaters radiate heat throughout the entire day.

Masonry heaters typically burn wood, but they have also been used to burn straw, dry vegetable matter, and even garbage. The fire burns very hot (over 1,400°F), leading to complete and rapid fuel consumption that releases very little air pollution. Despite the high temperature, the surrounding stone is massive enough not to be hot to the touch. The heaters offer exceptional (80-90%) efficiency because most of the energy is trapped in the masonry rather than vented up through the chimney.

However, there are several drawbacks to masonry heaters. They require a couple of hours to heat up, which can be a long wait on a

Courtesy of Bob Weaver Masonry

cold winter morning. They also do not have centralized heat distribution, leaving most of the radiant heat to remain in the room with the heater. Finally, anyone considering a masonry heater must take into account their weight and cost. The stonework can easily weigh two thousand pounds or more, often requiring that the floor be reinforced. Masonry heaters are custom built by expert craftsmen and can cost many thousands of dollars. Additional information, and a listing of licensed builders, can be found online at the Masonry Heater Association of North America.[163]

COAL/PELLET/WOOD STOVES

Coal, pellet, and wood stoves are in many ways the epitome of disaster preparedness. In many cases, they can serve as both heater and stove—meeting two very important needs simultaneously. Some stoves fit into existing fireplaces as inserts, while others are free-standing. Newer models control the oxygen level so that fuel lasts longer and burns more completely, making them more efficient and less polluting than stoves of the past. Stoves are excellent backup heaters, but they are fairly expensive, require periodic maintenance, and professional installation is definitely recommended. There are many vendors for fuel-burning stoves, including Woodstock Soapstone Company, Lopi, Harman, Napoleon, Reading Stove Company, Lehman's, and Vermont Castings.

Coal Stoves

Coal stoves emit more pollution than EPA-certified wood stoves. The primary advantage of a coal stove is its higher fuel efficiency and lower fuel costs. Table 8-2 gives a useful comparison of fuel efficiencies and costs for many types of vented room heaters. This table makes clear the advantage of coal over other fuels since costs can be half those of a pellet stove or one-third those of electric power.

Much like masonry heaters, coal and wood stoves allow burning of improvised fuels (e.g., lumber scraps, furniture, newspapers, books). However, when burning makeshift fuels, pay attention

Wood can be burned in coal stoves, but not vice versa.

Table 8-2 Fuel Comparisons for Vented Room Heaters[164]

Fuel Type	Fuel Unit	Fuel Heat Content per Unit (BTUs)	Fuel Cost per Million BTUs	Efficiency	Fuel Cost per Million BTUs (efficiency included)
Coal (Anthracite)	Ton	25,000,000	$8.00	75%	$10.67
Solid Wood	Cord	22,000,000	$9.09	55%	$16.53
Corn (kernels)	Ton	16,500,000	$12.12	68%	$17.83
Natural Gas	Therm	100,000	$12.27	65%	$18.88
Fuel Oil (#2)	Gallon	138,690	$17.01	78%	$21.81
Pellets	Ton	16,500,000	$15.15	68%	$22.28
Propane	Gallon	91,333	$21.27	65%	$32.73
Electricity	Kilowatt-hour	3,412	$33.85	100%	$33.85

that the chimney doesn't become clogged and catch fire. Burning wood in a coal stove is generally acceptable, but burning coal in wood or pellet stoves will quickly deteriorate the stove floor due to the higher burn temperatures.

Pellet Stoves

Pellet stoves are designed to burn cleaner and more efficiently than conventional wood stoves. They burn short, thin rods of compressed sawdust or other renewable materials. These "pellets" are poured into a hopper that feeds automatically into the stove, typically using an internal electric auger. Note that these stoves can be picky about the types of pellets they will handle without jamming, so be sure to experiment with products before stocking up.[165] Pellet stoves emit very little pollution and therefore do not require EPA certification.

Wood Stoves

There are two types of wood stoves: catalytic and non-catalytic. Most stoves are non-catalytic, which means they are essentially large metal fireboxes with baffles. Catalytic stoves are a bit more complicated since they pass the smoky exhaust through a coated, ceramic honeycomb inside the stove where the smoke gases and particles burn. The honeycomb elements must be replaced every two to six years. Catalytic stoves also come equipped with a lever-operated bypass damper that is opened when starting or reloading.

Be sure to do your homework and select an EPA-certified stove that provides adequate heat output and burns the fuel you have selected. The EPA's smoke emission, efficiency, and heat output ratings (in BTUs/hour) are listed on the back

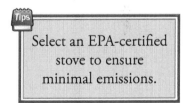

Select an EPA-certified stove to ensure minimal emissions.

of certified stoves. Modern wood-burning stoves emit much less smoke than older stoves. For a stove to be EPA-certified, particulate emissions must be below 7.5 grams per hour for non-catalytic wood stoves and 4.1 grams per hour for catalytic stoves. (Some states impose even more restrictive limits). Compare this to previous-generation stoves that emitted between 15 and 30 grams per hour.[166]

Fine Particle Emissions In One Hour

15 - 30 grams   2 - 7 grams

Old, Inefficient Stove   EPA Certified Stove

Certified Stoves Are 50% More Energy Efficient Than Non-Certified Stoves

When researching stoves, don't just read product descriptions; check user reviews to see what types of problems others have experienced. Also, visit the retailer and personally inspect each stove for durability and quality. This is an investment that your family will benefit from for many years, so take the time to make a well-informed selection.

Calculating Wood Needed

If you are relying on a wood-burning stove, either as your primary heat source or as a backup emergency heater, you will need to determine

Table 8-3 Fuel Equivalence[249]

Fuel Type	Equivalent Quantity
Wood	1 cord
No. 2 Fuel Oil	150 gallons
Liquid Propane	230 gallons
Natural Gas	21,000 cubic feet
Electricity	6,158 kilowatt-hours

your fuel needs. Wood is purchased in cords, with each cord measuring 4 feet × 4 feet × 8 feet. A cord should consist of tightly-stacked, cut wood. Most of the time, individual wood pieces are sold in lengths smaller than 4 feet to facilitate easier burning. The amount of energy in a cord of wood can be compared to other fuel sources as shown in Table 8-3.

Using these equivalence values and the fuel efficiencies given in Table 8-2, you can determine the number of cords of wood needed to meet your heating needs.

$$Cords = \frac{PF \times E_{PF}}{W \times E_W}$$

PF is the amount of primary fuel used, W is the wood equivalence number from Table 8-3, and E_{PF} and E_W are energy efficiencies of the primary fuel and wood (given in Table 8-2). An example is in order.

Example: Assume your 2,000-sq. foot home normally uses 60,000 cubic feet of natural gas per year. The efficiency of natural gas is about 65%, and the efficiency of wood is about 55%. The number of cords of wood needed to supply your heating needs for a full year would be given by:

$$Cords = \frac{60,000 \times 0.65}{21,000 \times 0.55} = 3.4$$

Cord of Wood

ELECTRIC SPACE HEATERS

Electric space heaters are inexpensive and easy to use; simply plug them in and set the desired output level or thermostat temperature. They obviously require electricity, provided either by your electric company, a generator, or an inverter and battery combination. The Electrical Code limits the size of residential electric heaters to a maximum of 1,500 watts. If you need more heat than that, you must use multiple heaters. Each heater should be plugged into a different circuit in your home (e.g., one in the living room outlet, one in the kitchen—assuming they are on separate breakers). If you plug two heaters into the same circuit, they will almost certainly overload and trip your breakers.

> **Tips**
> Plug each electric heater into a separate circuit to prevent overloading your breakers.

If you have consolidated your family to a small area, even a single 1,500 watt electric space heater may be adequate to keep warm. This depends on the size of the room, the insulation, and how cold it is outside. Electric heaters do not emit carbon monoxide. However, as with all heaters, ensure that there is adequate space around the heater to prevent a fire.

Features to look for in an electric space heater include:

- Automatic shutoff when tipped over
- Overheat protection
- Long power cord to allow easier placement of the heater
- Thermostat or multiple output settings
- Circulating fan (for convection models)

The two most common types of electric space heaters are *convection* and *radiant*. Convection heaters flow air across a hot thermal conductor (usually ceramic plates or metal coils). Air is circulated into the room either naturally through convection or by an electric fan. Convection heaters are useful for heating small rooms.

Radiant heaters produce directional heat using an element, such as quartz, and a reflector. They are best suited for heating a small area directly in front of the heater because very little heat is radiated at any other angle. The heat is immediate but dissipates quickly when the unit is turned off.

There are many manufacturers of electric space heaters including Bionaire, Soleus, DeLonghi, Duraheat, Honeywell, Vornado, Presto, and Lasko.

Vornado convection and Soleus radiant heaters

KEROSENE SPACE HEATERS

Kerosene heaters can either be vented or unvented. Larger units generally feed directly from outdoor kerosene tanks and vent back outside through pipes (similar to wood stoves). Smaller, unvented units have modest kerosene tanks attached directly to the unit and are meant to heat one or two rooms. Beware that the term "unvented" is misleading. Like all fuel-burning appliances, unvented kerosene heaters consume oxygen and emit poisonous fumes, meaning that venting of the room is still required. Kerosene heaters also emit an odor that many people find unpleasant—some heaters worse than others.

Portable, unvented kerosene heaters generate significant heat, most outputting from 10,000 to 30,000 BTUs/hour. Surface temperatures can reach up to 500°F, so use caution, and keep children a safe distance away from them.

Below are additional safety recommendations for using kerosene heaters.[154]

1. Use heaters that have been tested and listed in accordance with Underwriters' Laboratories (UL) Standard 647. This compliance should be present on the nameplate.
2. Use 1-K kerosene fuel, which has about 1/8 the sulfur content of 2-K kerosene. The use of 2-K kerosene leads to increased sulfur dioxide emissions and frequent wick maintenance. The terms "water clear" or "clear white" are often used to describe 1-K kerosene. Never use diesel fuel, gasoline, jet fuel, or No. 1 fuel oil in a kerosene heater.
3. Keep heaters at least 36 inches from anything combustible.
4. Perform periodic maintenance, including cleaning the unit, trimming the wick, and inspecting for fuel leaks.
5. Ensure adequate ventilation. Follow the manufacturer's guidelines. If recommendations are not given, provide a minimum of one square inch of window opening for each 1,000 BTUs of the heater rating.
6. Don't operate kerosene heaters when everyone is asleep. A malfunction could lead to asphyxiation.
7. Allow the heater to cool a minimum of 15 minutes before refueling. If kerosene is spilled onto a hot heater it can ignite and cause a fire.

Also, refuel the heater outside in a well-ventilated area. Don't overfill it; leave a space at the top for fuel expansion.

8. Keep fuel outside of the main living area, stored in approved blue safety containers with "Kerosene" clearly marked on them.

9. Have smoke and CO detectors in the area being heated, as well as fire extinguishers nearby.

Manufacturers of kerosene heaters include Sengoku, KeroSun, Toyostove, and Corona.

Sengoku kerosene heater

OIL-FILLED RADIATORS

Oil-filled radiators are sealed metal canisters filled with heating oil. When the heater is plugged into AC electrical power, the oil heats up and warms the air around the radiator. Oil-filled radiators have many advantages: they are easy to use, provide convective heat in all directions, are equipped with thermostats, and do not emit carbon monoxide. They are the safest of all space heaters and are the only type recommended to leave running while asleep. With outputs ranging from 600 to 1,500 watts, radiators are best suited to heating small rooms. Heat output is much slower than from electric or kerosene heaters, but radiators stay warm long after power is turned off. Manufacturers include Pelonis, Honeywell, Lakewood, and DeLonghi.

Tips

Oil-filled radiators are considered safe enough to use even while sleeping.

DeLonghi oil-filled radiator

PORTABLE PROPANE HEATERS

Portable propane heaters are a relatively new addition to space heaters. They come in many different sizes. There are large, outdoor units that provide up to 400,000 BTUs/hour of heat and run off 100-lb tanks. These units are not meant to be used indoors, being better suited to sporting events, barns, or construction sites.

There are also smaller hand-carried heaters that use standard 1 lb or 20-lb propane tanks. They typically output between 4,000 and 18,000 BTUs/hour. Small units can be used indoors as long as ventilation rules are followed—check the owner's manuals. If no specification is given in the owner's manual, allow a minimum of one square inch of ventilation for every 1,000 BTUs of heat.

> **Tips**
>
> Portable propane heaters can be a quick "grab-n-go" heating system.

The small, portable propane heaters offer the unique advantage of providing heat on the go. You can quickly pack the heater and a few bottles of propane and take them on the road. However, be aware that 1 lb propane tanks may only last a few hours, so be sure to stock enough fuel. If you decide to use portable propane heaters, invest in a disposable tank adapter that allows you to refill 1 lb bottles from a 20-lb tank.

Mr. Heater propane heater

PREVENTING PIPES FROM FREEZING

Water expands when it freezes and, as any homeowner who lives in a cold climate can attest, this expansion can crack pipes. The most susceptible pipes are those directly exposed to the cold, including sprinkler and swimming pool supply lines, and your home's main water line. However, pipes in exterior walls or unheated areas of your house, such as in the basement, attic, garage, or crawlspace, are also prone to freezing.

Depending on the size of your backup heating system, it may or may not keep the temperature of your entire home above freezing. If it doesn't, then some of your water pipes may freeze. This is an important consideration since being without water makes a bad situation far worse.

Below are several recommendations to help prevent pipes from freezing.[167]

Before the cold arrives

- Drain sprinkler and pool supply lines.
- Remove, drain, and store hoses.
- Cut off the water supply to external hose spigots. If that is not possible, cover hose spigots with insulating covers.
- Insulate all exposed pipes using fiberglass, pipe sleeves, or heat tape.

When the cold arrives

- Keep your garage doors and crawlspace access panels closed to keep in any available heat.
- Open kitchen and bathroom cabinet doors to allow house heat to warm the pipes in the walls more efficiently.
- Let water trickle from several faucets, especially overnight.
- If you have heat available, keep the thermostat set no lower than 55°F.
- Consider turning off the water entering your house, and draining your house pipes until the worst of the cold has passed. To do this, cut off the main line (typically located in your yard somewhere). It may require a special tool that can be purchased at most home improvement and hardware stores. An alternative is to use the interior cutoff (sometimes in the garage or a nearby closet), but

the water may still freeze as it comes into your home. Once you cut off the flow of water, turn on all faucets until the water drains out of the interior house pipes.

After the cold passes

- If your pipes freeze but don't crack, turn on your faucets and leave them open giving the pipes a way to flush themselves.
- If you can access the frozen pipe, try thawing it with a hair dryer or small electric heater—don't use a propane torch.

COOKING

Cooking and heating are often related preparations because the two can frequently be used interchangeably—stoves can be used to heat the house; fireplaces can be used to cook food. At a minimum, you should try to select cooking and heating equipment that uses the same type of fuel. This helps alleviate the burden of multi-fuel storage and allows you to use your limited fuel for the more pressing of the two needs.

> **Tips**
> Consider using the same type of fuel for cooking and heating.

There are several ways to do small scale cooking in an emergency. They include using a fuel-burning stove, fireplace, barbeque grill, microwave oven, camp stove, or solar oven.

FUEL-BURNING STOVE

Courtesy of Reading Stove Company

Many coal, wood, and pellet stoves have flat surfaces that are intended for cooking. This design is a great combination since it takes care of two very important needs with one appliance. These stoves generally don't allow traditional baking, limiting you to stovetop cooking. The disadvantages include high initial setup cost, difficulty in regulating temperature, and the need to store large quantities of fuel. But even with their limitations and drawbacks, fuel-burning stoves are an excellent method of providing both heat and a means of cooking.

FIREPLACE/OPEN FIRE

If you are going to cook over a fire, you will need some way to support the food. In the case of a fireplace, it is easiest to install a swinging-arm crane that folds out and allows you to hang a pot directly over the fire. A heavy, fire-safe pot, such as a Dutch oven, is definitely recommended since fire can wreak havoc on regular cooking equipment.

Likewise, when cooking over an open fire, you can either cook using a cast iron support tripod or a folding camp grill that straddles the fire.

Texsport campfire tripod

BARBEQUE GRILL

Americans love a good barbeque. When the power fails, breaking out the grill can be an excellent way to cook. One particular benefit of the barbeque grill is that you are probably already proficient with it. A good grill master knows not only how to prepare meats, but also fresh vegetables, foil-wrapped dinners, and food in a heavy pot.

If you are not experienced at cooking over the grill, there are numerous cookbooks available to teach you the necessary skills. Depending on the model of grill, you will need either a supply of propane or natural gas, or charcoal briquettes and starter fuel. Barbeque grills should only be used outdoors because they release deadly carbon monoxide. Never use them inside your home or garage, even with the windows or doors open.

Weber grill

MICROWAVE OVEN

You may have never considered your microwave oven to be an emergency cooking source, but it does offer several advantages. Most units require only 800 to 1,000 watts of electricity, well within the range of a small generator or inverter—see *Chapter 7: Electrical Power.* Microwave ovens cook very quickly and consume far less power than a range or conventional oven. If you rely on a microwave oven to be your backup cooking source, become proficient ahead of time at preparing many different types of foods.

CAMP STOVES

Camp stoves are portable cooking units fueled by small propane canisters or tanks. Some stoves can burn a host of different fuel types, including white gas, kerosene, diesel, and jet fuel. Smaller stoves are little more than a single burner centered over a fuel canister. Larger units resemble a conventional stove top with multiple burners and fit the needs of a family better.

The main advantage of a camp stove is its portability—great for packing up and taking with you on the road. One thing to note about any portable stove that burns fuel is that it is not safe to use indoors. Also, store the compressed fuel canisters or tanks in a safe place that is cool and dry.

Masterbuilt and Coleman camp stoves

SOLAR OVENS

You might think that cooking with the sun is the stuff of survivalist lore. In reality, solar ovens that can cook a daily meal using nothing more than the sun do exist.

The advantages of solar ovens are easy to identify: they use free energy, don't release any poisonous gases, and can be used to cook just about anything that your conventional oven can. But alas, nothing is perfect. The disadvantages are equally significant. Solar ovens cook significantly slower than other stoves, hours of direct sunlight are required, and winds can cool the food or disturb the reflectors.

Slow cooking can be partially offset by cutting the food into bite-sized pieces, and careful placement of the oven can remedy wind disturbances. The need for sunny days, however, precludes the solar oven from serving as a reliable, backup cooking source.

Sun Ovens International solar cooker

DP PLAN EXAMPLE

Table 8-4 Sample DP Plan Entry

Need: Heating/Cooling			
Danger	Goals	Needs	Implementation
Disruption of heating fuel source, *or* Loss of heating unit *addressing both dangers with the same preparations*	Heat the main living area for a minimum of 14 days without primary heating system	A backup heater capable of heating 800 square feet with a minimum inside-to-outside temperature difference of 50°F	Operate a vented, wood-burning stove in the living room that provides a minimum of 28,000 BTUs/hour. Seal off unused upstairs rooms to consolidate heat to the main living area. Sleep in main living area. Stock 2 cords of wood at rear of property, covered with tarp.
	Cook food without electrical or gas services	A stove capable of cooking two hot meals each day	Use the wood-burning stove as a stovetop. Use the microwave oven with backup electrical power.

Quick Summary - Heating/Cooling

➤ Hypothermia is caused by allowing your body to get too cold. Likewise, hyperthermia is a result of your body getting too hot. Both conditions can be deadly.

➤ Keeping cool can be accomplished by limiting your activities, wetting yourself down, drinking cold liquids, and establishing some basic air circulation in your home.

➤ When stockpiling blankets, consider the worst case scenario. Extra blankets can also benefit less-prepared neighbors or family members.

➤ Heat can be lost in two ways: a disruption in your fuel source, or a failure of your heating unit. You must be prepared for either one.

➤ Carbon monoxide poisoning, fire, and burns are very real dangers associated with backup heaters. Take the necessary precautions including installing CO alarms and fire extinguishers, and training everyone on how to safely operate the heater.

➤ Several methods exist to estimate the size of your secondary heater. Use them to establish a rough estimate of your heating needs. Trial and error is often needed to get the size right.

➤ Many backup heating options exist, including fireplaces, masonry heaters, fuel-burning stoves, and space heaters.

➤ Coal, wood, and pellet stoves are the epitome of disaster preparedness because they reliably serve two vital needs.

➤ Backup cooking can be accomplished with a fuel-burning stove, fireplace, barbeque grill, microwave oven, camp stove, or solar oven.

Recommended Items - Heating/Cooling

❑ A method to stay warm while asleep
a. Heavy blankets and/or sleeping bags

❑ An emergency heat source
a. Fireplace with Texas Fire Frame, *or*
b. Masonry stove, *or*
c. Coal, wood, or pellet stove, *or*
d. Propane, kerosene, oil-filled, or electric space heater

❑ Fuel for emergency heater *and* backup stove
a. Coal, wood, pellets, *or*
b. Gas or diesel for a generator, *or*
c. Kerosene, propane, or natural gas

❑ Backup stove or oven
a. Coal, wood, or pellet stove, *or*
b. Fireplace with swinging-arm crane, *or*
c. Barbeque grill, *or*
d. Microwave oven, *or*
e. Camp stove

CHAPTER 9

AIR

Chapter 9 Notes

AIR

Challenge

News outlets issue an urgent warning that an accident has occurred at a nearby chemical plant. Dangerous levels of unspecified pollutants have been released into the air. Authorities advise residents to shelter in place immediately. How will you protect your family from this airborne threat?

There are numerous disaster scenarios that can threaten your air supply. These threats could come in different forms, from an industrial accident releasing sulfuric acid into the air, to a volcanic eruption spewing ash across the country, to a terrorist attack spraying chemical or biological agents over metropolitan cities. To effectively respond to these types of airborne threats, you must learn to shelter in place as well as understand the benefits and limitations of air purifiers, facemasks, and respirators.

Before even considering disaster response, however, it is important to recognize that the world is already in the midst of a global air calamity.

AIR POLLUTION

On average, each person breathes about 3,000 gallons of air per day.[168] It is fair to say that air is the ocean we breathe. When the air becomes polluted, it affects not only *your* health but also plants, animals, and fish.

> Air pollution is particularly dangerous to the 30 million Americans with asthma.

Air pollution doesn't just hinder natural processes; it also damages buildings and monuments, and interferes with aviation. Those with respiratory problems are particularly sensitive to air pollution, including the 30 million people in the United States with asthma.

In October 1948, a polluted cloud lingered over Donora, Pennsylvania, for five days, killing 20 people and sickening 6,000 others. During a similar incident in 1952, over 3,000 people died in London from a polluted fog so thick that people had to carry lanterns to walk through it. These events and others alerted governments to the dangers of air pollution. In 1963, the United States adopted the Clean Air Act, which now targets reducing 189 different toxic air pollutants.[169]

The Environmental Protection Agency (EPA) has set national air quality standards for six common air pollutants:

- carbon monoxide
- ozone
- lead
- nitrogen dioxide
- particulate matter
- sulfur dioxide

Deadly London smog of 1952

Each year, the EPA tracks levels of these air pollutants across the country. There is no denying the effectiveness of the Clean Air Act. Since 1980, the pollution levels for these contaminants have decreased as much as 92% (in the case of lead).[170] Trends for your particular community can be found at *www.epa.gov/airtrends/where*.

Even with emission regulations adopted around the world, serious air pollution hazards remain. Poor air conditions can be found in developing countries, such as China, Vietnam, and India, as well as industrialized nations, such as Russia and Japan. While it is true that, comparatively

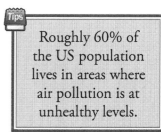

Roughly 60% of the US population lives in areas where air pollution is at unhealthy levels.

speaking, the United States is not as polluted as many other countries, its citizens still face very serious pollution-related health risks. Consider that the United States is currently ranked 17th in overall air quality, and roughly 60% of its citizens live in areas where air pollution is at unhealthy levels of either ozone or particulate contamination.[171]

As pointed out by the World Health Organization, even more sobering statistics exist if the entire globe is considered.[172,173]

- Air pollution causes approximately two million premature deaths every year. Most of these deaths are due to respiratory infections and chronic obstructive pulmonary disease (COPD).
- Indoor air pollution (primarily due to the burning of solid fuels) is estimated to be the 8th most important risk factor for disease, and responsible for 2.7% of all global diseases. In developing countries, this number rises to 3.7%, making it the most lethal killer after malnutrition, unsafe sex, and lack of clean water and sanitation.
- Globally, acute respiratory infections represent the single most significant cause of death in children under age five. Exposure to indoor air pollution more than doubles this risk.

Air pollution is both a local and a global problem—one that must be considered an ever present threat to every corner of the world. Just as with other potential threats, you need to better understand the air hazards that your community faces. Real-time air quality assessments and projected forecasts for the entire United States can be found at

Air pollution

www.airnow.gov. Likewise, a scorecard for your community's air, including a listing of the worst polluters, can be found at *www.stateoftheair.org.*

A COLLECTIVE SOLUTION

There is no short-term solution to air pollution. Remedies will take years, if not decades, to make a significant difference. Any sustainable solution to air pollution begins by recognizing that we all share one planet. What happens across the world ultimately affects you. If air pollution continues to worsen, humankind will collectively bring about a disaster of global proportions—one that may not be fixable. This prediction does not refer to global warming or other atmospheric issues still open to scientific and political debate but is based solely on current, measurable pollution levels and the deaths and disease caused by them.

Regardless of political views, it is impossible to deny that air pollution is a serious problem, one that no individual or single nation can remedy. Much of the solution lies in the hands of world leaders, including reducing the emissions of coal-burning power plants and responsibly managing deforestation. However, individuals must also play a critical role in ensuring cleaner air by adopting conservation-friendly actions (see Table 9-1), none of which should come as a surprise to anyone.[174,175]

Table 9-1 Individual Actions to Reduce Air Pollution

Conserve Resources
Turn off lights and appliances when not in use.
Install thermostats that shut off when you are away from home.
Replace incandescent with fluorescent bulbs.
Run the dishwasher only when full.
Wash clothes in cold or warm water.
Turn off the water when brushing your teeth.
Connect your outdoor lights to a timer or motion detector, or use solar lighting.
Buy Energy Star appliances (see *www.energystar.gov*).
Plant deciduous trees around your home to provide summer shade and winter warmth.
Lower your water heater's thermostat to 120°F.
Reduce the Impact of Your Car
Take shared transportation whenever possible, using car pools, buses, trains, and airplanes. Better yet, get some exercise by biking or walking.
Drive a fuel-efficient or low-emission vehicle. A useful tool to compare the environmental impact of different car models can be found at *www.epa.gov/greenvehicles*.
Don't leave your vehicle idling for more than 30 seconds (except when in traffic).
Keep your car tuned up and the tires properly inflated.
Reduce Waste
Recycle paper, plastic, glass bottles, cardboard, and cans.
Use rechargeable batteries.
Recycle cell phones, laptop computers, CRT monitors, and other electronics.

Minimize Your Pollution
Don't burn wood or trash unnecessarily.
Never smoke indoors.
If purchasing a wood, coal, or pellet stove, select one with reduced emissions, preferably EPA certified. Once in use, maintain wood stoves (and fireplaces) so that they burn efficiently.
Get Active
Influence your public transportation and local school systems to drive modern low-emission buses.
Get politically involved. Politicians will only take action if their voter base directs them to do so. Make it known that you are concerned about air quality and want steps taken to reduce emissions.

Tips

Clean air comes with a price in an industrialized society.

Realize that reducing air pollution (or at least stemming its growth) comes with a price, whether it be lost productivity, the inconvenience of recycling, sacrificing your gas guzzler, or increased production costs. In an industrial world, clean air isn't free, but the price of doing nothing and simply letting the corporate bottom line drive the rampant polluting of our planet will ultimately prove too high for everyone. Assume a responsible posture toward the planet and its citizens by doing your part, however small or large that may be.

INCIDENT-DRIVEN EVENTS

Air quality can also be affected by sudden, immediate disaster events, such as a volcanic eruption, chemical release, widespread fire, biochemical attack, or airborne pandemic. Protecting your family from these threats requires insulating them from the contaminated air as thoroughly as possible. Tools at your disposal include a well-sealed shelter, masks and respirators, and air filters.

UNDERGROUND SHELTERS WITH AIR FILTRATION

Underground shelters equipped with highly efficient air filtration systems clearly fall on the survivalist end of the preparedness spectrum. With that said, they can be designed to offer excellent protection from dangerous air hazards (as well as other threats). Many factors must be considered before constructing an underground shelter, including water level, air flow, temperature and humidity management, electricity, and access. If you are contemplating building an underground shelter, do your homework, consult professionals, and thoroughly plan *before* breaking ground. This topic is not covered in more detail here, because for most people, installing an underground bunker is prohibitively expensive and perhaps physically impossible (e.g., apartment dwellers). For additional information, consult Philip Hoag's, *No Such Thing as Doomsday*.

SHELTER IN PLACE

Even if a full-up underground bunker is out of the question, there are some basic measures you can take to create a mini-shelter in your own home. This process is typically referred to as sheltering in place, and is designed to protect against radiological, biological, and chemical threats. This creation of a contaminant-free area

> Tips
>
> Sheltering in place is designed to protect you from radiological, biological, and chemical threats.

is an addendum to the safe room discussed in *Chapter 5: Shelter,* but with additional consideration given to protecting against airborne threats. Sheltering in place is a short-term strategy, useful to insulate your family from an immediate threat that will diminish or pass quickly (i.e., within minutes, hours, or days). Specific recommendations are given below:[176,177]

1. Select an interior room in your home (ideally one without windows or exterior doors) to serve as your family's shelter. It should have a minimum of 10 square feet of space for each person, which will provide adequate air volume for at least five hours of sheltering. A room with an adjacent bathroom is often a good choice. You may wish to locate the safe room on the upper floor of your home because gases tend to settle.

2. Pre-stock your room with necessary emergency supplies, such as water, food (for you and your pets), a radio, television, first-aid kit, flashlights, hardwired telephone, medications, blankets, and material to effectively seal the room.

3. When directed by emergency management services, or when you feel that something poses an immediate threat to air quality, gather your family in the safe room. You may also wish to bring your pets into the room with you. At a minimum, bring your pets into your home from the outdoors.

4. Cut off all heating, air conditioning, and circulation systems. Close fireplace dampers. Close and lock all exterior doors and windows.

5. Cover all doors, windows, and air vents in the safe room with plastic sheeting (minimum thickness of 4 mils, where a mil is 1/1000 of an inch). Cut the plastic several inches wider than the openings being covered, and secure the sheeting with heavy-duty duct tape (minimum thickness of 10 mils). For expediency, pre-cut and label the plastic sheets, and have them ready in the room.

6. Seal any water pipes that enter the area using appropriate sealants.

Seal around doors, windows, air vents, and water pipes

Shelter in place

7. Use a portable HEPA air filter to help purify the air in the safe room. When properly sized to the room, HEPA filters have been shown to be effective in removing vapor contaminants and some poisonous gases.[102]

8. If appropriate to the threat, put on protective hoods or respirators. Although not as effective, you can also use inexpensive N95 disposable masks for limited protection. Disposable biochemical protection suits, such as Tyvek F, can also be worn to protect against skin contamination.

9. Monitor the radio or television for updates. Officials may call for evacuation, so be ready to move.

UNDERSTANDING RADIATION

Radiation is broadly classified as either low-energy, non-ionizing waves or high-energy, ionizing waves. Low-energy waves include visible light, radio waves, and microwaves. Non-ionizing waves of this type are generally not harmful to humans except in very high doses. High-energy waves include alpha, beta, gamma, and x-rays. Gamma and x-rays are particularly dangerous because they are able to travel through the air and disrupt the atomic structure of living creatures. This atomic disruption can lead to bleeding, cancer, mutation, and death. Table 9-2 compares the different types of radiation.

Radiation—a deadly threat

Table 9-2 Comparing Radiation Types[178,179]

Radiation Type	Examples	Range	Penetration	Shielding	Danger	Detectable
Low-energy, non-ionizing	Visible light Radio waves Microwaves	Long	Shallow	Easily blocked	None unless in very high doses	Naked eye, test equipment, or radio receivers
High-energy, ionizing	Alpha	Short (inches)	Generally unable to penetrate skin	Easily blocked	Harmful if swallowed or inhaled	Geiger-Mueller counters, scintillation counters, survey meters, dosimeters, film badges
	Beta	Medium (feet)	Can penetrate human skin to the germinal layer	Clothing offers some protection	Skin injury	
	Gamma, X-ray	Long	Can penetrate clothing and the human body	Dense materials (e.g., lead) required to block	Cellular damage, bleeding, cancer, and death	

RADIOACTIVE THREATS

As touched upon in *Chapter 5: Shelter,* radiation threats come in two different forms: radioactive contamination and radiation exposure. Radioactive contamination occurs when radioactive materials are released into the environment. This can be the result of a nuclear power plant accident, a medical or industrial device malfunction, or an intentional act of terrorism. When the contaminants are inhaled, ingested, or come into contact with your skin, they can cause tissue and organ damage, and ultimately death.

Radiation exposure occurs when you are exposed to high-energy, ionizing waves. This exposure causes atomic disruption, leading to sickness and death. The severity of illness depends on the exposure level and type of radiation. The immediate and latent biological effects of acute radiation exposure are summarized in Table 9-3. The latent effects are cumulative, meaning that all the lower-level effects are also suffered.

Radiation burns on Japanese woman following atomic bombing, 1945

Table 9-3 Biological Effects of Acute, Total Body Irradiation without Treatment[179,180,181,182]

Exposure (Rem)	Time to Onset, Duration	Immediate Effects	Time to Latent Effects	Latent Effects (Cumulative)	Lethality after 30 days
5-50	-	No detectable injury or symptoms	-	None	0%
50-100	3-6 hrs, up to 1 day	Headache, nausea, fatigue, vomiting, diarrhea (intensity and frequency increases with higher exposure levels)	-	Temporary male sterility possible	0%
100-200	3-6 hrs, up to 1 day		10-14 days	Illness, fatigue, premature childbirth possible	0-10%
200-300	1-6 hrs, up to 2 days		7-14 days	Loss of hair, permanent female sterility possible	10-35%
300-400	1-6 hrs, up to 2 days		7-14 days	Bleeding in mouth, under skin, and in kidneys	35-50%
400-600	½-2 hrs, up to 2 days		7-14 days	Same as 300-400, with greater intensity	50-90%
600-1,000	15-30 minutes, up to 2 days		5-10 days	Damage to bone marrow and intestinal tissue	Near 100%
>1,000	5-30 minutes		Hours to days	Same as 600-1000	100%

It is important to understand the difference between radioactive contamination and exposure because the preparations and subsequent actions are quite different. In the case of radiation exposure, put as much distance between you and the source of radiation as possible—distance means safety because the energy of the waves decreases rapidly with space and time. If evacuation is not possible, or if the radiation levels are too high to evacuate safely, retreat to a well-shielded location. This area could be an underground storm shelter, a fallout shelter at the local library, mall or subway, or even a cave in nearby mountains. The idea is to put as much solid material (e.g., dirt, concrete, metal, water) as possible between you and the radiating source. If you suspect that you have been exposed, contact local emergency management services for medical treatment.

In the case of radioactive contamination, remove your clothing and put it into a plastic bag away from other people. Next, wash yourself thoroughly with soap and warm water, and contact local authorities for decontamination and medical treatment.[183] The effects of internal radioactive contamination (i.e., contamination that is ingested or inhaled) may be reduced by taking medicines. The two most well-known medicines are potassium iodide and Prussian blue.

The blood, urine, and sweat of a contaminated person can be radioactive.

POTASSIUM IODIDE[184]

Potassium iodide (KI) is a salt of stable iodine used by your body to produce thyroid hormones. In the event of a radiological or nuclear event, radioactive iodine may be released into the air, food, or water. If you ingest or inhale this iodine, it will be quickly absorbed by your thyroid gland. This can injure your thyroid, leading to cancer and death. If you take potassium iodide in advance, it essentially fills your thyroid, preventing the absorption of radioactive iodine and potentially saving your life. The effectiveness of potassium iodide depends upon three things: (1) how much time has passed between the contamination of radioactive iodine and the taking of KI, (2) how fast the KI is absorbed into your blood, and (3) the total amount of radioactive iodine to which you are exposed.

> **Tips**
>
> Potassium iodide is *only* effective at protecting against internal radioactive iodine contamination.

It is also important to understand what KI cannot do. Potassium iodide only protects the thyroid against ingested or inhaled radioactive iodine. It will not protect against other radioactive materials such as those released by a "dirty bomb"; neither will it protect any part of the body except the thyroid. It will also not protect against the effects of radiation exposure.

The thyroid glands of unborn fetuses, infants, and young children are particularly susceptible to radioactive iodine, making KI pre-treatment critical. Potassium iodide will protect the thyroid for 24 hours, so depending on the duration of the threat, repeat dosing may be required. Potassium iodide comes in both tablet (65 mg and 130 mg) and liquid (65 mg per mL) forms. These concentrations align well with the FDA's recommended dosages.

> **Tips**
>
> **Recommended KI Dosing[189]**
>
> | | |
> |---|---|
> | Birth to 1 month: | 16 mg |
> | 1 month to 3 years: | 32 mg |
> | 3 years to 18 years: | 65 mg |
> | 18+ years or >150 lbs: | 130 mg |

Potassium iodide is generally considered very safe but can be harmful to people with certain medical conditions, so consult your doctor before taking KI. A prescription is not required to purchase KI; your pharmacist can dispense it directly to you. It is also widely available on the internet. The product iOSAT is recommended since it is the only full-strength, FDA-approved KI tablet for radiation blocking legally sold in the United States. It is best to purchase iOSAT directly from the manufacturer at *www.anbex.com* to guarantee optimal freshness. The only FDA-approved KI liquid is ThyroShield, and is especially useful for administering to young children (see *www.thyroshield.com*). Potassium iodide is inexpensive and has a shelf life of at least five to seven years, making it a low-cost, yet potentially life-saving preparation.

iOSAT KI tablets

PRUSSIAN BLUE[185]

Prussian blue is an FDA-approved drug used to treat internal contamination caused by radioactive cesium-137 or thallium. It is sold under the name Radiogardase, and has been available since 2003. Along with potassium iodide, Prussian blue is currently stockpiled by the United States government for emergency response.

Unlike potassium iodide, which blocks the absorption of a specific contaminant, Prussian blue helps to speed your body's excretion of radioactive cesium and thallium. It does not protect against radioactive iodine likely to be released from a nuclear power plant. However, it may offer some protection against a "dirty bomb" from which radioactive cesium has the potential to be released. Prussian blue is available only with a doctor's prescription. It is not taken as a preventive to radioactive contamination but rather as a treatment after poisoning has occurred. Table 9-4 provides a brief comparison between KI and Prussian blue.

Table 9-4 Comparing KI and Prussian Blue

	Potassium Iodide	Prussian Blue
Effective Against	Internal contamination from radioactive iodine	Internal contamination from cesium and thallium
Possible Source	Nuclear power plants	Dirty bomb
Taken	As a preventive before contamination	As a treatment after contamination
Prescription	Not required	Required

NUKALERT

As was previously discussed in *Chapter 5: Shelter,* a relatively inexpensive radiation detector that fits on your keychain is offered from NukAlert. It claims to reliably detect radiation levels from 100 milliRems per hour to more than 50 Rems per hour and can operate for 10 full years without a battery replacement. The detector remains active 24 hours a day, and sounds different alarms depending on the exposure level.[122] If you live in an area where nuclear contamination is a viable threat, the NukAlert detector is a reasonable precaution capable of providing your family with the early warning vital to evacuation or other preparatory steps.

AIR PURIFIERS

You should consider using a portable high-efficiency particulate air (HEPA) purifier in your safe room. HEPA filters were designed as part of the Manhattan Project to prevent the spread of airborne radioactive particles, and as such are capable of removing a significant number of very small airborne contaminants. HEPA filters operate using a combination of interception, impaction, and diffusion. Even for the most penetrating particle sizes (MPPS), they remove with an efficiency of at least 99.97%.[123,186] HEPA purifiers are routinely used in hospitals to remove bacteria and viruses from the air. They have also been shown to be effective in removing biological and radiological contaminants.[187] HEPA filters alone do not remove chemicals, gases, or odors, but are typically combined with carbon filters to remove such things as cigarette smoke and pet odors.

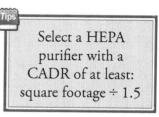

> **Tips**
> Select a HEPA purifier with a CADR of at least: square footage ÷ 1.5

The amount of air flow that a portable HEPA purifier provides is rated by its clean air delivery rate (CADR). The higher the CADR, the more air flow it provides— meaning it cycles the room air more frequently. The CADR value is expressed in cubic-feet-volume per minute. A CADR of 250 indicates that the filter cycles 250 cubic feet of air per minute. A rule of thumb is to size your unit so that the CADR multiplied by 1.5 is equal to or greater than the square footage of the room. For example, a purifier with a CADR of 250 would be effective filtering rooms up to 375 square feet in size. It is recommended that you purchase a purifier with a lifetime HEPA filter and a replaceable carbon pre-filter to significantly lower your ownership costs.

Larger HEPA filters can also be equipped onto your home's primary air circulation system. However, since your entire home is not well sealed, the protection from sudden high-levels of contamination will be limited. Whole-house filters are, however, excellent at reducing allergens in the home, such as pollen, pet dander, dust mites, and mold.

Honeywell HEPA filter

FACEMASKS/RESPIRATORS

Facemasks and respirators have proven to be effective at preventing respiratory illnesses in dangerous workplaces for many years. The term *facemask* usually refers to disposable cloth masks approved by the Food and Drug Administration for use as medical devices. They typically tie around the head and may be loose cloth or have a pre-molded shape. Facemasks are designed to provide limited protection from blood and body fluids. They are, however, not designed to protect against small airborne particles or gases. Facemasks should be used only once and then discarded.

The term *respirator* refers to more effective protective masks that are certified by the National Institute for Occupational Safety and Health

(NIOSH). Respirators are specifically designed to protect from chemical, biological, radiological, or nuclear airborne contaminants. As such, respirators must fit more snugly to the face than facemasks, making prolonged breathing through them more arduous (unless they have forced air systems). Many respirators cannot be used by people with beards or thick mustaches because facial hair prevents adequate sealing. Achieving the greatest protection requires training regarding proper fit and use.[188]

There are numerous types of respirators, each with its own limitations and capabilities. They range from single-use, disposable masks to reusable models with replaceable cartridges. Some masks cover the entire face, while others cover only the nose and mouth. Many masks allow you to speak or drink while wearing them, but some require that you keep a mouthpiece clenched between your teeth. The key points are to: select a respirator that protects from the right contaminants; ensure that it fits properly, and keep it ready and in working order.

Respiratory equipment is generally divided into five categories: particulate filtering facepiece respirators, negative pressure air-purifying respirators (APRs), powered air-purifying respirators (PAPRs), self-contained atmosphere-supplying respirators, and escape respirators.

PARTICULATE FILTERING FACEPIECE RESPIRATORS

Particulate filtering facepiece respirators use wool, plastic, glass, or other materials to capture contaminants from the air that pass through the filter. These budget respirators are worn in a manner similar to facemasks, although designed to fit more snugly and filter more thoroughly. The filters cannot be cleaned and should be discarded after each exposure. They are the least expensive type of respirator but also the least effective. Common types of particulate filters are the N95 (removes 95% of airborne particles), N99 (removes 99% of airborne particles), and N100 (removes 99.97% of airborne particles). There are also oil-resistant equivalent models (e.g., P95, P100). A listing of NIOSH-approved particulate filtering facepiece respirators can be found online at the CDC website.[189]

Particulate filtering facepiece respirators are low-cost safety devices that provide limited protection from airborne contaminants, such as during a flu pandemic. They are only designed to protect against particles, not

Facemask and particulate filtering facepiece respirators

gases or vapors. For people who wish to take a modest approach to protecting against airborne threats, these are likely the respirators of choice. Smaller sizes are also available to fit children.

> Particulate filtering respirators come in both adult and child sizes.

Tests conducted by the CDC showed that achieving a tight fit is critical for optimal mask effectiveness.[190]

AIR-PURIFYING RESPIRATORS (APRS)/A.K.A., "GAS MASKS" [191]

Air-purifying respirators (APRs) provide a much higher level of protection by removing air contaminants through filtering, adsorbing, absorbing, or chemical reaction. Most are negative pressure devices, requiring the wearer to force air through the filtration system by breathing. Some units are positive pressure systems, circulating forced air with battery-powered electric blowers.

APRs can be certified by the NIOSH to protect against chemical, biological, radiological, and nuclear (CBRN) contaminants. All CBRN-certified respirators provide a specified minimum level of protection against a host of dangerous atmospheres, including biological aerosols and chemical gases. They are rated by their protection duration (e.g., Cap 1 = 15 min, Cap 2 = 30 min, Cap 3 = 45 min). CBRN respirators are targeted primarily to emergency first responders but can be purchased by anyone.

Drager APR

POWERED AIR-PURIFYING RESPIRATORS

3M PAPR

A powered air-purifying respirator (PAPR) uses an electric blower to circulate filtered, ambient air into the facepiece. PAPR systems consist of a motor blower unit with filter cartridge, headpiece, battery, and breathing tube. The positive air pressure not only relieves the user from having to force air in and out of the filter, but it also creates a positive pressure in the face mask, preventing inward leaking.

SELF-CONTAINED ATMOSPHERE-SUPPLYING RESPIRATORS

Self-contained atmosphere-supplying respirators provide clean air from an uncontaminated source rather than filtering contaminants from the environment. There are three types: self-contained breathing apparatus (SCBA) devices (air is provided by a tank worn on the user's back), supplied air respirators (SARs) (air is provided by a tether), and closed-circuit SCBA systems known as "rebreathers" (the user's own air is scrubbed, oxygen enriched, and recycled). Firefighters often use SCBAs in oxygen-deficient conditions.

Avon Protection SCBA

A comparison of many APRs can be found in the Department of Homeland Security's *Guide for the Selection of Personal Protective Equipment for Emergency Responders*.[191] If you decide to purchase a respirator, it is highly recommended that you first consult this document.

ESCAPE RESPIRATORS

Escape respirators are relatively low-cost emergency devices used for rapid evacuation of respiratory hazard areas, such as burning buildings or contaminated subway tunnels. These devices are grouped into two categories: air-purifying escape respirators (APERs) and self-contained escape respirators. APERs are negative pressure systems that use filter canisters to remove contaminants, whereas self-contained escape respirators have an attached air tank. Escape respirators are designed to be used for a short duration, perhaps 5

Avon Protection escape respirator

to 60 minutes. Both types seal around the neck and are capable of providing the wearer with respiratory protection from CBRN threats.

For most people, the purchase of an air-purifying respirator cannot be easily justified. However, escape respirators may make sense if you work in a high-rise building or travel on the subway each day. But for most people, a simple particulate filtering respirator (e.g., N95) is sufficient to provide a modest level of protection from airborne contaminants. As with every aspect of disaster preparation, the decision is ultimately yours to make. Assess your risk and take the appropriate actions.

Escape respirators are particularly useful for people working in high-rise buildings or traveling on subways.

If you decide that a respirator is needed, consider the following list of questions when making your selection.[192]

1. What contaminants does the escape hood protect against?
2. Is there more than one size available? How do you ensure that the gas mask or escape hood will fit properly?
3. What type of training do you need to use the respirator?

4. Is data available to show that the escape hood has been tested against various contaminants, such as biological agents, chemical warfare agents, toxic industrial chemicals, and radioactive dust particles?

5. Who performed the testing? What were the tested levels and test durations? Are they representative of your concerns?

6. Is the escape hood certified by an independent laboratory or government agency?

7. Are there any special maintenance or storage requirements? What is the shelf life?

8. Will you be able to talk or drink while wearing the respirator?

9. Does the hood restrict vision or head movement in any way?

10. How would you carry the device to where it might be needed? In the trunk of your car? In your purse or brief case? Or would it be left in a drawer at work?

11. Is a training respirator available from the vendor to practice with?

12. Can you use the respirator more than once? Does it have replaceable filter cartridges? If so, where are they purchased?

Respirators are just one part of a complete ensemble of personal protective equipment needed to adequately protect you from biological or chemical threats. To be fully protected, clothing, gloves, and boots should also be considered. For a detailed discussion of CBRN protective clothing and respirators, refer to the *Guide for the Selection of Personal Protective Equipment for Emergency Responders*.[191]

DP PLAN EXAMPLE

Table 9-5 Sample DP Plan Entry

Need: Air			
Danger	Goals	Needs	Implementation
Air pollution	Reduce the air pollution levels in our community	Steps to conserve resources and reduce emissions	Follow Individual Action pollution checklist.
		A way to motivate public officials	Write local and national representatives to express support for Clean Air Act legislation.
Contamination	Protect family from airborne hazards	An area that can be sealed	Use the large bedroom closet for sheltering in place. Stock it with emergency supplies.
			Pre-cut and label plastic to cover windows and doors.
		Air purification devices	Use a 250 CADR HEPA air filter in the safe room.
			Equip everyone with appropriate fitting N95 respirators.
	Detect and respond to high levels of radiation	A portable device that warns of radiation threats	Keep a NukAlert on keychain.
		Medicine that mitigates radiation poisoning	Stock iOSAT KI tablets and administer if radiation threat is detected.

Quick Summary - Air

➢ Air pollution is a serious problem facing our world. Over 60% of the United States population lives in areas where air pollution reaches unhealthy levels.

➢ In the long term, a perhaps irreversible disaster is looming if pollution is not brought under control. Everyone needs to take steps to improve the situation.

➢ Numerous disasters can affect air quality, including a volcanic eruption, chemical release, widespread fire, biological attack, nuclear event, or airborne pandemic.

➢ Air hazards can be mitigated by sheltering in place, and through the use of air purification devices, such as HEPA filters and respirators.

➢ Sheltering in place involves sealing an internal room of your house or workplace using heavy plastic sheeting and duct tape.

➢ HEPA air purifiers can remove very small contaminants from the air, including radiological and biological.

➢ Radioactive contamination occurs when you come into physical contact with radioactive materials. This can be external, such as on the skin, or internal (inhaled or ingested). Potassium iodide is an effective preventive measure against thyroid damage caused by radioactive iodine.

➢ Particulate filtering facepiece respirators (e.g., N95, N99) are low-cost protective devices that offer limited protection from airborne contaminants.

➢ Advanced respiratory equipment includes air-purifying respirators (APRs), powered air-purifying respirators (PAPRs), and self-contained atmosphere-supplying respirators. Due to cost, these devices may not be practical for many families.

➢ Escape respirators are lightweight breathing devices to escape a burning building or CBRN-contaminated area.

Recommended Items - Air

❑ Shelter in place
  a. Roll of 4 mil thick plastic sheeting
  b. Roll of 10 mil thick duct tape
  c. Portable HEPA air filter

❑ Protection from radioactive contamination
  a. iOSAT potassium iodide pills or ThyroidShield liquid
  b. Optional: NukAlert radiation detector
  c. Optional: Dosimeter

❑ Individual air filtration
  a. Particulate filtering facepiece respirators (e.g., N95) for each family member, *or*
  b. Air-purifying respirators
  c. Optional: Escape respirators

CHAPTER 10
SLEEP

CHAPTER 10

SLEEP

Challenge

The stock market is crashing. Worrying over what might happen to your family's nest egg is keeping you awake at night. The lack of sleep is affecting you both physically and emotionally. What can you do to get more sleep?

Sleep is one of life's simple pleasures that isn't fully appreciated until you don't get enough of it. Up to 70 million Americans suffer from some form of insomnia.[193] It affects people regardless of status or profession, from entertainer (e.g., Michael Jackson) to political leader (e.g., Benjamin Franklin) to scientist (e.g., Thomas Edison).

During times of crisis, even otherwise sound sleepers can experience difficulties. People react to stress in varying ways. For many, stress can keep them awake at night worrying. For others, sleep comes quickly as a means of escaping from the pressures and decision making. It is no wonder that when your roof has a large tree poking through it, your car is floating in rising waters, or your children are coughing from the latest flu outbreak, sleeping may be unusually difficult. However, it is during these times of great stress that your body and mind need sleep the most.

There is strong evidence to support that getting enough sleep is important not only to your performance of routine tasks, such as driving or working, but also to your health. Heart disease, diabetes, and obesity have all been linked to lack of sleep.[194] Getting an adequate amount of quality sleep is akin to exercising and eating a balanced diet—they all lead to a longer, healthier life.

Tips

Lack of sleep can be just as deadly as food or water shortages.

This chapter is unique in that there's nothing to buy, no skill to learn, no community or government resources to draw upon. Sleep is a natural part of life, one of the few things not explicitly taught to humans. That is not to suggest that sleep shouldn't be given consideration in your preparations. Lack of sleep will affect you emotionally, physically, and mentally, and those effects can lead to lapses in judgement that could prove just as deadly as shortages of food or water.

RECOMMENDATIONS

There are countless reasons for having difficulty sleeping, from anxiety, to bodily pain, to uncomfortable sleeping conditions. Unless you are a master yogi, trying to force yourself into sleep usually only exacerbates the problem. The truth is that sleep is not something you can control; the sooner you accept that fact, the better. The most you can do is work to establish a comfortable environment that helps you to relax and take your mind off your troubles.

Below is list of recommendations shown to help people get a good night's sleep. Some of these suggestions are from reputable insomnia experts, while others are mere personal observations. Certainly not all of them apply to every situation, but together they present an overview of important considerations to overcoming sleeping difficulties.

- Establish a sleep schedule. Go to bed and wake up at the same time each day—even on the weekends.
- Don't drink alcohol or caffeine within three hours of bedtime.
- Invest in a comfortable bed and pillow.
- Keep the temperature in your bedroom comfortable; experts recommend 65° to 72°F.
- Put socks on your feet to keep them warm (if necessary).
- Turn off the TV or computer at least one hour before bedtime.

- Read a good book to get your mind on something else.
- Limit the size of any late night snack. Warm milk or caffeine-free tea may be better choices.
- Take a warm bath to help you relax.
- Exercise routinely—but not within two hours of bedtime.
- Enjoy sex with your partner.
- Budget more than enough time to sleep, relieving the feeling that you must fall asleep quickly.
- Manage stress by making a checklist of worries and the actions you will take to resolve them.
- Experiment with a sound machine. Most devices generate white noise, but some will also emit natural sounds, such as a trickling stream, rainfall, or chirping birds.
- If you are experiencing pain or sore muscles, consider taking an over-the-counter pain reliever. As a longer term solution, try stretching or yoga.
- If necessary, consult your physician for sleep aids, such as Ambien and Lunesta. Many people feel that drug-assisted sleep is not as restful as natural sleep, but medicines may be helpful when nothing else seems to work. Be aware that sleep aids may have side effects, including headaches, diarrhea, and dizziness, and can limit your sleep to perhaps only 4 to 6 hours.

For more information on insomnia and its treatments, review the many sleep-related articles and resources at *www.webmd.com* and *www.health.com*.

The good news is that if you get tired enough, you *will* sleep. There are no exceptions to this rule—save for the unfortunate people who suffer from a deadly hereditary disease, familial insomnia. The best thing you can do to facilitate healthy sleep is to give yourself a comfortable environment and adequate time to rest.

CHILDREN

Children are particularly susceptible to the effects of insufficient sleep. They need sleep not only to function, but also to grow and develop. It affects their mood, view of the world around them, alertness, social behavior, and learning ability. If you have children, you can surely testify

Ensuring that your children get adequate quality sleep will help your family to run smoother in times of crisis.

to this if you consider how difficult your children become when they haven't had adequate rest.

Perhaps this topic relates only peripherally to disaster preparedness, but consider how much more difficult a challenging situation can become if your children are bickering, misbehaving, and pushing all your buttons. Keeping your children well rested helps your entire family to function smoother and thus be better prepared for whatever challenges any given day might bring.

Children need significantly more sleep than adults. Table 10-1 lists the recommended number of hours of sleep required for children of different ages.[195,196] Each child is different, some requiring less than the

Children need adequate, restful sleep

Table 10-1 Hours of Sleep Needed by Age

Age	Sleep / Night (hours)
1-4 weeks	15½ to 16½
1-4 months	14½ to 15½
4-12 months	14 to 15
1-3 years	12 to 14
3-6 years	10¾ to 12
7-12 years	10 to 11
12-18 years	8¼ to 9½
19+	7-8

recommended amount, some more. One of the most important things you can do for your children is to provide them with adequate sleep.

Not only is it important to ensure that children sleep sufficient hours, but also that they have quality, uninterrupted sleep. This permits their developing brains to go through the various sleep cycles. Consider a few observations regarding the correlation of sleep quality and child behavior.[197]

- Children should not be expected to outgrow sleeping problems. Sleeping issues must be resolved before they become a part of a child's routine.
- Children who get adequate sleep have longer attention spans.
- Babies and toddlers who sleep more hours are less fitful and socially demanding.
- Even small sleep deficits can accrue and lead to long-term effects on the brain. Children with higher IQs have been shown to sleep longer.
- Children suffering from attention deficit problems, such as ADHD, can benefit dramatically from improved sleep. In fact, many learning and behavioral problems are improved with healthy sleeping.

TOGETHERNESS

During a crisis, you may find that having the entire family sleep together in the same room helps everyone to sleep better. Children in particular often benefit because they feel a heightened sense of security when close to their parents and siblings. With parents, this tactic tends to be more hit and miss. Some parents feel relief when close to their children; others may feel anxiety over the lack of privacy. Sleeping in close proximity also helps to keep your family members warm, which can be important in many situations.

Personal aside: I sleep better when I know that my children are nearby and safe. On the other hand, if I am under great stress, I sometimes have trouble sleeping in the same bed as my wife. I have no logical explanation for this, only the observation.

Reducing anxiety by sleeping in the same room

HOW LONG CAN YOU GO?

When everything is falling apart, it is easy to push too hard, telling yourself that you will sleep later. However, not getting the necessary rest can lead to irrational decision-making, perhaps with deadly consequences. A good night's sleep not only maintains your mental acuity, but also refreshes your body, preparing you for the physical challenges ahead. With that said, there are times when you may be forced to interrupt your regular sleep schedule, such as during an emergency evacuation or a particularly dangerous weather event that requires vigilant monitoring.

You may wonder how long a person can go without sleep. In December of 1963, Randy Gardner, a 17-year-old Californian boy, went without sleep for a record 11 days. His 264 hours of being awake is the longest verified period anyone has ever voluntarily gone without sleep.[198] Gardner suffered from mood swings, memory lapses, coordination difficulties, slurred speech, and hallucinations. He did not take stimulants, but people were constantly interacting with him.

Without constant interaction, staying awake for more than 36 hours is difficult, and more than 48 hours is nearly impossible. When you become very tired, your mind will force sleep on you in tiny bursts, some of which you may not even be aware. These

> **Tips**
> Staying awake for more than 48 hours is nearly impossible for most people.

sleep bursts can occur with your eyes open or closed. Testing on rats has proven that if you were forced to remain awake for a long period of time, it would kill you in less time than you would starve to death.

There are medications, such as modafinil, to help combat excessive daytime sleepiness often associated with obstructive sleep apnea or other sleep disorders. These drugs have also been used by militaries around the world to help soldiers remain alert for long periods of time. It is not difficult to imagine situations where you might need to stay alert for a long time, perhaps during an evacuation or a period of intense danger. However, stimulants of any kind should always be considered a last resort because they have side effects and may become physically addictive. Usually working with family members to sleep in shifts is a more judicious choice. With that said, your choices may be more limited when alone.

DP PLAN EXAMPLE

Table 10-2 Sample DP Plan Entry

Need: Sleep			
Danger	Goals	Needs	Implementation
Insomnia	Get adequate sleep, especially during stressful times	7-8 hours sleep per night for adults; 10-11 hours for three children	Budget one hour more than needed for sleep. Monitor the children for any signs of inadequate sleep. Don't exercise within three hours of bedtime. Don't drink any coffee or alcohol after supper. Make a to do list of any pressing items, with plan of action noted. Take ibuprofen at bedtime if suffering from aches or pain.
Sleepiness	Stay alert in the presence of any threat	Have someone remain alert during a lengthy evacuation or extended threat	When dangers are threatening, establish a sleeping schedule with wife or other DP network members.

Quick Summary - Sleep

➢ People of every class and profession suffer from insomnia.

➢ Sleep is important not only to remain mentally alert, but also to maintain good health. Many diseases have been connected to inadequate sleep, including diabetes, heart disease, and obesity.

➢ Sleep is not something you can control. Rather, you should establish a comfortable environment and consistent bedtime routine.

➢ Consider taking pain relievers to help with aches and pains, or seeing your doctor about sleep aids if absolutely necessary.

➢ Children need much more sleep than adults. Inadequate or poor quality sleep can cause children to develop slowly, have shorter attention spans, feel irritated, and experience behavioral problems. Their misbehavior can make a bad situation much more stressful.

➢ When a situation is particularly threatening, consider sleeping with the entire family in one room. Consolidating helps to keep everyone warm, and can relieve worry and stress—especially in young children.

➢ Going without sleep for more than 36 hours is very difficult and may eventually lead to mood swings, poor decision making, loss of coordination, and even hallucinations. Resist the temptation to push yourself too hard.

➢ Even when staying alert for a long period of time is required, sleeping in shifts is preferred to using stimulants.

Recommended Items - Sleep

❑ An environment that facilitates sleep
   a. A comfortable bed, pillow, and sheets
   b. Adequate temperature control of the room

❑ Medicine
   a. Optional: Pain killers (e.g., ibuprofen, acetaminophen)
   b. Optional: Sleep aids (e.g., Ambien, Lunesta)

CHAPTER 11
MEDICAL / FIRST AID

Chapter 11 Notes

CHAPTER 11

MEDICAL / FIRST AID

Challenge

Your spouse awakens you during the night complaining of chest pain and difficulty breathing. Should you administer aspirin, and if so, how much? Should you have him/her sit down, lie down, or stand up? Should you call emergency services or rush your spouse to the hospital? If he/she suddenly collapses and stops breathing, do you know how to correctly perform CPR?

Medical concerns are important every day, but even more so during times of disaster because services and supplies may be limited. Hospitals may quickly become overloaded, or worse yet, inaccessible. Doctors and pharmacists may be compelled to close their practices in order to handle their own family emergencies. This shortage of staff and supplies could force your family to rely on its own first aid abilities and existing stockpile of medicines.

MEDICINE

If anyone in your family has a serious existing medical condition, maintaining a stockpile of medicine may be critical to their survival. When a disaster occurs, you may be unable to gain timely access to a doctor or pharmacist, meaning that whatever supplies you have on hand must last until the situation improves. A few of the many possible concerns include insulin for diabetics, respiratory inhalers for asthmatics, opioids for those suffering chronic pain, and nitroglycerin for people with heart conditions.

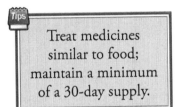

Treat medicines similar to food; maintain a minimum of a 30-day supply.

A reasonable approach to preparing is to handle medications in a manner similar to food—stockpiling a minimum of a 30-day supply. If your customary prescriptions don't support this, explain your preparedness rationale to your doctor to receive the additional prescriptions. Just as with food, rotate the newest medicine to the back, and use that which is oldest. If a crisis causes you to experience a shortage of medicine, make every effort to inform your doctor and family of your predicament *before* the issue becomes serious.

MEDICAL EMERGENCIES

Medical emergencies are to be expected when times are especially challenging. This is in part due to the immediate dangers posed by the threats, but also from having to adapt to difficult living conditions. Connecting a generator, foraging for water, cooking with portable stoves, and shoring up damaged shelters are all examples of activities that introduce additional risk of injury.

To better handle medical emergencies, take the following preparations.

- Teach everyone in the family how to call for emergency medical assistance (see *How to Call for Help*). This includes all children old enough to hold and dial a phone.
- Ensure that all adults in the household learn and practice basic first aid.

- Compile well-stocked first aid kits for your home and automobiles.
- Share information about any serious, existing medical conditions with family and friends.
- Memorize driving directions to at least two emergency medical facilities.
- Investigate which hospitals offer the best services and equipment. For example, some hospitals have specialized cardiac care centers, improving a heart patient's chances for survival.

HOW TO CALL FOR HELP

The United States uses 911 as its three-digit emergency number. This number can be called without charge from any landline, payphone, or cell phone (active or not). Once received, an operator or dispatcher requests that

EMERGENCY
DIAL 911

the caller specify the nature of the call: police, fire, or medical services. In the case of an operator, the call is then forwarded to the correct emergency service center. A dispatcher is specially trained to dispatch emergency services as well as provide urgent lifesaving advice.

Note that 911 is not a universal emergency number outside the United States. Every country has one or more of its own emergency phone numbers. For example, much of Europe uses 112.

When placing an emergency call, it is better to use a conventional landline rather than a cell phone. A landline enables the emergency operator to immediately identify your location. Location determination is slower and less precise when you call from a mobile phone.

Calling 911 from a landline helps the dispatcher to more quickly locate you.

The most important thing to remember when calling for emergency service is to *remain calm*. It may feel like the world is tumbling down around you, but staying calm improves your chances of a successful outcome, whether that is saving someone's life or getting the police to your home as quickly as possible. Explain your situation clearly, follow the dispatcher's directions, and do not hang up until directed to do so.

WHEN TO CALL FOR HELP

There are many health conditions that require emergency medical services. Recognizing those conditions is critical to increasing the victim's chances of survival. Most life-threatening conditions can be recognized by one or more basic warning signs. Consider the following list of symptoms that often indicate a medical emergency.[199] If you witness or experience any of these symptoms, immediately call for emergency medical assistance.

Symptoms of a Medical Emergency

- ➢ Loss of consciousness
- ➢ Chest or severe abdominal pain
- ➢ Sudden weakness or numbness in face, arm, or leg
- ➢ Sudden changes in vision
- ➢ Difficulty speaking
- ➢ Severe shortness of breath
- ➢ Bleeding that does not stop after ten minutes of direct pressure
- ➢ Any sudden, severe pain without an obvious cause
- ➢ A major injury such as a head trauma or broken limb
- ➢ Unexplained confusion or disorientation
- ➢ Bloody diarrhea with weakness
- ➢ Coughing or vomiting blood
- ➢ A severe or worsening reaction to an insect bite, food, or medication
- ➢ Suicidal feelings

APPLYING FIRST AID

First aid is defined as the initial medical assistance given to someone who is ill or injured. It may be required at home, in the workplace, or while traveling the roadways; medical emergencies can happen anywhere. In the case of minor illnesses or accidents, treatment can usually be rendered without any outside medical assistance. More serious conditions require that you stabilize the patient and call for emergency medical assistance.

First Aid

As a caregiver, your role begins with an understanding of the six first aid priorities:[200]

1. Assess the situation quickly but calmly.
2. Don't put yourself or the patient in additional danger.
3. Prevent cross contamination by cleaning your hands, using sterile supplies, and equipping yourself with protective clothing.
4. Provide comfort and reassurance to the patient.
5. Administer life-saving treatment first (e.g., stop the bleeding, clear the airway, administer chest compressions) before taking any other actions.
6. Never hesitate to call for emergency medical assistance, even if the victim is reluctant to have you do so.

First aid training can be acquired from your local Red Cross or medical "how to" manuals. With that said, there is no substitute for hands-on experience. Reading about injuries is one thing; feeling the flow of warm blood over your fingers as you try to stop the bleeding from a major wound is something altogether different. Beyond professional training, the single best way to become proficient at first aid is to practice. For example, to become proficient at applying bandages, take every opportunity to apply bandages over a variety of wound types.

Above all, follow the doctor's dictum, *primum non nocere* . . . first do no harm. The human body does a remarkable job of healing itself from many injuries, so be judicious when deciding your course of action. Perhaps the most important rule to remember is that if you are unsure about

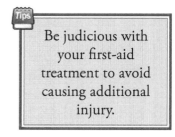

Be judicious with your first-aid treatment to avoid causing additional injury.

what to do, stabilize the person, and seek medical assistance.

Step-by-step treatments for a variety of first aid situations are outlined in this chapter. Recognize that gaining proficiency in administering first aid is very different from becoming a self-prescribed emergency room doctor. For serious medical situations, you should always seek a trained physician in a fully-equipped facility. With that said, there are times when you may have to handle medical emergencies on your own—even if it is only to stabilize the patient until help arrives.

This chapter should serve as a good start to your first aid preparations. The bulk of this material describes symptoms and treatments for a host of common first aid situations. For each situation, recommended actions are provided based on a number of reputable medical sources.[200,201,202,203] A list of supplies necessary to treat each condition is also given. The lists of supplies have been combined into a comprehensive first aid kit at the end of the chapter. The goal of organizing it this way is to ensure that you know how to use everything in your first aid kit.

Note: For ease of writing, the terms "him" and "he" are used throughout the descriptions of medical conditions, but they are meant to refer to both male and female patients.

FIRST AID CONDITIONS AND TREATMENT

ANAPHYLAXIS

Anaphylaxis is a severe allergic reaction that can result in respiratory distress and circulatory shutdown. Anaphylactic shock can occur immediately or take several hours from the time of exposure. In an anaphylactic reaction, blood vessels dilate, causing the victim's blood pressure to fall and air passages to constrict. Additional symptoms may include hives; swelling of the lips, eyes, tongue, and throat; wheezing and gasping; dizziness; abdominal cramping; nausea; vomiting; and diarrhea. There exists a wide variety of allergens, but some of the most common are nuts, insect stings, shellfish, latex, and eggs.

Recommended Actions:

1. Call 911 for emergency medical assistance.
2. Check to see if the patient is carrying an epinephrine auto-injector.

3. If epinephrine is available and the patient is conscious, help him to use the auto injector.
4. If the patient is unconscious or nonresponsive, administer epinephrine as directed:
   • Remove the safety cap.
   • Hold the injector in your fist and place the tip firmly against the patient's thigh—the shot can be given through most clothing.
   • Release the medicine and hold the injector in place for at least 10 seconds.
   • Massage the injection site to increase absorption.
5. Have the patient sit in whatever position feels most comfortable for his breathing. If he begins to appear pale or weak, have him lie on his back with his feet elevated about 12 inches.
6. Administer an over-the-counter antihistamine pill with a little water if the patient is able to swallow it without choking.
7. Loosen any tight clothing and cover the patient with a blanket. Do not give him anything else to drink.
8. If the patient begins vomiting or bleeding from the mouth, turn him on his side to prevent choking.
9. If the patient stops breathing, perform CPR.

Supplies needed:

• Epinephrine auto-injector—requires a doctor's prescription
• Antihistamine pills (e.g., Benadryl)

ANIMAL/HUMAN BITES

Domestic pets are the source of most animal bites. Dog bites occur more often, but cat bites are more likely to cause infection. Any bite from a wild or non-immunized animal should be immediately treated by a medical doctor due to the increased risks of infection, tetanus, and rabies. Bites from immunized animals that break the skin should also be treated. Rabies is most common in raccoons, skunks, bats, and foxes, and less likely in rodents, rabbits, and squirrels. Reptiles, fish, and birds do not carry rabies. Human bites can also cause infection or transfer potentially deadly viruses, such as HIV/AIDS, and should therefore be treated immediately by medical personnel.

Animal bites

Recommended Actions:

1. If the bite is from a wild animal, or if the immunization of the animal is unknown, seek medical care immediately. Rabies is a fast-acting, deadly disease that requires immediate diagnosis for the greatest chance of survival.
2. If the bite doesn't break or barely breaks the skin *and* is from an immunized, domesticated animal, wash the wound with soap and water (or Betadine antiseptic if water is unavailable), apply an antibiotic cream, and cover with a clean bandage.
3. If the bite is a deeper wound (i.e., punctured or torn), apply pressure with a clean cloth or bandage to stop the bleeding, and then seek emergency medical care.
4. As the wound heals, if you notice signs of infection, such as swelling, redness, or oozing, seek medical attention.

Supplies needed:

- Soap and water, or Betadine
- Antibiotic cream
- Adhesive bandages

BLACK EYE

A black eye is caused by bleeding under the skin around the eye. Most black eye injuries are not serious and can be handled without assistance.

Recommended Actions:

1. To reduce swelling, gently apply a cold pack or ice-filled cloth to the area. Apply it as soon as possible, and continue using the cold pack a few times a day for 24 to 48 hours.
2. If the patient experiences vision problems (e.g., blurring, double vision), severe pain, bleeding within the eye, or bleeding from the nose, seek emergency medical care.
3. If both eyes become black, seek emergency medical care since it may indicate a skull fracture.

Supplies needed:

• Cold pack

BLISTERS

Blisters are typically caused by friction (e.g., your foot rubbing against your shoe) or heat (e.g., grease splashing onto your hand from a hot pan). Most blisters are not serious and can be handled without medical assistance.

Recommended Actions:

1. Wash the blister and surrounding area with clean water. Gently pat dry with a soft, clean cloth.
2. If the blister isn't too painful, try to avoid popping it. Keeping the skin intact will help to prevent infection.
3. If the blister is small, cover it with an adhesive bandage. Larger blisters can be covered with porous, non-stick gauze pads.
4. If the blister must be drained due to its size or location, follow these steps:
   a) Wash your hands with soap and water.
   b) Apply iodine or rubbing alcohol to the blister.
   c) Sterilize a clean needle with alcohol.
   d) Use the needle to puncture the blister at several places near the blister's edge. Let it drain, but try to keep the overlying skin intact.
   e) Apply an antibiotic cream, and cover with an adhesive bandage or porous, non-stick gauze pad.

f) After several days, it may be possible to use sterile scissors and tweezers to gently cut away the top skin. After doing so, apply more antibiotic ointment and a fresh bandage.

g) Seek medical attention if signs of infection develop, such as pus, redness, increased pain, or warm skin.

Supplies needed:

- Antibiotic cream or ointment
- Adhesive bandages
- Porous, non-stick gauze pads
- Rubbing alcohol
- Needle

BRUISE

Bruises are pools of blood just beneath the skin, usually caused by a physical blow of some sort. They fade within a few days and are not a serious medical concern. Generally, the older a person is, the more easily bruising occurs.

Recommended Actions:

1. If the skin isn't broken, there is no need to cover a bruise with a bandage. However, some patients may prefer to cover particularly unsightly bruises.
2. To help a bruise heal faster:
   a) Elevate and rest the injured area if possible.
   b) Apply a cold pack to the bruise several times a day for 24 to 48 hours. Do not apply ice directly to the skin.
3. After about 48 hours, apply a warm washcloth for 10 minutes, twice a day, to help increase blood flow. This allows the skin to reabsorb the blood more quickly.
4. Seek medical attention if the bruise is unusually large or painful—particularly if the patient can't remember suffering any trauma to the region.
5. Seek emergency medical attention if the patient is experiencing abnormal bleeding elsewhere, such as from the nose, gums, or eyes, or if blood is present in the stool or urine.

Supplies needed:

- Cold pack
- Warm washcloth

BURNS

Burns are described by three classifications: first degree, second degree, and third degree. Each increase in degree indicates an increase in severity (i.e., third degree is more serious than second degree). The classification is based on the depth of the burn. It is important to recognize the symptoms of each type of burn because their respective treatments are different.

First-degree burns (a.k.a. superficial burns) damage only the outermost layer of skin, the epidermis. The affected area is usually red, swollen, and painful. Mild sunburn is the most common type of superficial burn. First-degree burns are generally treated as minor burns as outlined below. However, if the burn covers a large portion of the hands, feet, face, groin, buttocks, or a major joint, seek medical attention.

Second-degree burns (a.k.a. partial-thickness burns) damage down to the second layer of skin, the dermis. Symptoms include blisters, intensely red and splotchy skin, pain, and swelling. If the burn is smaller than three inches across, treat it as a minor burn as outlined below. If the burn is larger than three inches across, or is located on the hands, feet, face, groin, buttocks, or over a major joint, treat as a major burn.

Third-degree burns (a.k.a. full-thickness burns) are serious burns that involve all layers of the skin and sometimes even muscle and bone. The area may appear waxy, pale, or charred. Full-thickness burns require immediate emergency medical care and should be treated as major burns.

Recommended Actions (Minor Burns):

1. Immediately cool the burn by holding the area under cool running water for 10 to 15 minutes. If this is difficult to do because of the burn's location, soak the affected area in cool water or apply cold compresses. Do not apply ice directly to the burn.

First Degree Burn

Epidermis

Dermis

Subcutaneous

Second Degree Burn

Epidermis

Dermis

Subcutaneous

Third Degree Burn

Epidermis

Dermis

Subcutaneous

Three degrees of burns

2. Cover or wrap the burn loosely with a non-stick gauze bandage. Try to avoid breaking any blisters.
3. Administer an over-the-counter pain reliever as needed.
4. Watch for signs of infection such as increased pain, redness, fever, swelling, or oozing. If infection occurs, seek medical attention.
5. To minimize pigmentation color changes, apply sunscreen on the burned area for at least one year.

Recommended Actions (Major Burns):
1. Call for, or seek, emergency medical assistance.
2. Cool the injury by flooding the area or entire body with cold water. Be careful about overcooling the patient, especially when dealing with babies and the elderly.
3. Do not touch the injured area. If possible, remove any burned clothing as well as any watches or jewelry that might become constricting if the limb should swell. If there is a risk of injury, leave the clothing in place, but be sure that it is fully extinguished.
4. Cover the burned area with a non-stick gauze or gel-soaked bandage, such as those from Water-Jel. If bandages are not available, cover the wound with plastic wrap to keep out infection.
5. Reassure the patient and treat for shock if necessary.
6. If the patient stops breathing, administer CPR.

Supplies needed:
- Non-stick gauze or gel-soaked burn bandage

CARDIOPULMONARY RESUSCITATION (CPR)

Cardiopulmonary resuscitation (CPR) is a lifesaving treatment used on a person whose breathing or heartbeat has stopped. If you are interested in receiving formal CPR training, contact the American Heart Association at 1-800-AHA-USA1 or your local American Red Cross.

CPR consists of chest compressions and mouth-to-mouth rescue breathing. For adult patients, experts now recommend that untrained people only administer chest compressions, rather than the combination of compressions and rescue breathing. The reason for this change is that for the first five minutes after an adult's heart stops, the blood

Administering chest compressions

remains oxygen rich, and chest compressions are the highest priority for survival. The chest compressions help keep oxygenated blood flowing to the brain and organs until emergency personnel arrive.

For infants and children, however, both chest compressions and rescue breathing are necessary. The differences in treatment are outlined in the steps below.

Recommended Actions:

1. Check to see if the person is unconscious by touching him and asking "Are you okay?" Be sure he isn't just sleeping!
2. If he doesn't respond, have someone call for emergency medical assistance while you start CPR. If you are the only person on the scene and have immediate access to a phone, make the call before beginning CPR. However, if the patient is unconscious due to suffocation or drowning, or if the patient is a child, administer CPR for one full minute before calling for emergency assistance.
3. If you suspect the patient has suffered a heart attack, and an Automatic External Defibrillator (AED) is available, retrieve the unit, push the ON button, and follow the voice prompts. Otherwise, administer manual CPR as outlined below.

4. Before administering CPR, check to be sure that the patient's airway is clear and that he is not currently breathing.

a) Lay him on his back.

b) Kneel next to his shoulders.

c) Tilt back his head using his chin and forehead.

d) Check for breathing using the *look, listen, feel* technique. Look for chest motion; listen for breathing; feel for breath on your cheek. If he is breathing, wait for emergency personnel to arrive while monitoring his condition.

e) If the patient is not breathing, look to see if his airway is obstructed. If it is visibly obstructed, or you know the patient choked, follow the steps outlined in *Choking*. Otherwise, begin administering CPR.

5. ***Adolescent/Adult Patient:*** Administer chest compressions.

a) Place the heel of one hand over the center of the patient's chest directly between his nipples. Place your other hand on top of the first.

b) Keeping your elbows straight, use your upper body weight to quickly compress the chest about two inches. Repeat at a rate of 100 compressions per minute.

c) Continue chest compressions until the patient revives or medical personnel arrive.

6. ***Child Patient (age 1-8):*** Administer chest compressions and rescue breathing.

a) Administer chest compressions using the heel of one hand placed directly between the child's nipples. The compression should compress the child's chest by about one third. Administer 30 compressions at a rate of 100 compressions per minute.

b) Administer rescue breathing by tilting the child's head back, pinching his nose closed, and placing your lips around his mouth. Blow steadily for one second; the chest should rise. Remove your mouth, take a breath, and administer a second rescue breath.

c) Continue repeating 30 chest compressions followed by two rescue breaths until the child revives or rescue personnel arrive.

d) If alone, repeat the cycle five times before calling for emergency medical assistance.

7. *Infant Patient (<1 year old):* Administer chest compressions and rescue breathing.

a) Administer chest compressions using the two fingers of one hand placed directly between the infant's nipples. The compression should compress the child's chest by about one third. Administer 30 compressions at a rate of 100 compressions per minute.

b) Administer rescue breathing by tilting the infant's head back, and placing your lips around the infant's mouth *and* nose. Blow a gentle breath for one second; the chest should rise. Remove your mouth, take a breath, and administer a second rescue breath.

c) Continue repeating 30 compressions followed by two rescue breaths until the infant revives or rescue personnel arrive.

d) If alone, repeat the cycle five times before calling for emergency medical assistance.

Supplies needed:

• Optional: rescue breathing masks or face shields

CHEMICAL SPLASH IN EYE

Chemical splashes in the eye can cause serious injury if not treated quickly. It is important to thoroughly flush the eye with water or saline solution as rapidly as possible.

Recommended Actions:

1. Turn the patient's head sideways under a gentle running faucet (or shower), flushing the eye thoroughly with water for up to ten minutes. Orient the patient so that the affected eye is down toward the sink, preventing the contaminants from washing over into the uninjured eye. With a young child, it might be easier to have him lay back while you gently pour water onto his forehead or the bridge of his nose.

2. After cleaning his eye, wash your hands and have the patient wash his hands to remove any possible chemical contamination.

3. Have him remove any contact lenses if they haven't been removed already.

4. Try to prevent any rubbing of the eye, as this may cause damage.

5. If pain or irritation continues, seek emergency medical care. Take the bottle of chemical contaminant with you.

Supplies needed:

- Water or saline solution

CHEST PAIN

Chest pain can be an indication of many different medical conditions, ranging from minor to deadly. An accurate diagnosis is often very difficult for a layperson to make. A few of the many possible causes for chest pain are given below:

- Heartburn—stomach acid rises into the esophagus
- Sore muscles, injured ribs, or pinched nerves
- Heart attack—an artery providing oxygen to the heart becomes blocked
- Angina—plaque buildup causes reduced blood flow in the heart
- Pulmonary embolism—a blood clot lodges in an artery of the lungs
- Aortic dissection—a tear develops in the inner layer of the aorta (the heart's large blood vessel)
- Costochondritis—pain in the chest wall causes tenderness around the cartilage that connects the ribs to the sternum
- Pleurisy—membrane lining the chest wall becomes inflamed, causing sharp, localized chest pain, especially when inhaling

Recommended Actions:

1. If someone experiences unexplained chest pain that lasts for more than a few minutes, seek emergency medical care. Either call for emergency medical assistance and wait for an ambulance, or immediately drive the patient to the nearest emergency room. A patient should not be allowed to drive himself in case his condition worsens.
2. If you suspect the chest pain is due to a heart attack, follow the steps given under *Heart Attack*.

Supplies needed:

- None

CHOKING

Choking is usually the result of something lodged in the throat, partially or fully blocking the airflow. With adults, the cause is often a piece of food, but with children it can also be a toy, coin, or other small object. Teach everyone in your family the universally accepted sign for choking—clutching their throat with both hands. Symptoms of choking can include inability to talk or cough, difficulty or noisy breathing, skin and lips turning blue or dusty-looking, and loss of consciousness. Choking is a potentially deadly condition that requires immediate attention.

Recommended Actions (For Adult Patient):

1. Ask the patient if he is choking. If he is able to talk or cough forcefully, allow him to dislodge the food himself. Do not administer abdominal thrusts if the patient is coughing.
2. If you determine that his airflow is blocked, administer standing abdominal thrusts—see below.
3. If the patient collapses unconscious, examine his airway to see if the obstruction can be removed. If so, attempt to remove it, but be careful not to push it further into the airway.
4. If you cannot remove the object, administer prone abdominal thrusts—see below.
5. If you fail to clear the obstruction, call for emergency medical assistance, and administer CPR until emergency personnel arrive.

Administering abdominal thrusts (a.k.a. Heimlich maneuver):

Stand behind the patient and bend him slightly forward at the waist. Wrap your arms around his waist, making a fist with one hand and grabbing it with the other. Place your fist slightly above the patient's navel. Press hard up into the abdomen with a quick thrust—as if you are trying to lift him off his feet. In the case of an obese or pregnant patient, position your hands slightly higher.

If the patient is unconscious, deliver abdominal thrusts by straddling the patient and placing the heel of your hand just above his navel. Place your other hand on top of the first. Keeping your elbows straight, give several quick upward thrusts until the object is expelled.

Standing Victim

Unconscious Victim

Delivering abdominal thrusts, standing and prone

Recommended Actions (For Infant Patient):

1. Sit down, and place the infant face down on your forearm, resting the supporting arm on your thigh. The infant's head should be lower than his trunk.
2. Using your heel of your palm, thump the infant five times in the middle of his back.
3. If back blows fail to relieve the choking, roll the infant over and check his mouth and throat. Remove any obvious obstructions with your fingertips—don't sweep the object, since that may push the object further down the throat.
4. If the obstruction cannot be removed with your fingers, keep the infant face-up on your forearm with his head lower than his trunk. Using two fingers, give up to five quick chest compressions at the center of the infant's breastbone. The purpose of the compressions is to dislodge the blockage.

5. If chest compressions do not free the obstruction, call for emergency medical assistance, and repeat this routine of five back blows followed by five chest thrusts until the object clears or emergency personnel arrive.
6. If the infant loses consciousness, administer CPR.

Supplies needed:

- None

CUTS AND SCRAPES

Minor cuts and scrapes occur frequently and can usually be treated without medical assistance. However, if you can't stop the flow of blood or if it seems to spurt out, seek emergency medical care. Likewise, if the wound is deeper than about ¼ inch or is gaping open, seek emergency medical care to receive stitches or other treatment.

Recommended Actions:

1. Most small cuts and scrapes will stop bleeding on their own, but if they don't, apply gentle pressure with a clean bandage or cloth for 20 to 30 minutes. If possible, elevate the wound above the patient's heart.
2. Clean the wound by rinsing it with clean water. You can also use soap (or alcohol wipes) to clean the area, but try to keep the soap or alcohol out of the wound. If dirt or debris remains in the wound after rinsing, use tweezers dipped in alcohol to remove the debris.
3. Apply a thin layer of antibiotic cream or ointment to the cut or scrape.
4. Cover the wound with a clean bandage.
5. Change the bandage at least once daily or when it becomes wet or dirty.
6. Once the wound has healed sufficiently to make infection less likely, remove the bandage and expose it to the air to speed healing.
7. If you see signs of infection, such as redness, increasing pain, drainage, or swelling, seek medical attention.

Supplies needed:

- Bandages
- Antibiotic ointment
- Soap and water
- Rubbing alcohol
- Tweezers

DISLOCATION

Bones can dislocate as a result of a blow or fall. This type of injury occurs frequently in contact sports, such as football or hockey. Dislocation can occur in major joints, such as the shoulder or knee, or in smaller joints, such as the fingers and toes. Torn ligaments, damage to the synovial membrane, and fractured bones can also accompany dislocated joints.

Recommended Actions:

1. Do not move the bone or try to reposition it back in the joint. Keep the limb stationary in the position that causes the patient the least amount of pain. If possible, use a splint or sling to prevent movement.
2. Apply a cold pack to the injured joint to reduce swelling.
3. Seek emergency medical care immediately.

Supplies needed:

- Splint, sling
- Medical tape
- Cold pack

ELECTRICAL SHOCK

Minor electrical shock (i.e., one that causes no noticeable symptoms) doesn't usually require medical treatment. However, a major electrical shock can cause serious complications, including cardiac arrest, respiratory failure, burns, seizures, and loss of consciousness. A patient who receives a shock by alternating current (AC) may be unable to let go of the electrified object. Direct current (DC) tends to produce a single violent muscular contraction that throws the patient away from the electrified object.

If you witness someone being shocked or encounter someone who you suspect has been shocked, use extreme caution to prevent injury to yourself. Electricity can arc through the air from person to person or from object to person if you get too close. High-voltage power lines, for example, can arc through the air up to 60 feet.

Recommended Actions:

1. Carefully inspect the situation. Do not touch the person until you are certain that he is no longer being shocked.
2. If the patient is being shocked by a high-voltage power line, do not approach him. Call for emergency assistance immediately.
3. If the patient is being shocked by a house appliance or outlet, unplug the source or throw the circuit breaker. If that is not possible, use a non-conducting object, such as a wood broomstick, to push the source away from the person.
4. Check to see if the patient is breathing. If he isn't breathing, begin administering CPR, and call for emergency medical assistance.
5. If the patient is injured but still breathing, treat for shock by laying him down and elevating his legs. Then call for emergency medical assistance.

Supplies needed:

• None

FAINTING

Fainting is a brief loss of consciousness caused by a temporary reduction in blood flow to the brain. It can be brought on by dehydration, lack of food, exhaustion, reaction to pain, or emotional stress. It may also occur when standing up quickly after sitting for a long period of time because blood may pool in the legs and be unable to reach the brain fast enough. A person who faints is typically unconscious for only a brief time (less than one minute) until blood flow to the brain improves.

Recommended Actions:

1. If someone says he feels faint, have him sit or lie down. Do not have him put his head between his legs while sitting because he may fall and become injured. If he chooses to lie down, elevate his feet slightly.
2. If someone faints, first check to see if he is breathing. If he is not breathing, immediately begin administering CPR, and call for emergency medical assistance.
3. If he is unconscious but breathing, lay him on his back and elevate his feet above his heart level by about 12 inches. Loosen any constrictive clothing, and monitor his breathing.
4. Once he regains consciousness, have him rest a moment before slowly standing up.
5. If he does not regain consciousness within one minute, call for emergency medical assistance.

Supplies needed:

• None

FEVER

Fever is a symptom of many different medical conditions but is most often caused by a bacterial or viral infection. Every person's normal body temperature is slightly different, with the average being 98.6°F. A moderate fever is not usually harmful to adults, but may introduce seizures in young children.

Many doctors recommend not treating fevers below 102°F with medications. They argue that the body's elevated temperature will help fight off infection, but only at the expense of added discomfort for the patient.

Recommended Actions:

1. Keep the patient cool and comfortable, preferably remaining in bed.
2. Provide cool beverages to drink (non-alcoholic, caffeine-free).
3. Treat with fever reducers or pain medicine as needed.
   • Adult fevers can be treated with acetaminophen, ibuprofen, or aspirin (assuming there are no allergies).

- Children over 6 months of age can be treated with ibuprofen or acetaminophen. Do not give aspirin to children because it might trigger Reye's syndrome—a rare but deadly disorder.
- Children under 6 months of age should only be treated with acetaminophen.

4. Seek medical care if any of the following conditions apply:
  - A baby younger than 3 months has a rectal temperature of 100.4°F or higher. A rectal reading is generally about 1 degree higher than oral readings
  - A baby older than 3 months has a temperature of 102°F or higher
  - A newborn has a rectal temperature below 97°F
  - A child younger than age 2 has a fever longer than one full day, or a child older than age 2 has a fever longer than three days
  - An adult has a temperature of more than 103°F or has a fever for more than three days

Caution: Be very careful to give the correct dose of acetaminophen. Overdosing of acetaminophen can lead to liver failure and death. Tens of thousands of Americans are rushed to emergency rooms every year from acetaminophen overdose.[204] Be aware that acetaminophen may also be present in other medicines, such as cough suppressants, that when combined with fever-reducing medicine, can lead to a dangerous overdose.

Supplies needed:

- Fever-reducing medicine

FOREIGN OBJECT IN EAR

A foreign object can become stuck in the ear and cause pain or hearing loss. Common objects include cotton swabs and insects. In most cases, foreign objects can be safely removed without medical assistance, but care must be taken not to injure the patient's ear or push the object deeper into the ear canal.

Recommended Actions:

1. If the object is clearly visible, attempt to gently remove it using tweezers. Do not try to remove the object using a cotton swab, matchstick, or other ill-suited topl; you risk pushing it further into the ear and causing damage.

2. If you can't easily pull it out, try tilting the patient's head such that his ear faces the ground, and then gently try to dislodge it.

3. If the object is an insect (alive or dead), fill the ear with warm water, mineral oil, baby oil, or olive oil to float the insect out. Do not use this method if there is any pain, bleeding, or discharge from the ear.

4. If these simple methods fail to remove the object, seek medical attention.

Supplies needed:

- Tweezers
- Mineral, baby, or olive oil

FOREIGN OBJECT IN EYE

Most eye injuries involve the cornea—the clear protective coating at the front of the eye. Dust, dirt, sand, wood shavings, or other particles can scratch, cut, or become lodged in the cornea. Corneal abrasions are painful, but most are not serious unless they become infected or inflamed. Symptoms may include tearing, blurred vision, headache, and eye redness.

Recommended Actions:

1. Have the patient sit facing a bright light so that you can more easily inspect his eye.

2. Wash your hands with soap and water.

3. Using your thumb and forefinger, gently separate his eyelids (pulling the top one up and the bottom one down). Have the patient look left, right, up, and down, while you are examining the eye for foreign objects.

4. If you see a foreign object on the surface of the eye, rinse the eye with saline solution (or clean water if saline isn't available).

5. If rinsing is not successful, try to lift the object out by gently dabbing with a clean moist cotton swab. Try not to rub the eye, which can cause additional scratching.

6. You can also have him pull the upper eyelid over the lower one to help dislodge anything stuck on the undersurface of the upper eyelid.

7. Don't try to remove anything that is embedded in the eyeball.
8. If you are unable to remove the foreign object, or if it is embedded in the eyeball, cover the eye with sterile eye pad or gauze, and seek emergency medical care.

Supplies needed:

- Saline solution or eye wash
- Eye pad
- Bright light
- Cotton swab

FOREIGN OBJECT IN NOSE

Children are especially likely to lodge a small object in their noses. Common obstructions include marbles, candy, toys, or batteries. If the object is sharp, it can cause tissue damage, which can lead to infection. Likewise, batteries can cause tissue burns. Small objects lodged in the nose can usually be removed without medical assistance; however, care must be taken to ensure that the object isn't pushed further into the airway.

Recommended Actions:

1. Have the patient breathe through his mouth, preventing him from inhaling the object.
2. Have him blow his nose gently. If the obstruction is affecting only one nostril, plug the other nostril when blowing.
3. If the object can be easily grabbed, carefully use tweezers to remove it. Do not use a cotton swab or other ill-suited tool to try to pry the object out.
4. If the object is a marble and it will not blow out, try gently pinching the nose from the top down, pressing the marble down and out of the nose.
5. If you are unable to remove the object, seek emergency medical care.

Supplies needed:

- Tweezers

FOREIGN OBJECT IN SKIN

Splinters of wood, metal, glass, or fiberglass can become lodged in the skin. It is important to remove the splinter to prevent infection. Getting a splinter out can usually be done without medical assistance.

Recommended Actions:

1. Wash your hands and the affected area with soap and water. Sterilize a needle and tweezers using isopropyl alcohol.
2. If the splinter juts out above the skin, use tweezers to draw the object out in a straight line opposite the direction that it went in.
3. If the splinter is completely embedded in the skin, use a small sterilized needle to break the skin above it. Then gently lift the tip of the splinter out, and use tweezers to remove the object.
4. Gently squeeze the area to stimulate a little bleeding, which helps to flush out the wound.
5. Wash and dry the area again.
6. Apply a thin layer of antibiotic ointment and a small adhesive bandage as needed.

Supplies needed:

- Tweezers
- Needle
- Isopropyl alcohol
- Antibiotic ointment
- Adhesive bandage

FOREIGN OBJECT SWALLOWED

Most small foreign objects that are swallowed will usually pass through the digestive system without complications. However, sharp objects may become lodged in the esophagus (the tube connecting the throat to the stomach). Also, button batteries used in watches, calculators, and toys, can cause tissue damage and should be removed by a medical professional immediately. Finally, swallowing multiple magnets may cause internal complications and requires immediate medical consultation.

Recommended Actions:

1. If the object is small and doesn't cause choking, contact your family doctor. He will likely recommend that you allow the item to pass through the body.
2. If the object is sharp, lodged in the esophagus, or a battery, seek emergency medical care.
3. If the object causes choking, treat the patient as outlined under *Choking.*

Supplies needed:

- None

FRACTURES (BROKEN BONES)

A fracture is a break or crack in the bone. Open (compound) fractures are those where the broken bone penetrates the skin, whereas closed (simple) fractures leave the skin intact. Open fractures are particularly

Fractured hand

susceptible to infection. Fractures may be characterized by bleeding, swelling, deformity, bruising, pain, and difficulty in moving the limb. Fractures require professional medical attention.

Recommended Actions:

1. If the fracture is on the arm, hand, or foot, and there is no bleeding, immobilize the limb using a sling or structural aluminum malleable (SAM) splint. Apply a cold pack to the area, and seek emergency medical care.
2. If the fracture is elsewhere on the body, such as the neck, back, leg, or hip, call for emergency medical assistance and have the patient remain still until emergency personnel arrive.
3. If the fracture is bleeding, carefully apply pressure to the wound with a clean cloth or bandage, and call for emergency medical assistance. Keep the area immobilized, and do not try to realign or push a protruding bone back in.
4. If the patient feels faint, treat him for shock by laying him on his back and elevating his feet.

Supplies needed:

- SAM splint
- Sling
- Tape
- Cold pack
- Clean cloth or bandage

FROSTBITE

Frostbite is the result of the skin being exposed to very cold temperatures. Extremities such as hands, feet, nose, and ears are most likely to be affected. If left unchecked, frostbite can cause loss of sensation and tissue death. Symptoms include the skin appearing white or grayish-yellow, being very cold to the touch, and having a hard or waxy feel. Itching, burning, or numbness may also be present. As the skin thaws, it becomes red and painful. Frostbite is often accompanied by hypothermia, which must also be treated (see *Hypothermia*).

Recommended Actions:

1. Immediately get the patient out of the cold. Try to keep him from walking on frostbitten feet or toes.
2. Warm the affected area. You can warm hands or feet by placing them under your armpits. Hands and feet can also be warmed by placing them in lukewarm (not hot) water. Cover ears, nose, and face with warm hands.
3. Raise the affected limb to reduce any swelling.
4. Do not rub the affected area as this this can cause skin and tissue damage.
5. Administer over-the-counter pain medicine as needed.
6. Seek emergency medical assistance if numbness remains after warming or if skin damage is present.

Supplies needed:

- Over-the-counter pain medicine

GASTROENTERITIS

Gastroenteritis is a general term used to describe the inflammation of the stomach and intestines. There are many possible causes, including viruses, food- or water-borne bacteria, and stress. Symptoms may include nausea, vomiting, diarrhea, abdominal cramps, and occasionally a low-grade fever. The symptoms may last from 24 hours to more than a week. See *Chapter 3: Food* and *Chapter 4: Water* for additional information on food poisoning and water-borne contamination.

Recommended Actions:

1. Have the patient rest and drink plenty of liquids to prevent dehydration.
2. Have him gradually ease back into eating, starting with bland foods, such as crackers, toast, gelatin, bananas, and chicken soup. Have him avoid dairy products, caffeine, alcohol, nicotine, and fatty foods for a few days.
3. Generally, do not administer anti-diarrheal medications early in the sickness because they may slow the elimination of contaminant from the digestive system.

4. Seek medical care for any of the following conditions:
   - Vomiting persists for more than two days, or turns bloody
   - Diarrhea persists for more than a week, or turns bloody
   - High fever develops
   - Confusion, lightheadedness, or fainting occurs
5. Additionally, seek emergency medical care for a child for any of the following conditions:
   - Child becomes unusually drowsy
   - Child shows signs of dehydration such as marked thirst, sunken eyes, crying without tears, if the soft spot on an infant's head starts to become sunken, or if diapers remain dry for 8 or more hours
   - Fever remains longer than one day for child under age 2, or fever remains longer than 3 days for child over age 2

Supplies needed:

- Thermometer

HEADACHE

A headache may accompany many illnesses, particularly those with fevers. Headaches may also be the result of stress, fatigue, or excessive alcohol consumption. Most headaches are minor and can be treated with over-the-counter pain medications. However, headaches can also signal dangerous medical conditions, such as meningitis or a stroke.

Recommended Actions:

1. Have the patient sit or lie down in a quiet room. Provide a cold compress for his head.
2. If the headache is minor, consider treating with over-the-counter pain medication.
   - Treat adult headaches with acetaminophen, ibuprofen, or aspirin (assuming there are no allergies).
   - Treat a child's headache only with acetaminophen or ibuprofen. Do not give aspirin to children because it might trigger Reye's syndrome—a rare but deadly disorder.
   - Treat infants younger than 6 months of age with acetaminophen. Be very careful to administer the correct dose.

3. Seek emergency medical care for any of the following:
   - A severe headache develops suddenly
   - The headache is accompanied with a fever, stiff neck, rash, confusion, seizures, vision changes, dizziness, weakness, paralysis, or difficulty speaking
   - The headache is the result of a head injury or fall
   - The headache progressively worsens throughout the day or persists for several days

Supplies needed:

- Over-the-counter pain reliever

HEAD TRAUMA

Minor abrasions and cuts to the head are treated as they would be to any other part of the body (see *Cuts and Scrapes*). However, in the case of a more severe head injury, the patient requires careful monitoring because head trauma may cause more serious medical conditions, including a skull fracture, concussion, and bleeding in the brain.

Recommended Actions:

1. If the head trauma is minor, treat the abrasions as detailed in *Cuts and Scrapes*. An ice pack can also be applied to reduce localized swelling.
2. If any of the following symptoms occur at the time of the injury, or become evident within 24 hours, call for emergency medical assistance immediately.
   - Severe head or facial bleeding
   - Bleeding from the nose or ears (other than from a minor injury to the nose or exterior of the ears)
   - Severe headache
   - Loss of consciousness for more than a few seconds
   - Black and blue discoloration below the eyes or behind the ears
   - Cessation of breathing
   - Confusion
   - Loss of balance
   - Weakness or inability to use an arm or leg

- Unequal pupil size
- Vomiting
- Slurred speech
- Seizures

3. While awaiting emergency personnel, keep the patient still, stop any bleeding by applying pressure using a clean cloth or bandage, and stay alert for any changes in breathing.

4. If the patient stops breathing, administer CPR.

Supplies needed:

- Bandages
- Antibiotic ointment
- Cold pack

HEART ATTACK

A heart attack occurs when the artery supplying blood to the heart becomes partially or completely blocked. The loss of blood flow causes damage to the heart muscle. Symptoms can include any of the following: chest pressure; pain in the upper abdomen or back; pain spreading from the chest to shoulders, neck, jaw, and one or both arms; shortness of breath; dizziness; sweating; and nausea. The earliest warning sign may be episodes of chest pain that occur during physical exertion but are relieved by rest. However, a heart attack can also occur without any warning signs.

Recommended Actions:

1. If you suspect that someone is having a heart attack, call for emergency medical assistance.
2. Have the patient sit down, rest, and try to remain calm.
3. Have him chew one regular strength aspirin tablet (assuming no allergy), or if he has been prescribed nitroglycerin or other heart medication, have him take it as directed. Do not administer nitroglycerin to someone who has not had it prescribed.
4. If the patient stops breathing, administer CPR while waiting for emergency personnel.

5. If you are in a public building that has an automatic external defibrillator (AED), have someone else retrieve it while you administer CPR. Training is certainly desired when using an AED, but even if you are not trained, don't be afraid to use it on a patient who has stopped breathing. It is their best chance for survival.

Using an AED: An AED analyzes a patient's heart rhythm and determines if an electrical shock is required. After switching the unit on, attach the two pads to the correct location: one just under the patient's right collarbone, and the other along his left ribcage. Get everyone to stand clear while the AED analyzes his heart rhythm. The AED will then advise whether a shock is needed. If advised to do so, press the *Shock* button on the AED control box to administer the shock. The AED will then direct you to continue administering CPR for two minutes before it reanalyzes the patient's heart rhythm again. If at any time the patient starts to breathe, stop using the AED (but leave it attached), and help him to be comfortable while awaiting emergency personnel.

AED pad placement

Supplies needed:

- Aspirin
- AED (if available)

HEAT CRAMPS

Heat cramps are the first stage of hyperthermia (see *Chapter 8: Heating/ Cooling*) and consist of painful involuntary muscle spasms. They are most often the result of overexertion in hot environments. Inadequate fluid intake also contributes to heat cramps.

Recommended Actions:

1. Move the patient to a cool environment to rest.
2. Have him drink cool liquids that do not contain caffeine or alcohol.
3. Gently stretch and massage the affected muscle group.
4. Advise the patient to wait a few hours after the heat cramps subside before resuming any strenuous activity.
5. Seek medical care if the cramps don't go away within an hour.

Supplies needed:

- Cool liquids

HEAT EXHAUSTION

Heat exhaustion is the second stage of hyperthermia (*Chapter 8: Heating/ Cooling*). It is typically a result of overexertion in hot conditions. Symptoms often begin suddenly and may include heavy perspiration, dizziness, nausea, a rapid but weak heartbeat, low blood pressure, cool skin that may look pale, low-grade fever, heat cramps, headache, dark urine, and fatigue.

Recommended Actions:

1. Get the patient out of the sun and into a cooler location.
2. Lay the patient down and elevate his feet about 12 inches. Loosen any tight clothing.

---

3. Have him drink cool liquids that do not contain caffeine or alcohol.
4. Cool the patient by gently spraying or sponging him with water.
5. Monitor his temperature and condition for signs of heatstroke.
6. If any of the following symptoms occur, call for emergency medical assistance:
   - Fever greater than 102°F
   - Fainting
   - Confusion
   - Seizures

Supplies needed:

- Cool liquids
- Thermometer

HEATSTROKE

Heatstroke is the third and most severe stage of hyperthermia (see *Chapter 8: Heating/Cooling*). It is often a result of continue overexertion in hot conditions combined with inadequate fluid intake. Young children, older adults, and obese people are at higher risk of suffering from heatstroke. Heatstroke can also result from the use of some drugs, such as Ecstasy. The main symptom of heatstroke is an elevated body temperature, generally higher than 104°F. This condition may result in personality changes, confusion, coma, and even death. Other symptoms can include rapid heartbeat, shallow breathing, cessation of sweating, dizziness, headache, nausea, and fainting.

Recommended Actions:

1. Move the patient out of the sun to a cooler location, and remove as much of his outer clothing as possible.
2. Call for emergency medical assistance.
3. Have him drink cool liquids that do not contain caffeine or alcohol.
4. Cool the patient by covering him with damp sheets, or gently spraying with cool water and then fanning him.

5. Once the patient's temperature returns to normal, replace the wet sheets with a dry one. If his temperature rises again, repeat the cooling process.
6. If the patient loses consciousness, continue cooling while monitoring his pulse and breathing.
7. If the patient stops breathing, administer CPR.

Supplies needed:

- Cool liquids
- Sheets

HYPOTHERMIA

Hypothermia is a condition that occurs when the body temperature falls below 95°F, caused by prolonged exposure to the cold (see *Chapter 8: Heating/Cooling*). Severe hypothermia, in which the core body temperature falls below 89°F, is usually fatal. Becoming wet or not covering your head in cold weather increases your chances of suffering hypothermia. Symptoms include shivering, slurred speech, slowed breathing, cold pale skin, loss of coordination, fatigue, and confusion. Symptoms usually develop slowly, with a gradual loss of mental acuity and physical ability. Older adults, infants, young children, and people who are very lean are at higher risk of hypothermia. Alcohol and drugs can exacerbate the condition. If a person is submerged in cold water, hypothermia can develop very quickly.

Recommended Actions:

1. Move the patient out of the cold, preferably into a warm, sheltered location. If you must lay him on the ground, place a pad or other insulating material beneath him.
2. Call for emergency medical assistance.
3. Remove his wet clothing and replace it with something warm and dry. Handle the patient very gently, since rubbing frostbitten skin can cause severe damage.
4. Warm the patient gradually. Do not apply direct heat, such as a hot water, heating pad, or heat lamp. Instead, warm slowly with warm

compresses to the trunk of the body. Do not attempt to directly warm the arms and legs because that can cause a fatal condition in which cold blood flows back to the heart, lungs, and brain.

5. Give the patient something warm to drink as well as a small quantity of high-energy food, such as chocolate, to eat.

6. While awaiting medical help, monitor the patient's breathing. If he stops breathing, administer CPR.

Supplies needed:

* Warm liquids
* High-energy food, such as chocolate
* Dry clothing

INSECT BITES AND STINGS

Most insect bites and stings cause only mild symptoms, such as itching, stinging, or swelling, and can be safely treated without medical assistance. Only a small percentage of people develop severe reactions to insect venom (see *Anaphylaxis*).

Recommended Actions:

1. Move the patient away from the area to avoid additional stings.

2. If visible, remove any stinger with tweezers, or scrape it out using a playing card or other flat object. Be careful not to squeeze the stinger, which might inject additional venom.

3. Wash the area with soap and water.

4. Apply a cold pack or cloth filled with ice to reduce swelling and pain. Raise the infected limb above heart level if possible.

5. Have the patient take an antihistamine containing diphenhydramine (e.g., Benadryl).

6. Apply hydrocortisone cream, calamine lotion, or baking soda paste (3 teaspoons baking soda to 1 teaspoon water) several times a day until the symptoms subside.

7. For severe reactions, call for emergency medical assistance and follow the steps under *Anaphylaxis*.

8. If the sting occurs on the throat, give the patient ice water to sip. If swelling starts to occur, seek emergency medical assistance.

Supplies needed:

- Tweezers or flat card
- Cold pack
- Hydrocortisone cream, calmine lotion, or baking soda
- Antihistamine with diphenhydramine

NOSEBLEEDS

Most nosebleeds are not serious and are easily treated without medical assistance. In older adults, however, some nosebleeds originate from deeper within the nose and may be a result of hardened arteries or high blood pressure. These deeper nosebleeds can be difficult to stop and may require medical assistance.

Recommended Actions:

1. Have the patient sit upright and lean forward to avoid swallowing blood.
2. If bleeding is the result of an injury that may have broken the nose, seek emergency medical assistance.
3. Have him pinch his nose for 5 to 10 minutes to stop the bleeding.
4. If re-bleeding occurs, have him blow out forcefully to clear his nose of blood clots. Then spray nose with a decongestant nasal spray containing oxymetazoline (e.g., Afrin). Then have him pinch his nose for another 5 to 10 minutes.
5. If bleeding persists for more than 20 minutes, seek emergency medical assistance.

Supplies needed:

- Decongestant nasal spray containing oxymetazoline

POISONING

Poisons are toxic substances that once introduced into the body, can cause sickness and death. They can be ingested, inhaled, splashed into the eyes, or absorbed through the skin. The specific effects of each poison are unique, but common reactions are: vomiting and nausea (ingested

Poison

poisons), breathing difficulties (inhaled poisons), blurred vision and watering eyes (splashed poisons), and skin irritation (absorbed poisons). Other effects, including seizures, dizziness, and pain are also possible.

Recommended Actions:

1. If you suspect poisoning of any kind, immediately call the **Poison Control Center at 1-800-222-1222.** If the patient is already unconscious, call 911 for emergency medical assistance.
2. If a poison was ingested, remove anything still remaining in the patient's mouth. If possible, ask him what was swallowed. If he is unable to answer, look for clues, such as leaves, berries, pill bottles, or containers. Do not give the patient anything to induce vomiting unless directed to do so by the Poison Control Center.
3. If the patient was exposed to poisonous fumes, such as carbon monoxide, immediately move him to an area with fresh air.
4. If the poison spilled onto the patient's clothing or skin, or splashed into his eyes, remove the clothing and flush the skin and eyes with water.
5. If the patient stops breathing, administer CPR.

Supplies needed:

* None

PUNCTURE WOUNDS

A puncture wound, such as a nail through the foot, usually does not cause excessive bleeding but can be serious due to the depth of the wound and risk of infection. The puncturing object may have spores of tetanus or other bacteria, especially if exposed to the soil. Puncture wounds from mammals carry the additional risk of rabies (see *Animal Bites*).

Recommended Actions:

1. Apply gentle pressure to help stop the bleeding as needed. If bleeding persists, seek emergency medical assistance.
2. If the object remains embedded, seek emergency medical attention.
3. If the object is not embedded, flush the wound with clean water. Use tweezers disinfected in alcohol to remove any superficial particles. Clean around the wound with soap and water. If debris remains in the wound, seek emergency medical assistance.
4. Apply a thin layer of antibiotic ointment.
5. Cover the wound with a clean bandage.
6. Change the bandage at least daily or when it gets wet or dirty.
7. Watch for signs of infection including redness, drainage, or swelling. If infection occurs, seek medical care.
8. If the puncture is deep, or from an animal or human bite, or in the foot, seek emergency medical assistance. The doctor may recommend a tetanus booster or a series of rabies vaccinations.

Supplies needed:

- Tweezers
- Antibiotic ointment
- Isopropyl alcohol
- Bandages
- Soap and water

SEVERE EXTERNAL BLEEDING

Trauma can result in severe external bleeding, which can be distressing for both you and the patient. Keeping calm is critical to administer life-saving first aid successfully. If the bleeding is not stopped quickly, the patient will lose consciousness and die.

Recommended Actions:

1. Call for emergency medical assistance.
2. If possible, wash your hands and put on rubber or latex gloves.
3. Have the injured person lie down, and cover him to prevent loss of body heat.
4. Treat for shock by elevating his legs about 12 inches.
5. Remove or cut away clothing to expose the wound.
6. Remove any obvious dirt or debris from the wound. Do not try to remove any deeply embedded objects.
7. Using a clean cloth or thick sterile bandage, such as a trauma pad or bloodstopper compress, apply direct pressure to the wound until bleeding stops (at least 20 minutes). If a bandage or cloth is not available, use your hands directly (preferably with gloves on). If there is an object embedded in the wound, press to either side of it.
8. If possible, elevate the wound above the patient's heart while applying pressure.
9. If the bleeding continues and seeps through the bandage, do not remove it. Instead, add absorbent material over it.
10. If the bleeding doesn't stop, use one hand to compress a main artery that feeds the limb by pressing it against the bone. Use the other hand to maintain pressure on the wound.
    - Artery pressure points on the arm are on the inside of the arm, one above the elbow and one below the armpit.
    - Artery pressure points on the leg are behind the knee and in the groin.
11. Once the bleeding has stopped, secure the bandage with tape or gauze, and immobilize the injured part until emergency personnel arrive.

Supplies needed:

- Thick, sterile bandages such as trauma pads, bloodstopper compress bandages, or multi-trauma dressings
- Conforming gauze rolls
- Rubber or latex gloves

SHOCK

Shock is a life-threatening condition most often caused by a significant loss of blood (i.e., more than two pints). It may also be a result of trauma, heatstroke, allergic reaction, infection, poisoning, electric shock, heart failure, hypothermia, hypoglycemia, or severe burns. When in shock, a person's vital organs, such as his brain and heart, aren't getting enough oxygen. This deprivation can lead to organ damage and death. Initial symptoms of shock may include cool, clammy skin; weak, rapid pulse; and sweating. As shock develops, additional symptoms may include nausea, thirst, confusion, weakness, gasping for air, and loss of consciousness. If not treated, the patient's heart will eventually stop.

Recommended Actions:

1. If you suspect that a person is going into shock, call for emergency medical assistance.
2. Have the patient lie on his back and remain still. Elevate his feet about 12 inches.
3. Reassure the patient. Keep the patient warm and comfortable by loosening clothing and covering with a blanket.
4. If the patient begins to vomit or bleed from the mouth, turn him on his side to prevent choking.
5. Monitor the patient's breathing and heart rate. If he stops breathing, administer CPR.

Supplies needed:

- Blanket

SNAKEBITES

Fortunately, most North American snakes are not poisonous. Obvious exceptions are the rattlesnake, coral snake, water moccasin, and copperhead, all of which can deliver fatal bites. Snakes do not carry rabies.

Recommended Actions:

1. Call for emergency medical assistance immediately.
2. Do not try to capture the snake, but do try to remember its color and shape so you can describe it to emergency personnel. Also, note the exact time of the bite.

3. Have the patient sit upright and remain calm. Reassure him as needed.
4. Keep the bite below the level of the patient's heart if possible.
5. Remove any jewelry on the limb, and cover the wound with a clean, dry bandage.
6. Immobilize the bitten limb using a splint if possible. If a splint is not available, wrap the limb with heavy gauze up past the joint to prevent bending.
7. Do not use a tourniquet, apply ice, cut the wound, or try to suck out the venom.

Supplies needed:

- Splint
- Bandage
- Gauze roll

SPINAL INJURY

Injuries to the spine may involve the vertebrae, the disks of tissue separating them, the surrounding muscles and ligaments, and the spinal cord and associated nerves branching off from it. The most serious risk exists when the spinal cord is damaged, which can lead to temporary or permanent paralysis. Spinal injuries are often the result of an impact, such as falling off a ladder or horse, landing awkwardly on a trampoline, diving into a shallow pool, or suffering a misplaced football tackle. Symptoms often include pain in the neck or back, irregularity in the normal curve of the spine, paralysis, abnormal sensations, and loss of bladder or bowel control.

Recommended Actions:

1. If spinal injury is suspected, call for emergency medical assistance.
2. Keep the patient still. Brace his head on both sides using rolled up clothes or towels. Do not roll him over or straighten him out; instead, leave him in the position that you found him.
3. If the patient is wearing a helmet, do not remove it.

4. Provide emergency first aid if needed, such as stopping any bleeding. But try to do so without moving the patient's head or neck.
5. Monitor the patient's vital signs. If he stops breathing, administer CPR—chest compressions only.

Supplies needed:

• Towels

STRAIN OR SPRAIN

A strain is an injury to the muscles or tendons, and is the result of the muscle being overstretched. The muscle can be partially torn or fully ruptured. The injury often occurs at the junction between the muscle and the tendon that joins it to the bone.

A sprain is an injury to the ligaments connecting bones together or holding joints in place. The ligament can be stretched, partially torn, or completely separated. Ankle and knee sprains are the two most common types. Sprains cause rapid swelling and can be very painful. Generally, the greater the pain, the more severe the sprain. Most minor sprains can be treated without medical assistance by keeping the swelling down and treating the pain.

Recommended Actions:

1. Help the patient sit or lie down. Support the injured limb in a comfortable raised position using pillows or other soft materials.
2. Apply a cold pack to the area immediately after injury.
3. Compress the area with an ACE bandage or neoprene wrap.
4. Elevate the injured limb above the patient's heart whenever possible to prevent swelling.
5. Use over-the-counter anti-inflammatories/pain relievers to help with swelling and pain.
6. The injured person may require the use of crutches or splints for two to three days. During this time, apply a cold pack for 10 to 15 minutes at a time, four times a day.
7. If the sprain isn't improving after three days, consult a doctor.
8. If a fever develops, or if the joint feels unstable, seek emergency medical assistance.

Supplies needed:

- Cold pack
- ACE bandage or neoprene wrap
- Over-the-counter anti-inflammatories, pain relievers
- Crutches

STROKE

Strokes are the third most common cause of death in the United States. The condition is more common in older people and is often associated with circulatory system disorders such as high blood pressure.

A stroke is caused from bleeding in the brain or when the blood flow into the brain is interrupted (usually by a clot in a blood vessel). Within minutes, blood cells start dying—a process that may continue for several hours. The best ways to prevent brain damage are to recognize the symptoms and quickly seek emergency medical treatment.

Symptoms of a stroke may include:

- Sudden weakness or numbness in the face, arm, or leg on one side of the body
- Sudden dimness, blurring, or loss of vision, particularly in one eye
- Trouble talking or understanding speech
- Sudden and severe headache
- Dizziness

Recommended Actions:

1. Ask the patient to smile while you are looking at his face. If he is having a stroke, one side of his mouth may droop.
2. Ask the patient to raise both his arms out to his sides. If he is having a stroke, he may be able to lift only one arm out straight.
3. Ask the person several questions and see if he responds intelligibly. If he is unable to understand you or reply coherently, he may be suffering from a stroke.
4. Based on your assessment, if you suspect a person is having a stroke, call for emergency medical assistance.

Supplies needed:

- None

SUNBURN

Overexposure to the sun can cause sunburn. Numerous medicines, including some antibiotics and chemotherapy drugs, can trigger hypersensitivity to the sun, making the skin burn very easily. Sunburn is prevented by staying in the shade or applying protective sunscreen. Symptoms of sunburn usually appear within a few hours and may include pain, redness, swelling, and blistering. If sunburn covers a large portion of the body, it can also cause headache, fever, and fatigue.

Recommended Actions:

1. Cover the burn with a cool wet cloth, or have the patient take a cool bath.
2. Apply aloe vera, calamine, or moisturizing lotion several times a day. Do not use petroleum jelly, butter, or other home remedies.
3. Leave any blisters intact to speed healing and avoid infection. Apply antibiotic ointment to any that burst.
4. Administer over-the-counter pain reliever for pain as needed.
5. If complications develop, such as rash, fever, or blistering, seek medical care.

Supplies needed:

* Aloe vera, calamine, or moisturizing lotion
* Over-the-counter pain reliever

TOOTH LOSS

If an adult tooth is knocked out, it may be possible to replant it in the socket, either at home or at the dentist's office. Proper handling of the tooth is critical to improving the chances of a successful replanting.

Recommended Actions:

1. Retrieve the tooth, handling it only by the top, not the roots.
2. Do not rub or scrape the tooth to remove debris since this might damage the roots.
3. Rinse away any dirt with milk (or lukewarm water if milk is unavailable).

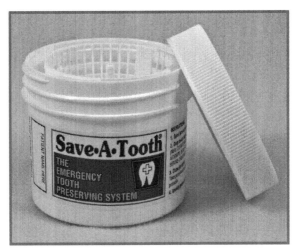

Save-A-Tooth

4. Try to replant the tooth back into the socket. If it doesn't fully reseat, have the patient bite down slowly and gently on a gauze or moistened tea bag. Have him hold the tooth in place while traveling to the dentist or hospital.
5. If you can't replace the tooth in the socket, put it in a plastic bag or container along with some milk or the patient's saliva. If you have a Save-A-Tooth preserving kit, use it.
6. Regardless of whether replanting is successful or not, seek immediate care from a dentist or hospital.

Supplies needed:

- Save-A-Tooth preserving system
- Gauze
- Milk

TOOTHACHE

Toothaches are often the result of tooth decay. The first signs might be a painful sensation when eating something sweet, hot, or cold. When these early symptoms become evident, the patient should seek out dental care to address the underlying cause. If an injury to the mouth causes tooth pain, the patient should see his dentist immediately.

Recommended Actions:

1. Have the patient rinse his mouth with warm water, and then use dental floss to remove any food particles that might be wedged between teeth.
2. Administer over-the-counter pain reliever as needed. You can also apply an over-the-counter antiseptic containing benzocaine directly to the irritated tooth or nearby gum.
3. Call the dentist or seek emergency care if:
    * There are signs of infection such as swelling, pain, red gums, or foul discharge
    * The pain persists for more than a day
    * A fever is present
    * The patient has trouble breathing or swallowing
    * The toothache is a result of injury to the mouth

Supplies needed:

* Over-the-counter pain reliever
* Antiseptic containing benzocaine

FIRST AID KIT

A good first aid kit is one stocked with items that *you* know how to use. There is no point in having a huge stockpile of medical supplies if you can't put them to use safely and effectively.

The following first aid kit is compiled to treat the first aid conditions described above (as well as many others). For the most part, the supplies are readily available from your local drug store or through online medical supply stores. The quantities listed are completely subjective, based on family size, likelihood of injury, and types of expected injuries. You should stock your kit with enough supplies to meet your family's needs. It is also recommended that you build up a smaller first aid kit, primarily focused on trauma, for inclusion in your roadside emergency kit (see *Chapter 14: Transportation*).

To keep your medical supplies fresh, as well as maintain familiarity with your kit's contents, use your first aid kit for your family's daily medical needs. As long as you are vigilent at replacing supplies as they are consumed, daily use in no way compromises your preparation for a more significant first aid emergency.

Qty	Item	Use
1	Large first aid bag with individual compartments	Contain your first aid supplies
1	Bottle of alcohol or alcohol wipes	Disinfect tweezers, needles, or around wounds
1	Bottle of Betadine or hydrogen peroxide	Clean wounds when soap and water is unavailable
1	Bottle of hand sanitizer or sanitizer wipes	Sanitize hands when water is not available
1	Bottle of mineral or baby oil	Float insects out of ear
1	Bottle of saline solution or eye wash	Flush contaminant from eye
1	Bottle of decongestant spray	Clean blood clots from nose
1	Tube of antiseptic containing benzocaine	Apply for mouth pain
10	Individual doses of burn gel (e.g., Water Jel)	Treat burns, sunburn
1	Bottle of aloe vera lotion or gel	Treat sunburn
1	Bottle of calamine lotion	Treat poison ivy, sunburn
1	Tube of hydrocortisone cream	Treat insect bites or itchy rashes
1	Tube of antibiotic cream or ointment	Apply to wounds or broken blisters to prevent infection
2	Pairs of rubber or latex gloves	Protect against infection
1	Tweezers	Remove foreign objects
1	Needle in protective case	Remove splinters

1	Penlight	Examine eyes, ears, throat
1	Bandage scissors	Cut gauze, tape
1	Rescue shears	Cut away clothing
1	Magnifying glass	Examine wounds, foreign objects in eye and skin
6	Safety pins or bandage clips	Secure bandages
1	Digital thermometer	Measure temperature
1	Small plastic bag	Dispose of trash, bloody bandages
1	Plastic measuring spoon	Administer correct dosages of liquid medicines
1	Roll of medical tape, 1 in. × 10 yds.	Secure bandages and splints
1	Bulb syringe, 3 oz.	Remove congestion from nose; irrigate wounds
1	Small package of cotton swabs (Q-tips)	Clean around wounds; remove foreign object from eye
3	Instant, disposable cold packs	Reduce swelling; relieve pain
1	SAM splints, 1 finger, 1 large (36 in.)	Immobilize limb
1	Roll of duct tape	Immobilize limb
1	Rescue blanket	Treat for shock
1	Epinephrine auto-injector	Administer for anaphylactic shock
1	Save-A-Tooth storage system	Transport tooth to dentist or hospital
1	Pocket mask	Protect against infection when administering rescue breathing
1	Bottle of acetaminophen or ibuprofen tablets	Relieve pain in adults

1	Bottle of acetaminophen or ibuprofen liquid	Relive pain in children
1	Bottle of aspirin	Treat heart attack
1	Bottle of diphenhydramine anti-histamine pills	Treat allergic reaction
1	Package of pink bismuth tablets (or bottle of liquid)	Treat upset stomach, diarrhea, and indigestion
50	Adhesive bandages, assorted sizes	Cover minor scrapes, cuts, and punctures
20	Gauze pads, assorted sizes	Cover wounds; clean around wounds; insert lost tooth
20	Non-stick gauze pads, assorted sizes	Cover burns, blisters, wounds
2	Conforming gauze rolls, 4 in. wide	Secure bandages; compress joints
2	Eye pads	Protect injured eye
10	Trauma pads, 5 in. × 9 in and 8 in. × 10 in.	Stop bleeding of deep wounds
1	Multi-trauma dressing, 10 in. × 30 in.	Protect and pad major wounds
2	Bloodstopper compress dressings	Stop bleeding of deep wounds
2	Water-Jel burn dressings, 4 in. × 4 in., 4 in. × 16 in.	Treat burns
20	Fingertip and knuckle bandages	Protect wounds on fingers and toes
1	Triangle bandage, 40 in.	Cover large wounds; secure limbs
25	Butterfly wound closure strips, assorted sizes	Hold wound edges together
1	Notepad and pen	Write down patient information, vital signs
1	First aid manual	Guide your actions

DP PLAN EXAMPLE

Table 11-1 Sample DP Plan Entry

Need: Medical / First Aid			
Danger	**Goals**	**Needs**	**Implementation**
Loss of access to medical care and medications	Establish an emergency supply of medicines and first aid supplies	30-day supply of medications	Explain preparedness rationale to family doctor and request additional prescriptions. Stock additional insulin and glucose for diabetic daughter.
		First aid kit capable of meeting emergency medical needs	Build up a first aid kit able to meet the needs of a family of five. Build a smaller kit with trauma supplies, and keep it in the car.

Quick Summary - Medical / First Aid

➢ Keep a minimum of a 30-day supply of medicine for everyone in your family. Give special consideration to any critical medicinal needs, such as insulin, nitroglycerin, or pain medicine.

➢ Everyone in your family should learn first aid. Critical life-saving first aid includes: administering CPR, stopping heavy bleeding, recognizing the signs of a stroke, treating for shock, responding correctly to poisoning, and delivering abdomen thrusts to a choking victim.

➢ When placing an emergency call, try to use a landline so the dispatcher can immediately determine your location.

➢ First aid care is not meant to replace professional emergency medical treatment.

➢ An effective first-aid kit is one that contains medical supplies that you know how to use.

Recommended Items - Medical / First Aid

❑ Minimum of a 30-day supply of medicines

❑ A well-stocked first aid kit for your home

❑ A smaller first aid kit for your car, primarily focused on trauma injuries

❑ A comprehensive first aid manual

CHAPTER 12
COMMUNICATION

COMMUNICATION

Challenge

Your city is attacked by terrorists, causing widespread panic and mayhem. Local television stations are off the air. Where else can you obtain information? Do you have a backup method of requesting help if the telephone lines become overloaded?

When a disaster threatens, your ability to communicate can mean the difference between life and death. Without communication, you are cut off from information as well as unable to request emergency assistance—both extremely important to survival during a widespread crisis.

Communication can be divided into two broad functions: *incoming* and *outgoing*. Incoming communications consist of radio, television, or Internet broadcasts for the purpose of providing warnings or situational updates. Critical information, such as evacuation orders, food and water restrictions, and early warnings of dangerous weather events, can be quickly relayed to large populations. Information may be your single greatest need during a disaster. Numerous questions require answers: How bad is the situation? What are the specific dangers? What should your family do to remain safe? Is evacuation necessary? If so, which are the best routes? How long will the threat last? What areas are affected? Are more threats expected?

Outgoing communications consist of radio transmissions, telephone, written, or even informal person-to-person messaging. Obvious uses are to request assistance from emergency services, provide updates to friends and family, and relay situational updates from the affected area.

Communication Needs

Incoming:
> Warn of approaching dangers
> Receive evacuation instructions and routes
> Receive timely situational updates

Outgoing:
> Request help from emergency services
> Contact family, friends, and DP network members
> Relay first-person updates out of the affected area

The benefits of a communication system are not only practical but psychological. Being cut off from the rest of the world can quickly cause people to grow fearful and perhaps make irrational conclusions about the state of things. These conclusions can lead to decisions that might ultimately prove dangerous or costly.

For many situations, a TV set, radio, computer, or a couple of well-placed telephone calls can answer your questions and help you to make informed decisions. During serious disasters, however, a more robust communication system may be required. In this chapter, different types of communication systems are discussed. Some allow you to receive information, while others enable you to reach out for help.

Your goal is to have a robust and reliable communication system.

Your goal should be to have a communication system that is robust and reliable—capable of working under nearly any set of circumstances. Unfortunately, there is no way to know which communication methods will be dependable because reliability tends to be a strong function of the surrounding conditions. For this reason, redundancy is especially important. Design your communication system with a fallback plan in mind, and perhaps another fallback to that fallback. If you prepare in this way, it is unlikely that *all* of your methods will become inoperable.

COMMERCIAL BROADCASTS

In this modern age of technology, information comes from a variety of broadcasters, including those who operate using radio, television, newspapers, cable, satellite, and the Internet. The Internet in particular serves as an immense and diverse information system capable of providing news in many forms, including text, audio, photographs, and video.

Together, these commercial services represent the primary methods of keeping citizens informed in times of emergency. However, depending on the type and severity of the disaster, some or all of your commercial services may become inoperable. This leaves you to gather your own information through less conventional services, such as shortwave radio or emergency service broadcasts.

EMERGENCY SERVICES

The United States government provides three important emergency notification services: the National Weather Service, the Emergency Alert System, and the Homeland Security Advisory System. The government also maintains a host of Internet websites with valuable disaster preparedness information (see *Internet Resources*).

NATIONAL WEATHER SERVICE

Americans live in the most severe-weather prone country on Earth with an average of 10,000 thunderstorms, 5,000 floods, 1,000 tornadoes, and 2 landfalling hurricanes each year.[205] To help combat these numerous threats, the National Oceanic Atmospheric Administration's National Weather Service (NWS) provides weather, flood, and climate forecasts and warnings.

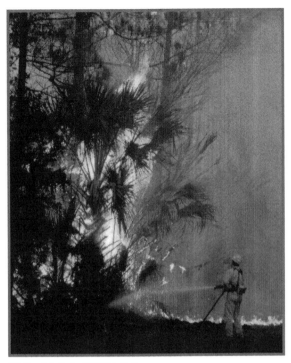

Wildfire *(photo by FEMA/Liz Roll)*

The NWS is organized as a collection of national and regional weather centers, as well as 122 Weather Forecast Offices (WFOs). The WFOs report local weather forecasts and conditions, such as temperature, humidity, and chance of precipitation, which are then combined in the National Digital Forecast Database. The NWS website, *www.weather.gov*, contains a great deal of useful information, including weather forecasts and warnings, weather radar, satellite imagery, water levels, and air quality maps. The NWS also provides information on sky conditions (for aviators), water warnings and advisories (for boaters), and fire conditions (for those concerned about wildfires).[206]

The NWS solicits help from over 290,000 SKYWARN® severe weather spotters, whose primary responsibility is to report local storm conditions. These volunteer weather reporters include police and fire personnel, EMS workers, public utility workers, and private HAM radio operators. If you are interested in becoming a SKYWARN® weather spotter, contact your local Warning Coordination Meteorologist.[207]

EMERGENCY ALERT SYSTEM

The Emergency Alert System (EAS) is a nationwide public warning system (audio only) that replaced the Emergency Broadcast System (EBS) in 1994. Radio and TV broadcasters, cable TV systems, and satellite providers are required to make available communications capabilities so that the president can address the American public during times of a national emergency. The system is also used by local and state authorities to deliver emergency information, such as weather warnings and missing children (AMBER) alerts.[208]

EAS messages are composed of four parts: a digitally-encoded SAME (Specific Area Message Encoding) header, an attention signal, an audio announcement, and a digitally-encoded end-of-message marker. The SAME header indicates who originated the message (e.g., the president, state or local authorities, NWS, or the broadcaster), a description of the event, the counties or states affected, the expected duration of the event, and the date and time it was issued. This information is translated by special receivers that decode the information (see *Weather Radios*).

Every broadcaster is required to test their EAS equipment on a weekly basis. As a courtesy to their listeners and viewers, broadcasters will typically announce that a test of the EAS is underway.

It is worth noting that the federal EAS (or its predecessor, the EBS) has never been officially used. This is in part due to the nearly universal access to news media throughout the country, making the EAS of questionable value. There are plans to eventually replace the EAS system with the Integrated Public Alert and Warning System (IPAWS), which will provide warnings through personal communication devices such as cell phones and computers.

HOMELAND SECURITY ADVISORY SYSTEM

The Department of Homeland Security (DHS) was formed following the terrorist attacks of 2001 and consists of 22 agencies, including the U.S. Customs Service, Coast Guard, Secret Service, and Immigration and Naturalization Service.[209] DHS's purpose is to protect the nation and its critical infrastructure from dangerous people and goods, as well as to strengthen the country's preparedness and emergency response capabilities.[210] DHS established a Security Advisory System that consists of Homeland Security Threat Advisories, Homeland Security Information Bulletins, and the Color-coded Threat Level System.[211]

HOMELAND SECURITY THREAT ADVISORIES

Homeland Security Threat Advisories are targeted toward federal, state and local government, private sector organizations, and international partners. They contain "actionable information" about an incident or threat that is targeting critical networks, infrastructures, or assets. The advisories recommend procedures or actions that are designed to improve security and provide protection from known threats.

HOMELAND SECURITY INFORMATION BULLETINS

Homeland Security Information Bulletins are also targeted toward federal, state and local government, private sector organizations, and international partners. They are used to communicate information to the nation's infrastructures that don't meet the timeliness, specificity, or significance of Threat Advisories. Examples of DHS bulletins include statistical reports and incident response guidelines.

COLOR-CODED THREAT LEVEL SYSTEM

The Color-coded Threat Level System was designed to communicate both to the public and public safety officials the relative likelihood of a terrorist attack. Graduated threat levels are represented by progressive colors, (e.g., red indicating imminent danger, and green indicating very low risk). Different threat levels can also be issued for various parts of the country, or even specific industries.

While it is certainly desirable to have a means by which to make the public aware of impending danger, the effectiveness of the color-coded system has been questioned. As a response to this criticism, DHS and the American Red Cross released the following set of guidelines regarding actions that should be taken for each threat level.[212,213]

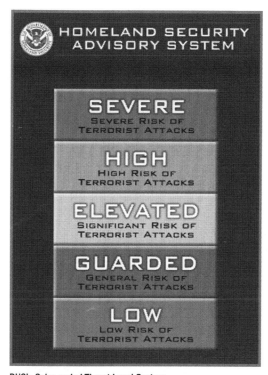

DHS's Color-coded Threat Level System

GREEN: Low Risk

- Develop a family emergency plan (see note). Share it with family and friends, and practice the plan. Visit *www.ready.gov* for help with creating a plan.
- Create an emergency supply kit for your household.
- Be informed. Visit *www.ready.gov* (or call 1-800-BE-READY) to obtain a copy of "Preparing Makes Sense, Get Ready Now."
- Know where to shelter and how to turn off utilities to your home.
- Examine volunteer opportunities in your community, such as Citizen Corps, Volunteers in Police Service, Neighborhood Watch or others. Consider completing an American Red Cross first aid or CPR course, or Community Emergency Response Team (CERT) course.

Note: A "family emergency plan" as defined by DHS is a collection of emergency contact information, meeting locations, and details of any special needs that your family members might have. To help you with this, an interactive family emergency plan tool is online at *www.ready.gov.* The tool allows you to enter your family's personal information and then print out worksheets that can be kept in your car and home. Worsheets in the *Appendix* allow you to record similar information. However, for your protection, it is recommended that you keep sensitive information like this on an encrypted flash drive as discussed in *Chapter 14: Transportation.*

BLUE: Guarded Risk

- Complete the level GREEN steps.
- Review your family's disaster supplies, and replace any items that have expired or are in poor condition.
- Be alert to suspicious activity, and report it to the proper authorities.

YELLOW: Elevated Risk

- Complete the level BLUE steps.
- Ensure that your family's disaster supplies are fully stocked and ready to use.
- Check that the telephone numbers in your family emergency plan are up to date.
- Develop and practice alternate routes to and from work.
- Continue to be alert for suspicious activity, and report it to the authorities.

ORANGE: High Risk

- Complete the level YELLOW steps.
- Exercise caution when traveling, and pay attention to travel advisories.
- Review your family emergency plan with all family members.
- Be patient. Expect delays, baggage searches, and restrictions at public buildings.
- Check on neighbors or others who might need assistance in an emergency.

RED: Severe Risk

- Complete the level ORANGE steps.
- Listen to local emergency management officials.

- Stay tuned to TV or radio for current information and instructions.
- Be prepared to shelter or evacuate if instructed.
- Expect traffic delays and restrictions.
- Provide volunteer services only if requested.
- Contact your school or business to determine the status of any cancelations.

It is worth noting that since the color-coded system was implemented in 2002, the country has always been at levels yellow or orange. It is likely to remain at one of these two levels for the foreseeable future, both of which provide the same general message, "Be prepared."

If the threat level is ever raised to RED, you should consider taking more drastic preparations, such as keeping your kids out of school, staying away from public places, and taking some time off from work.

INTERNET RESOURCES

The Internet is the worldwide, publicly accessible network of interconnected computers that transmit data by packet switching, using the standard Internet Protocol (IP). It consists of more than a billion computers on domestic, academic, business, and government networks, which together carry various information and services, such as electronic mail, online chat, file transfer, and the interlinked Web pages and other documents of the World Wide Web.[214]

Individual connection to the Internet is accomplished by connecting to dedicated servers using phone lines (dial-up or DSL), cable, fiber-optic, wireless, or satellite links. Vast amounts of information, only some of which is accurate, can be found on the Internet on every conceivable topic. Keep in mind that anyone can post anything, so information from personal webpages or organizations with particular agendas should be viewed with skepticism.

Nationwide news outlets, such as Reuters (*www.reuters.com*) and the Associated Press (*www.ap.org*), provide real-time updates and are likely to be valuable resources of information in times of crisis. Public bulletins, disaster preparedness information, and contact information can also be found on the Internet, both on official government and non-government sites.

Below is an alphabetical listing of numerous useful disaster-related public education websites.[212] Each has its own unique focus, such as infectious diseases (CDC), community readiness (Citizen Corps), and emergency preparedness (Ready.gov). The specific content of the websites changes frequently, and there is a great deal of overlap. If you want to change your perspective not only about disaster preparedness, but also about important issues facing the country, spend a few hours visiting these websites. Links to the websites are also available at *www.disasterpreparer.com*.

Government Websites	
Agency for Toxic Substances and Disease Registry Provides information regarding toxic substances, including exposure registries, medical education, emergency response, risk assessments for contaminated sites, and comprehensive information about toxic substances of all types.	**www.atsdr.cdc.gov**
Air Now Displays air quality index ratings, ozone, and particulate levels for every state in the United States.	**www.airnow.gov**
Be Ready Campaign Provides information to help people prepare for and respond to emergencies. Offers advice on assembling a simple emergency supply kit and creating a family emergency plan. Furnishes links to state and local emergency management services.	**www.ready.gov**
Centers for Disease Control and Prevention Offers information on many health safety topics, including diseases, healthy living, injuries, travelers' health, and environmental health. Provides weekly updates of influenza outbreaks and publications that discuss infectious diseases.	**www.cdc.gov**

Citizen Corps A grassroots organization of over 2000 local councils focused on citizen awareness and preparation. Offers online training and discusses Community Emergency Response Team (CERT) training. (The listing of Citizen's Corps Councils is a good way to find other *preppers* in your area.)	www.citizencorps.gov
Department of Health and Human Services Contains extensive information on preparing for natural and man-made disasters. Provides links to FEMA's daily National Situation Update, the National Weather Service, and NOAA weather radio broadcasts. Lists state emergency management and health agencies and Red Cross offices.	www.hhs.gov/disasters
Department of Homeland Security Provides a broad range of information relating to homeland security, including the national threat level, travel alerts and procedures, emergency preparation guidelines, immigration policies and border initiatives, school safety, and other security-related topics.	www.dhs.gov
Department of Interior Responsible for the conservation and management of federal land and administration programs relating to native Americans, Alaskans, and Hawaiians. Provides many useful links, including USGS, National Park Service, and US Fish and Wildlife Service.	www.doi.gov
Department of Justice Provides information on federal law enforcement, including the country's Most Wanted and Missing Persons lists. Furnishes links to report a crime, report or identify a missing person, locate an inmate or sex offender, or provide a tip to the FBI.	www.justice.gov

Disability Preparedness Provides information targeted to the physically disabled. Has discussions regarding evacuation, preparedness, and emergency planning.	www.disabilityprepared-ness.gov
Environmental Protection Agency Discusses environmental issues, including water, air quality, climate, waste/pollution, and ecosystems. Provides regional and national environmental news, and a listing of environmental laws and regulations. Contains links to report environmental violations or spills.	www.epa.gov
Federal Emergency Management Agency Provides extensive information about preparing for and recovering from numerous types of emergencies and disasters. Gives instructions on applying for disaster assistance; displays flood maps and declarations of disaster areas.	www.fema.gov
Food and Drug Administration Provides information concerning food safety, nutrition, bioterrorism, food bacteria outbreaks, animal-related illnesses, drug approvals and alerts, radiation-emitting products, and vaccines.	www.fda.gov
Food Safety Lists information pertaining to food handling, cooking temperatures, food illnesses, inspections, and product recalls.	www.foodsafety.gov
National Oceanic and Atmospheric Admin. Focuses on ocean and atmospheric conditions. Provides links to forecasts and weather alerts, atmospheric research, conservation activities, and environmental concerns.	www.noaa.gov
National Weather Service Gives up-to-date weather forecasts, warnings, radar, air quality, flooding, and weather safety information, including hazard assessments and weather radios.	www.weather.gov

Nuclear Regulatory Commission Oversees issues relating to nuclear energy production and safety, including reactors, materials, and waste. Provides recommendations for radiological emergency preparations, and maps of active nuclear reactors and waste disposal sites.	www.nrc.gov
National Traffic and Road Closure Information Displays maps and associated links to traffic conditions and road closures across the United States.	www.fhwa.dot.gov/ trafficinfo
U.S. Department of Agriculture Develops and executes policies on agriculture, farming, and food. Topics include pest control, weather, animal health, food aid, a plant database, food and nutrition, farm bills, and agricultural news.	www.usda.gov
U.S. Fire Administration Manages programs relating to fire fighting and fire safety, and collects statistics on incidents and deaths. Also provides fire safety and prevention information.	www.usfa.dhs.gov
U.S. Geological Survey Provides scientific information about the country's landscape, resources, and natural hazards, including earthquakes, floods, droughts, wildfires, climate change, volcanoes, and invasive species.	www.usgs.gov
U.S. Office of Personnel Management Maintains disaster preparedness information specifically targeted to federal employees.	www.opm.gov/emergency
The White House The official government website details policy, achievements, and challenges facing the United States. Also includes press briefings, presidential addresses, proclamations, and cabinet appointments.	www.whitehouse.gov

National Wildfire Programs Database A national database of state and local wildfire mitigation programs.	www.wildfireprograms.com
Pandemic Flu Furnishes extensive information about pandemic and flu outbreaks, vaccinations, and preparations around the world.	www.pandemicflu.gov
Non-government Websites	
American Red Cross Lists links to disaster preparation, including for those with special needs (children, elderly, and disabled). Also, provides information on how to receive assistance after a disaster, and take first aid or other training classes.	www.redcross.org
American Veterinary Medical Association Offers emergency preparedness information relating to pets and livestock.	www.avma.org/disaster/saving_family.asp
Equipped to Survive Furnishes information on first aid kits, position locator beacons, survival equipment, and other emergency gear.	www.equipped.org
Google Flu Trends Tracks influenza outbreaks around much of the world. Compares current year's flu activity to previous years'.	www.google.org/flutrends/
Institute for Business and Home Safety Offers practical information on preparing for earthquakes, floods, freezing weather, hail, high winds, hurricanes, tornados, and wildfires.	www.disastersafety.org
Kids Health Provides medical and first aid information relating specifically to children's needs. Contains useful instruction sheets for dealing with a host of medical and first aid issues.	www.kidshealth.org/parent

National Fire Protection Association Provides fact sheets and safety tips regarding prevention, fire proofing your home, and evacuation.	www.nfpa.org
Web MD An online resource that offers medical condition information, symptom-based diagnoses, and health-related news.	www.webmd.com

COMMUNICATION EQUIPMENT

The effectiveness of different communication methods will largely depend upon the type, duration, proximity, and extent of a particular disaster. Each method utilizes specific communications hardware, from commonplace TVs and AM/FM radios, to more specialized shortwave radios and scanners. Below are brief discussions of many communication devices designed to receive and/or transmit vital information during an emergency.

AM/FM RADIO AND TELEVISION

Tried and true, the AM/FM radio and television are very valuable tools to receive updates during a crisis. Not only will local stations broadcast the most up to date information, but the nation's Emergency Alert System also uses radio and TV broadcasts to inform the public of dangerous events.

One distinct advantage of AM radio over other broadcasts is that, in some weather conditions, it can transfer very long distances. This is known as skywave propagation, or more simply as "skip," and refers to the amplitude-modulated wave refracting back from the ionosphere and returning to the surface at a faraway place. The skipping phenomenon is much less likely to occur with TV or FM signals. AM skip can be especially beneficial during large scale disasters.

Tips

AM and shortwave broadcasts benefit from skywave propagation.

One disadvantage of AM, however, is that its signals don't penetrate well. For this reason, reception in an underground shelter is very limited without external antennas.

At a minimum, you should own at least one high-quality, portable, battery-powered AM/FM radio (e.g., Grundig, Sangean, Sony). Determine your radio's battery use, and stock enough spare batteries to run the radio for a minimum of 84 hours. If you listen to the radio for six hours per day, this represents two full weeks of listening. If you opt for rechargeable batteries, be sure you have the appropriate equipment to recharge them from your backup electrical source (see *Chapter 7: Electrical Power*).

Battery-powered radios with hand cranks and/or solar panels are another viable option. However, treat the hand crank or solar recharging as a backup capability only. Cranking the radio every few minutes can grow tedious, and the durability of the cranking system is often the radio's weak link. Likewise, recharging by solar means is slow and unpredictable (see *Chapter 7: Electrical Power*). Several companies, including Sangean, Freeplay, and Eton, offer quality hand-crank and solar units. Read numerous consumer reviews before purchasing a solar or hand-crank radio. Many units are not well built and won't stand up to continued use.

Portable, battery-operated televisions are also becoming fairly commonplace. If you plan to use a TV to pick up local stations without the use

Midland hand-crank AM/FM radio

of a cable or satellite box, select a unit with a built-in-digital tuner that supports digital TV (DTV). Analog broadcasts are no longer available.

WEATHER RADIO

Weather radios are special-purpose radios designed to receive weather-related announcements, forecasts, and emergency broadcasts. For many years, NOAA's National Weather Service has broadcasted continuous weather information, including forecasts, watches, and warnings on seven frequencies from 162.4 MHz to 162.55 MHz. Recently however, they have also begun working in conjunction with the Federal Communications Commission's Emergency Alert System to broadcast warning and post-event information for natural disasters (e.g., earthquakes, volcanoes) and technological emergencies (e.g., chemical releases, oils spills).[215] This "all hazards" capability makes weather radios critically important to disaster preparedness.

It is strongly recommended that you have a weather radio at home and another at work. These radios sound a loud tone as well as provide critical information when dangerous weather or other events threaten your

Every home should have a NOAA weather radio.

Midland weather radio

area. In case the threat occurs overnight, place the radio somewhere in your home where it will awaken you. Early warnings of this sort can mean the difference between life and death. Modern radios are also equipped with the Specific Alert Message Encoding (SAME) feature. SAME allows you to designate the particular area for which you want to receive alerts, specifying your local county, for example.[216] This reduces the number of alarms you receive to only those of greatest interest.

Additional information regarding weather radios and the SAME messaging feature can be found at NOAA's NWS website, *www.weather.gov/nwr.*[217]

SCANNERS

Scanners are radio receivers that allow you to listen to emergency service broadcasts, including police, fire, and rescue, as well as broadcasts by airports, trains, utility companies, the National Weather Service, and amateur radio operators. A scanner sweeps through the frequency ranges that you specify until it finds a broadcasted signal. Once that signal subsides, the scanner continues the cyclic scan, repeating continuously.

Previous generation scanners were bulky, expensive, and had very limited channel capacity. Modern units, however, can be handheld, mobile, or stationary, and are available in nearly every price range. Much like computers, scanners are now equipped with microprocessors and solid-state memory that enables them to store thousands of channels, monitoring hundreds of them in a single second.

> **Tips**
> Scanner selection requires an understanding of the types of transmissions used in your area.

Before purchasing a scanner, it is vital that you match your requirements to the receiver's capabilities. Otherwise, you may be sorely disappointed when you are unable to receive the signals in your area. All scanners enable you to easily dial in and listen to single discrete frequencies—like a conventional radio station. However, many agencies have replaced analog transmissions with APCO-25 digital transmissions. This means that broadcasts are transmitted using binary modulation (1's and 0's), which cannot be decoded by basic analog receivers. Note that digital receivers can receive both analog and digital transmissions.

Trunked systems, such as EDACS and LTR, are also becoming very common. Trunking refers to the sharing of a small set of frequencies by a number of broadcasters. Each time a user attempts to broadcast, he is assigned one of the frequencies from the set, and the receivers on his user group are automatically notified to tune into that new frequency. This frequency hopping is very efficient in using a small number of frequencies, but it also makes it impossible for someone to listen to the broadcasts without a receiver that also automatically hops between frequencies.

It is important to understand whether your local area emergency services use basic analog, trunked analog, digital, or digital trunked communications, so you can select a scanner that supports those transmissions. Most cities appear to be migrating to digital trunked technology, so it is a safer bet, albeit more expensive, to purchase a unit capable of this type of reception.

If you are interested in learning more about scanners, start by visiting *www.scannermaster.com* and *www.radioreference.com*. Between the two websites is a wealth of information on scanners and the transmissions in your local area. You may also post questions on their forums to solicit advice

Uniden scanners

from scanner experts. If you enjoy listening to emergency broadcasts and have the time to become familiar with this hobby, scanners can be a very valuable emergency preparedness tool.

TELEPHONES

Telephones are broadly classified as conventional, Internet, cell, or satellite. Conventional phones rely on hardwired telephone cables and remain the primary means of telephone communication due to their many benefits, including moderate cost, high reliability, and good voice quality. Internet calling uses conventional phones or computers to transmit voice data through Internet connections. There are many voice-over-internet products, including magicJack, Skype, and Vonage. The specific features and equipment for each differ, but the products all offer low-cost, internet-enabled, point-to-point communications.

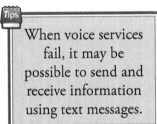

When voice services fail, it may be possible to send and receive information using text messages.

For many households, cellular phones are replacing conventional phones. This migration is in part due to the "always connected" society in which people now live. It is estimated that over 80% of the United States population has a cell phone.[218] The distinct advantage of cell phones is their portability. Disadvantages include cost and poor voice quality. Cell phones can also be used to text messages, which can be especially important because text messages can often get through when cell service is congested and otherwise unavailable.

Satellite phones use orbiting satellites to relay information, and thus offer communication to and from remote areas where other services are unavailable. Satellite phones are not part of the mainstream commercial market due to prohibitively high costs.

Depending on the type and severity of a disaster, some telephone services may no longer operate, or may be overwhelmed by users. Hardwired landline phones are preferable to cordless home ones because they will operate even when your power is out—assuming electricity is available to the phone company. For this reason, it is recommended that you have at least one hardwired landline phone in your home.

Compile a list of emergency phone numbers and keep a copy near the phone as well as in your safe room. An emergency contact worksheet is included in the *Appendix* for this purpose. Below are some phone numbers that might be useful:

Service or Agency	Phone Number
Emergency Services	911
Nationwide Traveler Information (Available in some states)	511
Poison Control Center	1800-222-1222
Federal Emergency Management Administration (FEMA)	1-800-621-FEMA
Centers for Disease Control and Prevention (CDC)	1-800-311-3435
Federal Bureau of Investigation	1-800-CALL-FBI

EMAIL

Due to its speed and convenience, email has largely replaced written correspondence, both for work and personal communications. Email can be a valuable method of communicating in times of crisis because it is less likely to be overwhelmed than telephone services and can send out messages to multiple recipients simultaneously. However, email depends on the availability of Internet or cellular phone service, as well as electrical power, making the loss of either a single point of failure.

If you are part of a disaster preparedness network, it is a good idea to create an email group to which you can quickly broadcast information in times of crisis. This allows your group to keep everyone up to date without the worry of accidentally forgetting someone in the network.

SHORTWAVE RADIOS

Shortwave radios operate in the frequency range from 3 to 30 MHz. There are several different types of transmissions including amplitude modulation (for general broadcasting), continuous wave (for Morse code transmission), single sideband (for long distance communication), and narrow band FM (for military communications).

In the United States, you do not need a license to own or operate a shortwave receiver. However, the privilege of operating a shortwave radio transmitter for non-commercial two-way communications (known as amateur radio) is granted through a licensing process by the Federal Communications Commission (FCC). Amateur radio operators often make themselves available to transmit emergency communications when normal communications channels have failed. In the case of a disaster, it is a good bet that shortwave operators will find a way to relay important information across the country. As with AM, shortwave radio signals also benefit from skywave propagation, meaning they can often transmit vast distances—even around the globe under certain favorable weather conditions.

There are many types of shortwave broadcasts, but most fall into the following categories:

- Amateur radio ("HAM") operators, many of who help local communities during times of crisis
- Domestic broadcasting from countries with widely dispersed populations
- World band radio broadcasting internationally to foreign audiences
- Political, religious, and conspiracy theory radio networks
- Numbers stations, believed to be operated by government agencies to communicate with clandestine operatives working in foreign countries
- Rebel and insurgent force communications

Of all the shortwave broadcasters, amateur radio operators should have a special place in the hearts of disaster preparers. HAM radio operators often serve as an information lifeline to affected communities when conventional broadcasts have gone offline. If you have an interest in becoming a HAM radio operator, consult the Internet and you will find many user groups that can help you get started. Even if you are not interested in becoming an operator, you should consider having a radio or scanner capable of receiving shortwave transmissions. This lets you function in a "listen only" mode, but at least you will become familiar with local area operators.

Kaito shortwave radio receiver

CB RADIOS, WALKIE-TALKIES

Walkie-talkies and CB radios are inexpensive, short-range communication devices that can be useful when cell phone service is unavailable. Don't rely on the mileage claims put forth by retailers. Actual effective operating distances are a strong function of the environment, but in general, walkie-talkies and CB radios should always be considered line of sight devices.

CB Radios—The Citizen Band is a 40-channel radio system operating in the 27 MHz band. CB radio technology is a bit dated, going back to its inception in 1945. Since the transmission does not propagate well through objects, CB radios are used predominantly outdoors. In the United States, these radios are used extensively by truckers communicating traffic information along the major roadways.

Cobra CB radio

Walkie-Talkies—Modern walkie-talkies operate using either the Family Radio Service (FRS) and/or General Mobile Radio Service (GMRS).

- **FRS**—The Family Radio Service is a frequency-modulated (FM), 14-channel walkie-talkie system authorized for use in the United States since 1996. It operates in the UHF band around 462 and 467 MHz, and thus does not suffer from the interference effects found with CB radios. FRS radios are limited by FCC regulations to a maximum of 0.5 watts. Channels 1 to 7 of FRS radios are shared with the GMRS. A license is required for those channels only if the power output exceeds the FRS 0.5 watt limit.
- **GMRS**—The General Mobile Radio Service is a 15-channel, FM, UHF radio service available for short-range two-way communications. GMRS operates in the same frequency band as FRS, but with a higher maximum allowed transmit power. By law, GMRS use requires an FCC license (costing about $75), although the vast majority of users are unlicensed. GMRS permits transmission on eight dedicated channels at up to 50 watts, but typical GMRS walkie-talkies transmit at only a few watts. GMRS licensees are also permitted to use the first seven FRS channels (the "interstitial" frequencies), but at the 5-watt maximum output power.

Uniden walkie-talkies

Recently, hybrid FRS/GMRS consumer radios were introduced that include all 22 channels (the 14 FRS and 8 dedicated GMRS). On this type of radio, only channels 8 through 14 are strictly license-free FRS channels. Transmitting on channels above 14 requires a license, and transmitting on the shared FRS/GMRS channels 1 through 7 also requires an FCC license if the effective radiated power of the radio is greater than the FRS limit of 0.5 watts. GMRS radios can be very useful short-range communication devices because of their higher output power.

ONSTAR

OnStar Corporation, a subsidiary of General Motors, offers a subscription-based communications service for use in your vehicle. The benefits

OnStar

of OnStar are quite significant. Below is a brief list of some of the important features.[219]

- Automatic Crash Response—Sensors monitor your car to determine when you are involved in an accident, and automatically dispatch emergency services to your location.
- Remote Door Unlock—Operators can remotely unlock your car in case you have lost your keys or locked them in the vehicle.
- One-button Call for Help—Press a single button to call for emergency or roadside services.
- Vehicle Diagnostics—Sensors monitor the health of your vehicle, reporting any anomalies or maintenance needs.
- Optional add-ons include voice-activated calling, turn-by-turn navigation, and stolen vehicle assistance.

One significant advantage over a cell phone is that OnStar transmits at three watts of power, about five times more than a typical cell phone. This extra transmit power enables you to call for help in areas where cell service is weak. OnStar also allows an operator to locate your car using embedded GPS. If you should become injured or ill, or break down in an unfamiliar area, the operator can guide emergency or repair services directly to you. Likewise, if you are reported missing, OnStar representatives can help rescue services to quickly locate you.

It should be obvious from the benefits discussed that having a vehicle equipped with OnStar is an excellent way to be prepared on the road. The most significant disadvantage of OnStar is that is only equipped in newer vehicles from General Motors. You cannot add OnStar to a vehicle that didn't have it factory installed as original equipment. Some people are also concerned with privacy issues relating to the tracking ability of the service. Finally, there is a cost associated with the service (currently $199/year). However, all things considered, if you have a car currently equipped with OnStar, it is highly recommend that you keep the service active.

LAST DITCH CALL FOR HELP! THE WHISTLE

One final form of personal communication device that shouldn't be overlooked is the whistle. A loud whistle can be useful in calling for help, such as when lost outdoors or trapped in a collapsed building. Blowing a whistle takes much less energy than screaming, and the sound travels farther. Keep a whistle in your safe room is a simple, but perhaps life-saving, precaution. Should your home ever collapse on top of you, a whistle can help you signal for help. Finally, everyone should always carry a whistle when hiking outdoors. Lost children and adults alike stand a much greater chance of surviving if they follow one simple rule: hug a tree and blow your whistle.

CRISIS JOURNAL

It is often helpful to create a crisis journal during an extended disaster. The journal can have many uses, including recording events, tracking the passing of time, listing worries and their potential solutions, documenting injuries or illnesses, and keeping up with supply lists. Creating a crisis journal can help you gain a sense of organization and control that is often critical not only to making sound decisions, but also to keeping a positive attitude.

First person accounts also serve as historical records for generations to come. A journal can be kept with pen and paper (both very portable), or with a word processor if electricity is available.

DP PLAN EXAMPLE

Table 12-1 Sample DP Plan Entry

Need: Communication			
Danger	Goals	Needs	Implementation
Loss of telephone	Request emergency assistance, and inform family of situation	Backup telephone systems	Use cell phone service as primary backup. Use magicJack plugged into computer to serve as a backup VOIP phone system.
		Electronic mail and texting	Set up DP network as an email group to quickly broadcast updates and warnings. Use cell phone text message capability to relay information when phones are overwhelmed.
	Communicate across short ranges with DP members	A two-way radio system	Use a GMRS walkie-talkie system for neighborhood and car-to-car communication.
Loss of radio and TV broadcasts	Receive news and emergency broadcasts	Online news	Use existing Internet connection to monitor online news channels.
		Emergency weather and other hazard news	Put NOAA weather radios in bedroom and kitchen.

Quick Summary - Communication

➢ Timely information is critical to making the correct decisions during a disaster. There are many possible sources of information, including radio and TV broadcasts, Internet websites, government emergency service announcements, and direct first person accounts.

➢ Commercial services, namely AM/FM radio and TV, will continue to be the primary methods used to distribute information from government agencies and media. More modern systems are underway that include using cell phones, text messages, and the Internet.

➢ Governmental emergency services include the National Weather Service, Emergency Alert System, and the Homeland Security Advisory System.

➢ The Internet offers access to numerous resources, including real-time news, evacuation routes, traffic conditions, medical advice, weather forecasts, disaster preparedness advice, and crisis assistance.

➢ Every home should have a weather radio. Modern weather radio broadcasts provide early warnings not only for dangerous weather events, but also for a variety of natural and man-made disasters.

➢ Specialty radios, including shortwave and scanners, may allow you to listen in on amateur broadcasts and emergency services. Before purchasing a scanner, be sure to understand the radio systems that your local emergency services use.

➢ Every home should be equipped with at least one hardwired landline phone that can operate without electricity services.

➢ Walkie-talkie and CB radios should be considered short-range, line of sight devices. GMRS radios have more transmit power than FRS radios, but require a license to operate.

➢ A crisis journal can help you make better decisions, track supplies; and it can serve as a record for historical purposes.

Recommended Items - Communication

❑ Receive information and situational updates
   a. AM/FM or shortwave radio (hand-cranked or battery operated)
   b. Television capable of receiving local and national news
   c. Computer with Internet access
   d. NOAA Weather radio
   e. Optional: Scanner

❑ Request assistance from home or while on the road
   a. Hardwired landline home phone (not cordless)
   b. List of emergency phone numbers
   c. Cell phone, preferably with text messaging
   d. Whistle
   e. Optional: OnStar
   f. Optional: GMRS walkie-talkies

❑ Keep a record of events
   a. Notebooks and pens

CHAPTER 13
FINANCIAL PREPAREDNESS

Chapter 13 Notes

CHAPTER 13
FINANCIAL PREPAREDNESS

Challenge

Your employer suddenly closes his doors, giving you only a week's severance pay. Do you have an adequate emergency fund with which to survive until you can find employment? Or have you burdened yourself so heavily with debt that you will quickly sink under its weight?

You may question the relevance of money management in disaster preparedness. Certainly it is not a topic covered in most handbooks. Its importance, however, is easy enough to see. Consider that your finances play three distinct roles in disaster preparedness.

1. Extra money enables you to purchase emergency supplies.
2. An emergency fund helps you to handle unexpected financial pressures.
3. A financial safety net protects your assets during times of loss.

Each of these three roles is vitally important and will be discussed in detail. Realize, however, that money is *not* the most important element of preparation. What you know is always more valuable than what you own.

You should never feel that you are not properly preparing because of budget constraints. Do what you can when you can. Being prepared is as much a frame of mind as it is a closet of supplies. There are many steps to becoming better prepared that cost nothing more than your time, including learning first aid, forming a community preparedness group, and ensuring that your home is protected from hazards.

For now though, let's turn our attention to money.

PRIORITIZING

When it comes to preparing, patience and persistence win the day.

By this point in the book, you have probably come to realize that preparing can be rather expensive. Throughout the chapters, every effort has been made to limit the recommended supplies to include only the most important items. Even with this limitation, costs can be significant. With all the various recommendations, you may wonder where to begin. Everyone has a limited budget, so becoming fully prepared will take time—perhaps months or even years. Patience and persistence win the day.

It would be satisfying to possess a simple linear checklist to run down to get prepared—buy item A, perform action B, learn skill C, etc. Unfortunately, such a general approach is impractical. Every family's priorities will differ because each is exposed to different types of threats. If you live on the East Coast and experience powerful nor'easters, you will want to prioritize shoring up your home to better weather those events. Likewise, if you live in the Northwest where heavy snowfall is common, a fully stocked pantry and secondary heat source are likely high priorities. The point is that every family's situation is unique.

The best way to start is to identify and prioritize *your* family's needs. This process begins with completing a DP Plan Worksheet (see *Appendix*) for each of the fourteen needs (e.g., food, water, shelter, etc.). To make it easier, sample DP plan entries have been furnished at the end of every chapter. The goal of using the worksheets is to map out the specific actions you will take, as well as the supplies you will purchase, to prepare for various types of threats.

Preparation is easier when accomplished in stages. For example, you might wish to first identify everything you need to reach an arbitrary minimum level of self-sustenance, that is, able to provide all of your family's needs for a brief time (perhaps

Start by reaching a minimum level of self-sustenance—perhaps a single week.

for a single week). This might require stocking the cupboards with extra food, purchasing a water filter, shoring up your home, getting a few lanterns, and other basic preparations.

After reaching this minimum level, you can then expand your capabilities based on the likelihood of the need and the cost of the preparation. Increasing your food stockpile to a 30-day supply and your water to a 14-day supply are often reasonable starting points for the second phase of preparation. The order of your preparations is dependent on the particular threats you may face, their likely impact, and the extent of your ability to prepare for them. For example, a generator is very expensive, but if you frequently find yourself without electrical power, it might be a high priority purchase for your family.

Once again, the idea is to methodically work through your DP Plan worksheets while considering which threats are most likely to affect your family.

ARE YOU FINANCIALLY PREPARED?

People come from all walks of life, each with his or her unique financial situation. Some people are unquestionably wealthy while others struggle to pay the rent. One commonality spanning all classes, however, is that we spend too much and save too little. Consider that Americans carry a revolving debt in excess of $900 billion (as of June of 2007). Add in loans, but still exclude mortgages, and the personal debt rises to a whopping $2.46 trillion.[220] These figures don't consider the trillions of dollars that the country's wasteful politicians have overspent.

One of the goals of this chapter is to provide you with common sense approaches to becoming better financially prepared. But the darker truth is that every citizen should be deeply concerned with the financial condition of our country. Both as individuals and as a country, we

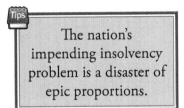

The nation's impending insolvency problem is a disaster of epic proportions.

are overspending. The solution to the nation's coming insolvency problems will surely involve government and citizens alike, but you should prepare for this coming debacle by getting your own financial house in order now.

Perhaps you haven't given much thought to your financial health. If that's true, use this foray into disaster preparedness to get financially fit. Some may shy away from the uncomfortable topic of money because it forces them to acknowledge some poor decisions they may have made in the past. Rest assured, from billionaires to paupers, *everyone* has made poor financial decisions at one time or another. Learn from your mistakes and move on.

A good place to start is to informally assess your own personal level of financial preparedness. Take a moment to answer the following questions as honestly as possible.

1. Are you living paycheck to paycheck?
2. Do you have an emergency fund set aside to handle a significant, unexpected expense?
3. Can you cope with the financially difficulties caused by an extended illness in your family?
4. If you or your spouse dies suddenly, will your family be able to maintain the same standard of living as it does today?
5. If your home or car is damaged or destroyed, can you afford to repair or replace it without excessive financial hardship?
6. Do you have a reasonable plan for retirement? (Hoping to win the lottery is *not* a plan!)

Your answers should give you insight into your current level of financial preparedness. Maybe your financial preparations are rock solid, in which case, you should stay the course. However, if your financial readiness is less than ideal, now is the time to turn things around. Sound money management will not only help you become better prepared, but also grant you a sense of control in your life. You are encouraged to read this chapter carefully, follow it up with your own research, and then put the principles into practice.

Unexpected financial hardship

THE MONEY PLAN

To accomplish anything difficult generally requires a plan, and becoming financially prepared is no exception. Readying your finances for the challenges that hard times are almost certain to bring begins by adopting a sound money management plan (a.k.a., the *Money Plan*).

Designing an effective money management plan is painfully simple. Putting it into practice is the hard part! Getting financially healthy is analogous to getting physically fit. On paper, it all sounds great . . . eat more vegetables, exercise 30 minutes a day, get plenty of sleep, etc. But once you see that cheesecake in the fridge, the best laid plans go out the window! This chapter will do its part to lay out a reasonable plan. You must do your part to resist the cheesecake.

The *Money Plan* is broken down into six steps (see tip box). Each and every step is crucial to your success. Together, they act as the foundation to your financial house. If any part is missing, the house quickly collapses.

> ### The *Money Plan*
> 1. Spend less than you make.
> 2. Save more.
> 3. Limit your debt.
> 4. Get the most bang for your buck.
> 5. Be adequately insured.
> 6. Don't get scammed.

As you will see, achieving financial preparedness will likely require you to adopt new spending and saving habits. This may lead to some dramatic changes in your way of living. For that reason, it must be a family commitment. Involving your children is especially important because they are the next generation either doomed to repeat our mistakes or to learn from them.

SPEND LESS THAN YOU MAKE

The first step of the *Money Plan* is certain to be the most difficult. But without it, you simply cannot succeed. You must learn to live below your means. Not *above* your means. Not even *at* your means. You must spend less than you make.

If our world was a cash-driven society, it would be much easier to keep from overspending. With cash, you can only spend what you have in hand. With the advent of debt, however, many people have adopted lifestyles that are beyond their means. People observe friends and neighbors living to a certain standard, and assume that they should live to that level too (a.k.a., *Keeping up with the Joneses'* syndrome).

One simple way to determine if you are living beyond your means is to answer this question:

Do you have short-term debt, such as credit cards or loans, that rolls over from month to month?

If the answer is yes, then you have borrowed money from your future to pay for your past. Said another way, you bought things you couldn't afford at the time. If it makes you feel any better, you are certainly not alone in this predicament. Debt is as seductive as the song of the Sirens.

Living below your means implies that you have extra money each month, thereby eliminating the need for short-term debt. By doing so, you will achieve a level of financial freedom. The word *freedom* may seem a bit extreme, but taking on debt is akin to placing yourself in the servitude of a company, organization, or individual. Is that really where you want to be? Being in debt is neither a natural nor desirable state for anyone.

HOW TO LIVE BELOW YOUR MEANS

Learning to live below your means sounds like such a simple thing. All you have to do is spend less than you make. What could be easier? In reality, living below your means will likely be a tremendous challenge, one that will require significant changes to your current lifestyle.

Living below your means is the single most important step to becoming financially prepared.

The process is straightforward. Begin by determining your monthly gross and net incomes. Gross income is the amount you earn before taxes and withdrawals. Net income is your take-home pay—the number of dollars you actually put into your wallet after the government takes its share. If your pay is not the same each month, then use the last 12 months to establish averages.

Next determine the amount that you would like to save. Most financial experts recommend that you save 10% of your gross income. As you become an experienced saver, you may wish to increase this amount. For now though, 10% is doing fantastic! Subtract that amount from your net income to get your available income—this is the money you have available to pay your bills, buy groceries, and keep gas in the car.

Once you determine your available income, calculate your monthly expenses. Determining your expenses is a bit trickier because some bills vary from month to month, and others may only come due once or twice a year. For those, determine the yearly totals and divide by twelve to determine average monthly expenses. With a bit of effort, you can get estimates that are close enough for budgeting purposes.

Finally, see how it all adds up. Any extra cash remaining each month is your available income minus your expenses. If this number is positive, congratulations are in order. You can live below your means without any appreciable changes to your income or spending. Unfortunately, for most people, the difference is more likely a negative number. This means that your monthly expenses are in excess of your available income. Your challenge is to increase your available income, decrease your monthly expenditures, or both.

Recognize that doing either one is difficult. Raising your income may require working extra hours, taking on a second job, or perhaps even making a job change. Lowering your expenses may require sacrifices that you simply don't want to make. Remind yourself that your financial readiness depends on working this out.

Numerous suggestions for increasing your income and reducing your expenditures are given in this chapter. They represent a smorgasbord of ideas, not all of which will apply to you. But don't dismiss them out of hand without consideration. Remember, the first and most important step to becoming financially prepared is to spend less than you make. Consider all the options, decide how you will make this happen, and then do it!

Increasing Money Flowing In

Below are suggestions to increase or supplement your income. As you take steps to raise your income, never lose sight of what you are trading for the additional money, whether it is simple "down time" or something more important like quality time with those you love. Make the appropriate choices.

- **Upgrade your skills.** Get the training or education you need to advance to a more highly paid position. Remember, if you have skill, energy, and a decent attitude, you are an employer's dream!
- **Become more valuable to your employer.** Put in the extra hours; volunteer for additional responsibilities; do exceptional work. Your employer *will* notice.

- **Take on a second job.** Burn the midnight oil and work a second job, at least until you can get some of your debt knocked out.
- **Maximize your investments for the best returns.** Put your money in the highest yielding accounts. Money under your mattress is losing its value in an inflationary economy.
- **Start up a small business.** Do something that you enjoy and are good at, such as a lawn cutting service, math tutoring, scrapbooking, etc.
- **Sell some stuff.** Look through your attic and closets and sell some of the things collecting dust. You can do this through consignment shops, online auctions, or garage sales.

When looking to increase your income, don't underestimate your abilities. The difference between a fast food restaurant manager and the CEO of a Fortune 500 company is not so great. Both handle daily business pressures, deal with difficult people, and are always on the lookout to raise revenue and cut costs. If you see jobs that are more rewarding than the one you currently have, take a practical approach to making the transition. Believe in yourself.

Decreasing Money Flowing Out

Below are suggestions to reduce your monthly expenses. Everyone has different priorities. You may feel that some of the suggestions are too great a sacrifice, but once again, give each item some honest consideration. The goal is to assess where your money is going each month, and then figure out ways to reduce or eliminate those expenses.[221]

- **Make a budget.** Manage your money using a formal budget. Start by planning how you will spend every dollar of your paycheck. Bills, savings, grocery money, and other necessities are budgeted first. Any additional money is then mapped out for leisure activities—movies, dinner out, amusement parks, etc. Numerous budget worksheets are available for free online.
- **Downsize.** It may be particularly painful to think about moving to a smaller house, or replacing that fancy new car with a used one, but these steps can free up a significant amount of money.
- **Get rid of high-interest debt.** Shop around for favorable rates on credit cards, car loans, home mortgages, and home equity lines of credit.

- **Stop smoking.** Quitting will not only reduce your monthly expenses but also help you to obtain more affordable life insurance—not to mention live longer.
- **Go out for bids on insurance.** Shop around for the best rates on your home, car, and life insurance.
- **Cut back on services.** Try living without cable, Internet, cell phone, caller ID, and other techno-luxuries.
- **Brew your own coffee.** Make coffee at home instead of hitting the coffee shop.
- **Learn to love water.** Drink tap water when eating out, rather than sodas, wine, or beer. Also, use a home water purifier instead of bottled water.
- **Avoid impulse buying.** Limit your purchases to real needs, rather than impulse buys. Always ask "Do I really need this?"
- **Carpool.** Establish or join a carpool to work.
- **Sell that second car.** Get by with only one car. It will reduce your debt as well as cut insurance and tax expenses.
- **Save energy.** Run the heater/AC less, weatherproof your house, turn down the water heater, cutoff unused lights, and run appliances less frequently to conserve energy.
- **Drop memberships.** Discontinue memberships if you are not getting your money's worth (e.g., gym, golf club, hunting club).
- **Avoid using ATMs.** Eliminate fees by keeping a little money in your sock drawer.
- **Limit trips to town.** Plan your trips to town to accomplish as much as possible.
- **Stay healthy.** Getting sick can cost you bundles. Take care of yourself, and it will fatten your wallet.
- **Buy store brands.** Try out those generic store brands. For many products, you will never notice the difference.
- **Thrift stores.** Check out the local thrift or consignment stores for great deals on secondhand products, particularly in well-to-do areas.
- **Generic or online drugs.** Generics can save 30% or more over brand-name drugs. Likewise, drugs can sometimes be ordered online for additional savings (e.g., *www.drugstore.com*).
- **Online shopping.** Compare local prices to those of online stores. Many online stores offer lower prices and have the advantage of not charging taxes.

- **Avoid eating out.** Cook at home. Not only is it cheaper, but it is often healthier.
- **Buy clothes off season.** Never pay the full retail price for clothing. Even designer clothes can be purchased at huge savings when out of season.
- **Use coupons.** Use coupons for groceries, restaurants, services, etc. Check out newspaper inserts as well as online coupon websites, such as *www.couponchief.com, www.fatwallet.com, www.retailmenot.com,* and *www.ultimatecoupons.com.*
- **Loyalty cards.** Use grocery store loyalty cards to receive special savings on promotional items.
- **Watch the register.** Monitor the checkout register for pricing errors.
- **Join a warehouse club.** Join Costco, Sam's Club, or other large warehouse stores to receive significant savings on bulk purchases.
- **Keep your car as long as possible.** Resist the urge to replace your car when the new wears off. Try to get at least 10 years (or 150,000 miles) out of a car.
- **Buy used cars.** When you must replace your vehicle, buy one that is a couple of years old to save on depreciation.
- **Learn to love the library.** Quit buying what you can get for free. Discover the treasure trove of books, CD's, and movies that libraries offer.
- **Rent instead of going to the movies.** Stay at home and watch movies using low-cost services like Netflix, Blockbuster, or Redbox.

The single most important thing you can do to cut your expenses is to learn to curb your consumerism. Quit accumulating stuff! When is enough really enough? The answer is different for each person, but even recognizing that there is a logical limit to just how much you want to accumulate in life is eye opening.

SAVE MORE

The second step to becoming financially healthy, and thus better prepared for unexpected financial burdens, is to save more. If you are like most Americans, you don't save enough. How much is enough? A respectable goal is to save 10% of your gross income. That means if your gross family income is $80,000, you should be saving $8,000 a year.

There are several important benefits to saving:

- Savings allow you to deal with unexpected hardships using an emergency fund.
- As your money grows, it serves as a new income stream.
- Savings help you to have a better life after you retire.
- With savings can come generosity, whether it is in the form of donations to your local animal shelter, paying for your grandchildren's college costs, or helping the church to build the new gymnasium. Prosperity can also be passed down to your children and other loved ones.

Your goal is to save 10% of your family's gross income.

There are many people who don't save a dime. Either they argue that they are living life to the fullest—mistakenly correlating spending to happiness, or more likely, they convince themselves that they simply can't afford to save.

Those in the first category will almost certainly come to regret their choices as they grow older and are forced to work to their dying day— assuming they are healthy enough to do so. As for the people who feel that they don't have enough income to save, it is generally more a matter of willingness to sacrifice. If your income was suddenly cut by 10%, would you still survive? Almost certainly you would. You might have to make some adjustments to how you live, but you would adapt and survive.

Also, recognize that savings is a sliding scale. If you make a lot, then you need to save a lot—enabling you to handle larger financial burdens and ultimately retire at the same standard that you have today. Likewise, if your income is small, then it is possible to save fewer dollars and still achieve your goals. Remember, 10% is your goal.

A STRATEGY FOR SAVINGS

The goal of saving is to become financially prepared—out of debt, socking away money each month, and prepared to deal with unexpected challenges. The obvious first step to achieving this goal is to establish an emergency fund.

However, there is another equally important goal of saving. Getting ready for the huge financial challenge nearly everyone faces. It's called retirement! There will very likely be a point in your life when you will be unable (or perhaps just unwilling) to work. If you have properly prepared, then retirement can be a wonderful and comfortable phase of life. But if retirement is forced upon you or arrives before you have fully prepared, it can become a disaster like any other.

A thorough savings plan should therefore meet both emergency *and* retirement needs. A four-step savings strategy is outlined below:

1. First, establish your emergency fund.
2. Once the emergency fund is fully funded, begin contributing to retirement accounts that offer employer matching. Invest enough to take full advantage of any employer matching. With any remaining money, pay off short term debt, such as credit cards.
3. When short-term debts are paid off, put the full 10% into retirement accounts, even if it is more than what your employer matches.
4. If you have more than 10% available to save, either supplement your retirement accounts, or put the extra aside for other savings goals, such as the kids' college accounts, travel, a new car, or leisure items.

Before anything else, you need to prepare for unexpected financial challenges. Establishing a strong emergency fund therefore comes first. If you don't have a suitable emergency fund, you will be forced to resort to using credit cards with the first unexpected financial setback.

After establishing your emergency fund, take advantage of any employer matching of retirement funds. The return on investment is simply too good to pass up. Apply what's left of your monthly savings to paying off short-term debt, starting with the accounts that have the highest rates and fees.

Finally, once all your short-term debt is knocked out, put the full 10% savings into your retirement accounts. If you have more than 10% available, apply the additional money toward other savings goals. Don't make the common mistake of saving for your kid's college needs at the expense of your retirement. There are many types of assistance available to pay for college (e.g., grants, loans, scholarships), but there is no one to help you with retirement. Let's apply the plan to an example situation.

Example: Assume that you have an income of $60,000 gross per year, $9,000 of credit card debt, and work for a company who offers 5% retirement matching. Through sacrifice and hard work, you have found that you can save 10% of your gross income, or $6,000 annually ($500 per month). You determine that your emergency fund should be $7,000. The savings plan would be applied as follows.

1. *Save the full $500/month for 14 months to fully fund your emergency fund.*
2. *After your emergency fund is established, begin contributing enough into your retirement account to take advantage of your employer's matching. In this case, your employer will match up to 5% of $60,000, which is $3,000 annually ($250/month). Therefore, invest $250 per month in your retirement account to receive the full matching. The other $250/month of the 10% savings goes toward paying off short-term debt.*
3. *Once the $9,000 in short-term debt is eliminated (taking about 36 months at $250/month), put the entire $500/month into your retirement accounts.*
4. *If you find that you have additional money beyond the 10% to save, put it toward specific goals. These could include college savings accounts, annual family travel, new car planning, or simply things that you would really enjoy having.*

This example shows that in a little over 4 years, you will have established a $7,000 emergency fund, paid off $9,000 of short-term debt, and begun establishing a retirement nest egg. Not a bad start to improving your financial preparedness!

EMERGENCY FUND

Establishing an emergency fund should be your first priority in savings. This fund will serve many important purposes, including handling the costs of unexpected car/house repairs, health care expenses, and weathering a job loss. It should be drawn upon only for emergencies, and only when no other options exist.

> **Tips**
> An emergency fund is your front-line defense against unexpected financial hardships.

Financial experts have differing recommendations about how big an emergency fund should be. A reasonable goal is to establish an emergency fund large enough to pay all your bills for at least three months. If your bills come to $3,000/month, then you should have a minimum of $9,000 in an emergency fund. Keep the bulk of your emergency fund liquid, not locked up in a CD or other account that isn't easily accessible. It is usually best to put the money in an FDIC-insured savings account or money market fund. The yields will be low from these accounts, but safety comes first when dealing with your emergency fund.

Check into using an online bank, since they frequently offer higher interest savings rates than your local bank or credit union. When you establish an online savings account, it links directly to your local bank account, making it very easy to transfer money between the accounts. Saving in an account like this also helps to keep the money out of sight, making it less likely to be used for things other than true emergencies.

The importance of an emergency fund cannot be overemphasized. It is the safety net that catches you when times get tough. If you draw money out of your emergency fund, immediately begin replenishing it with the money you set aside each month for savings. Maintaining the emergency fund is always your first priority, even if it means temporarily not putting savings into other accounts.

RETIREMENT

Planning for retirement is an exercise in wisdom. Unfortunately, people don't tend to gain this wisdom until later in life. Many people don't get serious about building their retirement savings until they see retirement on the horizon, perhaps when they are in

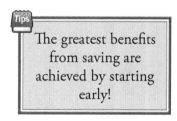

The greatest benefits from saving are achieved by starting early!

their 40s or 50s. This is unfortunate because the most benefit can be had if you begin saving for retirement when in your 20s (or even earlier).

Compound Interest

Albert Einstein is attributed with saying that the most powerful force in the universe is compound interest. Regardless of whether that is true or simply urban legend, it does highlight a very important savings phenomenon. In layman's terms, compound interest simply means that interest can earn more interest.

The equation for calculating compounded interest is given below:

$$FV = PV\left(1 + \frac{i}{k}\right)^{kt}$$

Where FV = future value, PV = present value, i = interest rate (e.g., 10% = 0.1), k = number of times the interest is compounded per year, and t = number of years. If you are not particularly math savvy, the equation may appear confusing. Don't worry over it. The coming conclusion is what's important.

Let's look two examples. First, assume that you have $1,000 in an investment account that earns 10% annually and is compounded monthly. Even if you never added another penny to the account, how much money would you have at the end of 10 years?

$$FV = \$1000\left(1 + \frac{0.10}{12}\right)^{12(10)} = \$2,707$$

At the end of 10 years, your $1,000 has grown to over $2,700. Almost a tripling of your money—not bad!

Now, what if you put the same $1,000 into an account when you were age 20 and let it sit until you were ready to retire 45 years later?

$$FV = \$1000\left(1 + \frac{0.10}{12}\right)^{12(45)} = \$88,354$$

When you were ready to retire, that single $1,000 investment would have grown to over $88,000!

These examples demonstrate that there are two significant impacts you can have on how much your money will grow: invest in an account with the largest rate of return, and invest as early as possible.

There is a very useful rule that can be used to estimate how long it takes money to double through interest accumulation. It is called the "Rule of 72." The rule states that if you divide the number 72 by the interest rate, it will indicate the number of years required to double an investment. For example, if you invest in an account with an interest rate of 6%, it takes about 72/6 = 12 years for that money to double. Likewise, if the interest rate is 10%, the money will double about every 72/10 ≈ 7 years.

GOLD

One issue frequently discussed when considering financial preparedness is the buying of gold or other precious metals. The concern is that the value of assets tied to paper currency will drop if inflation occurs. Gold is seen as a "hard asset" offering protection from inflation and wild stock market swings. If you listen to the radio and television commercials, you might think that gold is a *prepper's* financial salvation.

In reality, there are many drawbacks to buying physical gold. The worst of which is that you have to pay a premium both when you buy and sell the gold—typically losing 5 percent of the market price each way.[222] This means that gold has to rise 10% in value just for you to break even. To make

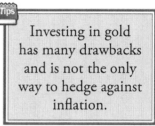

Investing in gold has many drawbacks and is not the only way to hedge against inflation.

matters worse, the IRS considers gold a collectible and taxes gains at much higher tax rates than stock gains. Finally, you have to store gold in special segregated vaults to guarantee its purity. If you keep it at home in a safe or in a bank's safety deposit box, you must have the gold re-assayed before selling it—yet another expense.

If you want to invest in gold while avoiding the many drawbacks, buy it through exchange-traded funds like SPDR Gold Trust (GLD) or iShares

Gold coins

COMEX Gold Trust (IAU). The shares are backed by gold bars stored in certified vaults in New York and London. Admittedly, it is not quite the same as holding a gold Krugerrand in your hands, but it is a better investment. Either way, if you decide to own gold (or any other precious metal), most experts advise that you limit the investment to no more than 10% of your portfolio.

A better option all around might simply be to put your money in inflation-protected index funds (available through all major investment brokers). Gold is far less predictable. It has been a good investment over the past few years, but if you look at it over the past few decades, the yield has not been very impressive. Even with the recent spike in prices, gold has risen only about 400% over the last 50 years. That corresponds to an average compounded yearly rate of less than 3%.

LIMIT YOUR DEBT

The third step to becoming financially prepared is to limit your debt. Consider the definition for debt as provided by Merriam-Webster Online:[223]

Debt - *sin, trespass; something owed, an obligation; a state of owing*

Wow. Does that cause you to pause for a second? Are these the words you want used to describe your financial condition?

Debt is so prevalent that it is taken for granted as a necessity in modern society. It enables you to purchase expensive items and amortize that cost over time. The problem arises when people use debt to fund everyday expenses. Worse yet is when debt is used to fund living expenses, essentially borrowing from the future to pay for the present. As the world's governments are now learning, this method of borrowed living is not sustainable.

CREDIT CARDS

The personal debt problem is largely the result of the ease of credit. Each year, the credit card industry mails out approximately six billion credit card offers across the United States.[224] Why do these companies go

Credit cards - friend or foe?

to the expense of such widespread solicitation? The answer is obvious—there is a lot of money to be made!

There are countless complaints about the unethical practices of credit card companies, including tacking on exorbitant penalty fees, delaying payments to incur late fees, charging rates higher than originally promised, targeting college kids with the expectation that their parents will pick up the expenses, and raising interest rates to outrageous levels when a borrower falls behind. Credit card companies are the modern day equivalent of the loan shark business, but on an unprecedented scale. Fortunately, the recently adopted Credit CARD Act legislation is taking steps toward protecting the consumer, but many questionable practices remain.

From the tone of the condemnation, you may think that credit cards should always be avoided. This is far from the truth. When used correctly, credit cards provide very real benefits.

- They provide buyer protection by limiting your liability to purchasing fraud.
- Many offer extended warranties on card-purchased items.
- Many offer rewards, such as cash back or frequent flyer miles.
- They are easily replaced if lost or stolen.
- They are necessary for certain purchases or rentals.
- They help you build a higher credit score, which is needed for mortgages or other large purchases.
- They can help you categorize your purchases for purposes of budgeting.

Despite the harsh words for credit card practices, you may wish to enjoy their many benefits. The key to credit of any type is using it correctly. So how do you do that with credit cards? Follow three simple rules and you can't go wrong.

1. Find a credit card with the best benefits. Cards can be compared online at *www.creditcards.com* and *www.cardweb.com*.
2. Use the credit card to make your purchases.
3. Pay off the credit card balance each month.

If you are unable to balance your checkbook well enough to guarantee your ability to pay off your credit card balance each month, then don't use credit cards. The bottom line is that credit cards can be a convenient tool or an irresistible temptation to overindulge.

Tips

Debit and business cards may leave you liable for significant expenses should they ever be lost or stolen.

Many people use debit cards—cards that charge directly against funds in your bank account. The advantage of a debit card is that you can't use it to put yourself into debt. The drawback is that debit cards don't provide the user the same protection that credit cards do. For example, when using VISA or MasterCard, you are limited to a $50 liability should the card be stolen and used fraudulently. The same is not generally true for debit cards. Likewise, business credit cards are often pushed on people (even those without a business). Why do credit card companies offer better deals on business credit cards? The answer once again comes back to consumer liability. If a business card is lost or stolen, the credit card company can claim that you were negligent with the handling of the card and hold you fully responsible for all fraudulent charges.

OTHER DEBT

There are of course many other types of debt besides credit cards. Car loans are one good example of this. The ideal way to purchase anything that depreciates in value is using cash. To borrow money to invest in something that depreciates is financially unwise. With that said, there is an argument for purchasing automobiles on credit. Cars are used to gain and keep employment, which in turn brings in income. Therefore, the case can be made for borrowing money to purchase a car *if* it is used to support employment. However, this does not suggest you borrow money to purchase a new Lexus to get back and forth to your job. If the cost of the debt prevents you from meeting your savings goals, then you can't afford it. Also, you will save significantly on depreciation by buying a car that is at least two years old.

Home mortgages are a unique class of debt. Most people are unable to purchase a home outright, so either they must rent for the majority of their lives, or surrender to this form of debt and take out a mortgage. Of all the types of debt, home mortgages are the best. There are several reasons for this. First, homes have historically appreciated in value, making them a reasonable investment. Second, they replace the expense of renting. The interest on home mortgages is also tax deductible, effectively lowering the borrowing costs. Finally, a mortgage gives an immediate return on the investment since you are able to enjoy living in the house. However, the same rules of affordability still apply. You can only afford a house if the mortgage, utilities, taxes, maintenance, association fees, and insurance costs don't prevent you from meeting your savings goals.

GET THE MOST BANG FOR YOUR BUCK

If you give two people one hundred dollars and ask them to go out and purchase a set of clothes, they will come back with very different results. A business man might come home with a pair of trousers and a tie. A frugal grandmother on the other hand might come home with two dresses, a pairs of shoes, some pantyhose, a new purse, and a pocket full of change. The difference being that one knows how to bargain shop. This is a classic example of getting the most bang for your buck. Learn to buy things off season or when they are falling out of fashion. Even high-end clothing can be found at huge discounts if you are willing to do end-of-season shopping. Online stores are also an excellent place to do comparison shopping and find bargains (especially on electronics).

One word of caution . . . if something sounds too good to be true, then it *is* too good to be true. There are rarely any exceptions to this rule. Be very careful when parting with your money! Remember what Thomas Tusser said, "A fool and his money are soon parted." Scams target everyone, rich and poor alike. The most common elements of scams are discussed a little later in this chapter.

BE ADEQUATELY INSURED

A very important step to financial preparedness is being adequately insured. There are countless disasters that can cause property damage, injury, and loss of life. Having appropriate safety nets in place is vital to your family's financial security.

HOME INSURANCE

Your home is likely to be your largest financial investment, both the structure and the contents. If you are a renter, then the property contained in your apartment, townhouse, or rental home is probably a large part of your assets. Having adequate homeowner's or renter's insurance is therefore imperative.

There are many companies that offer homeowner's or renter's insurance (e.g., State Farm, Allstate, Prudential). All of these companies have good and bad reputations depending on who you ask. It probably doesn't really make much difference which of the major insurers you choose. What does matter is that you select adequate coverage and sufficiently document your belongings.

The definition of "adequate coverage" is enough insurance to fully rebuild your home and replace all of your belongings with new items should they be lost to a major disaster, such as a fire, flood, tornado, or earthquake. Be sure to clarify that you want replacement cost insurance, not coverage that is pro-rated based on the age of the item. You may also need special endorsements known as riders to cover specialty items such as jewelry, guns, electronics, collectibles, or antiques.

Homeowner's insurance generally comprises two parts: property protection and liability protection. Property protection covers the dwelling, detached structures, personal contents, and costs associated with loss of use. Liability protection covers personal liability, such as damage to other people's property and medical expenses associated with an accident on your property. Do you know the details of your current policy? If not, take a few minutes to read through it. If your policy doesn't cover the worst case scenarios, make the appropriate changes.

One major problem that often arises when a catastrophic event completely destroys a home is convincing the insurer of what was actually lost. Insurers are all too familiar with customers claiming that every room

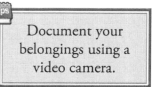

> Document your belongings using a video camera.

was filled floor to ceiling with Gucci handbags and Rolex watches. It is your responsibility to document what you actually possess and want insured. For this reason, you should create a home inventory video. Simply walk through your house with a camcorder (or camera), documenting every room and closet, as well as noting any high-value or irreplaceable items. Give a copy of the recording (or photos) to your insurer, and keep a copy for yourself somewhere other than inside your house. Repeat the process annually or when you have significant changes to your contents. Video documentation will help to protect you as well as make claims much easier to process.

Importance of home insurance *(photo by FEMA/Dave Gatley)*

AUTO INSURANCE

Auto insurance coverage is another financial necessity. Whether you drive a new BMW or a true junkyard classic, you need car insurance. At a minimum you will need liability insurance to pay for damages or injury to others, as well as comply with the law. If your vehicle is of any significant value, you will also want collision insurance, which pays for your car to be repaired in case of an accident. The only recommendation here is to find the best price on the best policy. It may make sense to use the same provider as do for your home since companies typically offer multi-policy discounts. Also, find an insurer with a local office and get to know the representative and staff.

DISABILITY INSURANCE

Disability insurance is likely to be the most difficult insurance decision you will have to make. This type of insurance provides a monthly stipend in case of disability. Depending on the type and coverage, it has a specific payout (paying a fixed amount each month) and duration (lasting a given number of years). If you opt for this coverage, be sure to ask many questions, such as how disability is determined, how insurance payments are affected by government disability payments, how long the payments will keep coming, and how long must you have to be out of work before the first payment is made.

One in three workers will become disabled before age 67.

It is estimated that one in three workers will become disabled for an extended period before age 67.[225] In a perfect world, every worker should therefore have disability insurance. In reality, few do. Disability insurance is relatively expensive, and often does not provide a comparable replacement income. It can, however, soften the financial impact of a disability.

MEDICAL INSURANCE

Medical insurance is another of life's necessities. Whether you are age 6 or 60, health problems can arise forcing you to seek medical services. It is truly unfortunate that nearly 50 million Americans have no medical insurance.[226] The problem is that medical insurance is very costly, to the point of being impossible to afford for people with serious pre-existing conditions. Without insurance, medical costs can quickly drain away emergency funds and even entire life savings.

If you are fortunate enough to work for an employer who provides (or at least supplements) health care insurance, take full advantage of the benefit. If your employer offers several plans, compare the trades between cost, co-pays, deductibles, and available network of doctors. If you are self-employed or unemployed, try teaming with groups of other individuals to get more attractive rates and coverage. Alternatively, look for plans through memberships or discount clubs. You can also comparison shop at websites like *www.ehealthinsurance.com*. Finally, if you are unemployed and can simply not afford health care, seek treatment through lower cost clinics or county-run health offices.

It is often possible to negotiate pricing with providers and hospitals. Specifically, if you have a large outstanding balance with a health care provider, you can often get that balance significantly reduced if you are willing to pay a negotiated amount in full.

Personal aside: Several years back, my mother had a large hospital bill (over $6,000). I called and explained that she was elderly, had little income, and would only be able to pay about $50 per month. As her son, I offered to pay a lump sum if they could lower the bill. Within 24 hours, they cut the bill to $1,200, which I promptly paid. The hospital was content with the partial payment because it was far more than they would have received otherwise. Likewise, I was happy with having paid off the debt at a fraction of the original cost.

LIFE INSURANCE

Life insurance is often misunderstood. The point to keep in mind is that life insurance is not designed for the person who has died; rather, it acts as a safety net for those left behind. Because of this, it is not a question of whether someone needs life insurance, but only *how much* they need.

How much to get?

When a person is young or without dependents, life insurance needs are very modest, perhaps only providing for burial expenses. Once a person gets married and has children, life insurance must provide for the family's continued well-being in case of the loss of the breadwinner. This can be quite substantial. As the family matures and children move away from home, life insurance needs will decrease, ultimately settling at the modest levels required to settle an estate.

Example: Jack, age 35, is a corporate salesman. His wife, Jill, is a homemaker who homeschools their three kids, ages 5, 7, and 10. Jack earns $100,000 a year. They live in a home with a mortgage of $300,000. Family debt (e.g., cars, credit cards) totals $40,000. The family's monthly expenses are $4,000 (half of which is a mortgage payment). Jack has a 401(k) retirement fund with a $100,000 balance. How much life insurance does he need and of what type? What about when he turns 70? Will he still have the same needs?

If Jack died today, his family would be without his significant income. His wife is a homemaker who has chosen to homeschool their children, meaning that her ability to replace his income is very limited. The amount of life insurance needed to act as a proper safety net could be calculated by summing up the following needs.

1. Pay off home mortgage.
2. Pay off other debt.
3. Establish savings large enough to provide an income stream to meet the family's long-term needs.

The mortgage payoff is easy to determine, $300,000 in this case. The additional debt adds another $40,000. The third part of the calculation is the hard part. How much money is needed to take care of future needs? Once the house is paid off, the monthly expenses will come down to $2,000. Let's assume that the remaining insurance money is put into a diversified investment account (stocks, bonds, money markets), with an average yield of 10%. Backing out the amount needed to earn $2,000 of interest each month, gives a net deposit of $240,000. The insurance breakdown would be:

Mortgage:	$300,000
Debt:	$ 40,000
Savings:	$240,000

The grand total comes to $600,000 in life insurance needs. This example neglects many things (e.g., Social Security survivor benefits, future education needs, inflation, investment variations, etc.), but it serves as a basis for the recommendation of many financial advisors. Many experts recommend that your life insurance be equal to 5 to 10 times your annual gross salary. In this simple example, it was shown that Jack needed about six times his annual income.

A person's life insurance needs change significantly during the course of a lifetime. The 5 to 10 times rule does not generally hold early or very late in life. For example, if Jack lives to be 70, his children will all be grown, his house will already be paid off, and he will likely have additional retirement assets for his surviving wife. Therefore, a large insurance policy is neither necessary nor cost effective at that age.

What about Jill's insurance needs? Since she is a homemaker, her insurance needs are significantly different than his. Even with Jill's death, Jack would continue to work, so his family's income would remain unchanged. Normally this would indicate that very little life insurance is needed for Jill. In this case, however, the family may decide that private schooling should replace homeschooling, and the costs of that schooling would need to be included in her insurance policy. This demonstrates how life insurance needs are unique to every individual. Once again the thing to keep in mind is that life insurance is about meeting the needs of those left behind.

Write a Will

Regardless of your net worth, you should have a Last Will and Testament. A will should name an executor who you trust to handle your affairs when you die. It should clearly spell out how your assets are to be distributed. If you have children, it should name who you would like take custody of them should both parents die together. A will serves all these vital purposes, but it does one thing more. It gives you a sense of peace. Death may come suddenly, or it may come slowly. Either way, knowing that you have prepared your estate and named caregivers for your children will give you peace of mind.

For most people, writing a will is inexpensive and easy to do. You can use online services, such as *www.legalzoom.com,* or software packages, such as Quicken's Willmaker. Another option is to hire a local attorney to draft up a will for a modest fee.

DON'T GET SCAMMED!

The final step in becoming financially prepared is to learning to hang onto your money. Scamming is big business. Billions of dollars are stolen from unsuspecting people each year. Being scammed and being robbed are tantamount to the same thing since both leave you with less cash in your pocket and the same violated and angry feelings. Below are a few basic observations about scamming.

1. At the root of nearly every scam is an exchange of money (or other valuable asset)—something leaving your hands and entering theirs.
2. In this electronic age, the most trusted form of payment is cash. Cashier's checks, money orders, bank checks, wire transfers, and personal checks are all readily forged.
3. Everyone is a target for scamming, from the single mother working two jobs to pay her rent, to the millionaire living in the Manhattan townhouse. Some scams amass money by targeting lots of "little people;" others shoot for the big payoffs.

What can you do about it? First and foremost, don't fool yourself into thinking that you are too smart to be scammed. Everyone is vulnerable. With that said, there are many things you can do to minimize your

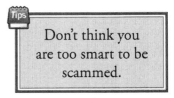

Don't think you are too smart to be scammed.

vulnerability by making yourself a tougher target than the next person.

Start by familiarizing yourself with the most common scams (some of which are discussed on the next page). Talk about them openly with your entire family, including your kids. A great resource for learning about scams is Clark Howard, heard on AM radio, seen on CNN, and found at *www.clarkhoward.com*.

Look at every financial transaction with skepticism. Ask yourself a few questions. What could go wrong? How will you handle problems? How can you protect yourself? Are you feeling rushed? Does something seem not quite right? Use a protected form of payment whenever possible (such as a credit card, PayPal, etc.). Most credit cards are protected against fraud if reported within 60 days. The maximum loss you will typically suffer is $50. For this reason, if you buy something and it hasn't arrived within 60 days, consider reporting it as a fraudulent transaction to your credit card company. You can always cancel that report should the item arrive later.

When selling something, don't release the item until you have a cleared payment from the purchaser. If payment is made through a personal check, have your banker contact the buyer's bank to verify funds. You should then wait until the check clears before releasing the item. Likewise, if payment is made with a bank-issued check, have your banker call the issuing bank to verify authenticity. For small transactions, you might consider using postal money orders with serial numbers that allow online verification. Don't accept wire transfers since they are often fraudulent.

COMMON SCAMS

A discussion of several common scams appear below.

- **Need Your Info:** Never give out personal or financial information to unknown callers or emailers. If someone calls or emails asking for your Social Security number or bank account information, it is a scam. There are many variations of this scam, including a court clerk claiming to be calling about jury duty, a bank representative claiming there is a problem with your account, or a prize company suggesting they want to deposit money into your bank account.
- **The Sure Thing:** Beware of any investment that claims to "beat the market." This is often a huckster trying to convince you to part with your life savings through a Ponzi scheme or by investing in very high risk activities. If anyone can reliably beat the stock market without added risk, they surely would not have to go looking for customers!
- **Money Up Front:** Don't pay for a service until the work is completed. If supplies are needed to perform the service, you may be required to pay enough to cover those costs. If the service is not done to your satisfaction, refuse final payment, and take up the issue with the parent company.
- **Online Hucksters:** Don't buy goods from questionable sellers. In the past, the shady salesperson might have been a street corner

peddler with a coat full of cheap knockoff watches. That danger is largely replaced with online auction hucksters. If you decide to purchase something through an online auction, understand that it is inherently riskier than making retail purchases. Once again, use only protected forms of payment.

- **Return to Sender:** Never refund money back for accidental overpayment. If someone overpays you for an item and then asks for a partial refund of the overpayment, it is *always* a scam. Their original payment will ultimately prove to be worthless—often taking weeks to bounce.
- **Lottery:** You will never receive a legitimate limited-time-only "act fast" lottery offer. Neither will you ever win the lottery through email. If you win any form of lottery, you will receive a certified letter as well as personal contact from the issuing company. You will never be required to pay any form of upfront payment, such as issuance, processing, registration, tax, or transfer fees. If it is truly your lucky day, there will be no doubt in your mind.
- **Nigerian Royalty:** If you receive a chain letter or email offering you a handsome commission for depositing a Nigerian prince's inheritance (or other such nonsense), it is a scam. If you reply, you will be led through a carefully crafted scheme that has you send money for one reason or another.
- **Hit Man:** If you receive a letter from a professional assassin claiming that he has a contract to kill you but will let you live if you pay him a fee, it is a scam. Report it to your local law enforcement agency or the FBI. But relax. No one is out to get you, only your money.
- **Gypsies and Curses:** If a gypsy, palm reader, tarot card reader, or anyone else tells you that your money is the source of a curse, it is a scam. They will ultimately try to convince you to give it to them to throw over a bridge, burn, or dispose of in some other way. Get away from them and seek better counseling.

FINANCIAL MISTAKES

In February of 2008, Consumer Reports published an article detailing 12 financial mistakes that could cost you $1,000,000. Let's wrap up this financial preparedness chapter with a quick listing of those common money-related blunders:

1. Investing too conservatively for retirement—limits your savings growth
2. Retiring before you can afford to—leaves you with inadequate savings for your leisure years
3. Having an expensive divorce war
4. Underinsuring your home—results in hefty losses when the structure or contents are damaged
5. Overpaying your mortgage by having a high interest rate
6. Carrying credit card balances—requires payment of significant interest (and perhaps fees)
7. Living an unhealthy lifestyle—leads to higher insurance costs and greater medical expenses
8. Not using Roth accounts
9. Cashing out retirement accounts early—results in loss of retirement accumulation as well as hefty withdrawal penalties
10. Underfunding retirement accounts
11. Paying excessive brokerage and fund fees
12. Falling for a scam

Avoiding these costly mistakes while following a reasonable money management strategy, such as the *Money Plan*, will help to ensure that you have adequate funds to meet the challenges that unforeseen events can bring.

DP PLAN EXAMPLE

Table 13-1 Sample DP Plan Entry

Need: Financial Preparedness			
Danger	**Goals**	**Needs**	**Implementation**
A significant, unexpected financial expense	Pay unexpected expenses without getting into debt	An emergency fund	Establish an emergency fund with three month's of expenses.
Death in the family	Continue current lifestyle despite the loss of spouse	Life insurance	Insure breadwinner at six times annual salary. Insure non-working spouse at $200,000.
Property loss	Rebuild house and replace contents if destroyed	House insurance with replacement cost coverage	Insure home at 1.25 times value, and contents at $150,000.
	Repair or replace car if damaged	Car insurance	Insure car for comprehensive and collision coverage.
Loss of income due to disability or retirement	Have a reasonable quality of life if the breadwinner becomes disabled	Disability insurance	Purchase disability insurance, covering 40% of salary.
	Have a comfortable quality of life during retirement	Retirement savings and income	Save 10% of salary in 401(k) retirement account; take advantage of 5% employer matching. Contribute to employer's pension plan.

Quick Summary - Financial Preparedness

➢ Prioritizing can be done using the personalized DP Plan worksheets. Begin by identifying everything you need to reach a minimum level of self-sustenance. Once that level is reached, expand your capabilities to support your family through a prolonged or more severe disaster.

➢ Financial preparedness plays an important role in disaster preparedness, enabling you to stockpile supplies, cope with unexpected financial pressures, and minimize losses.

➢ Six key steps to achieving financial preparedness are: living below your means, limiting your debt, saving 10% of your gross income, getting the most from your money, being adequately insured, and not getting scammed.

➢ The ultimate goal of saving is to become financially prepared—out of debt, socking away money each month—and thus prepared to deal with life's unexpected challenges.

➢ A savings plan begins by establishing an emergency fund of at least three months of expenses. The emergency fund is only used to cope with hardships from unexpected events.

➢ Adequately insure your property, life, health, and ability to work. Remember, life insurance should be determined by the needs of those left behind.

➢ Leave behind a properly executed will to dictate how your possessions will be distributed, and who will care for your surviving children.

➢ Protect your money by guarding against scams.

Recommended Items - Financial Preparedness

❏ A detailed budget

❏ Emergency fund (minimum of 3 months)

❏ Retirement savings

❏ Adequate life, health, home, and auto insurance

❏ Last Will and Testament

CHAPTER 14
TRANSPORTATION

TRANSPORTATION

Challenge

While traveling through the Colorado Rockies, you take a wrong turn and become lost. Your car becomes stuck in deep snow on an infrequently traveled mountain pass. Do you know how to free your vehicle? If you can't free your vehicle, how will you call for help? Should you leave your car and hike to safety? If rescuers are unable to find you, are you prepared to survive in your vehicle until weather conditions improve?

Reliable transportation, when coupled with accurate information and navigation, can save your life. Appreciate that, to be effective, they all have to work together. This is easiest to appreciate when you are trying to escape an immediate threat. For example, it would do you little good to hop in your car and race away from an approaching wildfire, only to discover that you have become hopelessly lost (navigation); that the winds had changed direction, putting the fire directly in your path (information); or worse yet, that your car has a leaking radiator (transportation).

Transportation, navigation, and information all offer valuable benefits, but when combined, they form a powerful defense.

- **Transportation**—keeps you mobile and able to get out of harm's way
- **Navigation**—allows you to efficiently travel from point A to B, as well as make detours without getting lost
- **Information**—helps you to avoid hazards that might interfere with your evacuation

More generally, transportation, navigation, and information serve two critical functions in disaster preparedness: (1) they help you to escape a dangerous area, should an evacuation be needed, and (2) they enable you to seek out supplies and assistance when you are unable or unwilling to evacuate.

TRANSPORTATION

Many times the best way to survive a disaster is to get away from it. Evacuation is addressed more fully in *Chapter 5: Shelter,* but warrants reiteration here. There are four basic steps to prepare for evacuation.

1. Fully fuel your vehicle and any spare gas cans. Store enough fuel to travel at least 500 miles—the specific number of gallons depends on your vehicle's fuel efficiency.
2. Identify multiple escape routes using maps or a GPS. Pick several possible retreat locations in case traffic flow prevents you from traveling to your preferred one.
3. Listen to TV or radio broadcasts to determine the best time to evacuate and the optimal escape routes.
4. Pack your vehicle with supplies, including things you might need for roadside emergencies—see *Roadside Emergency Kit* later in this chapter.

Once you make the decision to leave, take additional steps to prepare your home as outlined in *Chapter 5: Shelter.*

To successfully evacuate, you need a reliable vehicle capable of transporting your family, along with necessary emergency supplies, away from the disaster. Of course, not all disasters will require (or even permit) evacuation, but there are many cases when getting out of harm's way is the first and best choice.

Contrary to some suggestions, it is not necessary to have a heavy-duty off-road vehicle capable of climbing rocky ridges. Most of the time, evacuation will force you to vacate one city in favor of another that is less affected by the threat—meaning that a *dependable* car capable of traveling the road-ways is all that is needed. For many threats, having a vehicle with good fuel economy is of primary importance because it allows you to travel further on a given quantity of gas.

When evacuating, fuel efficiency is usually more important than off-road capability.

However, if you have prepared a specific retreat that requires off-road access, such as a cabin up in the mountains, then of course you should only attempt to reach it with a suitable vehicle. Four-wheel drive vehicles may also provide some additional capabilities in wintry conditions, but they are by no means a guarantee of safe travel.

SECONDARY TRANSPORTATION

For situations in which you cannot (or choose not to) evacuate a disaster area, a highly fuel-efficient backup method of transportation may prove valuable. It may also serve you well in cases where a collapse in the country's infrastructure has led to a major fuel shortage. Backup transportation might be a bicycle, moped, motorcycle, golf cart, or other fuel-efficient vehicle. Spare parts and maintenance items, such as inner tubes, air pump, batteries, and oil should be stockpiled.

NAVIGATION

In this modern technological age, it is possible to pinpoint your location nearly anywhere on the planet. The Global Positioning System (GPS) uses overhead satellites to triangulate a user's position. Commercial GPS receivers are available for vehicle-mounting and handheld use. Vehicle-mounted GPS systems provide information more of interest to drivers than those lost in the wilderness. Handheld GPS units, on the other hand, are useful when traipsing around the woods since they frequently provide additional topographical information.

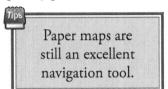

Tips

Paper maps are still an excellent navigation tool.

Using a GPS unit requires a fairly clear view of the sky. Systems don't work indoors without an outdoor antenna, and may have only marginal success during overcast conditions. It is worth noting that some disasters, such as a global war or large volcanic eruption, could leave the nation's GPS system inoperable. Finally, GPS systems are not particularly good at planning routes because they typically have very small screens. Old-fashioned paper maps are still the best choice, requiring neither batteries nor satellite signals. For this reason, it's a good idea to keep physical maps of your current location, any possible retreats, and the travel routes between them.

In the case of a widespread disaster, your evacuation routes may become extremely congested. What would normally take two hours to travel might now take a full day. To make matters worse, fuel is likely to be in short supply, leaving motorists stranded and further blocking the escape routes. If possible, before leaving home, you should carefully plan your escape route with consideration given to likely traffic flow and road conditions. Identify alternate routes in the event that your primary one doesn't work out. Finally, be prepared to violate conventional traffic rules in times of emergencies—but never risk endangering yourself or others.

INFORMATION

Important travel information could include: condition of the roadways, location of emergency shelters, recommended escape routes, coming weather events, curfews in effect, and availability of gasoline. This type of information may have to be collected from a variety of sources, including the Internet, public broadcasting (TV or radio), emergency services, short-wave radio, and friends/family outside the disaster area. Table 14-1 provides a few information resources relating to travel. Refer to *Chapter 12: Communication* for a more complete discussion of available information resources.

Table 14-1 Traveler Information Resources

Nationwide Traveler Information (only available in some areas)	511
National Traffic and Road Closure Information Maps and associated links to traffic conditions and road closures across the United States.	www.fhwa.dot.gov/trafficinfo
Google Maps Provides maps, street views, and driving directions.	www.maps.google.com

IMPORTANT PAPERS

One of the most important things you can do to prepare for a potential evacuation is to put copies of important documents onto a digital memory device, such as a USB flash drive, external hard drive, CD, or DVD.

A brief listing of some of the most important items to consider storing is given below:

- Addresses and phone numbers of points of contact (family, friends, insurer, doctor, etc.)
- Driver's licenses
- Social Security cards
- Birth and death certificates
- Adoption papers
- Insurance cards and policies
- Passports
- Recent photos of family members (suitable for missing person's posters)
- Property deeds
- Automobile titles
- Firearm serial numbers
- Weapon permits
- Marriage license
- Home inventory video or photos

- Bank and investment account information
- Tax records
- Computer account logins and passwords
- Last Will and Testament

A complete listing of all recommended information to store electronically is given in the *Appendix*. Having an easy to carry collection of important information can serve many purposes, including helping you replace original documents, provide proof of identity and ownership, and assist with insurance claims.

Tips

Store your information on password-protected or encrypted memory devices.

Given that the memory device will contain significant personal information, security becomes a major concern. To prevent the information from ever being compromised, you should use password protection, and if possible, data encryption. At a minimum, you can use password protection on zipped folders and individual documents. Password protection will deter the casual criminal but not the sophisticated computer hacker. A vastly more secure method is to store the information on hardware-encrypted USB flash drives (e.g., IRONKEY). These devices are more costly than conventional memory sticks, but they are nearly impossible for anyone short of the National Security Agency to access.

BEING PREPARED ON THE ROAD

Some people might question the need to be prepared while on the road. After all, what could possibly happen while driving to work or the grocery store? Once again, this is a very rational argument for the typical day. However, remember that being prepared is not about the typical day, it is about the exceptionally bad day. Every year there are reports of people becoming stranded and ultimately perishing from being unprepared while on the roadways.

Consider the following three reasons to be prepared when on the road.

1. People tend to spend a great deal of time in their vehicles, meaning that if you do find yourself in a dangerous situation, there's a reasonable chance that you will be in your car.

Roadside emergencies *(photo by FEMA/Walt Jennings)*

2. Some disasters force you to immediately evacuate the area, leaving you with only the supplies in your automobile.
3. When on the road, you are vulnerable to numerous hazards—especially when traveling in inclement weather. Consider the brief list of threats below:
   - Vehicle breakdown, such as a flat tire, dead battery, running out of gas, or mechanical failure
   - Dangerous weather events, such as tornados, hail, or heavy snowfall
   - Getting stuck in snow or mud
   - Auto accident
   - Flooded roads or submerged vehicle
   - Vehicle fire
   - Widespread disaster (e.g., nuclear leak, terrorist attack, volcanic eruption)

MAINTENANCE AND FUEL

The first step to being better prepared on the road is to keep your vehicle in good working order. Reliability, not curb appeal, is what's important when your life is depending on your car. Have your vehicle inspected regularly, and keep up on the routine maintenance items (e.g., tires, oil, radiator fluid, belts).

You should also endeavor to keep your vehicle's fuel tank at least half full at all times. Maintaining a minimum level of fuel gives you the ability to immediately evacuate an area without having to hunt for an open gas station. This obviously requires more frequent trips to the gas station but could give you a life-saving head start over other motorists. Certainly with an imminent threat, such as a dangerous weather event, you should fill your vehicle as one of your readiness steps. Having a tank full of gas also helps you to survive if you ever become stranded in the cold.

ROADSIDE EMERGENCY KITS

To be better prepared for roadside emergencies, every *prepper* should keep some basic supplies in their vehicle. The recommended supplies are divided into two kits: the "Just the Basics" kit (things that everyone should keep in their car), and the "Kitchen Sink" kit (less critical items that might be useful when dangers are more likely, such as when traveling on a long trip).

Table 14-2 "Just the Basics" Roadside Emergency Kit

Item	Use
Cell phone with car charger	Call for help
Small gas can	Retrieve gas
Folding shovel	Dig out tires; make a fire pit
Jumper cables or Jumpstart battery booster	Jump a dead battery
Flashlight with spare batteries and car adapter	Safely navigate the dark; wave down assistance
Roadside triangle reflectors or flares	Warn others of a disabled vehicle, accident, or roadside hazard

Small tool kit (e.g., screwdrivers, adjustable wrench, pliers)	Perform basic repairs
First aid kit	Assist those with medical needs
Tow strap	Free a stuck vehicle; tow a disabled vehicle a short distance
Notepad and pen	Leave notes when you abandon your vehicle; write down tag numbers of a drunk driver
ResQme device	Cut seat belt if trapped; break out windows if vehicle becomes submerged
Roll of heavy-duty duct tape	Tape broken windows; fix tears; build shelters; secure enemy's hands; countless other uses
Windshield ice scraper	Clean snow and ice from window
Spare tire, jack, lug wrench, and small board to put under jack	Change flat tire
Warm blankets	Keep warm when stranded
Pair of comfortable walking shoes and socks	Walk to safety
Maps and/or GPS unit	Navigate to safety
A few bottles of water	Stay hydrated

A more thorough roadside emergency kit can be stored in a large duffle bag. Having it in a bag allows you to quickly load or unload it. Ideally, the duffle should have shoulder straps, enabling you to easily carry it should you be forced to abandon your vehicle. Below is a general list of emergency supplies. You should review the list and tailor it to your specific needs and any likely threats for your area.

Table 14-3 "Kitchen Sink" Roadside Emergency Kit

Item	Use
Everything from the "Just the Basics" kit	Takes care of most common needs
Heavyweight canvas bag	Store your emergency supplies; easier to carry if you must abandon the vehicle
Class ABC or BC fire extinguisher	Extinguish small car fires
Leather work gloves	Protect your hands while changing tires, digging out car, etc.
Warm weather clothing (e.g., hats, gloves, coat)	Keep warm when stranded or hiking to safety
Large funnel	Fill radiator; add oil; funnel urine into plastic bag
Gallon-size freezer bags	Urinate in bag when stuck in traffic, or unable to go outdoors
Bulb-style siphon	Siphon fuel from a vehicle or gas container
Bag of kitty litter	Provide traction in mud or snow
Fix-a-Flat tire sealant	Quick temporary fix to a flat tire
Tire pump	Fill a leaky tire
Tire gauge	Check tire pressure
Hand-ratcheted winch (a.k.a., a "come-along")	Pull your vehicle out of the mud or snow
Permanent marker and plastic transparencies	Leave a weatherproof note on your windshield
Pack of wet wipes	Clean up after treating injury, or being contaminated
Bungee tie down cords	Strap down supplies to roof or truck bed

Plastic wire ties	Secure shelters; tie enemy's hands; make repairs
Disposable camera	Snap evidence at scene of accident
Oversized Heatsheet reflective blanket	Use as lightweight, portable blanket
Emergency food, such as high calorie food bars	Eat when stranded, or when needing energy
Drinking water	Drink when stranded, or when unable to get to water source
Respirator; either low-cost Type N95 or gas mask	Protect from airborne threats
12-hour Cyalume chemlights	Provide night safety
Waterproof matches	Start a fire when stranded
TinderQuik (to start a fire even when wet)	Use as tinder for fire
Parachute cord	Make shelter; secure items
Lightweight rain poncho	Keep from getting wet; also doubles as a temporary shelter
Rescue whistle	Call for help
Quality fixed or folding-blade knife	Used for self defense, cutting supplies, shaving wood, cleaning animals, etc.
Position locator beacon	Signal for rescue from anywhere in the world
NukAlert	Detect high levels of radiation

Just as with the bucket survival kit described in *Chapter 2: Staying Alive,* most retail roadside emergency kits are grossly inadequate. It is much better to assemble your own kit with quality, hand-picked supplies that will adequately meet your needs.

MIT roadside emergency kit - is this adequate?

FREEING A STUCK VEHICLE

Many travel-related tragedies begin when a vehicle becomes stuck in the mud or snow. If you travel with a well-stocked roadside emergency kit, you will have either a tow strap or what is known as a "come-along." In which case, freeing the vehicle requires that you either attach the come-along to a solid object, such as a tree or pole, or have another vehicle use the tow strap to pull you free. If you don't have either item, then you will have to free your automobile the hard way (i.e., pushing and rocking).

There are two cases to consider:

- **Help is available**—perhaps there is an adult passenger in your car, or a good Samaritan stops to render aid, or you can easily ask for help from someone nearby
- **Help is not available**—perhaps you are alone on a road that is not well-traveled, and you have no way to call for assistance

In the first case, take the help. Freeing a stuck vehicle is much easier to do with a few extra hands to push. Try following the steps outlined below to free your vehicle.

1. Put your hazard lights on. This warns other drivers to be careful when passing you.
2. Use a shovel or other stiff object to remove snow, mud, or obstructions from in front of the wheels (or behind it if going in reverse).
3. Determine which wheel is slipping and put sand, cat litter, an old piece of carpet, or a board in front of the wheel (or behind it if reversing). In a pinch, you can use your car's floor mats for traction. Regardless of what you use, warn everyone to be careful about the items dislodging and flying out from under the wheels.
4. If your car is an automatic, put the transmission into Low gear or Reverse (depending on which way you are trying to pull out). If the car is a manual, put the transmission into 1st or Reverse. These low gears give you the most torque at the wheels. If you have a four-wheel drive vehicle, enable that feature.
5. Gently drive forward or backward, having everyone push in the direction of travel. Try not to spin the tires. Slow and easy wins the day.

If help isn't available, try the same procedure listed above on your own. If this doesn't work, try rocking the vehicle back and forth by shifting from Low to Reverse repeatedly. The secret to being successful is to time the oscillation of the vehicle with the gear changing, rocking the vehicle further and further out of the ruts with each cycle.

If you are unable to free your vehicle, don't hesitate to call for help. If you have a cell phone, contact family or friends, or call for a tow truck. If the situation is serious, such as in very cold weather, call 911 for emergency assistance. If you are on an interstate, you can also put on your emergency flashers and wait for a state trooper to stop and assist you, although there is no guarantee as to how long it will take for you to get noticed—perhaps a minute, an hour, or longer.

If you can't call for help, consider waving down a passing motorist. Be aware of the risk in doing this. You are introducing an unknown person into a compromising situation and that can be dangerous—especially

Freeing a stuck vehicle

if you are a woman or appear to be wealthy. Proceed with caution and follow your instincts. It is usually a better idea to ask a good Samaratin to drive up the road a bit (perhaps where cell coverage is better) and relay your request for help to family or friends. Do not accept a ride from someone you don't know unless the situation is so dire that you feel that your survival depends on it. If you do accept a ride, leave a detailed note on your vehicle's dashboard describing where you went, along with a description of the person, their car, and the tag number.

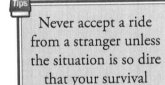

Tips

> Never accept a ride from a stranger unless the situation is so dire that your survival depends on it.

STRANDED

There are numerous ways that you can become stranded in your vehicle, such as your vehicle breaking down, becoming stuck in snow or mud, being trapped by impassible roadways (perhaps due to snow or flood-water), or losing control of your vehicle and sliding off the roadway. All of these scenarios (and many others) could leave you vulnerable, miles from home, and with limited options.

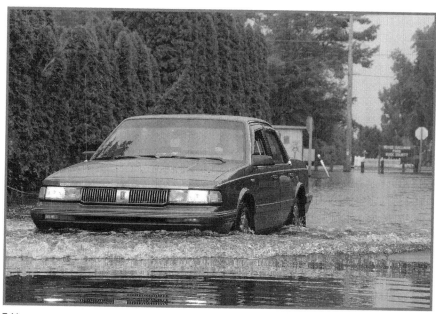

Taking unnecessary risks can leave you stranded

BENEFITS OF AN AUTOMOBILE

If you should ever become stranded, your automobile may save your life. A vehicle offers many benefits, and you should take full advantage of them. Consider the list of benefits that your car can provide.

1. It functions as an excellent shelter, keeping you dry, out of the wind, and off the cold ground.
2. If your car still runs and has fuel, it will help you stay warm for several hours.
3. It offers useful supplies:
   a) fuel for a fire (gasoline, oil, tires)
   b) a method of starting a fire (cigarette lighter, sparking across the battery, focusing with a headlamp reflector)
   c) a method of signaling for help (horn, headlights, emergency flashers)
   d) a radio for keeping up to date on emergency events
   e) a way to recharge your cell phone (cigarette lighter)
   f) a high-power two-way emergency radio (if equipped with Onstar)

g) traction for getting a stuck vehicle free (floor mats placed under the wheels)

h) lights to help you function at night (overhead light, headlights)

4. It is much more visible—generally, you are easier for rescue services to find if you remain with your vehicle.

If things turn desperate, don't hesitate to scavenge from your vehicle. Use anything that will help you survive, even if it means damaging your vehicle. For example, people who have been stranded in very cold weather have discovered that burning the tires not only provides warmth, but also acts as a smoky signal fire.

LESS SERIOUS SCENARIOS

If you should become stranded and can access a phone to call for help, there is a very good chance that the situation will be resolved within a couple of hours. For these less serious circumstances, your priorities are to stay comfortable and remain safe. The biggest threat you face is a collision with another motorist, especially during inclement weather with hazardous road conditions or limited visibility. If you have flares or other warning triangles, space them along the roadway behind your vehicle. Beyond that precaution, put your hazard lights on and wait for assistance to arrive.

To conserve battery power, turn off everything else that uses electrical power that isn't absolutely necessary, including headlights, overhead lights, heating/cooling blower motor, and the radio.

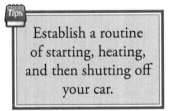
Establish a routine of starting, heating, and then shutting off your car.

If the weather is very cold, you may need to establish a routine that carefully balances conserving fuel, maintaining your battery power, and staying comfortable. Follow a regimen of starting the vehicle, warming the vehicle thoroughly (perhaps for 5-10 minutes with the heater blowing wide open), and then shutting it back off until it becomes cold again. Continue this routine until you determine that the battery is getting weak, at which time allow the vehicle to run 20 to 30 minutes to recharge the battery before returning to the regimen. Limit getting in and out of the vehicle to preserve the heat contained within. However, do open at least one window a small amount to introduce fresh air into the car. Also, be sure to check that the exhaust pipe is clear before starting your routine. If it becomes blocked, deadly carbon monoxide gas can back up into the vehicle's cabin.

In warmer weather, you will probably be fine shutting off your vehicle and opening all the doors, or finding shade nearby. Obviously, don't remain in a hot vehicle with the doors closed and windows rolled up. It is better to open the doors rather than rolling down the windows because if your battery fails, it may be impossible to roll back up the windows—leaving you exposed should the weather turn colder. Opening the doors also signals others that you are having difficulties and require assistance. In very hot weather, you may wish to follow a regimen of turning the engine on and running the air conditioner for a brief time (as described above), although it is usually better just to rest in a shady area.

MORE SERIOUS SCENARIOS

If you should become stranded in a remote region, or in conditions that make your discovery unlikely, the situation can go from simple annoyance to something truly life-threatening. The biggest dangers are hypothermia and carbon monoxide poisoning in cold weather, and dehydration in hot weather. Make every effort to address these three dangers, and you will go a long way to ensuring your survival.

Hypothermia is a condition in which your body gets too cold to regulate its temperature. Symptoms may include gradual loss of motor skills and mental acuity, fatigue, mumbling, slowed breathing, slurred speech, and cold pale skin. Hypothermia is best avoided by prior planning—packing warm blankets and spare clothing as part of your roadside emergency kit. Pay special attention to your hands and feet since they are often the first body parts affected by the cold.

Stay in your car to avoid exposure to cold winds, as well as to help conserve your body heat. Depending on how much fuel you have in the vehicle, you may get several hours of heat by cycling the vehicle on and off, running the heater for a few minutes each time (as discussed previously).

Tips

> Keep your exhaust pipe clear to prevent CO from backing up into your vehicle.

Carbon monoxide (CO) poisoning can occur when the vehicle's exhaust pipe becomes blocked or clogged, most likely from snow, causing CO gas to back up into the cabin. Symptoms of CO poisoning include headache, fatigue, lightheadedness, shortness of breath, nausea, and dizziness. Before running your vehicle, check that the exhaust pipe is clear. If there is a possibility that melting or falling snow might cause a subsequent blockage, re-check and clear the pipe periodically.

Dehydration can occur at any temperature but happens most quickly during hot weather when you sweat. Once again, dehydration is best avoided by prior planning—packing supplies of water in your roadside emergency kit. In hot weather, your car can act as an oven, so it is better to seek shade from a nearby tree.

Your primary goal when stranded in a remote location is to get noticed, ideally leading to your rescue. Open all your car doors and the hood to signal to any potential motorists that you are in distress. Also, if another car (or a rescue helicopter) approaches, do everything possible to get their attention—honking the horn, flashing your headlights, waving your arms, etc. Don't let vanity or pride kill you. If you are stranded in the vehicle with someone else, take turns sleeping so that one person is always on the lookout for potential rescuers.

If rescue is slow in coming, perhaps requiring you to spend one or more nights in your vehicle, you will have to weigh staying put and waiting for help against abandoning your vehicle and seeking help.

ABANDONING YOUR VEHICLE

All too often there are accounts of families stranded in their cars for days or even weeks. Many end tragically, usually because one or more family members leave the vehicle in search of help. Remember the order of needs discussed early in the book: shelter, water, and then food. Your stranded automobile can serve as a very good shelter, and leaving it should only be done when you determine that the danger of staying is greater than the danger of leaving.

How do you make this assessment? Ask yourself a few questions:

- Can you call for help using a cell phone, CB radio, position locator beacon, or OnStar?
- If you don't have cell coverage, is it possible to get to higher ground and call for help?
- How long will it take for someone to notice that you are missing? Do they know the route you are traveling?
- How likely is it that you will be discovered by a passerby?
- Can you signal for help?
- Are you properly equipped to weather it out for a few days?
- Do you know which direction to go for safety? Are you sure?
- Can you reach safety without getting lost or injured? Again, are you sure?

In most cases, the decision should be to stay with your vehicle. Of course there are exceptions—perhaps your vehicle has been submerged in water, or you have run so far off the roadway that it would be difficult for anyone to spot you, or you recall passing a gas station just a quarter of a mile back.

If you decide to leave your vehicle, consider taking the following precautions.

- Leave your vehicle only during the daytime. Wandering around at night is far too dangerous.
- Initially venture only to a distance such that you can still see your vehicle. This distance may be adequate for you to spot a gas station, house, or large road with passing traffic.
- If you expand your search further, take supplies with you. Assume that you *will* get lost and be unable to return to your vehicle. Be prepared to spend a cold night sleeping under the stars.
- Leave a clear, descriptive note on the vehicle's dashboard detailing who you are, where you went, as well as contact information for people who might be looking for you (see *Appendix* for note).
- Take the obvious path out, staying on the roadways if possible. If you have to make a turn at an intersection, clearly mark the way back to your vehicle.
- If the route is complicated, or you feel forced to explore, leave a trail of "breadcrumbs." One way to do this is to cut up strips of colorful cloth, string, or duct tape and hang them along your path.

DP PLAN EXAMPLE

Table 14-4 Sample DP Plan Entry

Need: Transportation			
Danger	Goals	Needs	Implementation
Roadside emergencies	Handle a medical emergency, vehicle breakdown, or engine fire	First aid supplies	Keep a trauma-based first aid kit in car.
		Tools and repair supplies	Keep a small tool kit along with a Jumpstart, car jack, spare tire, and gas can in the trunk.
		Fire extinguisher	Stock a 10BC fire extinguisher in trunk.
Immediate evacuation	Be ready to evacuate immediately	Reliable transportation	Maintain the car diligently.
		Adequate fuel	Keep gas tank at least half full. Keep 10 additional gallons in two gas cans in garage.
	Map alternative routes out of an area as necessary	Maps or GPS	Keep maps of Virginia and surrounding states in glove box.
	Receive situation updates	Radio	Store talk radio stations in car radio memory.
Vehicle stuck in snow or mud	Free a stuck vehicle	Supplies for digging out tires and pulling vehicle free	Keep shovel, tow strap, and kitty litter in trunk.
Stranded in vehicle	Call for help	Radio or phone capable of calling for help in nearly any conditions	Keep cell phone and spare battery in car. Equip car with 3-watt cell phone signal booster.
	Stay warm	Blankets and clothing to keep entire family warm in wintry conditions	Stock wool blankets in trunk, along with spare hats, gloves, and wool socks.
	Remain hydrated	Enough water for two days	Stock a case of 24 water bottles in trunk.

Quick Summary - Transportation

➤ Safely escaping a disaster area requires transportation, navigation, and information, all of which must work together.

➤ Use a reliable vehicle capable of taking your family out of harm's way. For most situations, fuel efficiency is more important than off-road capability.

➤ Try to keep your vehicle at least half full of fuel at all times.

➤ Prior to departure, stock your vehicle with emergency supplies.

➤ Store enough fuel to travel a minimum of 500 miles.

➤ Stay abreast of emergency information so that you can properly time your escape and choose the correct evacuation route.

➤ Keep a roadside emergency kit in your car. More exhaustive supplies can be added to the kit when you are traveling long distances or through dangerous regions.

➤ Keep electronic copies of important papers on encrypted memory devices. Electronic copies can help when requesting replacement documents, as well as prove ownership and identity.

➤ When stranded, try to stay comfortable and out of harm's way while awaiting assistance. For more serious situations, you may have to scavenge supplies from your car, take more drastic measures to get noticed, or evacuate to safety.

➤ Your vehicle can serve as an excellent shelter. Under most circumstances, you are more likely to survive if you stay with your vehicle rather than abandon it.

➤ If you must abandon your vehicle, take every precaution, including venturing only a short distance, taking supplies with you, leaving a clearly written note behind, and marking your path with "breadcrumbs."

Recommended Items - Transportation

❑ Reliable vehicle capable of transporting your entire family plus emergency supplies

❑ Roadside emergency kit

❑ Enough fuel to travel a minimum of 500 miles

❑ Fuel-efficient backup transportation (e.g., bicycle, moped, motorcycle)

CHAPTER 15
PROTECTION

Chapter 15 Notes

CHAPTER 15

PROTECTION

Challenge

A dangerous riot is underway in your community. Small groups of violent criminals have taken to the streets, looting houses and stores as well as assaulting families. How will you secure your home? Do you have the weapons and expertise necessary to protect your family?

There are numerous situations in which you might be required to protect yourself, your family, or your property. Most of these threats come from common criminals perpetrating violence on the innocent. Even under ideal conditions, police are unable to respond quickly enough to meet every threat. The reality is that sometimes you must take a stand and defend yourself.

During serious disaster situations, you may also be forced to protect your family when law and order breaks down due to widespread panic or chaos. Likewise, some events leave communities isolated with authorities unable to provide protection (e.g., perhaps due to high flood waters, impassable roadways, or widespread devastation). It is during these times of lawlessness that you and your fellow citizens must band together to establish order and security for your community.

TYPES OF VIOLENT THREATS

Violent threats can generally be categorized into three groups:

- Good people who are driven to do bad things because of need
- Career criminals, or those who use disasters to commit crimes of opportunity
- Terrorists or other extremists whose intention is to cause harm

Otherwise good people can be driven to violence by desperation.

The first group could include your neighbors, people you might otherwise wave to while fetching the newspaper from your front yard. Under normal circumstances they pose no threat, and might even render assistance. However, when a serious situation arises, it may be these same people who find themselves hopelessly unprepared. Consider the actions *you* would be willing to take if your family was dying of dehydration and you believed your neighbor was hoarding a large stockpile of water. Desperate times can force people to take desperate measures. These people might convince themselves that you are being unfair, and even rationalize that it is your duty to provide for them. If you fail to offer your supplies, they might resort to stealing or even taking your supplies by force. The best way to avoid this potential confrontation is to be discreet and not broadcast that you have stockpiles of supplies.

The second group of people are criminals, either traditional career offenders, or those exploiting the chaos of the situation. Sensing that they are less likely to be caught by the authorities, they perpetrate crimes of opportunity: robbery, rape, even murder. While these individuals invariably emerge during city riots, gangs of violent criminals are also prevalent after major natural disasters. A good example of this is the small bands of marauders who roamed the streets following Hurricane Katrina.

The third and final group is made up of people whose only intention is to cause death and destruction, perhaps due to their political or religious agenda. These people are the most dangerous because there is no room for negotiation or reason. There is no appeasing them, except through suffering and death. Terrorists often view human life as expendable for purposes of making a statement or progressing their cause. Many are willing to sacrifice their own life for these purposes.

Each of the three types of threats must be handled differently, but all should be recognized as very real dangers. Perhaps in the first scenario, you might assist those in need by providing training or helping to meet their most pressing needs. It is easy to argue that every citizen shares an obligation to help one another in times of need. However, that obligation should not extend to the point of endangering your own family.

Citizens share an obligation to one another, but that obligation only extends so far.

In the case of criminals, your goal is to avoid conflict while removing your family from harm's way. This may require nothing more than a show of force to indicate that you are not an easy target, or a little extra caution about where you travel. It is not your responsibility, neither is it particularly wise, to adopt the role of police officer. It is better to take care of your own backyard by pooling with others to establish a sense of order to your neighborhood and immediate community.

When dealing with terrorists or other extremists, there is little choice but to step outside your normal civilized behavior and operate with the mentality of a ruthless soldier fighting his enemy. There is no room for negotiation or restraint. Forgiving yourself later is easier than living with a lifetime of regret and sorrow. Terrorists' actions are often designed to be widespread and horrific, so stopping them is in everyone's interest.

DEPENDING ON THE POLICE

During large-scale disasters, local police may be unable to maintain law and order, leaving you to defend your family and property. This is in no way meant to suggest that you should give anything but your complete respect to those in uniform; only that you should be prepared for the authorities to be slow, or even completely unable, to respond to your calls for help.

Riot control

During widespread disasters, policemen have also been known to abandon their posts to care for their own families—certainly an understandable course of action. Those who remain are often tasked first with
evacuating people in need. Crimes, both property and violent, are re-
luctantly tolerated by authorities until conditions improve. When faced
with a breakdown in conventional law enforcement, citizens have been
known to band together into small neighborhood militias to protect
themselves from looters and gangs of violent criminals.

YOUR RIGHTS AND RESPONSIBILITIES

The United States has a proud history of protecting the rights of its
law-abiding citizens to own weapons for the stated purposes of self-

protection and maintaining a free state. The Second Amendment to the Constitution states:

> "A well regulated Militia, being necessary to the security of a free State, the right of the people to keep and bear Arms, shall not be infringed."

Exactly what this right guarantees is the subject of countless arguments and court decisions. What is clear, however, is that with only a few restrictions, Americans can legally own numerous types of firearms, including rifles, shotguns, and handguns. Militarized weaponry, such as automatic assault rifles and explosives, are more controlled, requiring special licenses for ownership.

As the head of a household, it is your responsibility to provide some measure of protection for your family. This is not to suggest that you must own a closet full of firearms. Protection comes in many forms,

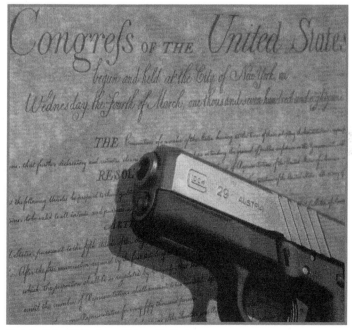

Photo by Robert H. Boatman, *Living with Glocks*

including having a strong support group willing to come to your aid should the need arise. Many people do, however, choose to own firearms for the purpose of home defense.

When taking protective measures, there is a temptation to go overboard and adopt the position that if a little is good, then a lot is better. Why stop at a handgun, when you can have an assault rifle with armor-piercing shells? This view is not only overkill, but it also transforms people who claim to be preparing for possible disasters into "paramilitary nuts" in the eyes of neighbors, friends, and the authorities. Once again, it is best to take reasonable, judicious measures when preparing.

> Tips
>
> In this country of personal freedoms, gun buffs and pacifists are to be equally respected.

Regardless of the moderation with which this topic is approached, there will undoubtedly be some people who are unwilling to consider owning weapons due to their strong aversion to violence. Likewise, there are adamant gun buffs who cherish their right to own a wide assortment of firearms. In our country of personal freedoms, both viewpoints are to be equally respected.

FIREARMS

Irrespective of your position regarding firearms, recognize that we live in a world of guns—with roughly 200 million firearms in the United States alone.[227] If you don't own a firearm, you will be at a distinct disadvantage if violence comes your way. You don't have to like guns, but you should at least recognize that they are highly effective weapons. Dating back to the 19th century, Samuel Colt's revolvers inspired the old saying: "God created man, Sam Colt made them equal." The underlying message being that a firearm gives even the smallest person the ability to defend himself against the largest.

The three types of firearms to consider are: rifles, shotguns, and handguns. As outlined in Table 15-1, each type has distinct advantages and disadvantages when it comes to personal protection.

For most people, a handgun or shotgun is the best option for home defense. Handguns are easier to handle, and good for close range com-

Table 15-1 Firearms Comparison

Weapon Type	Advantages	Disadvantages
Rifles	Excellent range and accuracy; small calibers can be easily handled by women; larger calibers have excellent stopping power	Not concealable; small calibers have limited stopping power; high penetration; prone to be taken away
Shotguns	Excellent stopping power; less accuracy required; limited penetration; intimidating	Not concealable; heavy ammunition; limited capacity; somewhat limited range; prone to be taken away
Handguns	Concealable; lightweight; easily handled by women; good for close range protection; good stopping power; large capacities available; not prone to be taken away	Very limited range; requires skill to be accurate; low calibers have limited stopping power; automatics can jam

bat, whereas shotguns have considerably more stopping power, and can be very intimidating. When loaded with the correct ammunition, both weapons have limited penetration, making it less likely that the bullet will pass through the walls of your house to hit a family member or neighbor.

AUTOMATICS VERSUS REVOLVERS

People tend to have strong, differing opinions about which is better, an automatic or a revolver. Either is adequate in the hands of someone who knows how to use them. An automatic offers greater capacity, but a revolver is generally considered more reliable and easier to use. If you are experienced with handguns, then an automatic is a reasonable choice. Otherwise, a revolver would probably serve you better.

What is more important than choosing between a revolver and an automatic, is selecting the right caliber of handgun. Don't fall into the trap of thinking that bigger is better. A firearm is not only useless but also dangerous to innocent bystanders if you can't use it accurately. A .38 caliber

Automatic and revolver

handgun, which has a mild recoil, will serve you better than a supersized .44 magnum if the kick and weight of the larger gun prevent you from hitting your target.

GUN SAFETY

To be a responsible gun owner, you *must* be diligent in practicing gun safety. At a minimum, this means keeping trigger or cable locks on every firearm, with the keys kept in a location inaccessible to children. Storing your firearms unloaded, with the ammunition in a separate location, adds another degree of safety. Additional safety can be had by locking the firearms and ammunition in a gun safe.

The argument is often made that if a gun is kept secured, then it will not be readily accessible, and thus be of limited value for fast-acting situations. This may well be true, but in households where children are present, *safety should always trump readiness.* On average, about 200 children die in the United States every year from accidental shootings, with about 20 times that number injured.[227] If proper safety precautions are not taken, the chances are far greater that a child will be injured or killed in your home playing with your firearm than at the hands of an intruder. When it comes to guns, be safe above all else.

Trigger lock, by Homak Security

THE "RULE OF 43"

An often-cited statistic claims that having a firearm in your home leaves you 43 times more likely to have it used for suicide, criminal homicide, or accidental shooting than for killing someone in self-defense.[228] At first glance, this would lead any rational person to seriously question ever having a gun in the home. However, as pointed out by experts who analyzed the report, the data was not properly presented and the conclusions not fairly drawn.[229] Most people would agree that it is not the number of dead intruders that should be tabulated when determining the effectiveness of having a gun in your home, but rather the comprehensive protective benefits, including how many lives were saved and injuries prevented.

Gun statistics are often interpreted to favor the reviewer's agenda.

This point is best made through a hypothetical example. Assume there are one thousand homeowners who *don't* have guns, and one thousand homeowners who *do* have guns. Of the homeowners who don't have guns, ten are murdered by intruders. Likewise, of the homeowners who do have guns, only one is murdered by intruders. One intruder is also killed by the homeowner, with the other intruders being scared away. Also, assume that there are four fatal gun accidents in the second group of homes.

The data could be presented with two very different but equally accurate statements:

- **Anti-gun group:** In homes where guns were present, four times as many innocent people were killed by guns than were intruders.
- **Pro-gun group:** Guns reduced the number of murders caused by home intruders by 90%.

You get the point. Data is often about how you present it. With the Rule of 43, one must consider what the data actually means. There may indeed be far more unintentional than intentional deaths in the home due to guns, but considering that less than 0.2% of defensive gun usages actually result in the death of a criminal, the Rule of 43 may not tell the entire story.[230] Gun ownership is a family decision that requires careful consideration of much more than simple statistics.

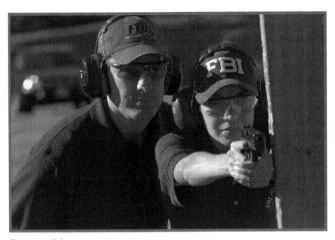

Firearm training

GUN HANDLING

If you own a firearm, take the training necessary to learn how to use it safely and effectively. Gun safety classes are offered from local firearm clubs, as well as the National Rifle Association (NRA) and Civilian Marksmanship Program (CMP). In these classes you will learn about many gun-related topics, including:

- Handling a firearm
- Understanding how a gun operates
- Selecting the right ammunition
- Shooting safely and effectively
- Selecting, cleaning, and storing a firearm

Gun handling skills are essential to everyone in your family old enough to safely handle a firearm. You are strongly encouraged to gain expertise with firearms before bringing one into your home.

LESS LETHAL WEAPONS

There are situations when you might want to defend yourself without resorting to using deadly force. Fortunately, there are many weapons that can deter an attacker without killing him. However, when dealing with "less lethal weapons," it is important to realize that they can, and fre-

Taser X26

quently do, kill people accidentally. Also, understand that the weapons mentioned in this section are not a replacement for firearms.

A list of less lethal weapons is given below:

- **Taser**—very effective; works through most clothing; range up to about 15 feet; commercial devices aren't as capable as those used by law enforcement; outlawed in some states.
- **Chemical spray (tear gas, pepper spray)**—safe to use on an attacker without risk of serious injury; not very effective; can help to escape from an attacker.
- **Bludgeoning weapon (baton, bat, pipe)**—effective; requires you to get fairly close; has the risk of causing serious injury or death to your opponent.
- **Knife**—often deadly; requires getting close; has a high risk of injury to self.
- **Contact Stun Device**—moderately effective; requires sustained direct contact; works through thin clothing; can easily injure self; requires you to be very close.
- **Non-lethal Bullets**—large rubber, bean bag, or plastic projectiles can be effective, but are only available to law enforcement personnel.
- **Bare hands**—can be effective with proper training, such as boxing or martial arts.

HAND-TO-HAND FIGHTING

There will undoubtedly be some time in your life when you find yourself in a violent, physical altercation. To effectively handle the situation, it will be to your advantage to have three things: skill, courage, and physical prowess. These desired attributes are listed in order of importance. Countless competitions have demonstrated that skill can overcome physical disadvantages. Consider that no-holds-barred competitions are frequently won by smaller men (e.g., the Gracie family).

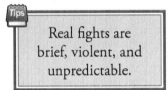

> Real fights are brief, violent, and unpredictable.

Fights should be avoided for numerous reasons, not the least of which is that you might be injured or arrested. However, if you do have to fight, fight like hell. More fights are lost by being hesitant than for any other reason. Fights are usually brief, violent, and unpredictable. They do not resemble what you see in the movies. Nothing is choreographed, meaning that you must adapt and focus on winning rather than putting on a show.

If you want to become skilled at unarmed combat, you must train. Enroll in a good martial arts or boxing club to get some hands-on experience. Recognize that many martial arts studios are designed more for sport than for practical defense, so choose your school carefully.

Martial arts training

DP PLAN EXAMPLE

Table 15-2 Sample DP Plan Entry

Need: Protection			
Danger	Goals	Needs	Implementation
Home invasion, robbery, looting, or other violent crime	Defend family and property	Firearms capable of being used for home defense or riot crowd deterrence	Use a Beretta 92FS for home defense. Use a Remington 870 Police Magnum for riots, or other external threats.
Accidental shooting	Keep firearms safe and away from children	Safety measures for all firearms	Keep firearms unloaded with trigger locks. Store ammunition in a locked fire safe. Teach everyone in the family about the dangers of firearms and proper handling techniques.
Assault by unarmed assailant	Protect self and family	Skill in unarmed combat	Attend weekly mixed-martial arts training classes at local studio.

Quick Summary - Protection

➢ Disasters can force law-abiding individuals to resort to violence in an effort to survive.

➢ When the authorities are unable to keep order, criminals are more likely to commit crimes of opportunity, including looting, rape, theft, robbery, and vandalism.

➢ Be discreet by not broadcasting your level of preparedness.

➢ There are approximately 200 million guns in the United States. Without a firearm, you are at a distinct disadvantage when defending yourself.

➢ Three types of firearms to consider are shotguns, handguns, and rifles. Each has its respective advantages and disadvantages. Handguns and shotguns are particularly suited to home defense.

➢ Select a firearm you can comfortably handle. Accuracy takes priority over stopping power.

➢ With children in the house, safety should always precede readiness. Safety methods include using trigger guards, separating weapons from ammunition, and storing weapons in a gun safe.

➢ Gun safety statistics are open to interpretation. The bottom line is to be safe above all else.

➢ If you own a firearm, take professional training in safety and proper handling techniques.

➢ As an alternative to firearms, consider less lethal weapons, including tasers, chemical sprays, knives, stun guns, and bludgeoning instruments.

Recommended Items - Protection

❏ Lethal weapon
   a. Shotgun with an 18- to 22-inch barrel (e.g., Remington 870, Mossberg 500), *or*
   b. Handgun (e.g., Beretta 92, Colt Python, Ruger GP100)

❏ Less-lethal weapon
   a. Taser, *or*
   b. Fixed-blade knife, *or*
   c. Baseball bat, baton, or other bludgeoning instrument

CHAPTER 16
SPECIAL NEEDS

CHAPTER 16

SPECIAL NEEDS

Challenge

A major earthquake has struck your community. Roadways are so badly damaged that you are unable to evacuate. You have three children and an infirmed, elderly neighbor who are depending on you. What special needs do they have, and how will you meet those needs?

From the very beginning, this handbook has focused on addressing *family* preparedness needs. Most of the topics presented thus far affect everyone equally—we all have to eat, drink, and stay warm. The only exceptions are the two chapters targeted at adult concerns, specifically *Chapter 13: Financial Preparedness* and *Chapter 15: Protection*. This chapter addresses the special needs of the elderly, people with disabilities, children, pregnant women, and pets. The goal of the chapter is to motivate you as a responsible family member and citizen to be aware of, and try to assist with, any special needs others may have.

THOSE WITH SPECIAL NEEDS

Many people have family members, neighbors, or friends with special needs. This could range from the elderly neighbor who requires nightly help preparing his meals,

Be careful not to stereotype people.

to the child born with a hearing disability. For purposes of identifying unique concerns, those with special needs have been grouped here into four categories: the elderly; people with disabilities or other medical needs; children; and pregnant women. This is not to suggest that these people are any less capable of caring for themselves than anyone else. Rather, it is simply a method of sorting a collection of preparations that may be useful in assisting others. The reader is strongly cautioned to avoid stereotyping any group of people.

THE ELDERLY

The definition of "elderly" is neither exact nor uniform in this country or anywhere else in the world. Certainly there are 80 year-old people who run marathons or hike mountains and suffer no physical limitations. For purposes of this discussion, however, an elderly person will be defined simply as someone whose age introduces limitations in their ability to handle disaster situations.

Special needs of the elderly

This section is divided into two parts. The first is targeted to elderly readers; the second is for those wishing to assist an elderly person during a time of crisis.

IF YOU ARE ELDERLY

Every person's capabilities are unique, and those in their "golden years" are no exception. Whether you climb mountains or are confined to a wheelchair, there are steps that you can take to better cope with a disaster. Begin by recognizing that regardless of age, nearly every topic in this book applies directly to you. You still need food, water, clean air, and life's other basic necessities. In order to be properly prepared, you *must* make the preparations outlined in the preceding chapters. However, as a senior, you should also recognize that you may have a few additional unique considerations.[231,232]

Start by answering a few questions to help you identify any limitations that you or your spouse may have.

Personal Assessment Questions[233]

- **Medical Conditions**—Do you have any existing medical conditions that might require immediate attention during a disaster? Do you have an adequate supply of medications? How will you get to the hospital in an emergency? Are others aware of your medical conditions?
- **Personal Care**—Do you need assistance with bathing and grooming? Do you use any personal care equipment to help you bathe or get dressed? What will you do if your care provider is no longer available?
- **Water Service**—Do you have access to purified water, or if not, are you able to safely boil water?
- **Food Service**—Can you prepare your own meals, or do you rely on services such as Meals on Wheels? How will you eat if your food service is interrupted?
- **Feeding Devices**—Do you use any special devices or utensils to eat? What will you do if one breaks and you cannot quickly get a replacement?

- **Electricity-Dependent Equipment**—Do you rely upon medical equipment that requires electricity? Do you have a backup power supply, and if so, how long will it last? Is the electric company aware of your dependency?
- **Transportation**—Do you require a specially equipped vehicle to travel? Can you safely drive at night or in bad weather? Do you need assistance entering or exiting your vehicle? Can you travel alone?
- **Mobility**—Do you use a wheelchair or walker? Can you navigate your house if it becomes cluttered with debris? If your wheelchair or walker is damaged and inoperable, how will you evacuate your home?
- **Errands**—Do you need others to run errands, such as obtaining groceries and medications? What will you do if the person you rely on is unable to reach you because roads are impassible?
- **Building Evacuation**—Can you evacuate your home or office independently and without assistance? Are you able to cope with debris that might block your exit? Can you reach and activate an alarm? Do you need an elevator to evacuate?
- **Calling for Help**—Can you call for help by shouting as well as using a telephone? Do you require hearing aids to communicate? If your hearing aid becomes lost or inoperable, how will you communicate?
- **Service Animals/Pets**—Will you be able to care for your service animal or pets during and after a disaster? Do you have appropriate licenses and certificates for your service animal such that you can keep it with you at an emergency shelter?

Once you have identified any personal limitations or concerns, take the steps necessary to minimize their impact. Below is a list of recommended actions that might be applicable to an elderly person.[234] Many of these suggestions are also applicable to a person with a disability or serious medical condition.

Recommended Actions

- Identify and stock any special backup supplies that you may need, such as spare oxygen bottles, wheelchair or hearing aid batteries, medications, and eyeglasses.

- If you are dependent on electricity for medical needs, notify your local power company. Also, equip your home with a backup power supply.
- If you receive periodic medical treatments or services such as home health care or food delivery, talk to your providers about their ability to continue services during an emergency.
- Wear medical alert tags or bracelets to help others quickly identify your disability or medical needs. Alert bracelets may be found online at *www.medids.com.*
- Consider getting an emergency medical alert system that allows you to call for assistance should you become immobilized.
- Compile a folder of your medical information. Give a copy of this information to a DP network member or trusted friend who lives outside your home. The folder should include:
  - o A list of prescription medicines, including dosages
  - o Descriptions of your medical conditions
  - o Allergy information
  - o Copies of your medical insurance and Medicare cards
  - o Descriptions of your medical devices, including models and serial numbers
  - o A list of contact information for your doctors and care providers
- Teach others in your home to operate your wheelchair. This will allow them to more easily transport you, should you become incapacitated.
- When making an emergency call, try to use a conventional landline rather than a cell phone. The landline will enable the dispatcher to more quickly identify your location. Be prepared to provide clear, specific instructions to rescue personnel. Equip your home with several phones, or keep one with you.
- Be careful about getting too hot or cold. Elderly people are more susceptible to temperature-related injuries.
- Millions of children live in households headed by grandparents. If you are raising grandchildren, be sure to consider their special needs as well (see *Children* later in this chapter).
- Don't forget the needs of your pets (see *Pets* later in this chapter).
- Establish a support network with your family, friends, neighbors, doctors, etc. Keep their contact information handy, and don't hesitate to call on them.

- Give a spare house key to someone in your local network. This will allow them to better check on you, as well as to keep an eye on your house in the event you have evacuated.
- If you decide to evacuate, let numerous people in your network know where you are going. Contact them once you arrive safely at your destination, and continue to stay in contact with them throughout the disaster.
- If you receive federal benefits, sign up for electronic payments, which are paid directly from the government to your bank account or a debit MasterCard. Disasters can disrupt the mail service for days or even weeks. Direct deposit also eliminates the risk of anyone stealing your benefit checks. You can sign up for direct deposit of federal benefits by calling 1-800-333-1795, or visiting *www.godirect. org*. Electronic payment will be required for all recipients beginning March 1, 2013.[235]
- Following a disaster, beware of fraudulent home repair contractors. Don't hire a contractor who comes to your door and solicits. Rather, find a reputable, insured contractor through the Yellow Pages or other conventional methods. Get more than one estimate for the repairs. Only deal with a contractor who is willing to put everything in writing, including firm repair costs. Ideally, pay for the work only after it has been completed.

ASSISTING THE ELDERLY

The elderly are particularly susceptible in the event of a disaster because many have medical conditions or physical limitations that make it more difficult for them to evacuate or perform rigorous activities. Some elderly people may be unwilling to leave their home for fear of having their belongings stolen or destroyed. They may also be reluctant to reach out to others because they don't want to be seen as a burden. As a good citizen, you are encouraged to assume some responsibility for caring for the elderly in your community. Below is a list of things you can do to help the elderly during a crisis.[231,232]

- Get to know the elderly in your neighborhood. Don't be offended if they seem suspicious of your intentions. The elderly are often the victims of scams (see *Chapter 13: Financial Preparedness*). Be patient and understanding of their caution.

- If you see a disaster coming, approach your elderly friends and neighbors beforehand, and let them know that you will be checking in on them. Ask if there are any preparations that you can help with, such as refilling prescriptions, picking up a few extra groceries, and removing any home hazards. Make it clear that you don't want payment for your assistance. Leave your phone number, and ask them to call you if they need anything.
- When a disaster does occur, periodically check on the elderly. Make sure that they have the necessary supplies to meet their needs, including food, water, medication, and heating/cooling.
- Continue checking on them after the disaster passes. Studies have shown that the elderly often have more economic and health-related issues after a disaster than younger people.
- If it is clear that an elderly person is suffering from a health problem, help him or her to seek medical attention.
- Help them to register for disaster recovery assistance should they require it.
- Keep an eye out to make sure they don't become targets of a fraudulent contractor. Intervene on the elderly person's behalf to let the perpetrator know that you are scrutinizing his activity.
- Don't treat the elderly as helpless! Many elderly people are perfectly capable of caring for themselves, so don't stereotype anyone.
- Encourage elderly people to receive electronic deposits of any federal benefits they may receive. Disasters can often disrupt the mail for days or even weeks. This also eliminates the risk of anyone stealing their checks. People can sign up for direct deposit of their federal benefits by calling 1-800-333-1795, or visiting *www.godirect. org*. Note that all federal benefits recipients will be required to use electronic payments beginning March 1, 2013.[235]

Medical ID tag

PEOPLE WITH DISABILITIES

The term "people with disabilities" is very broad in scope. The Americans with Disabilities Act defines a person with a disability as:[236]

- anyone with a physical or mental impairment that substantially limits one or more major life activities; or
- someone with a record of a physical or mental impairment; or
- any person who is regarded as having such an impairment.

People may suffer from physical disabilities, requiring a wheelchair, cane, prosthetic, or other device. Or they may suffer from mental or cognitive impairments, including autism, psychiatric disabilities, speech impediments, and learning disabilities. As a result, providing a single set of general disaster preparedness recommendations is simply not possible.

From a preparedness point of view, the challenges facing people with disabilities are often comparable to those facing the elderly, since many of these challenges result from limited mobility or impaired senses. For this reason, much of what has been written earlier, including the *Personal*

Evacuating people with disabilities *(photo by FEMA/Win Henderson)*

Assessment Questions, Recommended Actions, and *Assisting the Elderly,* directly applies to people with disabilities or other serious medical conditions. The extent to which the particular recommendations apply largely depend on the type and severity of a person's disabilities.

For a person with a disability, being ready for a disaster is another aspect of maintaining personal independence. They face the same needs as every other citizen, including food, water, shelter, protection, etc. Each individual must answer, and subsequently address, how their disability might introduce special needs in the event of a catastrophe.

CHILDREN

Having children in your home requires you to make some special preparations. There are differing points of view regarding the best ways to handle dangers faced by younger family members. Many experienced parents would probably agree that children respond better to honest, clear discussions about threats—whether it is a neighborhood sex offender, the school bully, or more suited to this discussion, the approaching tornado.

Openly discuss the disasters that can affect your area. Explain the likelihood and expected impact of each. Encourage your children to think about how your family should prepare. Actively solicit their inputs, giving each suggestion the appropriate level of consideration. At no time should you make the discussion frightening. Instead, try to make this a positive, bonding experience in which everyone feels that they have contributed part of the solution. Explain to your kids that not everyone prepares adequately, but by doing so, you can not only help yourself but also those who are less prepared.

Teach your children not to panic. Kids mimic what they see. If you are calm and in control, they will draw strength from you. Practice emergency situations. This might include such things as sheltering in place,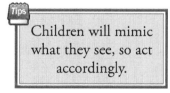
Children will mimic what they see, so act accordingly.

evacuating your home, and functioning without electrical power. Make sure that they know how to call 911. Practice how they would interact with the dispatcher. Roleplay to make this both informative and fun.

Teach your children how to evacuate from every room in the house. Most important, show them how to escape from their own bedrooms in case they should ever become trapped by a house fire. If old enough, teach them to use a fire extinguisher (see *Using an Extinguisher* in *Chapter 5: Shelter*). Finally, if your children will ever be exposed to firearms, teach them to handle them safely.

For younger children, consider providing them with comics, games, and coloring books that relate to disaster preparedness (found on FEMA's Ready Kids website at *www.ready.gov/kids*).[237] These materials strive to make learning fun while still providing accurate and useful information.

Older children might find the discussion of disaster types found at *www.fema.gov/hazard/types* to be more interesting. Consider assigning a project, such as assembling a small disaster kit, or writing a report on the dangers of a specific threat relevant to your area.

COPING WITH A DISASTER

When a disaster occurs, children may feel even greater stress than their parents. At the root of their anxiety, is a loss of control and normalcy. Daily routines are disturbed. Friends may not be accessible. Sleeping conditions may have changed. Food and water may be in short supply. Worst of all, they may have witnessed devastation, physical injury, and emotional trauma. All this can add up to terrible anxiety. As an adult, you

Children coping with disaster *(photo by FEMA/Andrea Boohers)*

are able to put logical bounds on how bad things can get. You can see beyond the immediate chaos to a longer term solution. Children, on the other hand, may feel their world has been turned upside down, uncertain that it will ever right itself.

Every child reacts to stress differently. Some may grow irritable, while others may become clingy, emotionally upset, or withdrawn. The best way to help them is to be calm and reassuring. Talk to your children about what they are feeling, and work to address their concerns. But don't lie to them. Trust is something that is difficult to regain once it is lost. Below are a few additional suggestions regarding helping children to cope with stress.[238,239,240]

Be honest with your kids; trust is very hard to regain once lost.

- Be mindful of *your* behavior. Children watch their parents for clues on how they should act. If you begin shouting and acting frantic, they may become frightened. Put on a brave face, and let your children know that you will keep them safe.
- Try to understand your children's fears, and provide the necessary reassurance. These fears often center around three concerns:
  o The disaster will never end.
  o Someone they love will be killed or injured.
  o They will be separated from their family.
- Give each child a specific job, and praise their efforts when they rise to the challenge.
- Establish a routine. Children and adults alike are able to adapt to new conditions, and routines help to relieve the stress that uncertainty brings.
- Maintain discipline. Allowing your children to turn their anxiety into disrespect or argument can make the entire family less functional and heighten the level of stress.
- If possible, allow them to have contact with family or friends.
- Demonstrate your love. Give your children plenty of pats, hugs, and kisses. Physical contact can be very reassuring. Spend extra time with them, perhaps reading a book or playing a game. It is during times of greatest stress that love can shine the brightest. How you treat your children in these times of crisis is what they will remember their entire lives.

Once the disaster has passed, children may display very different reactions. FEMA provides the following descriptions of common reactions based on a child's age:[240]

- **Birth to 2 years**—Children who are not yet able to effectively communicate may become irritable, upset, or clingy. When they grow older (perhaps years later), their games may involve acting out elements of the traumatic event.
- **Ages 3 to 6 years**—Preschool children often feel helpless, small, and unable to protect themselves or others. This may cause intense fear and insecurity when separated from their parents. Preschool children generally cannot grasp the concept of permanent loss. In the weeks following the traumatic event, their play may involve reenacting the incident.
- **Ages 7 to 10 years**—By age seven, children have the ability to understand permanent loss. Some kids may become preoccupied with the details of the disaster. This preoccupation can interfere with their school or other activities. They may also display a wide range of reactions, including sadness, fear, anger, and guilt.
- **Ages 11+**—Pre-adolescent and adolescent children will have a more sophisticated understanding of the disaster event. Some may become involved in risk-taking behaviors, such as alcohol or drug use. Others may become fearful and avoid activities they were previously comfortable doing. They may also have difficulty expressing their emotions and worries.

SCHOOL EMERGENCY PLANS

If your children attend a public or private school, contact the school administrator and ask a few basic questions about their emergency plans:

- How will school officials communicate with families during an emergency? Do they have your emergency contact information, including work, home, and cell phone numbers? What will they do if you are unreachable?
- Does the school store food, water, and other basic supplies?
- Is the school prepared to shelter-in-place?
- What are their evacuation plans?

In cases where schools institute procedures to shelter-in-place, be aware that you may not be permitted to pick up your children. Even if you go to the school, the doors may be locked or inaccessible for safety reasons. Also, if you want someone else to have the authority to pick up your children in case of an emergency (such as a grandmother or close friend), sign the necessary release paperwork with the school ahead of time.

PREGNANT WOMEN

The needs of pregnant women (or people with other medical conditions) during a disaster can be very unique. The suggestions given below are tailored to pregnant women, but most can be easily modified to fit people with other medical conditions.[241]

If you think you might need to evacuate, contact your health care provider ahead of time and get copies of your prenatal records. Also, let your doctor know the specifics of your new location. If you are close to your delivery date, or have a high-risk pregnancy, ask your caregiver for guidance as well as a referral for a doctor in the evacuation area. Also, compile a list of your medications, both prescription and non-prescription.

If you decide to evacuate, take an adequate supply of medications and prenatal vitamins, as well as your prenatal records and health care provider's contact information. If you are traveling by car, be sure to stop periodically to stretch and walk around. Wear and pack comfortable clothing and shoes. Also, take along some

A time for special care *(photo by USDA/Ken Hammond)*

healthy snacks and water, so you won't have to survive on roadside junk food. Be extra careful about not consuming food that might be contaminated or spoiled.

Try to get adequate rest and relaxation. Avoid overexerting yourself or getting too hot. The bottom line is to give yourself permission to take it easy. Even though it might be difficult given the circumstances, try to keep your stress level down. If you feel anxiety, consult a trusted friend, family member, or clergy member.

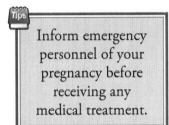

Inform emergency personnel of your pregnancy before receiving any medical treatment.

Inform emergency personnel or relief services that you are pregnant before receiving any immunizations, medications, or x-rays. If your health care provider closes or becomes inaccessible, contact a local hospital or health department about receiving prenatal, delivery, and medical care.

PETS

Americans have over 360 million pets, and that does not include exotic or wild animals. The simple truth is that people all over the world love their pets. A dog, cat, bird, horse, or even a turtle can feel like part of the family. Unfortunately, some disasters leave pet owners with very difficult decisions to make if prior planning was not done.

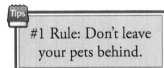

#1 Rule: Don't leave your pets behind.

The starting point to pet planning is to *do everything possible not to leave your animals behind.* History tells us that animals left behind will suffer terribly, with many perishing. You certainly don't want to be responsible for the death of your animal companion. Fortunately, proper planning can help. A very useful video regarding pets in a community emergency is provided online by Oak Ridge National Laboratory.[242] Every pet owner is encouraged to watch the video (see *Bibliography* for the web link).

The two basic disaster scenarios to consider are: (1) you must immediately shelter in place—perhaps due to a biochemical threat, or (2) you must evacuate—perhaps due to an approaching wildfire or hurricane.

Evacuating with pets *(photo by FEMA/Leif Skoogfors)*

In the case of sheltering in place, you would normally just take your animals into your home's makeshift shelter (see *Chapter 5: Shelter*). If the animals are too large, you will need to make other accommodations, perhaps a barn, basement, or garage. The important thing is to get them out of harm's way.

If you decide to evacuate, take your animals with you. If that is not possible, shelter them in a safe location, such as a friend's house or boarding kennel. In 2006, the Pets Evacuation and Transportation Standards Act (PETS) was passed, mandating that communities have plans for evacuating, transporting, and sheltering animals. However, don't expect extensive assistance from government officials. They will have their hands full with many other pressing needs. The responsibility ultimately falls on you as the pet owner to ensure your pet's well-being.

This section is divided into three time frames: before a disaster arrives, when the event is occurring, and after it has passed. The material draws heavily from FEMA's guide, *Information for Pet Owners* and the American Veterinarian's Medical Association's guide, *Saving the Whole Family*.[243,244]

BEFORE A DISASTER

The time to take action to ensure that your pets will be properly cared for is *before* a disaster strikes. There are numerous preparatory steps to consider:

- Understand your local risks. Every region faces different hazards, ranging from flooding, to extreme weather events, to wildfires. Consider how these threats will affect your pets.
- Take clear photos of each pet. If your animal ever becomes lost, you can use the photos to create posters or show them to shelter workers.
- Make certain that your pets have up-to-date identification tags. If you know where you will be evacuating to, put that location and a phone number on the back of your pet's tag or on the collar using duct tape. Microchips placed under the skin can also greatly assist veterinarians or shelter workers when trying to reunite lost pets with owners.
- Locate a place to board your pet. This could be a professional boarder, veterinarian, or friend not affected by the disaster. For health and safety reasons, most emergency shelters *will not* accept pets. The one exception to this is service animals. By law, service animals are allowed into emergency shelters if the owner has proof of a medical need and the pet's current vaccinations. Some hotels and motels will also allow pets, but you should confirm this ahead of time. Your local animal shelter may also be able provide information regarding available shelter and boarding locations.
- If you decide to evacuate your pets with you, take adequate pet food, water, medications, veterinary records, vaccination certificates, litter, clean up material, muzzles, tie out materials, and other supplies that might not be available during transit.
- Take pet carriers, leashes, and harnesses as appropriate. Pet carriers should be large enough to have a small water bowl and a litter pan (for cats), and must have your contact information on them.
- Supplement your first aid kit with any additional specialty supplies needed for your pets. See FEMA's *Information for Pet Owners* for a complete listing of first aid supplies for various pet types and sizes.[243]

- Don't leave your pets unattended in your vehicle in hot weather. Temperatures can become far hotter in the car than outside and can quickly kill your animals.
- If you have livestock or other large animals, work with local and state authorities to evacuate them. During some emergencies, state authorities may not allow large animal trailers on the roadways.
- Identify a trusted neighbor or friend who will serve as the designated caregiver for your animals in case the emergency happens while you are away from home. Give him or her a spare key and simple instructions on how to care for your pets.
- Understand that it may be impossible to take any animal (except service animals) on a plane, bus, or train. Plan accordingly.

If you absolutely have no choice but to leave your pets behind, there are a few precautions you can take to improve their chances for survival:

1. Confine your pets to a safe area inside the home. Do not leave them chained or tied up.
2. Leave plenty of food and water.
3. Remove the toilet tank lids, raise the seats, and brace the bathroom doors so they can drink from the toilets as needed.
4. Leave a notice on your front door that details what types of pets are inside, their names, where they are located, and when you left them. Also, provide your contact information and that of your veterinarian.
5. Return to your pets as promptly as possible. If you will be delayed, have someone else check on them.

Understand that these steps will *not* ensure your pets' survival, only help to give them a fighting chance. Leaving a pet behind should always be considered a last resort.

DURING A DISASTER

If a disaster is imminent or underway, you need to take immediate action to protect your pets.

- Bring them inside to a safe, manageable area of your home. If you have an indoor kennel, you may wish to keep them in it for their protection and comfort. If the animals are too large to be brought indoors, accommodate them in a barn, basement, garage, or other structure.

- If you have different types of animals (such as a cat and dog), keep them separated. The anxiety of an emergency situation can cause them to act dominant and aggressive.
- Provide reassurance to your pets. If you have children, ask them to help comfort the animals. This will help your pets relax, and give your kids a sense of participation.
- Be sure to have adequate food, water, and cleanup supplies available. Consider feeding moist food to reduce your pet's additional water needs. Don't overfeed your pets in an effort to keep them happy.
- Clean up any animal urine or feces immediately and thoroughly.

AFTER A DISASTER

Once the disaster passes, take a few final precautions to ensure your pets' safety.

- Begin by assessing if there are any immediate threats to your pets. These could include rising waters, downed power lines, roaming animals, and debris. If threats exist, keep your pets on a leash or indoors until the dangers subside.
- Recognize that your outdoor animals may act strangely or try to wander off because of new smells and sounds. Keep a close eye on them until things return to normal.
- If pets were left behind, they may require additional care. This may include professional decontamination, especially if they were exposed to high waters. Discuss your pets' needs with local emergency management officials or your veterinarian.
- Discard any contaminated pet supplies, including food and water bowls, bedding, and toys.
- If your pet is lost, check with animal control, local shelters, and veterinarians daily to see if it turns up. Also, put up missing posters, and ask neighbors to be on the lookout for your pets.
- Animals left unattended during a disaster may become violent and dangerous. If you see signs of personality changes in your pets, seek counsel from your veterinarian.

Quick Summary - Special Needs

➤ Those with special needs may include the elderly, people with disabilities or medical conditions, pregnant women, and children.

➤ Elderly *preppers* should assess their physical limitations, if any, and take steps to minimize the impact of those limitations. Such steps may include stocking medicines or medical equipment, compiling medical information, and establishing a trusted network of supporters.

➤ From a preparedness point of view, the challenges facing people with disabilities are in many cases similar to those facing the elderly since challenges often result from limited mobility or impaired senses. However, every case is unique, and needs must be addressed with individual consideration.

➤ Children respond better to honest, clear discussions about threats. Don't frighten them, but don't lose credibility either.

➤ When around children, be mindful of your behavior. Kids watch their parents for clues as to how they should act. Put on a brave face, and let your children know that you will keep them safe. Maintain discipline and work to establish a daily routine.

➤ Contact your children's school administrator and ask about their emergency plans. Be sure that they have your current emergency contact information.

➤ The time to prepare for your pets is before a disaster strikes. Do everything possible *not* to leave your animals behind. If you must evacuate with your pets, take adequate supplies to care for them.

CHAPTER 17
CREATING A DP NETWORK

CHAPTER 17

CREATING A DP NETWORK

Challenge

A serious pandemic has swept across the country. Unfortunately, your family has been infected. Medical services have treated your family's symptoms and advised them to stay away from other people for at least 10 days to prevent spreading the disease. Who will you call on to help meet your family's needs?

One of the most important things you can do to prepare for a disaster is to form a support network. To do this, you must first recognize that you are stronger in a group of like-minded individuals than you are alone. Sometimes this is a difficult idea to accept because most people see themselves as independent and able to handle anything. However, if history has taught us anything about surviving widespread crises, it is that those affected find increased support and strength in numbers.

Everyone has unique capabilities and skills. Individually, these skills may prove valuable, but when combined with others, a much more cohesive solution can be found. Consider the contributions of a doctor, policeman, elementary school teacher, fisherman, lawyer, and cook. Any one of these people's skills might be valuable during a disaster, but when combined, forms a more powerful and effective entity.

You might believe that people will think you are bonkers if you talk about the need to establish a disaster preparedness support network. Perhaps ten years ago this would have been true, but today there is a growing sense that being prepared is vitally important. Simply put, you are not alone! People in large numbers around the world are beginning to consider and prepare for worst-case, "what if" scenarios.

Invite others to be part of this grass roots movement to become better prepared.

Even if the people you approach have not previously considered the importance of an emergency preparedness group, it is not a hard sell. Nearly everyone has witnessed the widespread catastrophes of the past few years, including the gulf oil spill, the earthquake in Haiti, the stock market collapse, Hurricane Katrina, and the Indian Ocean tsunami to name but a handful. Events of this magnitude affect vast numbers of people, from relatives of victims, to business owners, to medical care providers. When inviting others to participate in this grass roots movement, you may find that many people will have a story to share about how their lives have already been affected by a recent disaster event.

PURPOSE OF A DP NETWORK

The purpose of a DP network is to more effectively meet life's basic needs during a disaster. Your group must decide how to meet those needs as a collective rather than as individuals. This is generally accomplished by pooling resources, sharing supplies, and leveraging skills. A few examples of each are given below:

- *Pooling resources*—A member of your network has a large pickup truck that can be used to transport debris to the local dump. Another member has a chainsaw to help cut fallen trees. A third person has a portable electric generator to help recharge batteries. Resources such as these can be shared to the benefit of everyone in the group.
- *Sharing supplies*—A member of your network has a large vegetable garden with more food than his family can consume. Another person has a 250-gallon Super Tanker that can be used to store

extra water. A third member has several cords of cut wood in his backyard that can be used as fuel for wood-burning stoves. Once again, these supplies can be shared to the benefit of the entire team.

* ***Leveraging skills***—A member of your network is a shortwave radio operator and can receive and relay information about your situation. Another member is an insurance salesman who can offer advice on how best to document and file claims. A third person works a taxi cab driver and can provide details on alternate evacuation routes out of the city. Leveraging these skills can benefit everyone in the network.

NETWORK MEMBERS

It is important to distinguish between contacts and network members so as to correctly set your expectations. Contacts are people who exchange information with you. A neighbor who keeps you informed of weather events is an example of a contact. When it comes to contacts, nothing is expected, and no agreements or understandings are reached. It is a simple exchange of information, which sometimes can be extremely valuable. Network members are different in that they have pledged to work as part of a team and have accepted specific responsibilities.

The fundamental rule for establishing an effective network is that everyone must bring something to the table. For some members, this might be tangible contributions, such as stored food or water. Others may elect to contribute a valuable service, such as emergency medical care or home repair.

> **Tips**
> Everyone must contribute something, but not all contributions will be equal.

Contributions will never be exactly equal, and that's okay. However, everyone should adopt the mindset that they are part of a group and be fully committed to share and contribute to the welfare of the team.

Your network should strive to have a few members outside your immediate community. Their contribution to the group may simply be that of information conduits, relaying information to and from emergency services or concerned family members. This is particularly important for situations where local communication services have failed.

Disaster preparedness networks can include anyone, but most often consist of people from four distinct groups:

- Family and friends
- Neighbors
- Service providers
- Church or civic groups

FAMILY AND FRIENDS

You will likely have the greatest success if you start your DP network with close friends or family members. These are the people with whom you feel most comfortable, and who are most likely to share similar values and concerns. They may live next door, across town, or halfway around the globe. Friends and family are typically the easiest to enlist because there already exists a longstanding trust.

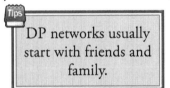

DP networks usually start with friends and family.

One way to broach the subject is to begin by discussing the tragedies currently affecting others, and then move on to express your concerns about how threats might affect your respective families. From there, you can suggest ways to work together to prepare for the most worrisome events. A DP network can start very informally—two people sitting around the kitchen table discussing how to keep their families safe.

It is usually easy to tell if someone understands the importance of disaster preparedness. If your friend or family member doesn't initially respond to your invitation with enthusiasm, be patient and give them time for the idea to settle in. Certainly, be careful not co come off as an overzealous alarmist, which might endanger your relationship.

NEIGHBORS

Inviting neighbors to be part of a disaster preparedness network is very much like inviting them to part of a neighborhood watch program. In fact, the two can often be combined. Start with a discussion of the need and the benefits, much like a friendly business proposition. Then progress to discussing individual contributions. Be patient and give everyone a chance to come to terms with your proposition. You don't want to be seen as a pushy neighbor. The good news is that neighbors tend to band together when times get tough. Everyone enjoys knowing that the people living next door are watching their back.

An important task for a neighborhood-based DP network is to identify people in the immediate community who might have special needs, such as the elderly or someone with a disability. Certainly, these people

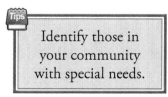

Identify those in your community with special needs.

should be invited into your network as well, but even if they decline to participate, you should consider how best to help them through challenging times (see *Chapter 16: Special Needs*).

SERVICE PROVIDERS

Your doctor, accountant, hair dresser, pastor, veterinarian, and day-care provider are all examples of service providers. A person possessing such skills can be extremely valuable during a time when normal services are unavailable. Understandably, your relationship with these people might not be as strong as with family or friends, but these people may still be interested in being part of a network of fellow preparers.

A good way to begin is to discuss relevant concerns and preparations with them—perhaps asking your doctor about prescribing additional medications, or your pastor about providing shelter in the case of a family who becomes suddenly homeless. The conversation can then easily migrate into a more personal invitation if the person expresses an interest.

CHURCH OR CIVIC GROUPS

Churches and civic organizations (e.g., Lion's Club, Masonic Lodge, Kiwanis club) are excellent places to find individuals who might be interested in being part of a preparedness network. Both churches and civic groups are well versed in providing food and other relief, and the feeling of community care and kinship is inherent in their belief structures.

A reasonable approach is to start by explaining what you are trying to accomplish to the church or civic organization's leaders. Encourage them to make an announcement to their broader audience. From there, hold a small question and answer session to work out the details of how the members will work together. Many local preparedness groups even hold meetings in their local church.

CREATING AN EFFECTIVE NETWORK

How do you establish an effective network? First and foremost, find people who share similar concerns. Everyone wants to survive, and many people are coming to realize that the world presents very real dangers. Your success in recruiting network members is more a matter of timing—connecting with people who are at the point in their life where they recognize and wish to prepare for these dangers.

Once you have identified interested parties, determine the best way for everyone to work well together. People tend to get in the right frame of mind when reminded that the activity is motivated by love and concern for one another. Being part of a disaster preparedness network requires you to be part Scout and part charity worker.

A DP network is a mini-community that shares goods, services, and information.

At its core, a DP network is simply a mini-community that looks out for one another. Its members share goods, services, and information; more important, they watch out for one another. Many modern communities have lost this sense of unity. There was a time when neighbors lent a hand, held potluck dinners, and worked together as part of an informal family. Sadly, for the most part, the "I'll watch your back if you'll watch mine," mentality has been replaced by "I'll leave you alone if you'll leave me alone." A preparedness network is an opportunity to reverse this trend by reestablishing a sense of working toward the common good.

YOUR FIRST MEETING

At your first meeting, consider inviting everyone's families to attend. Try to make it a social gathering: share food, let the kids play; and get to know one another's families. The goal is to introduce everyone, talk about the basic purpose of the group, share war stories, and in general, ensure that everyone has compatible goals and agendas.

Have everyone tell a little about themselves, describing their jobs, hobbies, families, pets, and personal concerns. This will help the group to better understand the strengths that each person brings to the team. Keep politics and religion out of it, unless these are intentionally going to be a cornerstone of your group.

Some people may come well versed on disaster preparedness, while others may be new to the subject—perhaps affected by a recent crisis. Try to make everyone feel that their participation is important, regardless of how much they appear willing to contribute to the group at this initial stage.

Discuss the basic goals of the network, but don't make any specific assignments at this stage. Rather, suggest that everyone buy or borrow a copy of your favorite disaster preparedness book—this or another one. Ask them to read it by the next meeting and jot down suggestions and concerns. By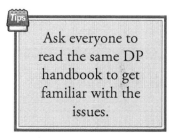

Ask everyone to read the same DP handbook to get familiar with the issues.

doing this, everyone will come to the second meeting with a similar understanding of the specific preparations that need to be addressed. Also, ask each person to consider what contributions they would be willing to make the group.

THE FOLLOW-UP MEETING

Hold a follow-up meeting—perhaps a few weeks later, giving everyone time to read the handbook and think about their respective roles on the team. The follow-up meeting can either be another large family event, or something a little quieter with just the adults. The goal of the second meeting is to begin to outline emergency plans. Keep things simple. The simpler the plans, the more likely they are to actually work.

Collect and combine everyone's contact information, and arrange to distribute the list to every member—perhaps through email. Much like a book club, discuss the disaster preparedness book you will be using. If members read different (or additional) books, this is a good time to swap with one another.

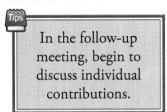

In the follow-up meeting, begin to discuss individual contributions.

Begin working through the list of 14 basic needs (see *Chapter 2: Staying Alive*), prioritizing those that need to be met first. Determine who has interests in specific areas, and let them take the lead on those. People tend to volunteer solutions to things. If you bring up the concern that the group needs some sort of water storage, a member may quickly step forward with a solution that he already has in hand. Make sure that everyone has something to do. Don't expect to find good solutions to all the needs in this initial meeting. Preparing takes time.

KEEPING THINGS MOVING

An effective network is constantly evolving. Members join, others may drop out or move away. As the group changes, so will its needs and capabilities. The network should keep a list of what every member will provide. Careful notetaking will help to identify shortages or overlaps as the group evolves, as well as make responsibilities clear to its members.

Have each member identify someone in the group to share a house key with. There are many situations that require someone have access to your house, perhaps to care for a pet, cut off utilities, or retrieve emergency supplies, not to mention when you lock yourself out and just need someone to let you in. But don't push the key sharing too quickly. Give everyone a chance to get to know and trust one another first.

No matter how mild or severe the crisis, work together as a group to meet your member's needs.

When a disaster event does occur, reconnect as a group and take action to ensure that everyone's needs are being met. If the situation is mild—perhaps the power goes out for a few hours one evening—check in with your network members and see how they are doing. It is this sense of camaraderie that goes a long way when things become more challenging.

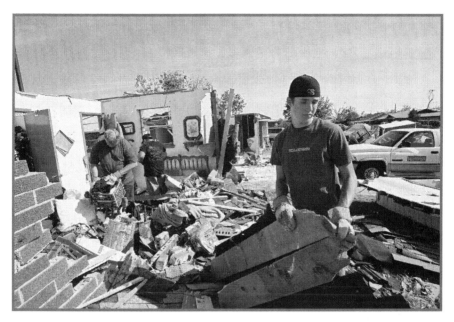

Working together, *(photo by FEMA/Bob McMillan)*

If the event is serious, have the group gather together and determine how best to handle the situation. Your network's response will depend on the particular crisis. For example, if the community gets snowed in, perhaps one member who owns a four-wheel drive vehicle can help distribute supplies. If an ice storm brings trees down in a member's yard, the group can gather to help with cleanup. Or, if heavy rains flood one member's home, another member can take that family in until the water recedes. Every situation will be different and thus require different responses. Being part of the preparedness network is a commitment to helping one another through difficult times.

Quick Summary - Creating a DP Network

➤ You are safer and more likely to survive a serious disaster in a group of like-minded individuals.

➤ The DP network is most effective when members strive to pool resources, share supplies, and leverage skills.

➤ DP networks can include anyone, but often consist of friends and family, neighbors, service providers, and members from church or civic organizations.

➤ Hold an initial social gathering so that everyone can get to know one another. Identify a DP handbook that everyone can read to get a clearer understanding of the needed preparations.

➤ At the follow-up meeting, begin to discuss the group's needs, allowing members to volunteer taking the lead in different areas. Also, gather and distribute contact information.

➤ When a disaster event occurs, no matter how small, connect with your network members to make sure that everyone's needs are being met.

CHAPTER 18
TRIAL BY FIRE

CHAPTER 18

TRIAL BY FIRE

The only way to determine if your family is truly prepared is to put your supplies and skills to the test. Too often people do a good job of stocking the basics, but miss small items that end up being critical to their survival. The classic example of this is having a pantry full of canned foods but no manual can opener. Such oversights are easily remedied by testing your preparations before a disaster strikes.

Below is a list of trials that your family should consider working through. Each trial is designed to help identify any shortcomings in your preparations. Some of the trials may not be relevant to your family, so pick and choose accordingly. Also, try to come up with your own challenges that might be germane to your family or com-

Create your own challenges by considering the most likely or most worrisome threats facing your family.

munity. The best way to do that is to identify the most likely threats; and then simulate those conditions.

Some of the tests outlined below should ideally be taken on a day when everyone is off work and available. This way the whole family can

---

participate. Try to make this fun, but be forewarned, you are likely to hear a few complaints. No doubt you will have to remind everyone that these trials are meant to simulate hard times, so some level of discomfort is to be expected.

Of course, many disasters are more far-reaching than these short-lived experiments. However, by completing these tests, you will learn quite a bit. You will determine your family's daily food and water consumption, verify that your energy resources (batteries, flashlights, wood, generator fuel, etc.) are adequate, learn about hygiene in the absence of running water, practice evacuating the single most deadly danger you will likely face—the house fire—and realize firsthand the importance of having a solid grab-and-go strategy.

UNPLUGGED

Scenario: A powerful storm rolls through your community overnight, causing a loss of electrical power.

As soon as you climb out of bed, turn off your main power breaker— something you should know how to do. For the next 24 hours, operate without utility power. If you have a generator and/or an inverter (see *Chapter 7: Electrical Power*), practice using them. Discover the capabilities and limitations of your equipment. Can you power your house lights? If not, do you have adequate substitute lighting for nighttime? Can you stay warm (or cool)? How will you cook? Operate under the assumption that the whole community is without power. This means that you must pre-pare your own meals—no running out to a restaurant. Keep the power turned off until the following morning. It is advisable to try this test in both the heat of summer and the middle of winter.

BOIL ORDER

Scenario: Your county health department issues a boil order for all tap water.

Treat the water coming out of your taps as contaminated. Start by dis-carding all the ice made from your water supply on the assumption that it too is suspect. If you have a true purifier (see *Chapter 4: Water*), you can use the purified water without boiling it beforehand, but only the water from that single tap. If you do not have a purifier, then you must boil all water before using it. If you wash your hands in contaminated water, you must use an alcohol sanitizer afterward. Give this a try for a day and see what impact it has on your family.

DRIED UP

Scenario: *Local authorities have shut off tap water because heavy rains caused sewage to contaminate the water supply.*

Start by cutting off the water main coming into your home—something you should know how to do. For the next 24 hours, use stored water for your family's drinking and sanitary needs. Be sure to prepare for this challenge by storing adequate water. This is a great experiment to determine how much water your family really needs in an emergency. It is best to try this test in the heat of summer when your water needs are at their greatest.

RUNNING ON EMPTY

Scenario: *Due to war needs, gasoline is in short supply and being rationed.*

Challenge your family to cut their fuel usage by 50% for an entire week. Consider carpooling with your spouse, limiting the number of shopping trips, eating at home rather than dining out, walking or riding a bike to nearby places, and a host of other fuel-saving actions.

LIVE FROM YOUR CUPBOARDS

Scenario: *Terrorists attack the food supply system, preventing supermarkets from resupplying.*

For two full weeks, have your family live off what you have in the house— no trips to the grocery store or restaurants. This is a great way to assess how much food you really need to store, as well as clear out some of the food that has cluttered up the cupboards and freezer for months. It may also help you to learn to pull together some creative menus.

ESCAPE

Scenario: A dangerous event occurs at your location, such as a fire breaking out at the movie theater.

This is more of an ongoing challenge than one done over a single day or week. Over the next few months, challenge your family to identify escape routes from public locations. This could include such places as a movie theater, supermarket, restaurant, bowling alley, or shopping mall. Ask them some basic questions: If there was suddenly a fire or explosion how would they get out alive? What route would they take if the main exit was blocked? Why would some exits be better than others? Where would they go once they escaped?

FIRE IN THE HOUSE

Scenario: Your house catches fire in the middle of the night.

Before doing this trial, discuss and practice emergency evacuations from your home. To keep panic to a minimum, let everyone know that you will be conducting an overnight fire drill, but don't tell them the specific day that it will occur.

On the night of the trial, wait until everyone is asleep and then activate a fire alarm farthest from where your family sleeps. You can activate it by holding the test button, or blowing out a few matches underneath it—put in ear plugs first. See how long it takes your family to wake up and rendezvous safely at a predetermined location just outside the home. Ideally everyone should be outside in less than one minute. If your children don't wake up quickly, investigate alternative alarm types, such as voice alarms.

ON THE ROAD

Scenario: Due to approaching wildfires, an evacuation order has just been issued for your community.

Without prior preparation, give your family 15 minutes to grab whatever they think they might need to evacuate. Take only a single change

Anything can happen, *(photo by FEMA/Michael Rieger)*

of clothes. Use the little time you have to gather important supplies, irreplaceable things, and important documents. Pick a hotel that is at least 50 miles away, and travel to it using an alternate route—no main interstates. Spend the night there and talk about the things you may have forgotten.

IT IS IN THE AIR

Scenario: *A chemical plant has issued an urgent warning that an airborne hazard has accidentally been released. Authorities are urging residents to immediately go indoors and shelter-in-place.*

Following the instructions provided in *Chapter 5: Shelter,* have your family retreat to a single room in your home. Seal the doors and windows as described. Remain in your safe room monitoring the radio for a couple hours. Discuss ways with your family to prepare the room more quickly or make it more livable for a longer stay.

BIBLIOGRAPHY

1. **Dictionary.com.** Definition: Disaster. [Online] http://dictionary.reference.com/browse/disaster.

2. **CBC News.** The World's Worst Natural Disasters. [Online] October 2, 2009. http://www.cbc.ca/world/story/2008/05/08/f-natural-disasters-history.html.

3. **Cummings, Bruce.** We Look at it and See Ourselves. *London Review of Books.* [Online] December 15, 2005. http://www.lrb.co.uk/v27/n24/bruce-cumings/we-look-at-it-and-see-ourselves.

4. **Blong, Russell J.** *Volcanic Hazards: A Sourcebook on the Effects of Eruptions.* City Unk.: Academic Press, 1985.

5. **US Geological Survey.** Historic Earthquakes. *Earthquake Hazards Program.* [Online] http://earthquake.us-gs.gov/earthquakes/world/events/1970_05_31.php#huayco.

6. **World Health Organization.** *Health Effects of the Chernobyl Accident and Special Health Care Programmes.* Geneva: WHO Press, 2006.

7. **Simmons, Janet A., Irwin, Donald B., and Drinnien, Beverly A.** *Psychology - The Search for Understanding.* New York: West Publishing Company, 1987.

8. **US Department of Agriculture.** MyPyramid.gov Steps to a Healthier You. [Online] http://www.mypyramid.gov/.

9. **Wake Forest University Baptist Medical Center.** Study Confirms Health Benefits of Whole Grains. [Online] 05 10, 2007. http://www1.wfubmc.edu/News/NewsARticle.htm?ArticleID=2081.

10. **General Mills.** Health Benefits. *General Mills with Whole Grain.* [Online] http://www.wholegrainlife.com/Benefits/HealthBenefits.aspx.

11. **Whole Grains Council.** Whole Grains 101. [Online] http://www.wholegrainscouncil.org/whole-grains-101/what-are-the-health-benefits.

12. **American Heart Association.** Prevention and Treatment Options. [Online] http://www.americanheart.org/presenter.jhtml?identifier=3046113.

13. **NutritionData.** NutirtionData Know What You Eat. [Online] http://www.nutritiondata.com/facts/dairy-and-egg-products/111/2.

14. **US Food and Drug Administration, Center for Food Safety and Applied Nutrition.** Qualified Health Claims. *Letter of Enforcement Discretion - Nuts and Coronary Heart Disease.* [Online] July 14, 2003. http://www.fda.gov/Food/Labeling-Nutrition/LabelClaims/QualifiedHealthClaims/ucm072926.htm.

15. **American Heart Association.** Fat. [Online] http://www.americanheart.org/presenter.jhtml?identifier=4582.

16. **FitDay.** Nutrition Information for All Foods. [Online] http://www.fitday.com/webfit/nutrition/BrwsFoods.html.

17. **Layton, P.** *Emergency Food Storage & Survival Handbook.* Roseville: Three Rivers Press, 2002.

18. **GLAD Products Company.** GLAD Frequently Asked Questions. *GLAD Trash Bags.* [Online] http://www.glad.com/faqs/trashbags.php.

19. **Spigarelli, Jack.** *Crisis Preparedness Handbook: A Comprehensive Guide to Home Storage and Physical Survival.* Alpine: Cross-Current Publishing, 2002.

20. **Arizona Department of Health Services.** *Safe Food Storage Times and Temperatures.* [Online] http://www.azdhs.gov/phs/oeh/fses/sfstt.htm.

21. **New Zealand Food Safety Authority.** *A Guide to Calculating the Shelf Life of Foods.* 2005.

22. **US Department of Agriculture.** Freezing and Food Safety. *Fact Sheets: Safe Food Handling.* [Online] http://www.fsis.usda.gov/factsheets/focus_on_freezing/index.asp.

23. **US Food and Drug Administration Center for Food Safety and Applied Nutrition.** The A to Z. *Science and our Food Supply.* [Online] http://www.cfsan.fda.gov/~dms/a2z-term.html.

24. **Proquantum Corporation.** Local Health Departments in the USA. *Health Guide USA.* [Online] http://healthguideusa.org/local_health_departments.htm.

25. **Brewer, M. S.** *Food Storage, Food Spoilage, and Foodborne Illness.* Urbana-Champaign: University of Illinois at Urbana-Champaign, College of Agriculture, 1991. Vol. Circular 1313.

26. **US Food and Drug Administration.** Center for Food Safety and Applied Nutrition. *Bad Bug Book: Foodborne Pathogenic Microorganisms and Natural Toxins Handbook.* [Online] http://www.cfsan.fda.gov/~mow/intro.html.

27. **Centers for Disease Control and Prevention.** *Foodborne Illnesses, Frequently Asked Questions.* Department of Health and Human Services. 2005.

28. —. Division of Foodborne Bacterial and Mycotic Diseases. [Online] http://www.cdc.gov/nczved/dfbmd/disease_listing.html.

29. **Milton S. Hershey Medical Center College of Medicine.** Food Poisoning. *Health and Disease Information, A to Z Topics.* [Online] http://www.hmc.psu.edu/healthinfo/f/foodpoisoning.htm.

30. **US Department of Health and Human Services.** Your Gateway to Federal Food Safety Information. [Online] www.foodsafety.gov.

31. **Partnership for Food Safety Education.** Fight BAC! Keep Food Safe from Bacteria. [Online] http://www.fightbac.org/.

32. **US Department of Agriculture.** Food Safety Education. *Food Safety and Inspection Service.* [Online] www.isitdoneyet.gov.

33. —. Fact Sheets: Food Labeling. *Food Safety and Inspection Service.* [Online] http://www.fsis.usda.gov/Fact_Sheets/Food_Product_Dating/index.asp.

34. **University of Nebraska Cooperative Extension in Lancaster County.** Food Reflections: Decoding Food Product Dates. [Online] http://lancaster.unl.edu/food/ftjan05.htm.

35. **Garden-Robinson, J.** *Food Storage Guide.* Fargo, ND: North Dakota State University Extension Service, 1998. FN-579.

36. **US Food and Drug Administration.** Refrigerator & Freezer Storage Chart. [Online] http://www.cfsan.fda.gov/~pregnant/refrfrez.pdf.

37. **World Food Programme. Food Quality Control.** [Online] http://foodquality. wfp.org/FoodSpecifications/Shelflifeoffoods/Overviewtableshelflifeoffoods/tabid/471/Default.aspx.

38. **Willenberg, Barbara.** Food Safety. *How Does Freezing Affect Food Quality?* [Online] Nutritional Sciences, University of Missouri-Columbia. http://missourifamilies. org/quick/foodsafetyqa/qafs327.htm.

39. **United States Congress.** Public Health Security and Bioterrorism Preparedness and Response Act of 2002. [Online] 2002. http://www.nj1dmat.org/Default. asp?Page=24. Public Law 107-188.

40. **US Food and Drug Administration.** The Bioterrorism Act of 2002. [Online] http://www.cfsan.fda.gov/~dms/defterr.html.

41. **US Department of State.** FACT SHEET: Guidance for Responding to Radiological and Nuclear Incidents. *Radiological and Nuclear Incidents.* [Online] http://travel. state.gov/travel/tips/health/health_1184.html.

42. **Flint, Vivekan.** Contraindications and Possible Adverse Effects of Therapeutic Diets and Supplements. [Online] http://www-ksl.stanford.edu/people/kpfleger/multivitamins/cached/my.webmd.com_content_dmk_dmk_article_58947.html.

43. **Sine, Richard.** Vitamins: Separating Fact from Fiction. *WebMD.* [Online] http://men.webmd.com/features/vitamins-separating-fact-from-fiction.

44. *Mortality in Randomized Trials of Antioxidant Supplements for Primary and Secondary Prevention.* **Bjelakovic, Goran, et. al.** 8, s.l.: The Journal of the American Medical Association, 2007, Vol. 297, pp. 842-857.

45. **Miller, Edgar R., et. al.** Meta-Analysis: High-Dosage Vitamin E Supplementation May Increase All-Cause Mortality. *Annals of Internal Medicine.* [Online] American College of Physicians, January 4, 2005. http://www.annals.org/cgi/content/short/142/1/37.

46. **World Health Organization.** *Global water supply and sanitation assessment.* Geneva: World Health Organization and United Nations Children's Fund, 2000.

47. **Mayo Clinic.** Hand Washing: An Easy Way to Prevent Infection. *Adult Health.* [Online] http://www.mayoclinic.com/health/hand-washing/HQ00407.

48. **US Department of Homeland Security.** *Emergency Supply List.* 2009.

49. **Raloff, Janet.** How to Disinfect your Salad. *Science News Online.* [Online] September 28, 1996. http://www.sciencenews.org/sn_arch/9_28_96/food.htm.

50. **US Environmental Protection Agency.** Ground Water and Drinking Water. [Online] http://www.epa.gov/safewater/.

51. *Survival of bacterial enteropathogens in the ice of popular drinks.* **Dickens, D., DuPont, D., Johnson, P.** s.l.: JAMA, 1985, Vol. 253, pp. 3141-3.

52. **Centers for Disease Control and Prevention.** *Global WASH-Related Diseases and Contaminants. Global Water, Sanitation, and Hygiene (WASH).* [Online] http://www.cdc.gov/healthywater/global/wash_diseases.html.

53. **US Environmental Protection Agency.** *National Drinking Water Standards.* Office of Water. s.l.: EPA, 2003. EPA 816-F-03-016.

54. **National Sanitation Foundation International.** Drinking Water Contaminant Testing Protocols. [Online] http://www.nsf.org/consumer/drinking_water/dw_contaminant_protocols.asp?program=WaterTre.

55. **Baxtel Company.** Microorganisms. *Microtrack.* [Online] http://www.microtack.com/html/microorganism.htm.

56. **Centers for Disease Control and Prevention.** Water-related Diseases, Contaminants, and Injuries By Type. [Online] http://www.cdc.gov/healthywater/disease/type.html.

57. **Wikipedia.** Bacteria. [Online] http://en.wikipedia.org/wiki/Bacteria.

58. **US Environmental Protection Agency.** Radionuclides in Drinking Water. *Safewater.* [Online] http://www.epa.gov/safewater/radionuclides/index.html.

59. **Water Filters and Purifiers Guide.** Radionuclide in water - Exposures to radionuclides from drinking water can result in the increased risk of cancer or kidney problems. *Water Filtes and Purifiers Guide.* [Online] http://www.waterfilters-camping-water-purifier.com/radionuclide-in-water.html.

60. **US Environmental Protection Agency.** Local Drinking Water Information. [Online] http://www.epa.gov/safewater/dwinfo/index.html.

61. **Wikipedia.** Water Purification. [Online] http://en.wikipedia.org/wiki/Water_Purification.

62. *Microbiological water purification without the use of chemical purification.* **Gerba C., Naranjo J.** 1, 2000, Wilderness and Environmental Medicine, Vol. 11, pp. 12-16.

63. **Wisconsin Pharmacal Company.** Portable Aqua Water Purification Technology. [Online] http://www.potableaqua.com/faq.shtml.

64. **Katadyn Products, Inc.** US military choose Katadyn Micropur MP1 purification tablets. *Katadyn, Making Water Drinking Water.* [Online] http://www.katadyn.com/usen/service/news/detail/article/2009/08/27/us-military-choose-katadyn-micropur-mp1-purification-tablets/.

65. **Polar Equipment, Inc.** Frequently Asked Questions. *Polar Pure Water Disinfectant.* [Online] http://www.polarequipment.com/questions.htm.

66. **The Clorox Company.** Frequently Asked Questions Biological Safety Topics. *Cornell University Office of Environmental Health and Safety.* [Online] http://www.med.cornell.edu/ehs/faq/biological_safety.htm.

67. *Occurence and control of Cryptosporidium in drinking water.* **Rose, J.** [ed.] G. McFeters. New York: Springer-Verlag, 1990, Drinking water microbiology, pp. 294-322.

68. **US Environmental Protection Agency.** *Guide Standard and Protocol for Testing Microbiological Water Purifiers.* Washington, DC: Office of Pesticide Programs and Criteria and Standards Division, Office of Drinking Water, 1987.

69. —. Emergency Disinfection of Drinking Water. *Ground Water & Drinking Water.* [Online] http://www.epa.gov/safewater/faq/emerg.html.

70. **Federal Emergency Management Agency.** *Earthquake Safety Checklist.* 2009. FEMA P-526.

71. *Use of water for iodine disinfection: iodine toxicity and maximum recommended dose.* **Backer, H., Hollowell, J.** 108, s.l.: Environmental Health Perspect, 2000, pp. 679-84.

72. *Effect of turbidity on chlorination and bacterial persistence in drinking water.* **LeChevallier M, Evans T, Seidler R.** 42, s.l.: Appl Environmental Microbiology, 1981, pp. 159-167.

73. **Backer, H.** Water Disenfection for International and Wilderness Travelers. *Travel Medicine.* Clinical Infectious Diseases, 2002, Vol. 34, pp. 355-64.

74. **Centers for Disease Control and Prevention.** A Guide to Drinking Water Treatment Technologies for Household Use. [Online] http://www.cdc.gov/healthywater/drinking/travel/household_water_treatment.html#remember.

75. **North Dakota State University.** Reverse Osmosis. *Treatment Systems for Household Water Supplies.* [Online] 1992. http://www.ag.ndsu.edu/pubs/h2oqual/watsys/ae1047w.htm#disadvantage.

76. **Enriquez, C., Gerba, C.** *Evaluation of the Steri-Pen® Water Treatment System According to the US Environmental Protection Agency Guide Standard And Protocol For Testing of Microbiological Water Purifiers.* Tucson, AZ: University of Arizona, Dept. of Soil, Water, and Environmental Science, 2001.

77. **U.S. Army Center for Health Promotion and Preventive Medicine.** *Technical Information Paper; Ultraviolet Light Disinfection in the Use of Individual Water Purification Devices.* Aberdeen Proving Ground: US Army, 2005.

78. **Vin and Gwen Backpacking.** The Steri-Pen. [Online] http://www.angelfire.com/trek/vinandgwen/gear/steripen/results.html.

79. **SODIS.** SODIS-Safe Drinking Water in 6 Hours. *SODIS: Safe Drinking Water for All.* [Online] http://www.sodis.ch/index_EN.

80. **Plasticsinfo.org.** FAQ's: The Safety of Plastic Beverage Bottles. *Better Living with Plastics.* [Online] http://www.plasticsinfo.org/s_plasticsinfo/sec_level2_faq.asp?CID=705&DID=2839.

81. **US Environmental Protection Agency.** Filtration Facts. *Water Health Series.* 2005, 816-K-05-002.

82. **National Sanitation Foundation International.** NSF Product and Service Listings. [Online] www.nsf.org/certified/dwtu.

83. **Underwriter Labs.** UL Water Quality Services. [Online] www.ul.com/water.

84. **Water Quality Association.** Gold Seal Product Certification. [Online] www.wqa.org.

85. **National Sanitation Foundation International.** Drinking Water Treatment Standards. [Online] http://www.nsf.org/business/drinking_water_treatment/standards. asp?program=DrinkingWatTre.

86. **Andrew, R.** *NSF International, DWTU Program, Operations Manager.* July 2007.

87. **National Sanitation Foundation.** Importance of Changing Water Filters. [Online] http://www.nsf.org/consumer/newsroom/fact_water_filters.asp.

88. —. Emergency Drinking Water Treatment. [Online] http://www.nsf.org/consumer/newsroom/fact_disaster_water_treatment.asp.

89. **Atkins, R.** How to Find Water and Make It Safe to Drink. [Online] 2007. http:// grandpappy.info/wwater.htm.

90. Water and Food Group. *Equipped to Survive.* [Online] http://www.equipped.com/ watrfood.htm.

91. **Hoag, Philip L.** *No Such Thing as Doomsday.* Emigrant, Montana: Yellow River Publishing, 2001.

92. **Federal Emergency Management Agency.** Are You Ready? [Online] January 2008. http://www.fema.gov/areyouready/getting_informed.shtm.

93. **Colorado Farm Bureau Insurance Company.** *Protect your Home against Flood Damage.* s.l.: Colorado Farm Bureau Insurance Company, 2003.

94. **Federal Emergency Management Agency.** Before a Flood. [Online] http:// www.fema.gov/hazard/flood/fl_before.shtm.

95. —. Map Service Center. [Online] http://msc.fema.gov/.

96. **Canada Safety Council.** Crime and Home Invasion, Be Prepared. [Online] 0901, 2008. http://safety-council.org/safety-canada-online/issues/2007/10/4/crime-and-home-invasion-be-prepared/.

97. **Glendenning, Anna.** Tips for Preventing a Home Invasion. *Families.com.* [Online] 05 03, 2006. http://insurance.families.com/blog/tips-for-preventing-a-home-invasion.

98. **Canada Mortgage and Housing Corporation.** How to Lock Out Crime. [Online] http://www.cmhc-schl.gc.ca/en/co/maho/holooucr/.

99. **Barrie Police Service.** Home Security: Re-securring your Home. [Online] http:// www.police.barrie.on.ca/?q=node/71.

100. **Better Homes and Gardens.** *Home Security, Your Guide to Protecting Your Family.* Des Moines, Iowa: Meredith Publishing Group, 1999.

101. **The National Terror Alert Response Center.** Safe Room. *The National Terror Alert.* [Online] http://www.nationalterroralert.com/saferoom/.

102. *Air Cleaners add Safety to Shelter-in-Place Rooms.* **National Institute for Chemical Studies.** Charleston, SC: National Instituite for Chemical Studies, Summer 2003, NICS NEWS, Vol. 12, pp. 1, 3.

103. **Associated Press Online.** *Three Israelis Suffocate in Sealed Room.* March 17, 2003. Associate Press News.

104. **Minnesota Department of Health.** *Carbon Dioxide (CO2) in the Indoor Environment.* Minnesota Department of Health. St. Paul, MN: Minnesota Department of Health, 2008. Fact Sheet.

105. **InspectApedia.** Toxicity of Carbon Dioxide Gas Exposure, CO2 Poisoning Symptoms, Carbon Dioxide Exposure Limits, and Links to Toxic Gas Testing Procedures. *Building & Environmental Inspection, Testing, Diagnosis, Repair, & Problem Prevention Advice.* [Online] http://www.inspect-ny.com/hazmat/CO2 gashaz.htm.

106. **US Fire Administration.** USFA QuickStats. [Online] http://www.usfa.dhs.gov/statistics/quickstats/index.shtm.

107. **National Fire Protection Association.** A Few Facts at the Household Level. [Online] July 2009. http://www.nfpa.org/search.asp?query=fire+extinguishers+1evel+home. USS81.

108. **Ahrens, Marty.** *House Structure Fires.* s.l.: National Fire Protection Association, 2009. Order # USS12G.

109. **National Fire Prevention Association.** Fire Sprinkler Initiative, Bringing Safety Home. [Online] May 2009. http://nfpa.typepad.com/firesprinklerinitiative/2009/05/index.html.

110. **US Consumer Product Safety Commission.** Test All Smoke Alarms (Detectors) and Annually Replace Batteries. [Online] http://www.cpsc.gov/CPSCPUB/PUBS/5077.html. CPSC Document #5077.

111. Fire Extinguisher Types (What Kind do I Use?). *Fire Extinguishers: 101.* [Online] http://www.fire-extinguisher101.com/.

112. **GALT Technology, Inc.** Fire Extinguishers and Buying Guide. *GALT Buying Guide.* [Online] http://www.galttech.com/research/household-DIY-tools/best-fire-extinguisher.php.

113. **Occupational Safety and Health Administration.** Fire Extinguisher Use. *Evacuation Plans and Procedures.* [Online] http://www.osha.gov/SLTC/etools/evacuation/portable_use.html.

114. **Consumer Product Safety Commission.** Carbon Monoxide Questions and Answers. *Consumer Product Safety Commission Publications.* [Online] http://www.cpsc.gov/CPSCPUB/PUBS/466.html. CPSC #466.

115. **Consumer Search.** Carbon Monoxide Detectors Reviews. [Online] http://www.consumersearch.com/www/house_and_home/carbon-monoxide-detectors/.

116. **National Safety Council.** Frequently Asked Questions about Radon. [Online] http://www.nsc.org/search/results.aspx?k=radon testing.

117. **US Environmental Protection Agency.** Radon. *United States Environmental Protection Agency.* [Online] http://www.epa.gov/radon/.

118. **Consumer Reports.** Lead & Radon Test Kits Challenging Choices. September 2008.

119. **National Safety Council.** Radon. [Online] http://www.nsc.org/resources/issues/radon/index.aspx.

120. **Office of Civilian Radioactive Waste Management.** Americans' Average Radiation Exposure. *Fact Sheet.* [Online] http://www.ocrwm.doe.gov/factsheets/doeymp0337.shtml.

121. **Massachusetts Institute of Technology.** Radiation, How Much is Considered Safe for Humans? *MIT News Office.* [Online] January 1994. http://web.mit.edu/newsoffice/1994/safe-0105.html.

122. **KI4U, Inc.** NukAlert. [Online] www.nukalert.com.

123. **Centers for Disease Control and Prevention.** Radioactive Contamination and Radiation Exposure. *Emergency Preparedness and Response.* [Online] http://www.bt.cdc.gov/radiation/contamination.asp.

124. *The Developing World and the Electricity Challenge.* **International Energy Agency.** Paris: International Energy Agency, 2005. IEA Workshop 2005.

125. **Surefire, Inc.** Flashlight Comparison/Specification Chart. *Surefire, The Worlds Finest Flashlights and Tactical Products.* [Online] http://www.surefire.com/Flashlight-SpecChart.

126. **Shake-Flashlights.com.** Shake Flashlights Info. [Online] http://www.shake-flashlights.com/buying-guide.html.

127. **Vandervort, Don.** Lighting and Bulb Types Comparison. *Don Vandervort's Home Tips.* [Online] http://www.hometips.com/buying-guides/light-bulb-types.html.

128. **Harris, Tom.** How Light Sticks Work. *How Stuff Works.* [Online] http://science.howstuffworks.com/light-stick1.htm.

129. **Eartheasy.** Energy Efficient Lighting. [Online] http://www.eartheasy.com/live_energyeff_lighting.htm.

130. **Wikipedia.** Luminous Efficacy. [Online] http://en.wikipedia.org/wiki/Luminous_efficacy.

131. **Klipstein, Donald.** Incandescent Including Halogen Light Bulbs. *The Great Internet Light Bulb Book, Part I.* [Online] http://members.misty.com/don/bulb1.html#hle.

132. **Brillianz Ltd.** Lux, Lumen and Watts, What's the Difference. [Online] http://www.brillianz.co.uk/data/documents/Lumen.pdf.

133. **Briggs & Stratton.** *Elite Series Portable Generators.* s.l.: Briggs & Stratton Power Products Group, LLC, 2005. Manual No. 197386GS.

134. How Much Electricity do you Need to Produce. *GeneratorSales.com.* [Online] http://www.generatorsales.com/wattage-calculator.asp.

135. **Chevron Corporation.** Recommended Storage Practices. [Online] http://www.chevron.com/products/prodserv/fuels/technical_safety_bulletins/ltg_storage.aspx.

136. —. Chevron Products: Mr. Gasoline Answers. [Online] http://www.chevron. com/products/ourfuels/mrgas/?&aID=130&cID=24.

137. **Federal Emergency Management Agency.** Important Tips to Ensure When Using Generators. [Online] March 2006. http://www.fema.gov/news/newsrelease. fema?id=24340.

138. **Jaycar Electronics.** *Understanding & Using DC-AC Sources.* 2000.

139. Do Batteries Really Last Longer if they are Stored in the Refrigerator? *WiseGEEK.* [Online] http://www.wisegeek.com/do-batteries-really-last-longer-if-they-are-stored-in-the-refrigerator.htm.

140. Should you Refrigerate Batteries to make them Last Longer? *The Straight Dope.* [Online] http://www.straightdope.com/columns/read/1896/should-you-refrigerate-batteries-to-make-them-last-longer.

141. **Consumer Reports.** Digital Cameras and Photography. [Online] November 2007. http://www.consumerreports.org/cro/electronics-computers/cameras-photography/peripherial-devices/aa-batteries-11-07/ratings/aa-batteries-rate. htm.

142. **USA Today.** Cyberspeak - Batteris Up! With more power. [Online] February 2006. http://www.usatoday.com/tech/columnist/edwardbaig/2006-02-01-battery-test_x.htm.

143. **Aqualab.** Research Topic - Which battery will do? [Online] May 2007. http:// www.videofoundry.co.nz/ianman/laboratory/research/battery_1.shtml.

144. **Consumer Search.** Batteries Full Report. [Online] June 2008. http://www. consumersearch.com/batteries/review.

145. **Wikipedia.** Lithium Ion Battery. [Online] http://en.wikipedia.org/wiki/Lithium_ ion_battery.

146. **BatteryUniversity.** How to prolong lithium-based batteries. [Online] http:// batteryuniversity.com/parttwo-34.htm.

147. **Peterson, Bill.** Understanding Amp Hours. *Windpower Unlimited, LLC.* [Online] http://www.windpowerunlimited.com/batteries/Amp_Hours.htm.

148. **World Wind Energy Association.** *World Wind Energy Report 2008.* s.l.: World Wind Energy Association, 2008.

149. **Windstream Power LLC.** Innovations in Renewable Energy. [Online] www. windstreampower.com.

150. **Mayo Clinic Staff.** Hypothermia. *Mayo Clinic.* [Online] http://www.mayoclinic. com/health/hypothermia/ds00333.

151. The word: Paradoxical Undressing. *NewScientist.* 2007, 2600.

152. **USA Today.** Health Scout. [Online] http://www.healthscout.com/ency/68/271/ main.html.

153. **Mayo Clinic Staff.** Heatstroke. *Mayo Clinic.* [Online] http://www.mayoclinic. com/health/heat-stroke/DS01025.

154. **David E. Baker.** Unvented Portable Kerosene Heaters - Safety Considerations. *National AG Safety Database (NASD)*. [Online] http://www.nasdonline.org/document/1098/d000884/unvented-portable-kerosene-heaters-safety-considerations.html.

155. **Alsnetbiz.com.** Weatherproofing Your Home. *How to Series*. [Online] http://alsnetbiz.com/homeimprovement/info10.html.

156. Performing Heat Loss Calculations on a Structure. *Activair*. [Online] http://www.tombling.com/heaters/heat-loss.asp.

157. **Gas-Lights.com.** Online Calculator. [Online] http://www.gas-lights.com/form.html.

158. **Heater-Store.com.** Determining your Heater Size. [Online] http://www.heater-store.com/heater_calculator_info.htm.

159. **ehow.com.** How to Calculate Heater Size. [Online] http://www.ehow.com/how_2083985_calculate-heater-size.html.

160. **Bobvila.com.** Sizing Residential Heating and Air Conditioning Systems. [Online] http://www.bobvila.com/HowTo_Library/Sizing_Residential_Heating_and_Air_Conditioning_Systems-Air_Conditioning-A1967.html.

161. **Bob Formisano.** How to Size an Electric Room Heater - Baseboard or Wall or Cove Heater. *About.com*. [Online] http://homerepair.about.com/od/heating-coolingrepair/ss/size_elec_htr.htm.

162. **Time.com.** Science: The Physicists Fire. [Online] December 22, 1975. http://www.time.com/time/magazine/article/0,9171,879592,00.html.

163. **The Masonry Heater Association of North America.** What's a Masonry Heater? [Online] http://mha-net.org/.

164. **Energy Information Administration.** Heating Fuel Comparison Calculator. [Online] http://www.eia.doe.gov/neic/experts/heatcalc.xls.

165. **Consumer Reports.** Alternative Energy. October, 2009.

166. **US Environmental Protection Agency,** Choosing the Right Wood Stove. [Online] http://www.epa.gov/burnwise/woodstoves.html.

167. **Prepare.org.** Preventing and Thawing Frozen Pipes. [Online] http://www.prepare.org/basic/frozen.htm.

168. **US Environmental Protection Agency.** Why Should You Be Concerned About Air Pollution? *The Plain English Guide to the Clean Air Act*. [Online] http://www.epa.gov/air/peg/concern.html.

169. —. The Plain English Guide to the Clean Air Act. [Online] http://www.epa.gov/air/peg/index.html.

170. —. Air Trends. [Online] http://www.epa.gov/airtrends/.

171. **American Lung Association.** State of the Air: 2009. [Online] http://www.stateoftheair.org/.

172. **World Heath Organization.** Air Quality and Health. [Online] http://www.who.int/mediacentre/factsheets/fs313/en/index.html.

173. **World Health Organization.** *Indoor Air Pollution: National Burden of Disease Estimates.* 2001.

174. **US Environmental Protection Agency.** Ways to Reduce Air Pollution. *The Plain English Guide to the Clean Air Act.* [Online] http://www.epa.gov/air/caa/peg/reduce.html.

175. **American Lung Association.** 10 Tips for Cleaner Air. [Online] http://www.lungusa.org/associations/states/california/advocacy/fight-for-air-quality/sota-2010/tips-for-california.html.

176. **Ready.Gov.** Frequently Asked Questions. *Ready America.* [Online] http://www.ready.gov/america/other/faqs.html#q2.

177. **National Terror Alert.** Shelter-in-Place. [Online] http://www.nationalterroralert.com/shelterinplace/.

178. **NuclearTourist.com.** Radiation Safety. [Online] http://www.nucleartourist.com/systems/rad.htm.

179. **Oak Ridge Institute for Science and Education.** Types of Radiation Exposure. *Guidance for Radiation Accident Management.* [Online] http://orise.orau.gov/reacts/guide/index.htm.

180. **US Environmental Protection Agency.** Health Effects. *Radiation Protection.* [Online] http://www.epa.gov/radiation/understand/health_effects.html.

181. **JP Laboratories, Inc.** Effect of Radiation. [Online] http://www.jplabs.com/html/effect_of_radiation.HTM.

182. **Wikipedia.com.** Radiation Poisoning. [Online] http://en.wikipedia.org/wiki/Radiation_poisoning.

183. **Weitz & Luxenberg, P.C.** Learn More About the Harmful Effects of Radiation Contamination. [Online] http://www.weitzlux.com/radiation/contamination_4175.html.

184. **Centers for Disease Control and Prevention.** Potassium Iodide (KI). *Emergency Preparedness and Response.* [Online] http://www.bt.cdc.gov/radiation/ki.asp.

185. **US Food and Drug Administration.** Questions and Answers on Prussian Blue. [Online] http://www.fda.gov/Drugs/EmergencyPreparedness/BioterrorismandDrugPreparedness/ucm130337.htm.

186. **US Department of Health and Human Services.** *Primary Containment for Biohazards.* 2007.

187. **Federal Emergency Management Agency.** Biologial Threats. *Are You Ready?* [Online] http://www.fema.gov/areyouready/biological_threats.shtm.

188. **Centers for Disease Control and Prevention.** Interim Recommendations for Facemask and Respirator Use to Reduce 2009 Influenza A (H1N1) Virus Transmission. [Online] September 2009. http://www.cdc.gov/h1n1flu/masks.htm.

189. —. NIOSH-Approved Particulate Filtering Facepiece Respirators. [Online] http://www.cdc.gov/niosh/npptl/topics/respirators/disp_part/default.html.

190. —. Laboratory Performance Evaluation of N95 Filtering Facepiece Respirators, 1996. *MMWR Weekly.* 1998, Vol. 47(48), December 11, 1998.

191. **Preparedness Directorate Office of Grants and Training.** *Guide for the Selection of Personal Protective Equipment for Emergency Responders.* s.l.: US Department of Homeland Security, 2007. Guide 102-06.

192. **National Institute for Occupational Safety and Health.** NIOS Respirator Fact Sheet: What you should know in deciding whether to buy escape hoods, gas masks, or other respirators for preparedness at home and work. *Electronic Library of Construction Occupational Safety and Health (eLCOSH).* [Online] http://www.elcosh.org/en/document/593/d000570/niosh-respirator-fact-sheet%253A-what-you-should-know-in-deciding-whether-to-buy-escape-hoods%252C-gas-masks%252C-or-other-respirators-for-preparedness-at-home-and-work.html.

193. **Consumer Reports.** How did you sleep last night? September, 2008.

194. **Davis, Jeanie Lerche.** The Toll of Sleep Loss in America. *WebMD.* [Online] http://www.webmd.com/sleep-disorders/guide/toll-of-sleep-loss-in-america.

195. **Breus, Michael J.** How Much Sleep Do Children Need? *WebMD.* [Online] http://www.webmd.com/parenting/guide/how-much-sleep-do-children-need.

196. **WebMd.com.** Sleep 101. [Online] http://www.webmd.com/sleep-disorders/guide/sleep-101.

197. **Marc Weissbluth, MD.** *Healthy Sleep Habits, Happy Child.* s.l.: Ballantine Books, 2005.

198. **Lawton, Graham.** Maxed Out: How Long Can You Go Without Sleep. *New Scientist.* [Online] http://www.newscientist.com/article/mg20627562.100-maxed-out-how-long-can-you-go-without-sleep.html.

199. **Reader's Digest.** 35 More Secrets the ER Staff Won't Tell You. [Online] http://www.rd.com/your-america-inspiring-people-and-stories/35-more-secrets-the-er-staff-wont-tell-you/article175030-1.html.

200. **American College of Emergency Physicians.** *First Aid Manual.* New York: DK Publishing, 2009.

201. **Mayo Clinic.** First Aid. [Online] http://www.mayoclinic.com/health/FirstAid Index/FirstAidIndex.

202. **British Broadcasting Corporation.** First Aid Procedures Index. *Health Treatments.* [Online] http://www.bbc.co.uk/health/first_aid/procedures_index/index.shtml.

203. **WebMD.** First Aid Shortcuts. [Online] http://firstaid.webmd.com/.

204. **UAB Health System.** Acetaminophen. *UAB Medicine.* [Online] http://www.health.uab.edu/65703/.

205. **National Oceanic Atmospheric Admininstration.** StormReady! *National Weather Service.* [Online] http://www.stormready.noaa.gov/.

206. **National Weather Service.** NWS Offices and Centers. [Online] http://www.weather.gov/organization.php.

207. **National Oceanic Atmospheric Administration.** Local Contact Information. *National Weather Service.* [Online] www.stormready.noaa.gov/contact.

208. **FCC Public Safety and Homeland Security Bureau.** Emergency Alert System. [Online] http://www.fcc.gov/pshs/services/eas/.

209. **Department of Homeland Security. History:** Who Became a Part of the Department? [Online] http://www.dhs.gov/xabout/history/editorial_0133.shtm.

210. —. The Secretary's Five Goals. [Online] http://www.dhs.gov/xabout/gc_1207339653379.shtm.

211. —. Homeland Security Advisory System. [Online] http://www.dhs.gov/xinfoshare/programs/Copy_of_press_release_0046.shtm.

212. —. *Are you Ready? An In-Depth Guide to Citizen Preparedness.* s.l.: Department of Homeland Security, 2008.

213. **American Red Cross.** Homeland Security Advisory System Recommendations (Individual). [Online] http://www.redcross.org/services/disaster/beprepared/hsas/individual.pdf.

214. **Wikipedia.** Internet. [Online] http://en.wikipedia.org/wiki/Internet.

215. **NOAA National Weather Service.** NOAA Weather Radio All Hazards. [Online] http://www.weather.gov/nwr/nwrback.htm.

216. —. NWR Receiver Consumer Information. [Online] http://www.nws.noaa.gov/nwr/nwrrcvr.htm#residential.

217. —. NOAA Weather Radio All Hazards. [Online] http://www.weather.gov/nwr/.

218. U.S. Cell Phone Penetration Tops 82%. *Gearlog, A Gadget Guide by Geeks, for Geeks.* [Online] http://www.gearlog.com/2007/11/us_cellphone_penetration_tops.php.

219. **General Motors.** OnStar by GM. [Online] www.onstar.com.

220. **Woolsey, Ben.** Credit Cards (2006-2007). *CreditCards.com.* [Online] http://www.creditcards.com/statistics/credit-card-industry-facts-and-personal-debt-statistics.php.

221. **Consumer Reports.** *The Ultimate Money Guide.* New York, NY: Consumers Union of US, 2009.

222. —. How not to Invest in Gold. *Consumer Reports Money Adviser.* March, 2010.

223. **Merriam-Webster.** Merriam-Webster Online. [Online] http://www.merriam-webster.com/dictionary/debt.

224. **Credit Cards.com.** How to reduce credit card offers in the mail. [Online] http://www.creditcards.com/credit-card-news/no-more-credit-card-offers-in-the-mail-1268.php.

225. **Chura, Hillary.** Disability, the Insurance That Is Often Sadly Overlooked. *New York Times.* [Online] 06 30, 2007. http://www.nytimes.com/2007/06/30/business/30disability.html.

226. **Appleby, Julie.** Ranks of uninsured Americans grow. *USA Today.* [Online] August 29, 2006. http://www.usatoday.com/money/industries/health/2006-08-29-health-insurance-coverage_x.htm.

227. **Oregon.gov.** Firearms. *Safe Kids Oregon.* [Online] http://www.oregon.gov/DHS/ph/safekids/firearms.shtml.

228. *Protection or peril? An analysis of firearm-related deaths in the home.* **Kellermann, A.L., Reay, DT.** 24, June 12, 1986, New England Journal of Medicine, Vol. 314, pp. 1557-1560.

229. *Guns in the Medical Literature -- A Failure of Peer Review.* **Suter, Edgar.** 3, San Ramon: s.n., March 1994, Journal of the Medical Association of Georgia, Vol. 83, pp. 133-148.

230. **Kleck, G.** *Point Blank: Guns and Violence in America.* New York: Aldine de Gruyter, 1991.

231. **Santa Clara County Government (SCCGOV).** Emergency Preparedness for Elderly People. [Online] http://www.sccgov.org/portal/site/scc/chlevel3?path=%2Fv7%2FSCC%20Public%20Portal%2FHandling%20Emergencies%2FPeople%20with%20Special%20Needs%2FDisaster%20Planning%20%26%20Response%20for%20the%20Elderly.

232. **Ready.Gov.** Older Americans. *Ready America.* [Online] http://www.ready.gov/america/getakit/seniors.html.

233. **American Red Cross.** Preparing for Disaster for People with Disabilities and other Special Needs. [Online] http://www.redcross.org/www-files/Documents/Preparing/A4497.pdf.

234. **Ready.gov.** People with Disabilities and Other Special Needs. *Ready America.* [Online] http://www.ready.gov/america/getakit/disabled.html.

235. **US Department of Treasury.** Treasury Goes Green, Saves, Green. *Press Room.* [Online] April 19, 2010. http://www.ustreas.gov/press/releases/tg644.htm. TG-44.

236. **Department of Justice.** Americans with Disabilities Act of 1990, As Amended. *Americans with Disabilities Act.* [Online] http://www.ada.gov/pubs/adastatute08.htm#12102.

237. **Ready.gov.** FEMA Ready Kids. [Online] www.ready.gov/kids/fun/index.html.

238. **US Department of Education.** Tips for Helping Students Recover from Traumatic Events. *Lead & Manage my School.* [Online] September 2005. http://www.ed.gov/parents/academic/help/recovering/part_pg3.html#p3.

239. **American Red Cross.** Children. *Prepare - Home and Family.* [Online] http://www.redcross.org/portal/site/en/menuitem.d8aaecf214c576bf971e4cfe43181aa0/?vgnextoid=e4a20c45f663b110VgnVCM10000089f0870aRCRD&vgnextfmt=default.   .

240. **Federal Emergency Management Agency.** Helping Children Cope with Disaster. *Recover & Rebuild.* [Online] http://www.fema.gov/rebuild/recover/cope_child.shtm.

241. **March of Dimes.** Prepare for Disaster: Information for Pregnant Women. *Pregnancy & Newborn Health Education Center.* [Online] http://www.marchofdimes. com/pnhec/159_21889.asp.

242. **Oak Ridge National Laboratory.** Animals in Emergencies for Owners. *Chemical Stockpile Emergency Preparedness Program.* [Online] http://emc.ornl.gov/CSEPPweb/ animals/animals_emergencies_owner.htm.

243. **Federal Emergency Management Agency.** Information for Pet Owners. [Online] http://www.fema.gov/plan/prepare/animals.shtm.

244. **American Veterinary Medical Association.** Animal Health: Saving the Whole Family. [Online] http://www.avma.org/disaster/saving_family.asp.

245. **Maritime and Coastguard Agency.** Captains Medical Guide - check this!! *Medical Certification and Advice.* [Online] 2010. - http://www.mcga.gov.uk/c4mca/ mcga-seafarer_information/mcga-dqs_st_shs_seafarer_information-medical/ mcga-dqs_st_shs_ships_capt_medical_guide.htm.

246. **National Geographic.** Yellowstone Volcano: Is "the Beast" Building to a Violent Tantrum? *National Geographic News.* [Online] February 05, 2001. http://news. nationalgeographic.com/news/2001/08/0828_wireyellowstone.html.

FOOD STORAGE LIST

Food Category	Type	Full Stock Qty	Size	Current Stock	Qty Needed

TELEPHONE NUMBERS

Name	Telephone #
Emergency Services	
Police, Fire, Ambulance	911
Poison Control Center	1-800-222-1222
Emergency Management (FEMA)	1-800-621-FEMA
Centers for Disease Control (CDC)	1-800-311-3435
Federal Bureau of Investigation (FBI)	1-800-CALL-FBI
Local Chapter of American Red Cross	
Medical/School	
Family Doctor	
Child Doctor	
Dentist	
School	
Utilities	
Gas Company	
Electric Company	
Sewage Service Provider	
Water Service Provider	
Family/Friends	
Cell Phone	
Work	
Neighbor	
Babysitter	
Local Emergency Contact	
Out-of-Town Emergency Contact	
Insurance Companies	
Other	
Local Animal Control	

IMPORTANT PAPERS

- ❏ Addresses and phone numbers of points of contact (family, friends, insurer, doctor, etc.)
- ❏ Driver's licenses
- ❏ Social Security cards
- ❏ Birth/Death certificates
- ❏ Adoption papers
- ❏ Insurance cards and policies (medical, dental, vision, auto, home, life)
- ❏ Credit cards (front and back)
- ❏ Passports
- ❏ Recent photos of family members (suitable for missing person's posters)
- ❏ Military discharge papers (e.g., DD214)
- ❏ Diplomas, certificates
- ❏ Property deeds
- ❏ Description of all vehicles (e.g., make, model, photo, VIN, and license number)
- ❏ Automobile titles
- ❏ Firearm serial numbers
- ❏ Weapon permits
- ❏ Pay stub
- ❏ Marriage license
- ❏ Home inventory video or photos
- ❏ Bank/Investment account information
- ❏ Tax records
- ❏ Computer account logins and passwords
- ❏ Medical information (allergies, medicines, medical history)
- ❏ Resume (for job hunting)
- ❏ First aid information (see the Captain's Medical Guide (245))

- ❑ Survival reference information (collection of e-books, online tips, how-to manuals)
- ❑ GPS locations and driving directions of house, rally points, local medical emergency services, and other key places—see *www.maps.google.com*. For GPS coordinates, right click and select "What's here?"
- ❑ Last Will and Testament
- ❑ Professional licenses
- ❑ Bible and other e-books
- ❑ Relaxing music
- ❑ Foreign language dictionaries (e.g., Spanish)
- ❑ _____
- ❑ _____
- ❑ _____
- ❑ _____
- ❑ _____
- ❑ _____
- ❑ _____
- ❑ _____
- ❑ _____
- ❑ _____
- ❑ _____
- ❑ _____
- ❑ _____
- ❑ _____
- ❑ _____
- ❑ _____
- ❑ _____
- ❑ _____
- ❑ _____
- ❑ _____

HOME ASSESSMENT

Threat	Likelihood (1-10)	Protection (1-10)	Steps to Improve

HOME HAZARDS CHECKLISTS

Outdoor Hazards

Indoor Hazards

LIST OF MEDICATIONS AND ALLERGIES

Medications		
Family Member	**Medication**	**Dosage**
Allergies		
Family Member	**Allergy**	**Reaction**

Attention!

I have (abandoned my vehicle) / (evacuated my home) due to an emergency situation.

My Name: _____

Telephone: _____

Address: _____

My travel plans and emergency contact information are given below. I am requesting that emergency personnel confirm my safe arrival before discarding this note.

My Travel Plans:

_____

_____

_____

_____

_____

_____

_____

_____

_____

_____

Emergency Contact Information

Name: _____

Phone Numbers: _____

Address: _____

PERSONALIZED DP PLAN

Dangers	Goals	Needs	Implementation

_____ Plan

INDEX

CONTACT ME

Disaster preparedness is an important subject for *every* family. If you found this book to be helpful, I would kindly ask that you do two things: (1) give a copy to your loved ones (or simply pass this one along when finished), and (2) post a review on Amazon.com to let others know that reading this handbook is time is well spent.

Every author enjoys hearing from his readers, whether it be praise or criticism. If you would like to contact me regarding this book or any DP-related subject, please send an email to *ab@artbradley.com*. You can also send written correspondence to the mailing address shown on the Order Form.

Best wishes to you and your family!

ORDER FORM

If you would like to order an autographed copy of this handbook for yourself or a loved one, please include payment along with a copy of the order form below. You can also order the book online at *www.disasterpreparer.com*, or through any book retailer.

Order Form

Qty	Item	Total
	A Practical Handbook to Disaster Preparedness for the Family, *Autographed Copy, ($24.95 each)*	
	Process of Elimination, A Novel, *Autographed Copy, ($18.95 each)*	
	Free Shipping!	-
	Total Price	

Mail your order to:

Arthur Bradley
112 Zanca Turn
Yorktown, VA 23693

Address to where you would like the book sent:

Name: _____

Address: _____

_____

_____

Any special instructions?

_____

_____

Made in the USA
Lexington, KY
25 April 2011